Comments on the first edition:

'The book is highly successful in its stated goal of ⸜ to international law; one that foregrounds (rather than, as is customary, back-grounds) the operation of power and politics deep within the discipline itself and international law's deep connectedness to the (usually asymmetrical) exercise of power.'

Obiora Okafor, Professor of International Law at Osgoode Hall,
York University, Toronto

'The first edition to this wonderful work promised that its critical approach would be "skeptical rather than cynical". In analysing international law through a political lens, it was extremely successful. I am delighted that the publishers have had the foresight to commission a second edition to enlighten us all.'

Roger S Clark, Board of Governors Professor,
Rutgers Law School, New Jersey

'*International Law: A Critical Introduction* reaches below the surface of international law to interrogate the assumptions on which the system rests and bring to light its intimate connections with power. The work deepens our understanding of grand projects of global regulation through law, their capabilities and ultimate constraints.'

Patrick Thornberry, Emeritus Professor of International Law,
Keele University

'This text provides an effective and efficient compass for the reader to navigate the current contemporary international law landscape. The text is easily read, and international legal principles are clearly and lucidly explained in a way which is commensurate with their complexity. The book covers the traditional topics of an international law module but the critical analysis of the exposition provides insight by painting with a broad brush the international political background against which law is played out. *International Law: A Critical Introduction* is welcome and timely.'

Professor Rebecca Wallace, Research Professor,
Robert Gordon University, Aberdeen

'This is a welcome addition to public international law scholarship. There is much to criticise in international law's conventional representation as a politically neutral, rules-based system that often contrasts sharply with practice, and this book does well to peel off the layers of dogma to reveal a credible portrayal of the subject in terms of its ambitions, actors and methods.'

Michael Addo, Professor of Law, University of Notre Dame,
and Director of the London Law Program

INTERNATIONAL LAW – A CRITICAL INTRODUCTION

This book provides a critical introduction to the concepts, principles and rules of international law through a consideration of contemporary international events. It reflects on the relevance of international law to particular disputes and on the possibilities and limitations of legal method as a means of resolving them. This in turn necessitates an examination of the relationship between international law and power. Thus, rather than studying international law as a system of rules that purports to govern, or at least constrain, the international community, this book considers the actual effects of international law upon international disagreements.

Such an approach is sceptical rather than cynical, intending to provide the means by which the role of international law may be evaluated. This entails discussion of the legal quality of international law; of the relationship between international law and international relations; of the apparent 'Eurocentricity' of international law; and of the relationship between political power and the ability to use or abuse (or ignore) international law.

Underlying the book is the assertion that international law is political in content (in the sense of being concerned with the exercise of power) but that it draws much of its effectiveness from its self-portrayal as being apolitical, or at least politically neutral.

"AFTER YOU —"

26 April 1945. At the United Nations Conference at San Francisco, charged with drafting the Charter, a crucial dispute emerged between those (powerful) states who wished to stress the importance of an alliance of the great victorious Powers for the maintenance of international peace (a Security Council), and those smaller states who wanted to rely upon a juridical world institution. The dispute continues to reverberate.

Cartoon: 'After You –' by David Low reproduced courtesy of the British Cartoon Archive.

International Law

A Critical Introduction

Second Edition

Wade Mansell
and
Karen Openshaw

•HART•

OXFORD • LONDON • NEW YORK • NEW DELHI • SYDNEY

HART PUBLISHING

Bloomsbury Publishing Plc

Kemp House, Chawley Park, Cumnor Hill, Oxford, OX2 9PH, UK

HART PUBLISHING, the Hart/Stag logo, BLOOMSBURY and the Diana logo are
trademarks of Bloomsbury Publishing Plc

First published in Great Britain 2019

First edition, 2013

A catalogue record for this book is available from the British Library.

Library of Congress Cataloging-in-Publication data

Names: Mansell, Wade, author. | Openshaw, Karen, author.

Title: International law : a critical introduction / Wade Mansell and Karen Openshaw.

Description: Second edition. | Oxford ; Chicago, Illinois : Hart, an imprint
of Bloomsbury, 2019. | Includes bibliographical references and index.

Identifiers: LCCN 2019021109 (print) | LCCN 2019022292 (ebook) |
ISBN 9781509926725 (pbk. : alk. paper) | ISBN 9781509926701 (ePDF) |
ISBN 9781509926718 (EPub)

Subjects: LCSH: International law.

Classification: LCC KZ3410 .M357 2019 (print) | LCC KZ3410 (ebook) | DDC 341—dc23

LC record available at https://lccn.loc.gov/2019021109

LC ebook record available at https://lccn.loc.gov/2019022292

ISBN: PB: 978-1-50992-672-5
        ePDF: 978-1-50992-670-1
        ePub: 978-1-50992-671-8

Typeset by Compuscript Ltd, Shannon
Printed and bound in Great Britain by CPI Group (UK) Ltd, Croydon CR0 4YY

To find out more about our authors and books visit www.hartpublishing.co.uk.
Here you will find extracts, author information, details of forthcoming events
and the option to sign up for our newsletters.

We would like to dedicate this book to the memory of Alistair Berkley, whose untimely death in the Lockerbie tragedy robbed the world of a humane, kind and clever man who would have contributed much to the promotion of a just world. His demise is the clearest lesson of the futility and lunacy of violence randomly directed, and the need for an international legal regime committed to international justice.

Table of Contents

Table of Cases

International Criminal Tribunal for the Former Yugoslavia

Iran–US Claims Tribunal

Israel

Permanent Court of Arbitration

Permanent Court of International Justice

United Kingdom

United States of America

Table of Legislation

Table of Conventions, Treaties, etc

Introduction

There are so many books that claim either to introduce the subject of public international law or to be textbooks that encompass the subject, or even indeed books that purport to illustrate the relationship between international law and international relations (or the world of politics), that the justification for yet another needs to be made at the outset. The intentions of this book are rather different from others, in that it will be concerned to argue that international law, while having an important, distinctive and real function, nevertheless, under a veneer of political neutrality, demonstrably reflects a particular distribution of power among states, and this in turn dictates the interests that international law serves. Obviously, this is a gross generalisation but one the book will seek to sustain. It will also argue that the very process of international law is inevitably and irrevocably imbued with a legal way of thinking that is both time- and place-specific.

These arguments will obviously not meet with universal approval, but our hope is that, whatever the political views of readers, the book will be read and accepted as an introduction to a way of understanding and appreciating international law. Certainly, the political premises that underlie the thesis pursued will always be apparent, and these may be simply stated. They are premises that arise from value judgements not always amenable to objective proof. In particular, the central premise is that the extraordinary disparity between rich and poor (both nations and individuals) is absolutely incompatible with any notion of 'justice' and is for that reason unacceptable.[1] Nevertheless, for those who do not accept that premise there is yet an arguable case that, regardless of 'justice', the present state of the international world is simply unsustainable. The late UK prime minister Margaret Thatcher's well-known defence of capitalism – 'There is no alternative' – seems inevitably to be overtaken by a recognition that 'Things can't go on like this.' It is perhaps ironic that it is the astounding economic growth of China that has made many people realise that the entire world will never be able to live with wealth comparable to that of the citizens of the US (or indeed of Western Europe). Such levels of consumption are simply unsustainable. Further, as will be suggested below, many of the contemporary international crises may best be understood as manifestations of poverty versus wealth.

---

[1] For a recent discussion, see Samuel Moyn, *Not Enough: Human Rights in an Unequal World* (Cambridge, Harvard University Press, 2018).

Finally, a quick explanation of what we intend to be understood by our use of the greatly abused word 'critical'. Here its meaning is limited. Some years ago a professor who had once been one of our external examiners at the Kent Law School told us (with some amusement) of the rubric of the examination paper of one of our colleagues, which read 'Question any four of the following eight answers'. To us this rubric encapsulates the essence of what we mean here by a critical perspective, and indeed the more an answer seems to be uncontroversial and common sense, the greater should be the suspicion of its political neutrality. The book is intended to develop this perspective while recognising that *any* answer is of course itself still open to question.

I. International Law and Domestic Law

All legal practitioners who specialise in international law would accept that international law has a very different feel from domestic law. Indeed, the most sceptical domestic lawyers often query whether international law should really be described as law at all. International law often seems to be indistinguishable from general international relations. For those of that view, such rules as there are in international law seem excessively malleable and negotiable, and often the very sources of international law are questionable. Such perspectives will be considered at the beginning of the book and remain relevant throughout.

Nevertheless, the book will argue that international law, while different from domestic law, is also sufficiently distinctive from international relations to fall easily within the definition of law, and that this label is important. It is important because the *legal* quality of international law has consequences. In particular, if rules are accepted as legal, compliance tends to be much more automatic (although with obvious exceptions). And the centrality of international treaties in international law indicates that states, through their representatives, enter into what they regard as binding legal relations. It is often said that the principle *pacta sunt servanda* – translated as 'pacts (or promises) must be respected (or kept)' – underlies the whole of international law.

International law remains a developing and dynamic subject. When the United Nations (UN) was created in 1945, only 51 states became members immediately; today it has in excess of 190 members, so it is clear that the international community, not least the community of states, has changed considerably. The great period of decolonisation and self-determination created a myriad of new states that were faced with an existent international legal regime which they had had no part in creating. (Much international law had been developed in the interaction between colonial powers.) This led not only to stresses and tensions but also to some quite fundamental developments.

Perhaps the first and greatest difficulty posed by a study of international law for those trained in domestic law is the breadth of the subject itself. For almost every international dispute involving a state, international law will be relevant. Thus the potential topics for study are vast in number. Those that have been chosen for consideration in this book have been selected either because they are central to an understanding of the international legal regime, or because they are illustrative of the way in which international law impacts upon international problems. Those that have been ignored are often no less important (the environment, refugees, world trade, and development, to name but a few) and their exclusion is for reasons of length rather than relevance.

The second major difficulty lies in the relationship between international law and international politics and power. The exact relationship is impossible to define, as it will vary from case to case. Nonetheless, comprehension of the relationship is important and will be found easier by readers familiar with contemporary international disputes involving states.

II. Paradoxes in the Contemporary World

The fall of the Berlin Wall in 1989 presaged, and perhaps precipitated, stupendous changes in the realm of international politics. These changes, which remain ongoing, have greatly altered not only the realm of international organisation and relations, but also the rule regime which ordered them. While the focus of this book will be upon that rule regime, it is obvious that it cannot properly be considered without recognition of the developments in the world it attempts to regulate.

The introduction to the first edition of this book, in 2013, referenced as seminal occurrences the terrorist attacks on the US in September 2001 and the so-called Second Gulf War of 2003, in which an allied force led by the US, with the UK in a supporting role, invaded Iraq and removed the regime of Saddam Hussein. It suggested that the effects of these events continued to reverberate in the world of international law, as did such phenomena as the proliferation of nuclear weapons and their development, and the purported secession of territories to form new states. It was suggested that concepts central to international law, such as self-defence, the pre-emptive use of force and even sovereignty itself, might have been undergoing a process of transformation. Additionally, at that time, the Israeli war in Gaza in December and January of 2008–09 (Operation Cast Lead); the military intervention in Libya by some NATO members in 2011; the increased use of so-called drone warfare; and the 'extra-judicial execution' of Osama Bin Laden all presented challenges to the established international legal regime. Although this largely remains true six years later, at the beginning of 2019, events have also been overtaken and/or modified by subsequent developments in the international arena.

The foreign policy priorities of a new US presidential administration seem to support Gideon Rachman's thesis that the US, once the undisputed unipolar super-power, has now, whether for reasons of choice or necessity, elected to retreat from internationalism to an 'America First' stance, bewildering erstwhile allies and empowering competitors.[2]

China's rise, both economically and militarily, has continued, and has been accompanied by assertions of regional hegemony and an aggressive foreign policy often disguised by substantial loans to poor states, or to states with deplorable human rights records. In the Middle East, the US seems to have lost much influence, except in relation to Israel and perhaps Saudi Arabia. The ongoing Syrian civil war has led to greatly increased Russian and Iranian intervention, with Turkey also an active participant, while the US seems intent on withdrawing from direct involvement not only in Syria but also in Iraq and Afghanistan. The proxy war between Saudi Arabia and Iran continues to play out in Yemen's civil war, where Saudi Arabia's indiscriminate bombing campaign has left thousands of civilians dead and injured. One indisputable effect of these changes, probably (ironically) initiated by the US's decision to deny the rights guaranteed by the Geneva Conventions to prisoners suspected of terrorist activities, as well as its willingness to turn a blind eye to the use of torture through 'extraordinary rendition', has been a considerable diminution in the universal acceptance of human rights. Meanwhile, poverty, repressive governments, and ethnic conflict has continued to afflict many African states, provoking, along with those fleeing war-torn states, an exodus seeking refuge elsewhere (primarily in Europe). The resulting tragedy, with many drowned or attacked, shows little sign of abating. A similar phenomenon can be observed in Central America, where many are choosing to seek refuge in the US regardless of the Trump administration's determination to deny entry. Finally, Russia's dispute with Ukraine shows little sign of being peacefully resolved, although its assertion of sovereignty over Crimea would now seem to be a *fait accompli*, regardless of whether this is perceived as an unacceptable act of aggression or a justified (if unlawful) response to Russian fears of NATO's movement eastward.[3] As for the European Union (EU), the refugee crisis that has threatened Europe's solidarity has been accompanied by (and to a certain extent has partly caused) a rise in support for so-called populist parties, most of which champion the nation state over international institutions and ties, and many of which are openly xenophobic or racist. One manifestation of

---

[2] Gideon Rachman, *Easternisation: War and Peace in the Asian Century* (London, The Bodley Head, 2016).

[3] John Mearsheimer, *The Great Delusion: Liberal Dreams and International Realities* (New Haven, Yale University Press, 2018) 172–74.

this has been the decision of the UK to leave the EU, in spite of the obvious (to us at least) negative effects this will almost certainly have both upon the UK and upon the cause of European unity and harmony.

Another reverberation after 1989 concerned the centrality of the role of the United Nations, and particularly the United Nations Security Council, in the promotion and maintenance of world peace and order, which became, even if temporarily, highly problematic. The 'unipolar world' which resulted from the disintegration of the Soviet Union and the changes in Eastern Europe left but one state with unchallenged and, as it seemed at the time, almost unchallengeable power. In terms of military strength, the US appeared unassailable, and explicitly intended to remain so for the foreseeable future. With its military spending outpacing that of all other states, its power seemed arguably sufficient for it to act unilaterally, whether to 'effect regime change', or to punish what it perceived to be 'rogue states' – either directly through force or indirectly via economic sanctions. This in turn was reinforced by its political, economic and physical power, which often allowed objectives to be achieved without the need for action, with other states coerced by the weight of reality into supporting US international policy goals.

In the earliest years of the twenty-first century, this distribution of power among nations seemed, if not permanent, at least destined to continue for some decades. It was not to be. With the economic and military rise of China especially, but also of India, 'unipolarity' came to appear an anachronistic understanding of the world, even while the US retains its huge conventional military advantage – an advantage largely countered by the economic strengths of emerging powers and the comparative economic decline of the US. This is also a time of many paradoxes. One of the most significant for our purposes is that, in an era when imperialism has given way to a recognition of the validity of a diversity of cultures no longer 'on the road to civilisation', globalisation seems to imply a homogeneity of goals quite incompatible with such real diversity and multiculturalism. So-called 'economic reality' seems to continue to dictate but one economic ideology and one particular form of government, both inherent in the idea of 'liberal democracy'. That this ideology is at the heart of the government of the world super-power is clearly not coincidental. Some indeed have effectively argued (although they would probably not accept that this is the argument) that the 'road to civilisation' has been replaced by the 'road to democratic governance'. Again, however, such comfortable assumptions no longer clearly represent any international consensus. Since the first edition, there has been a move away from respect for democratic governance towards rising intolerance of opposition and pluralism, as well as increasing persecution of those who attempt to assert or defend human rights. This is true in such disparate states as China, Russia, Turkey, Saudi Arabia, Egypt, the Philippines, Cambodia, Bangladesh, Rwanda and even EU members Poland and Hungary. Both in the US and Brazil, those in power have asserted the legality of human rights abuses – torture not least, which almost all lawyers in democratic states had long regarded as indisputably beyond the pale. The word 'liberal' preceding 'democracy' no longer seems totally, if at all, appropriate.

Perhaps it might also seem paradoxical to suggest that, at such a time as this, international law can have any real effect or be of any real importance in governing or constraining international events. If realism dictates an appreciation of dramatic political changes, should international law now be seen as either irrelevant or itself subject to such changes as will reflect this new power reality? And if it is the latter, does this not suggest that the true role of international law might be less to constrain than to legitimate (give legal authority to) what is done through power?

These are substantial questions and ones which underlie much of this book. Before considering them directly, however, basic ideas and methods of international law must be understood. The book begins with a discussion of the meaning of international law.

Before proceeding, one caveat must be entered. Because international law is so much about the law relating to states there is an almost irresistible urge to speak of states not simply as institutions but rather as animate entities – and indeed in international law they do enjoy 'legal personality'. Such anthropomorphism should be recognised for what it is. It is important to remember that when the book refers to states it is really just a shorthand way of referring to those with the power within the state.

III. Law and Power

A major concern of this book will be a constant consideration of the relationship between law and power. It is of course the role of law in any dispute resolution, whether domestic or international, to resolve the dispute by reference to rules rather than through force. If the rules are accepted then the effect is to negate the difference in power or access to force that the disputants might enjoy. This is in fact the essence of the 'Rule of Law': a move from the rule of the bigger stick to the rule of rules. Obviously, this negation of physical (or monetary, or intellectual) power difference acts in the interests of the less powerful, but, equally obviously, in international relations powerful states are often unwilling to see their power advantage negated by rules. This unwillingness may be reinforced if either the rules themselves can be questioned, or if, in the event of non-compliance, there are either no sanctions available or those that are, are unenforceable.

As we shall see, a major criticism of international law, voiced particularly by domestic lawyers and others not conversant with the subject, is concerned with this apparent lack of sanction. The suggestion will be made, however, that this does no more and no less than reflect one of the limitations in reality of the law way of seeing the world – a point that will be elucidated in due course.

IV. The Structure of the Book

Finally, we add one further caveat. Writing an introduction that is more than descriptive of a complex subject has proved more difficult than we had anticipated. In particular, there has been a constant dilemma as to how much 'hard' information (background facts) should be included. While attempting to avoid such inclusion wherever possible, we nevertheless felt bound both in the chapter on the UN and the chapter on human rights in international law to include information about the structure and organisation of the UN, and the documents forming the International Bill of Rights. Readers familiar with this information will, we hope, not allow its repetition to obscure the arguments that are being made.

The opening two chapters are intended to set the scene by discussing the meaning and structure of international law and why it should be seen as a dynamic legal regime. This necessitates a discussion of what international law is and how it relates to sovereignty and territory. The third chapter, utilising the concept of self-determination in international law, considers the interplay between international law and international politics and diplomacy, and this in turn leads, in chapter four, to a consideration of the obligations of a state both through treaties and the concept of state responsibility. Chapter five considers the centrality of the UN in the international legal regime, while chapter six deals with human rights and the rise of the individual as a partici-pant in international law. This is followed, in chapter seven, by a discussion of the peaceful resolution of disputes through international law, including the role played by the International Court of Justice, while chapter eight concen-trates on international law and the use of force. The final chapter effectively returns to the opening discussions of the relationship between law and power. In focusing upon the US and Israel, the conclusion is reached that powerful states and their closest allies are both able to ignore international law and to avoid direct sanction; however, such conduct imperils the very international legal regime with incalculable, but necessarily unfortunate, results.

1

The Distinctive Nature
of International Law

I. What is International Law?

There is no absolute consensus as to what is meant by the term 'international law', and it is more illuminating to describe the role that international law plays and the tasks it performs (or is intended to perform) than to rely on a dictionary definition. However, one useful attempted definition is provided by Professor Ivan Shearer, in *Starke's International Law*:

> International law may be defined as that body of law which is composed for its greater part of the principles and rules of conduct which states feel themselves bound to observe, and therefore, do commonly observe in their relations with each other, and which includes also:
>
> 1. the rules of law relating to the functioning of international institutions or organisations, their relations with each other, and their relations with states and individuals; and
> 2. certain rules of law relating to individuals and non-states so far as the rights or duties of such individuals and non-state entities are the concern of the international community.[1]

To fully understand such a description or definition, however, depends on some prior knowledge of the subject. In this respect, it is helpful to consider some of the topics with which international law is concerned. These include the questions of how states come into existence; how states may acquire territory; the law relating to the sea and the seabed; laws relating to the international use of force and warfare; the law relating to treaties; the settlement

---

[1] Ivan Shearer in JG Starke and Ivan Shearer (eds), *Starke's International Law* (London, Butterworths, 1994) 3.

of international disputes; and laws governing human rights, international crimes and the treatment of aliens. Moreover, useful though definitions such as the one above are, they do fail to take account of the dynamic quality of international law, which has led, and is leading, to changes both in the subjects of international law and its content. Although states are still central to the international legal regime, other international organisations, such as the United Nations (UN), the International Labour Organization (ILO) and the World Bank, have increasingly been brought within its remit. Individuals, too, have acquired subject status in some respects, as have private entities, such as corporations.

Since there was a time when only states were considered fit and proper subjects of international law, the sole function of which was to regulate relations *between* them, it followed that international law had no effect upon states' domestic arrangements. Furthermore, as each state was said to be sovereign, this implied that each nation was free to conduct itself entirely as it wished within the confines of its own borders (that is, the rulers of states were unconstrained by international law as to how they exercised their authority internally). However, even if such a statement were ever true in practice, it certainly requires modification now. In particular, the rapid development of human rights law from the second half of the twentieth century onwards has increasingly obliged states to conform to international norms in matters of domestic governance.

It should also be observed (but will be considered in more detail in chapter nine) that international law is often claimed not to amount to 'real' law, on the ground that there is no supranational authority able to issue sanctions in the event that a state fails to comply with a legal rule or breaches an obligation. Such an objection may be quickly dealt with by observing that sanctions are not a necessary part of a legal regime. Nevertheless, this is a criticism which, while it seems to us misplaced, continues to affect perceptions of international law by some writers and some states.

For certain authors, such as the late Antonio Cassese, international law is still insufficiently evolved, having so far failed to usher in an era of world governance, or perhaps even world government, in which the role played by international law more closely resembles that performed by domestic legislation.[2] Others, however, believe that such an outcome is to be resisted, and point to the ways in which international law already constrains what states are able to do within their own territories, and warn of the dangers of transferring powers from the elected governments of democratic states to a central and largely unaccountable body. This perspective, too, will be considered more fully in the concluding chapter.

---

[2] Antonio Cassese, *International Law*, 2nd edn (Oxford, OUP, 2005) 5.

II. How International Law Differs from Domestic Law

It is indisputable that there are distinct differences between international law and domestic or municipal law. In the international realm, there is no supreme – or, indeed, any other sort of – legislature or law-making body capable of promulgating binding legal rules. Instead, the international legal regime is overwhelmingly, but not exclusively, reliant on the consent of those whom it purports to govern. International law can, by and large, be created only through agreement; it can rarely coerce those who refuse to comply. In some ways it is analogous to members of a club making the club rules. It is this that led Cassese to suggest that the international legal regime is best understood as a *horizontal* system of organisation rather than a *vertical* one.[3] By this, he meant that, whereas in domestic legal systems, laws are passed down to the subjects from the law-making body, in international law it is the parties them-selves who make the laws by which they will be bound. Cassese regarded this as unsatisfactory, but it might better be seen as the inevitable result of inter-national law being concerned *primarily* with rules directed at sovereign states.

Similarly, there is no international court before which states in breach of international law may consistently be forced to appear. The International Court of Justice (ICJ) (considered in chapter seven) is empowered to decide disputes between states (and only states have such standing if the Court is to make an authoritative ruling in a contentious case), but it can do so only if the states in question have consented to this. And, although some states have accepted the compulsory jurisdiction of the Court, this will be effective only if all the states parties to the dispute have accepted that compulsory jurisdic-tion. At present, only a minority of states have done so. More frequently, the Court will have jurisdiction only where the states parties to a dispute consent to the Court adjudicating in respect of that particular dispute. The Court has no role in punishing states that have contravened their international law obli-gations, nor can it compel a state to comply with its judgment. Thus, here too, the emphasis remains upon consent.

The importance of such consent rests upon two crucial, but not natural, facts. The first is that each state is said to be sovereign in its own territory. This does not mean that the rulers of a state can govern with utter impunity: as mentioned above, it has been accepted (generally, if not in particular cases) that human rights law places constraints on what states are able

---

[3] ibid 5–6.

to do within their own borders. Notwithstanding this, and although subject to some important qualifications, sovereignty is still regarded as allowing states to exercise full control in their domestic jurisdictions (discussed further in chapter two). This remains true even though a state may willingly accept limits upon its sovereignty, as have, for example, the states of the European Union (EU).

The second fact is that there is universal acceptance of the sovereign equality of states: that is, each state is equal in its sovereignty. Needless to say, and this does have implications for the arguments presented in this book, such sovereignty is formal and legal in its equality rather than actual. The relative power of states does not alter this aspect of equality, however: just as, under the rule of law, each individual has formal equality before the law, so in international law each state is equal. The respect accorded to sovereignty and sovereign equality explains why it is generally unrealistic to expect a greater level of coercion and sanction in international law than is currently the case.

III. The Changing Nature of International Law

Few areas of law have changed as radically as has international law over the last 150 years or so. According to Cassese, it is helpful to think of international law as having evolved over four major periods.[4] His suggested division reinforces the argument that the development of international law in the modern era is to be found largely in the history of Europe. This is certainly true of his first two stages, and partly true of the third. While there is a history of international law that precedes Cassese's, this is largely concerned with treaties concluded between ancient states, dealing with such matters as territory, trade and financial obligations, and is probably best viewed as forming the backdrop to the crucial transformation that was ushered in by the Peace of Westphalia, which brought an end to the Thirty Years' War in 1648 and also instituted the modern system of sovereign states.

What emerged as international law in this first period, from 1648 to the end of the First World War in 1918, consisted almost exclusively of rules governing relations between states. The individuals that resided within those states figured scarcely at all. Of course, in so far as states have always been inanimate entities, the reality was that international law governed the relationships between state governments, which in turn were composed of individuals, albeit acting in an official capacity. This period is normally characterised as

---

[4] ibid 22–45.

one in which international law was primarily descriptive, in that it described how states generally conducted their affairs with one another, but which was hardly normative, meaning that it did not seek to direct states as to how they should behave. In particular, little or no restraint was placed upon the threat or use of force by states powerful enough to do as they wished. Such international law as existed was informed by the mutual interests of those same states (well-exemplified by rules relating to the world of diplomacy and diplomats) and was also reflective of a world of colonies and the colonial powers which ruled over them.

Cassese's second period runs from the end of the First World War to the end of the Second World War in 1945. The aftermath of the 1914–18 conflict saw the establishment of the League of Nations and the Permanent Court of International Justice (the forerunners of, respectively, the UN and the ICJ), and was the era during which perspectives on world organisation changed significantly. The founding of the League of Nations represented the first real acknowledgement of the need for an institution to assist in regulating relations between states. One of its central goals was to limit the right of states to wage war to a number of stated causes, and also to discourage states from resorting to war at all – by providing for cooling-off periods, by instituting a scheme of disarmament, and by promoting the peaceful settlement of disputes. It was in furtherance of this latter aim that the Permanent Court of International Justice was created in 1922.

The League obviously failed to preserve the peace; however, two aspects of its functioning remain historically important (three if one remembers the contribution to socio-economic progress made particularly by the ILO). The first concerns 'minority treaties', the significance of which lay less in any success they achieved in their own right than in the fact that they served as a precursor of human rights protection under international law. Peace treaties negotiated at the end of the First World War insisted that, in return for recognition, certain nation states with significant ethnic minorities entered into agreements to protect the rights of these minority populations. The responsibility for guaranteeing and supervising these minority treaties was allocated to the League, which developed a (rather ineffective) 'minority petition procedure', viewed as the process that initiated transnational claims-making. However, although the minority treaties dealt implicitly with human rights issues, they were concerned not with the rights of individuals but with those of groups or collectivities. The other notable development (explored in chapter three) originated with the League's mandate system, which appeared, at least tacitly, to accept that subjected peoples should be 'brought towards' self-government, thereby sowing the seeds for the great wave of decolonisation that was to take place in the two decades following the Second World War.

The transformations that occurred in Cassese's third period, spanning the end of the Second World War to the end of the Cold War in 1991, encompass, most prominently, the creation of the UN (in place of the League);

the holding of the Nuremberg trials, which affirmed that individuals could be held responsible for their conduct under international law; the development of the concept of self-determination (along with the accompanying demise of West European empires); and the debut onto the international stage of a great number of new states, as many colonies gained their independence and were, for the first time, able to contribute towards the formation of international law. Also of great and continuing significance was the drafting and signing of the Universal Declaration of Human Rights in 1948, not least for the emphasis it placed on individual human rights. Most of these developments will be discussed in subsequent chapters, since they continue to occupy an important place in the history of international law.

Cassese's final period, covering the end of the Cold War to 2005, when his book was published, is still unfolding, although the full significance of the changes brought about by the disintegration of the USSR is still not entirely clear. What is apparent, however, is the dramatic effect that this initially had on the balance of power. Owing to the frequent use of the veto in the Security Council between 1948 and 1990, the ability of the UN to preserve or create peace had been very limited. Many thought that the break-up of the USSR would enable the UN to become much more powerful and active, and certainly the 1990–91 Gulf War (aimed at restoring the sovereignty of Kuwait) offered some hope that this might be the case. In fact, the outcome has been distinctly mixed. Another major consequence of the dissolution of the USSR was the elevation of the US to the status of the world's only super-power. In 2005, it did seem that the world could be described as 'unipolar', so superior was the US in comparison with all its rivals both militarily and in terms of productivity. The other seminal event in this period for the development of international law was of course the terrorist attacks against the US on 11 September 2001, although quite how international law has been affected is still a matter for debate.

Regrettably, Antonio Cassese died in 2011, before he had time to publish his thoughts on events after 2005, when the last edition of his book was issued. Nevertheless, it is perhaps appropriate to consider how significantly the international world of 2019 differs from that of 14 years ago, and how this might alter the Cassese assessment of the place and role of international law. From a Western perspective, the greatest challenge was posed by the financial crisis of 2007–08, the adverse consequences of which are by no means resolved. Whether this event was a cause of current upheavals or merely a catalyst is arguable, but what is certain is that its effects have reverberated throughout the economic, social, political and cultural worlds to an extent that could not have been foreseen in 2005.

It is now clear that the idea that the world is 'unipolar', with only one world superpower, requires at least some qualification. The rise of China, and its refusal to accept the world and its borders and divisions as defined by the US and its allies as immutable, is undeniable. Although the US's military spending continues to greatly exceed that of its potential competitors,[5] its continued unchallengeable superiority can no longer be assumed. Indeed, the limitations of military power and threats have become increasingly evident since 2001, and it is difficult to point to any US military triumphs from that time. In economic terms, the threat posed to the US is easier to discern, with China having surpassed the US in GDP based on purchasing-power parity in 2017.[6] Furthermore, certain states which are incomparably economically weaker than the US (among others, Russia, Pakistan and North Korea) possess arsenals of nuclear weapons capable of jeopardising the future of humanity, thus rendering technical inequality of arms irrelevant.

Not entirely coincidentally, there has also been a considerable change in attitudes to nation states. Whereas in 2005 there was almost universal and unquestioning acceptance of the obvious morality of decolonisation, 2019 allows us to see that the break-up of the USSR and Yugoslavia presaged a radical reassessment of both nationhood and self-determination. Nation states had come to be depicted as 'natural' phenomena, the continuing existence (and borders) of which were to be found guaranteed in the UN Charter and in UN membership – a portrayal strengthened by the rejection of Iraq's purported annexation of Kuwait in 1990 and Kuwait's subsequent 'liberation' seven months later by US-led coalition forces. It was also of the essence of nationhood (at least theoretically) that a state exercised complete control (sovereignty) over its internal affairs, enjoying a monopoly over the legitimate domestic use of force and the freedom to design its own financial and monetary structures and policies. This 'common sense' view of sovereignty is increasingly under threat, even in the case of more affluent and powerful nations, which in turn has significant implications for international law.

First, it is now ever clearer that decolonisation was, for a number of reasons, hardly an unalloyed success. The continent of Africa serves as the most obvious example, although this is not to suggest that colonialism was in any way a preferable system of administration: indeed, in many ways, it was responsible for the manifest failures of many now 'independent' African states (more fully discussed in chapter three). Instead of decolonisation (albeit within borders defined by the colonial power) bringing democracy, unity, financial viability and a measure of equality to the newly recognised state's citizens, too often it has brought continued economic exploitation, authoritarian government (often approximating dictatorship), environmental degradation, ethnic and

---

[5] Reaching $610 billion in 2017, over two-and-a-half times more than the estimated $228 billion spent by China, the next largest source of military expenditure. See Stockholm International Peace Research Institute data on military expenditure by country for 2017 at www.sipri.org/sites/default/files/1_Data%20for%20all%20countries%20from%201988%E2%80%932017%20in%20constant%20%282016%29%20USD.pdf.

[6] Vittorio Valli, *The American Economy from Roosevelt to Trump* (London, Palgrave Macmillan, 2018) 185.

religious conflict, wholesale corruption and a complete rejection of accountability and the rule of law. Internationally, a major effect of this inability
or unwillingness to govern in the interests of the populace has been a vast
increase in displaced persons, both internally and externally (as refugees).[7]
Indeed, the number of refugees now exceeds that of those seeking refuge after
the Second World War, fleeing the chaos and violence of war-torn and 'failed'
states, including, but by no means limited to, Syria, Afghanistan, Democratic
Republic of the Congo, Somalia, Myanmar and South Sudan (still the world's
youngest state, admitted to the UN as recently as 2011).

Secondly, globalisation has greatly affected the very nature of nationhood. Although it was never entirely clear what sovereignty implied, or quite
where its limits lay, Article 2(7) of the UN Charter reaffirmed the principle of
non-interference in 'matters which are essentially within the domestic jurisdiction of any State' – a reaffirmation which, while palpably ambiguous,
was not without meaning. However, from the earliest days of decolonisation,
newly independent states were immediately confronted with the realities
of the economic world of which they formed part. As will be discussed in
chapter three, political self-determination did not necessarily entail economic
self-determination, and the ability of the decolonised to assert control over
their economic affairs was limited by constraints of fact, such as the difficulty
of asserting title to property held by the colonising power or its commercial
enterprises, at least without the payment of full compensation.

The twenty-first century and the intensification of globalisation has
greatly complicated and muddled the old concept of a 'society of nations'
as envisaged in the UN Charter and by those who drafted it. No longer can
state governments, whether of colonial or colonised origin, exercise the level
of control over their economies that once seemed, at least to Western countries, natural and obvious. This becomes evident when comparing government
revenues with corporate turnover: in 2016, of the top 100 global economic
entities, 69 were multinational corporations, scarcely controllable by the
nation state.[8] Notwithstanding the crisis of 2007–08 – arguably largely caused
by financial deregulation at both the national and international level – there
has been no substantial strengthening of financial governance; and currently
the Trump administration is exploring reducing such regulation even further.
National regulation, even where politically acceptable, often lacks the power
to be effective. As a result, the ability of individual states to determine such

---

[7] Totalling 68.5 million in 2017, according to statistics compiled by the United Nations High
Commissioner for Refugees, of which 40 million were internally displaced persons; 25.4 million,
refugees; and 3.1 million, asylum-seekers. This was equivalent to an average of 44,400 displace-
ments every day in 2017. Around 16.9 million refugees, 85% of the total of refugees worldwide,
were being hosted in developing regions. UNHCR, 'Global Trends: Forced Displacement in
2017', 25 June 2018, available at www.unhcr.org/5b27be547.pdf.

[8] According to the World Bank in September 2016; see https://blogs.worldbank.org/
publicsphere/world-s-top-100-economies-31-countries-69-corporations.

economic fundamentals as capital flows, interest rates and the taxation of foreign enterprises has been greatly diminished. Some idea of the velocity of the movement of capital can be gauged from the startling figures of April 2016, which revealed that the average daily turnover in foreign currency trading in London was $2.426 billion, with worldwide daily currency trading amounting to $5.1 trillion. Any intimation of possible national restrictions upon the free movement of capital risks provoking capital flight, to the immediate detriment of the national economy and currency in question. Consequently, individual states are locked into a capitalist world that is becoming increasingly difficult to influence.

The financial crisis did have other consequences of indirect importance for international law. In the first place, many states adopted 'austerity policies' in order to redress the losses that the banking crisis had caused – some, such as the UK, voluntarily; others, under intense international pressure, of which Greece is a prime example (John Maynard Keynes's view that 'austerity is the enemy of prosperity' having fallen out of favour). State austerity has implications for policy not unlike those that resulted from the old 'structural adjustment policies' insisted upon by the International Monetary Fund in exchange for loans to heavily indebted poor countries, and which closely followed the mandate of the Washington Consensus – privatisation of state-owned property and state-run services, reductions in government expenditure (impacting health, welfare and education, but not normally defence), the abolition of subsidies (covering basic food and fuel necessities), coupled with policies thought likely to attract foreign investment and facilitate a return to private credit markets: liberalisation of capital flows, an increase in interest rates, and reductions in corporate and income tax (mainly of benefit to the wealthy). Secondly, as a result of such policies, even where the gross domestic product of a state increased, the beneficiaries were few in number and to be found in foreign investors and the already rich. Consequently, in almost every state, while the 'affluence' of the working and middle class has remained at best static, the percentage of wealth held by a tiny minority of individuals has burgeoned considerably.[9] As summarised by Rana Dasgupta, in an article tellingly entitled 'The demise of the nation state': 'In brief, 20th century political structures are drowning in a 21st century ocean of deregulated finance, autonomous technology, religious militancy and great-power rivalry.'[10] His point about autonomous technology is also important for the development of international law, as may be illustrated, to give two very different examples,

[9] Despite a significant increase in the income of the poorest half of the world's population (mainly owing to high growth in China and India), Oxfam reported that rising global inequality meant that, between 1980 and 2016, 'the top 1% richest individuals in the world captured twice as much growth as the bottom 50%'. Oxfam, *World Inequality Report 2018* 7 and 9, available at wir2018.wid.world/files/download/wir2018-summary-english.pdf.

[10] *Guardian*, 5 April 2018.

by electronic trading in worldwide stock exchanges, and by the development of 'drones' in warfare.

Much of the resulting discontent at stagnating or deteriorating living standards has arguably been channelled into – or has been co-opted by – populist parties and politicians,[11] often with scant regard for democratic niceties and the rule of law.[12] This has had ramifications at both the domestic and the international level. Within states, one can point, for example, to the constitutional 'reforms' initiated by President Recep Erdoğan of Turkey or President Viktor Orbán of Hungary aimed at arrogating more power to themselves and their parties, the attempt of the governing Law and Justice Party (PiS) in Poland to remodel the country's Supreme Court more to its ideological liking,[13] and the threats made by Donald Trump and Jair Bolsonaro before assuming presidential office in the US and Brazil respectively that they would refuse to accept as legitimate the election of any other candidate. As to the international realm, disillusion with globalisation and the supposed benefits brought by international trade has led many populations, in the West in particular, to align with those who advocate a renewed strengthening of the nation state, disparage supranational and global institutions, and embrace economic protectionism and an anti-immigration agenda. This has been demonstrated

[11] A careful examination of populism and what constitutes a populist politician or party can be found in Jan-Werner Müller, *What is Populism?* (London, Penguin Books, 2017). Müller makes clear that what distinguishes populists from other political actors, and makes them a potential threat to democracy, is not their adoption of an anti-establishment stance or a willingness to rail against governing elites, but their anti-pluralism. That is, populists assert that they are the only true representatives of the people, regard all political opponents as illegitimate, and portray those who refuse to support them as not forming part of the people proper. Indeed, the 'real people' they claim to represent are less actual citizens than a symbolic construction whose views conveniently happen to coincide with the policies that the populist wishes to impose. Thus, in the current UK context, the various, often wildly diverging, visions of different British politicians regarding the UK's future relationship with its European neighbours after the country departs from the EU are each said to represent 'the will of the people'.

[12] Although see Roger Eatwell and Matthew Goodwin, *National Populism: The Revolt Against Liberal Democracy* (London, Pelican, 2018), whose research demonstrates that a diverse range of people vote for populist politicians, including the relatively affluent – as well as the young, people from ethnic minorities, and women; ie the populist-supporting demographic is certainly not confined to the 'angry old white men' of popular liberal imagining. They point to four main factors driving support for populist movements: distrust of established parties and institutions; a sense of relative deprivation (ie the feeling of falling behind relative to others in society, including immigrants); fear that social and cultural changes in society are destroying traditional identities and ways of life; and an erosion in allegiance to traditional political parties (what the authors term 'de-alignment'), which has created a more unstable political landscape and opportunities for newcomers, including populists.

[13] Roughly a third of the judges serving on the Court lost their jobs after the PiS Government lowered the retirement age for the posts in question from 70 to 65. This resulted in the European Commission condemning the action as politically motivated (the Government had described the measure as necessary in order to remove Communist-era judges from the Court) and initiating proceedings under Art 7 of the Treaty of the European Union to remove Poland's voting rights in the EU. In compliance with a temporary ruling issued by the European Court of Justice in October 2018, the Government reversed the retirement legislation, reinstating the judges.

most starkly by the Trump administration's 'America First' stance (discussed in chapter nine), which has seen the withdrawal of the US from many international institutions, treaties and accords, the triggering of a trade war with China, and the implementation of harsh, at times inhumane, border controls, accompanied by unequivocally racist rhetoric. It can also be witnessed in the UK's deeply divisive decision to leave the EU ('Brexit'), as well as in a rise in support across much of Europe for parties situated both to the left and right of the traditional political spectrum, including increased support for clearly xenophobic and/or racist parties (for example, the UK Independence Party, Alternative für Deutschland in Germany, Fidesz in Hungary, La Liga in Italy, Rassemblement National (formerly Front National) in France, the Freedom Parties in Austria and the Netherlands, the Finns Party in Finland, and Vox in Spain). Such parties oppose the admission of refugees and are hostile to immigration in general, blaming immigrants for job losses, declining living standards, crumbling infrastructure and rising crime rates. They are also generally antagonistic to the EU both in relation to its economic policies, especially in the Eurozone (budget constraints in order to meet deficit targets, austerity measures after the financial crisis), and what the Hungarian and Polish governments in particular have criticised as an over-liberal social and cultural agenda (supportive, for example, of gay marriage and rights to abortion), which they argue is alien to the conservative mores of their respective states.

It is these challenging political realities that now provide the setting for international law in 2019 and the years to come.

IV. International Law and Common Sense

It is often said that the international law way of understanding the world is essentially Eurocentric. According to this view, although the assumptions that underpin international law and the methods that it employs appear very reasonable and obvious to those trained in the common law or civil law tradition, it is important to realise that they are in fact contingent rather than necessary. This means that we have to be able to appreciate that international law is not common sense, but rather a particular way of attempting to deal with international relations and problems, and one that continues to be heavily informed by a European perspective, although this is not to suggest that such a perspective is uncontested.

The foundations of current international law were laid down in an era that predates the creation of the majority of nation states. Equally clearly, the antecedents of international law are overwhelmingly European (within which, for this purpose, we can include the US), since the system evolved at a time of European hegemony, most overtly expressed through colonialism. Because of this, it can be persuasively argued that the international legal regime is fundamentally European in its processes and its ideology. What is meant by this is that international law reflects a *particular* way of perceiving the world, in which even the most basic premises underlying the system, such as those concerning the nature of sovereignty, and even the acceptance of the underlying principle of *pacta sunt servanda* (roughly translated as 'treaties must be observed', but with rather wider implications), are arguably the product of a Western mindset.

Before discussing the significance of this further, a broader but related point must be made. It is not insignificant that most (British, in particular) international law textbooks seem implicitly to reject the assumption that international law is intimately and necessarily interrelated with contemporary international events. The inference to be drawn from the content of some of the most eminent texts is not only that law is separate and distinct from political relationships and international relations, but that, because of this, a study of international law can be a very pure one indeed. To the extent that politics does impinge upon such texts, it tends to be from the vantage point of history rather than that of the contemporary world, and is a history that is often decontextualised and 'objective' – ie treated as a series of uncontested facts. Very often, if the greatest international events appear at all, they appear only in the form of desiccated legal decisions or opinions, bringing to mind a remark attributed to the late Harvard law professor Thomas Reed Powell: 'If you think that you can think about a thing inextricably attached to something else without thinking of the thing which it is attached to, then you have a legal mind.'

The majority of such doctrinal texts also have a remarkably standard set of contents, with the main differences to be found in the depth of analysis and the variety of emphasis. Such orthodoxy should breed suspicion, particularly if it is accepted that any study of international law must be concerned with the politics that underlie it, the power relations it may disguise, and the ideology that the 'law way of thinking' conceals. In turn, it should be clear that the ideological assumptions that underpin international law are not confined to the substantive content of the discipline, but also permeate its very processes and procedures. One clear example of this is the International Court of Justice case *Nicaragua v USA* (actually, there are two separate decisions, one dealing with procedural questions of jurisdiction and admissibility,[14] and the other concerned with the substance of the dispute[15]). International law textbooks tend to approach this case by isolating the many legal propositions

---

[14] *Military and Paramilitary Activities in and against Nicaragua (Nicaragua v United States of America), Jurisdiction and Admissibility, Judgment,* ICJ Reports 1984, 392.
[15] *Military and Paramilitary Activities in and against Nicaragua (Nicaragua v United States of America), Merits, Judgment,* ICJ Reports 1986, 14.

asserted, particularly those that relate to the use of force. But they usually do so without mentioning the factual background to the case or the international relations saga that both preceded and followed it. Unless, however, something is known of the Sandinista revolution that overthrew the tyrannical Samoza regime, together with the subsequent activities of the US-backed 'Contras' in attempting to destabilise the newly installed government, as well as the aftermath of the affair after the US withdrew from the Court's jurisdiction and refused to comply with its final judgment, then any understanding of the case's legal points must be at best partial. In other words, the power relationship between the parties cannot be totally ignored. To illustrate this proposition about decontextualisation (in itself an essential element in European legal dispute resolution) it is useful to consider one exception: Antonio Cassese's *International Law in a Divided World*,[16] which, although written while the Soviet Union was still in existence (in 1986), remains relevant, and does address the lack of universal acceptance of international law method. Cassese drew attention to the fact that the so-called 'developing' countries and 'socialist states' (inappropriately labelled but nevertheless significantly different from the liberal capitalist states of the West at the time when he was writing) had very different perceptions of what international law was and what it was for, compared with their Western counterparts. For example, Cassese points out that, for certain African states, informed by a different cultural tradition, based on lineage and clan, and having suffered under colonialism, international law is not viewed as an abstract problem-solver (as it often appears in Western textbooks and international texts), but rather 'is relevant to the extent that it protects them from undue influence by powerful states and is instrumental in bringing about social change with more equitable conditions stimulating economic development'.[17]

We may not be comfortable with such a sweeping statement, but what is particularly important is the conclusions that Cassese draws from it. He argues that it is because of such generalisation that we can see many developing states very much preferring to 'elaborate general principles as opposed to detailed and precise legal rules',[18] citing in this regard the eminent Egyptian international lawyer Professor Georges Abi-Saab:

> [I]n dealing especially with the Western countries, anything which could be formulated in the very precise terms of an operational rule was considered nonsense [by developing countries] while Third World representatives in general attached great weight to general principles which sometimes could not be refined into operational rules. If we look at the same thing from a different point of view I would say that in most cases the attitude of the Third World was defined by the total effect of a proposed solution ... I think that the Western powers put too much emphasis

---

[16] Antonio Cassese, *International Law in a Divided World* (Oxford, Clarendon Press, 1986).
[17] ibid 119.
[18] ibid.

on the mechanistic elements [of law] while for Third World countries if by going through all the motions and respecting all the procedural rules you end up with an unjust solution, this would be bad law. And if you have a general directive, even if you cannot reduce it to very precise procedural rules, it is still good law, though it may be imperfect in terms of application.[19]

In certain respects this observation summarises a fundamental distinction in the way in which international law in particular (but also municipal law to some extent) is perceived. It is of the essence of the law way (meaning the 'rule of law way') of dealing with the world that the rules precede the facts to which they are to be applied. Indeed, it is this that makes the writing of 'pure international law textbooks' apparently sensible. It is also of the essence of both contract law and treaty law that, in general, rules are laid down providing for future possibilities. To most of us this seems, no doubt, obvious and sensible, but the above remark highlights the potential shortcomings of structuring rules to ensure justiciable disputes (disputes presented in a form that enables them to be decided by a court of law). If the outcome of applying rules, or treaty provisions, or even contractual terms leads to results which one party is very unwilling to accept, especially when they arise from situations unforeseen or unexpected at the time when the rule, or treaty, or contract was devised, then those who do not identify with the Western view of international law might well consider it dysfunctional. The preoccupation of international lawyers with the need to structure problems in a way which makes them justiciable is of central importance. From the perspective of Western international lawyers, indeed, treaties or rules which do not allow the formulation of problems in this way are often accorded significantly less respect than those that do. (A point to which we will return later in our brief discussion of so-called 'soft law'.)

Crucially (and this proposition underlies much of the argument of this book), only if the 'rule of law' approach to international law is seen as a *particular* way of organising the world, rather than as common sense, can we begin to appreciate the significance of international law in the international community as a whole. What has been suggested to be singular about the international law way of encompassing the world is both 'rule magic', which means that situations in the future are governed by rules that, when made, either did not have within their contemplation the facts of all subsequent cases, or were made without the participation of a party now said to be subject to them; and also the need for social facts to be translated into legal ones. What always distinguishes legal disputes from other kinds of dispute is the structuring of the issues, whereby many of the facts that the parties to the dispute think important (or at least one party might) are irrelevant for the purposes of legal resolution. Indeed, in the *Nicaragua v USA* cases mentioned

[19] ibid 119–20.

above, the ICJ was clearly concerned to avoid making judgments about the parties' conduct, except insofar as this conduct was amenable to legal resolution.

What is the significance of this? First, it should be made clear that, in transposing issues from the social and political world into the legal realm, one effect is often to apparently depoliticise a dispute. Legal questions have an appearance of objectivity and neutrality: it is the law which is being considered, and this seems very different from a political dispute. (This is discussed further in chapter four.) Nonetheless, it should be appreciated that legal questions do, in fact, always have a political dimension, as indeed does the law itself.

V. What Makes International Law 'Law'?

Most international lawyers would claim that what distinguishes international law from international relations, bringing it within the definition of law, is that it is a 'distinctive mode of discourse' (although that might not be the phrase they would use!). In other words, the law way of discussing international issues is distinctive because of the rules, procedures and processes that it brings to bear on the matters concerned. Indeed, even the formulation of the issues in a dispute will be shaped in accordance with legal principles and rules. Moreover, every state does accept the existence of international law as something distinct from ordinary international intercourse. Dealing with the last point first, this acceptance of the reality of international law by states stands as an important refutation of the argument that international law is not really law because it has no means of enforcing compliance. After all, in the realm of domestic law, the fact that legal rules are regularly broken and those that break them routinely escape any form of sanction is of only marginal importance in determining whether a particular rule or body of law exists or amounts to 'real law'. Of much more significance is the fact that most citizens internalise the legal values of their societies, particularly those that are embodied in criminal law, even if they do not always obey the law's rules and regulations. Even wrongdoers very seldom attempt to deny the authenticity of the law, and will commonly seek to justify their actions as being lawful. This is just as true at the international level.

When Iraq's Saddam Hussein ordered the invasion of Kuwait in 1990, he did not announce that he intended to flout or, worse still, ignore international law. Rather, he attempted (albeit hardly convincingly) to defend his actions as being consistent with international law. Hence, he not only suggested that the invasion was an act of legitimate self-defence, but also referred to historic Iraqi claims over Kuwaiti territory. Similarly, when the US invaded Grenada in 1983, it too, albeit belatedly and a little half-heartedly, attempted to justify the invasion as a lawful exercise of self-defence in order to protect US citizens. The fact that this 'justification' withstood little scrutiny is less important for our purposes than the fact that the US Government felt bound to make it. Very much the same was true of the US's invasion of Panama to capture General Noriega in 1989. Even the claim by China that both Tibet and Taiwan are integral components of China's territory is couched in terms calculated to appeal to international law. NATO's intervention in the former Republic of Yugoslavia in 1999 was defended as being consistent with international law, while even Israel's activities in Gaza in 2008–09, which resulted in the deaths of 1,400 Gazans and 13 Israelis were said (at least by Israel and the US) not necessarily to amount to a breach of international law as they were a 'legitimate' response to rockets being fired from Gaza into Israel. There was also, of course, the vigorous and often vituperative debate ignited by the 2003 invasion of Iraq by the US and certain of its allies, including the UK, which toppled Saddam Hussein. The legality (or not) of this operation assumed centre stage, with many, including some prominent political figures, maintaining not only that the intervention was illegal, but also that this illegality was determinative of the matter: that is, if the invasion was in contravention of international law, then it should not have been undertaken, and any other possible justification, whether political or moral, was simply irrelevant. The argument that the UK had participated in an illegal war even featured prominently in the political debates leading up to the country's general election in 2005. Also interesting was the sheer effort that was expended by both the US and UK Governments, both before and after the Iraqi war, in attempting to persuade the international community and their respective nationals that the course of action they had chosen to undertake did in fact comply with international law. More recently, when, in March 2014, Russia purported to formally incorporate Crimea into the Russian state, it denied that this was an unlawful annexation, arguing, among other matters, that this represented a lawful act of self-determination, justified by the concept of 'remedial secession' (the supposed right of a people to secede when suffering severe oppression).

As Brierly (an eminent UK authority on international law) wrote in 1944:

> The best evidence for the existence of international law is that every actual state recognises that it does exist and that it is itself under an obligation to observe it. States may often violate international law, just as individuals often violate municipal law, but no more than individuals do states defend their violations by claiming that they are above the law.[20]

As to international law's 'distinctive mode of discourse', this derives in part from its sources and origin. International law essentially comes into existence

---

[20] James Brierly, *The Outlook for International Law* (Oxford, Clarendon Press, 1944) 5.

either through treaties (requiring the consent of those states that are to be bound by them) or as a result of custom, and usually, but not always, custom which has been long established. Of course, not all custom is held to be international law: only that which states have come to regard as legally binding. Thus, custom becomes international law only when the states observing the custom do so in the belief that the custom forms part of international law. The fact that there is no legislature in the international realm able to create law is simply reflective, it can be argued, of the reality of sovereignty. As Shabtai Rosenne points out:

> International law is a law of co-ordination, not, as is the case of most internal law, a law of subordination. By law of co-ordination we mean to say that it is created and applied by its own subjects, primarily the independent states (directly or indirectly), for their own common purposes.[21]

Returning to the point that the law way of dealing with international issues is a distinct one (that is, legal discourse is distinguishable from the language of general international relations), it can be argued that what differentiates the law way from the social way of resolving disputes is that the law always requires a translation of social facts into legal facts. This is true of both domestic and international law. However, this necessary translation is arguably both law's greatest strength and, paradoxically, its greatest weakness. Its strength is that, when a dispute is cast in legal terms involving legal issues, it becomes legally resolvable, in that there will (almost invariably) be a legal solution to the legal problem. But this can also be a major weakness, depending on the nature of the dispute, because a resolution of the legal issues will not in itself solve the social ('untranslated') problem. Consequently, the law way of settling disputes works 'best' when all the parties to the dispute accept the 'legalisation' of the dispute.

This is one of the main reasons why only a minority of states accept the compulsory jurisdiction of the ICJ. There is little point in having a dispute legally resolved if the underlying political problems remain. Unless the parties to the dispute, together with the constituencies they represent, accept that the legal outcome truly disposes of the issue, the resolution itself may have little effect or may simply lead to further disagreements. In due course, when we consider at some length the role, effect and politics of the ICJ, this argument will be made by reference to selected cases that have come before it. Suffice to say at this point, that, while any number of cases could be selected to illustrate the proposition, a prominent feature of the translation of a social or political dispute into a legal one will be the initial selection of *legally relevant facts*.

[21] Shabtai Rosenne, *Practice and Methods of International Law* (New York, Oceana, 1984) 2.

Almost invariably, the selection of these facts not only structures the legal issues and thus the questions that will be adjudicated, but also involves, at the very least, a modification of the political arguments.

We will now consider more fully the sources and method of international law that facilitate its singular function.

VI. Why is it Necessary to Identify the Sources of International Law?

By 'sources of international law' is meant the processes or means by which rules of international law are created or determined. Given the points made earlier about the significant dissimilarities between domestic and international law, it clearly follows that their sources will also be different. As there is no international equivalent of a legislature, the rules of international law are of a quite different nature from those of municipal law, and are overwhelmingly derived from either or both of the two major sources creating legally binding obligations: treaty and/ or customary international law.

In the domestic realm, the source of a rule or law is seldom controversial. Common law systems rely upon statutes and the decisions to be found in court judgments for evidence of the existence of such a rule; civil law systems rely upon the appropriate legislation or codes. It is rarely necessary in either system to inquire whether a legal rule is in fact a legal rule, and its existence, if not its interpretation, will be uncontroversial. Exceptionally, a further question may arise as to the legitimacy of the rule. If so, this will usually concern the status of the rule, which may be affected by procedural defects, or it may be that the rule is deemed ultra vires (that is, the body that purported to create the rule in fact lacked the power to do so). When such a difficulty does arise, there are almost always other rules and procedures that allow for the testing of the validity of the rule in question.

Various authors have described such domestic systems in terms of primary and secondary rules. The rules that simply govern conduct are the primary rules, while the 'rules about the rules' (that is, those used to determine their legitimacy) are said to be secondary. International law presents different problems, which is why all international law textbooks have a section devoted to the question of sources. Notably, however, there is no absolute agreement about what constitutes a source of international law. Consequently, questions relating to the secondary rules not only occur with much greater frequency in international law contexts, but are also more difficult to resolve. International customary law presents particular difficulties, and many cases turn on whether the existence of a customary rule can actually be proven.

A. Article 38(1) of the Statute of the International Court of Justice

The closest approximation to an authoritative list of the relevant sources of international law, and the one that is most often cited, is found in Article 38(1) of the Statute of the ICJ. This states:

> 1. The Court, whose function is to decide in accordance with international law such disputes as are submitted to it, shall apply:
>   a.   international conventions, whether general or particular, establishing rules expressly recognized by the contesting states;
>   b.   international custom, as evidence of a general practice accepted as law;
>   c.   the general principles of law recognized by civilized nations;
>   d.   subject to the provisions of Article 59 ['The decision of the Court has no binding effect except between the parties and in respect of that particular case'] judicial decisions and the teachings of the most highly qualified publicists of the various nations, as subsidiary means for the determination of rules of law.

What will be noticed is that this is not intended as a general statement of sources of international law, but is rather an instruction to the ICJ as to the law the Court is to apply in deciding cases brought before it. Moreover, it has been pointed out that, even on its own terms as a general instruction to the Court, the list is inadequate, because it is incomplete. (It does not, for instance, refer to UN General Assembly resolutions, which under some circumstances have been used to evidence international law. Nor yet does it allude to UN Security Council resolutions, even though, under Article 25 of the UN Charter, all UN members agree to accept and give effect to Security Council decisions.) This is perhaps not surprising, as the wording of Article 38 replicates almost exactly that of Article 38 of the statute of the ICJ's predecessor, the Permanent Court of International Justice, which was established as far back as 1922. Notwithstanding this, so overwhelmingly dominant are the sources of 'international conventions' (ie treaties) and 'international custom, as evidence of a general practice accepted as law' (customary international law) that it is these with which we will be primarily concerned.

Obviously, custom and treaty can be seen as closely related. Both rely on the consent of the parties to be bound, but, in the case of customary international law, the consent is often tacit or implicit, whereas, in regard to treaties, it is expressed and explicit. Nonetheless, they do differ, in that customary law usually ends up binding all states, whereas treaties are generally confined in their effect to the states which are parties to them. Sometimes, however, a treaty may explicitly state a rule of customary international law, and sometimes, where the terms of a treaty are very widely accepted by states not parties to the treaty, they may over time come to be accepted as customary international law.

Treaties and customary international law are closely related in another way as well. Although treaties have multiplied and continue to do so, it can be argued that they depend for their legitimacy and efficacy upon customary international law. The principle underlying much of the international law between nations is, as mentioned above, *pacta sunt servanda*.

B. International Treaties

Although treaty law is discussed in chapter four, it is appropriate to consider it briefly here, because it is *the* major contemporary source of international law. Treaties may be bilateral (between two states only) or multilateral (involving three or more states). Generally speaking, treaties will be binding only upon the states that are party to them, and the nature of the relevant obligations will be defined in the treaty.[22] The generic term 'treaty' covers a multitude of international agreements and contracts between states. As well as those instruments that specifically describe themselves as treaties, the term may include conventions, pacts, declarations, charters, protocols and covenants. The binding nature of treaties lies at the very heart of international law and is derived from the principle of *pacta sunt servanda*, which roughly translates as 'promises must be kept', or, more precisely with regard to treaties, as: 'Every treaty in force is binding upon the parties to it and must be performed by them in good faith.' The status of this principle is a more profound issue than it may at first appear. Some writers have argued that it is a basic customary international rule, others that it is simply a premise upon which the edifice of international law depends. Either way, it is difficult to envisage any international legal system in which state promises were not, on the whole, regularly kept, and even sometimes enforced. However, it is important to realise that the principle is not as neutral as is often assumed. As will be seen in the ICJ case of *Gabçikovo-Nagymaros* (discussed in chapter four), the effect of the principle may directly impact upon, and constrain, democratic decision-making. Furthermore, and as pointed out in the previous section, the very concept of being bound by an agreement even when faced with changed (but not fundamentally changed) circumstances is a quintessentially Western legal way of interpreting the world.

While treaties have obvious similarities with contracts in domestic law, there is no need for consideration (in the legal sense that, for a contract to exist – at least in common law – there must be benefit flowing reciprocally),

---

[22] An exception concerns 'dispositive' treaties, which give rise to rights and obligations in relation to territory. Where, for example, two adjacent nations establish by means of a treaty the location of the boundary separating their two states, the international community as a whole, and not simply the states concerned, will then be obliged to respect that boundary line. However, this is not really a case of states being bound by a treaty to which they were not a party, but rather of them acknowledging the legal consequences that have flowed from an agreement concluded by others.

since, with regard to an international treaty, the benefit may be all one way. And, although Article 52 of the Vienna Convention on the Law of Treaties 1969 provides that a treaty will be void if its conclusion 'has been procured by *the threat or use of force* in violation of the principles of international law embodied in the Charter of the United Nations' (emphasis added), this is the *only* type of coercion deemed sufficient to invalidate a treaty. The fact that the Vienna Conference issued a separate Declaration on the Prohibition of Military, Political or Economic Coercion in the Conclusion of Treaties strongly suggests that coercive measures falling short of the threat or use of force will not necessarily be contrary to international law, and their employment will not automatically render a treaty void. This is an important point and one to which we will return, since mere sovereign equality cannot disguise extraordinarily unequal economic or other bargaining power in treaty negotiation. One example where a coerced treaty would not have been void had it been concluded was the so-called 'Rambouillet Accords' (Interim Agreement for Peace and Self-Government in Kosovo) of February 1999, which Serbia was pressed hard to accept. Had it done so it would certainly have been very unwillingly. Others are less controversial because they are less well known, and this is particularly true of trade agreements.

There is one significant constraint upon the terms that may be included in a treaty. Article 53 of the Vienna Convention on the Law of Treaties provides that:

> A treaty is void if, at the time of its conclusion, it conflicts with a peremptory norm of general international law. For the purposes of the present Convention, a peremptory norm of general international law is a norm accepted and recognized by the international community of States as a whole as a norm from which no derogation is permitted and which can be modified only by a subsequent norm of general international law having the same character.

This is extended by Article 64, which states that, where new peremptory norms of international law arise, any existing treaty which is in conflict with the norm becomes void and terminates. These peremptory norms (also known as *jus cogens*, meaning 'compelling law') are, at their broadest, rules of almost international constitutional importance. They are a body of principles accepted by the international community as a whole that are of such fundamental gravity as to ensure that no treaty which contemplated their breach would, or could, be valid. Examples are prohibitions on slavery, genocide, torture and apartheid, together with the crimes enumerated in the Statute of the International Criminal Court.

Unfortunately, while some principles, such as the prohibition of genocide, are fully accepted as peremptory norms, there is a wide measure of disagreement as to whether others have achieved this special status. Thus, while many would argue that the principle prohibiting the use of force in international relations as laid down in the United Nations Charter is now a peremptory norm, subsequent state practice has rendered this doubtful. This is so notwith-standing the ICJ's finding in *Nicaragua v USA* that both parties to the case (as well as the International Law Commission) were of the view that the prohi-bition of the use of force had come to be recognised as a rule of *jus cogens*.[23]

The final aspect of treaties considered here concerns the effect of a reservation on a state's obligations under a treaty. A reservation is defined in Article 2(1)(d) of the Vienna Convention on the Law of Treaties as

> a unilateral statement, however phrased or named, made by a State when signing, ratifying, accepting, approving or acceding to a treaty, whereby it purports to exclude or to modify the legal effect of certain provisions of the treaty in their application to that State.

Reservations are of significance here for two reasons. The first is that reserva-tions essentially recognise the necessity of consent by a state to all the terms of a treaty by which it is to be bound. This in turn, owing to the principle of reciprocity, means that, where a reservation has been successfully established by one state party to a treaty in regard to another party, then (as explained in Article 21 of the Convention) this:

(a) modifies for the reserving State in its relations with that other party the provisions of the treaty to which the reservation relates to the extent of the reservation; and

(b) modifies those provisions to the same extent for that other party in its rela-tions with the reserving State.

In other words, any reservation made by a state against other parties to a treaty will have the effect of limiting the obligations of those other parties to the reserving state in exactly the same way. Hence, no party to a treaty can be bound to a greater extent as against any other party than that party is itself bound.

The second point to note is that reservations can often have a profound impact upon the obligations apparently accepted and undertaken by a state. One important example concerns the so-called compulsory jurisdiction provi-sion in the Statute of the ICJ (Article 36(2)), which provides that the states parties to the statute:

> may at any time declare that they recognize as compulsory ipso facto and without special agreement, in relation to any other State accepting the same obligation, the jurisdiction of the Court in all legal disputes concerning:
>
> a. the interpretation of a treaty;
> b. any question of international law;

---

[23] *Military and Paramilitary Activities in and against Nicaragua (Nicaragua v United States of America), Merits, Judgment,* ICJ Reports 1986, 14, para 190.

    c.   the existence of any fact which, if established, would constitute a breach of an international obligation;

    d.   the nature or extent of the reparation to be made for the breach of an international obligation.

This provision is currently accepted by 73 states (as at February 2019).[24] However, many of these states have submitted reservations that exempt substantial areas of dispute from the Court's compulsory jurisdiction. (This is further discussed in chapter seven.) There are some limited restrictions on what reservations are permitted. If a purported reservation is incompatible with the actual purpose of a treaty, then it will not be valid (as was held by the ICJ in the *Genocide Convention (Reservations) Case* of 1951[25]). This point is further discussed when we consider the 1979 Convention on the Elimination of all Forms of Discrimination against Women in chapter six. Otherwise, unless restricted or prohibited by the terms of the treaty itself, reservations will generally be acceptable.

C. Customary International Law

The concept of customary international law is not easy to grasp. It is usually said (as in Article 38(1) of the ICJ's statute) that there are two elements required before a rule of customary international law can be said to have come into existence. The first is the custom itself, but only custom which evidences a general practice accepted as law. The second element, commonly entitled *opinio juris sive necessitatis* (opinion as to law or necessity), and normally shortened to *opinio juris*, means that only where a state complies with custom *in the belief that it is legally required so to do* will the custom in question be deemed to form part of international law. As to the element of custom, it has been held by the ICJ that the requirement is that state practice should be 'both extensive and virtually uniform',[26] although it need not be absolutely consistent. On the assumption that this may be proven (evidenced by state practice), this may not present a difficulty. The second element, however, *opinio juris*, is sufficiently opaque to have warranted a myriad of academic articles and discussions within textbooks.

    The concept of customary international law derives from a time when international law was overwhelmingly the law of (and between) nations. In the nineteenth century, international law was very much more concerned to *describe* the actual conduct of states in their relationships with each other, rather than to *prescribe*: that is, its focus was on what nations in fact did,

---

[24] See the ICJ website at www.icj-cij.org/en/declarations.

[25] *Reservations to the Convention on the Prevention and Punishment of the Crime of Genocide, Advisory Opinion*, ICJ Reports 1951, 15.

[26] *North Sea Continental Shelf, Judgment*, ICJ Reports 1969, 3, para 74.

rather than on what they ought to do. Under those circumstances, it was perhaps easier to infer *opinio juris* from state conduct. Now, however, it is much more difficult to do so. The assertion that it is necessary to show that compliance arose because of a state's belief that it was legally obligated to act in a particular way attributes a mental element to a non-sentient legal personality which is merely an institution, albeit one which is reified (turned into a social fact). Institutions as such are capable of many things but this mental apprehension is not one of them. The *opinio juris* is therefore to be inferred from the words and actions of personnel within the institution, whose status so empowers them. More specifically, evidence of *opinio juris* may be gleaned from official government statements, diplomatic exchanges between governments, the opinions of national legal advisers, national legislation, bilateral treaties, decisions of national courts and, possibly also, the voting patterns of a state in an international organisation.

Even more problematic is what Michael Byers, in a book he wrote about customary international law, calls 'the chronological paradox',[27] and which has been observed by many writers. According to the ICJ in the *North Sea Continental Shelf* cases:

> Not only must the acts concerned amount to a settled practice, but they must also be such, or be carried out in such a way, as to be evidence of a belief that this practice is rendered obligatory by the existence of a rule of law requiring it. The need for such a belief, i.e., the existence of a subjective element, is implicit in the very notion of the *opinio juris sive necessitatis*. The States concerned must therefore feel that they are conforming to what amounts to a legal obligation.[28]

However, it is difficult to see how new customary rules could ever develop, since the required *opinio juris* could exist only where the custom or rules already had that legal element.

To some extent, this apparent paradox has been resolved in the Final Report of the International Law Association's Committee on Formation of Customary (General) International Law (2000),[29] in which it addresses this problem of customary rules needing to be evidenced both by state practice (the objective element) and a belief by the states concerned that the practice in question amounts to a legal obligation (the subjective element). The report suggests that 'it is only sometimes necessary to establish the separate existence of a subjective element,'[30] adding that:

> Part of the confusion may be caused by a failure to distinguish between different stages in the life of a customary rule. Once a customary rule has become

---

[27] Michael Byers, *Custom, Power and the Power of Rules: International Relations and Customary International Law* (Cambridge, CUP, 1999).

[28] *North Sea Continental Shelf, Judgment*, ICJ Reports 1969, 3, para 77.

[29] International Law Association Committee on Formation of Customary (General) International Law, *Final Report of the Committee: Statement of Principles Applicable to the Formation of General Customary International Law*, 2000.

[30] ibid 7.

established, States will naturally have a belief in its existence: but this does not *necessarily* prove that the subjective element needs to be present during the *formation* of the rule. [Emphasis in original.][31]

Another important concept in this context is that of the persistent objector. As customary international law can develop only with the consent of the states it comes to bind, it has been accepted (with some qualification) that, where a state makes it clear that it does not agree with a rule that appears to be crystallising into a legal norm, then that objecting state will remain unbound by the rule in question. The qualification is that, where a rule has won overwhelming acceptance over a period of time by very many states, then even a persistent objector may find itself bound. Again, the International Law Association's Final Report, referred to above, makes the useful distinction between a 'general' rule of customary international law, which may not bind a state that has objected to the rule while it was in the process of forming, and 'universal' rules, which all states must obey.[32]

As well as the persistent objector, there is another problem that besets the formation of customary international law. On the one hand, customary law is said to be constantly developing, and yet, on the other, quite how it develops is unclear. US Attorney-General Bill Barr[33] was reported to have said: 'Well, as I understand it, what you're saying is the only way to change international law is to break it.'[34] This aptly captures the difficulty of determining exactly how new customs are created and then entrenched to the point where they can be said to have given birth to new legal rules. Here, too, the question of power is relevant. Rosenne once observed that the creation of customary international law was rather analogous to animals creating a track through a jungle, in that each animal following the trail left its imprint, but, the bigger the animal, the bigger the impact on trail creation. Certainly, after the 1999 intervention in Kosovo, there was a great deal of debate as to whether customary legal rules were developing in a direction that would allow one or more states to intervene in the territory of another for humanitarian purposes. Some suggested that such an outcome was more likely because of the greater power wielded by the states and the organisation (NATO) involved in the intervention. (For further discussion of humanitarian intervention, and the newer concept of responsibility to protect, see chapter eight.) Malcolm Shaw offers the following example of how a new customary legal rule may (or may not) be formed:

> If a state proclaims a twelve-mile limit to its territorial sea in the belief that, although the three-mile limit has been accepted law, the circumstances are so

---

[31] ibid.

[32] ibid 10.

[33] Bill Bar was Attorney-General from 1991–93 in the administration of George H W Bush; in February 2019, he became Attorney-General in the Trump administration, after receiving the confirmation of the US Senate.

[34] Cited in John Bolton 'Is There Really "Law" in International Affairs?' (2000) 10 *Transnational Law & Contemporary Problems* 1, 6.

altering that a twelve-mile limit might now be treated as becoming law, it is vindicated if other states follow suit and a new rule of customary law is established. If other states reject the proposition, then the projected rule withers away and the original law stands, reinforced by state practice and common acceptance.[35]

Of course, if new customary international law really can be created by ignoring the old, then this raises real concerns about the quality of legality in international law. This was one of the central concerns of John Bolton, now National Security Adviser to President Donald Trump, and formerly US Ambassador to the United Nations in George W Bush's administration, who argued forcefully that, at the very least, customary international law should find no unlegislated place in US domestic law. Perhaps, ironically, the area of established customary international law that has been most under threat in recent years has been that relating to the prohibition on the use of force except as permitted under the Charter of the United Nations: a challenge that arose in particular from an assertion by the US of a right to pre-emptive (or preventive) forcible intervention to counter threats to its national security (see chapter eight).

There is one final difficulty with customary international law that has been observed by some authors. This concerns the proof of custom. The argument is that the ICJ has chosen (when it wished) to find evidence of custom either in passive acquiescence by states or even in their inactivity. The difficulty here is that inactivity or passivity provides no evidence in itself of reason or intent, and, in either case, cannot be taken to indicate acceptance of a legal rule. When the first satellite (Sputnik) was launched in 1957 it was of course over-flying (without permission) all of the states below its orbit. In the absence of states attempting to insist upon what had been international law, new customary international law was quickly established distinguishing over-flight from space from over-flight within the atmosphere.

D. Other Sources of International Law

It is important to remember that international law is overwhelmingly derived from treaty and custom, and that other international law 'law-making processes' are very much subsidiary to these two sources. However, as Article 38(1) of the ICJ's statute mentions two further sources, these are also briefly considered for the sake of completeness.

The 'general principles of law' referred to in Article 38(1)(c) are those legal principles which exist in almost all domestic legal systems. These principles will be applied (if their existence can be proven) in cases where neither treaty nor customary international law seems applicable. As the international law

---

[35] Malcolm Shaw, *International Law*, 8th edn (Cambridge, CUP, 2017) 65.

regime is not totally comprehensive (that is, there are not legal rules cover-ing every eventuality), recourse to general principles is sometimes necessary. Examples include recognition of the principle that violation of an obligation leading to injury or damage should lead to reparation; the right of parties to a dispute to be heard before judgment is given; and the concept of limited liability. The general principles also probably encompass principles of equity, in the sense of legal fairness (as opposed to 'equity' as the distinct body of legal rules and principles that have developed in common law jurisdictions to supplement and modify the operation of the law in the interests of justice). Martin Dixon makes the very sensible point that even if such 'principles' have not attained the status of binding law, they may nonetheless 'have a profound impact on the development of international law, either as furnishing a reason why specific norms *should* be adopted or as a catalyst for state practice leading to the creation of customary and treaty law'.[36]

The second subsidiary source, set out in Article 38(1)(d), consists of 'judi-cial decisions and the teachings of the most highly qualified publicists of the various nations' (publicist in this context referring to someone learned in international law). Debate has been lengthy and intense as to precisely what the meaning of this statement is. The subsection in question specifically states that judicial decisions and the teachings of publicists are to be regarded as 'a subsidiary means for the determination of rules of law' – that is, they do not constitute a source of law in themselves but rather act as a means by which such rules may be discerned. The first point to be understood here is that international law makes no use of the common law system of *stare decisis*. In international law, no court binds either itself or any other court by its decisions, and it is explicitly stated in the ICJ statute that decisions have no binding quality beyond the parties to a particular case (Article 59). Never-theless, as will be appreciated after reading ICJ decisions, the judgments do often refer to earlier relevant cases in order to identify the law. And, although the analogy is not exact, judicial decisions and the writings of highly quali-fied publicists are drawn on in rather the same way that the common law system draws on decisions from different jurisdictions and the writings of legal academics: that is, they may be more or less persuasive not because of the formal status of the court or person from whom they emanate but owing to the cogency of reasoning deployed.

Finally, there are some resources recognised as potential sources of inter-national law that do not appear in Article 38(1). The most important of these are resolutions of international organisations (particularly those of the General Assembly of the United Nations) which may carry weight of their own in addition to evidencing state practice.

---

[36] Martin Dixon, *Textbook on International Law*, 7th edn (Oxford, OUP, 2013) 45.

E. 'Soft' Law

In the previous section, in discussing the singular nature of international law, we saw that not everyone agrees with the law way of resolving disputes, at least not as understood in the Western tradition. Instead, some have contended that, rather than attempting to lay down binding rules for future situations, both foreseen and unforeseen, an obligation to conform only when the rules lead to an acceptable outcome may be fairer. Such arguments have, in part, been encompassed by the development of what has come to be known as 'soft' law. It is here that we can observe 'law' moving away from our usual understanding of the concept and back towards the political world and the world of international relations. A number of meanings may be assigned to soft law, some seemingly more legal in character than others.

At its nearest approximation to the 'legal', soft law may encompass agreements between states that have no provision for enforcement, regardless of any default. Such agreements will often refrain from explicitly defining rights and obligations, and are normally found in cases where the parties simply want to oblige themselves in good faith to endeavour to promote a particular objective. Occasionally, agreements that may at first appear to be orthodox treaties will come within soft law definitions because they contain a provision explicitly stating that they are not intended to create legal relationships. More often, however, the status of such agreements will depend on the intentions of the parties, as inferred from the wording of the document itself and the circumstances surrounding its creation.

It is important to realise that such 'law' is not without consequences. One of the earliest examples of this is to be found in the Helsinki Final Act of 1975, which established the Conference on Security and Cooperation in Europe. Despite closely resembling a treaty in its format, the agreement contains an express provision that there is no intention to create legal relations. Nonetheless, the agreement proved to be enormously important, both because it led to the creation of a significant international organisation (which later became the Organization for Security and Co-operation in Europe) and because the principles it enunciated had the effect of reviving the concept of self-determination. The Helsinki Final Act Declaration on Principles Guiding Relations between Participating States (also known as 'The Decalogue') consists of the following 10 principles:

   I.   Sovereign equality, respect for the rights inherent in sovereignty
  II.   Refraining from the threat or use of force
 III.   Inviolability of frontiers
 IV.   Territorial integrity of States
  V.   Peaceful settlement of disputes
 VI.   Non-intervention in internal affairs
VII.   Respect for human rights and fundamental freedoms, including the freedom of thought, conscience, religion or belief

  VIII.   Equal rights and self-determination of peoples
   IX.   Cooperation among States
    X.   Fulfilment in good faith of obligations under international law.

This commitment to fulfil the obligations in good faith had enormous influence in the subsequent 'progress' and demise of the Cold War.

   Another important example of soft law is the Universal Declaration of Human Rights (UDHR) of 1948. This was certainly not intended to have any legally binding effect, and was instead meant to serve as a precursor to a subsequent binding convention (in the event, two covenants on human rights were eventually drafted – one covering civil and political rights and the other dealing with economic, social and cultural rights; see chapter six). Nevertheless, and in spite of the words of Eleanor Roosevelt, who chaired the UN Commission on Human Rights during the drafting of the Declaration – 'It is not a treaty; it is not an international agreement. It is not and does not purport to be a statement of law or of legal obligation. It is a declaration of basic principles of human rights and freedoms' – the UDHR may be seen as an illustration of soft law. Since the adoption of the 1948 UN General Assembly resolution that incorporated the UDHR, the Declaration has often been referred to as either evidencing a consensus in some provisions that may amount to state practice or even as providing evidence of *opinio juris.* In summary, therefore, 'soft' law is important both for the obligations it may impose and because the differences between it and 'hard' law do help to clarify the essence of international law itself.

VII. Conclusion

This chapter has sought to draw together a number of apparently disparate threads in order to explore the concept of international law, briefly considering how it may be defined, and how it has changed over the centuries, evolving from its original preoccupation solely with relations between states to encompass a wider range of issues, concerns and actors. It has described international law as a 'distinctive mode of discourse', with its own principles and procedures, and which is notable for its translation of social facts into legal ones. It has also been suggested that, far from embodying universally shared values, international law reflects a very specific, Western cultural heritage. In addition, the status of international law *as* law has been examined, necessarily entailing a 'compare and contrast exercise' with national legal regimes. Perhaps the one common factor underlying the topics dealt with in this chapter is that of indeterminacy: that is, little in the chapter is amenable to definitive statements; however, as will be seen throughout the book, this is a fundamental feature of international law itself.

2

The Dynamic Quality
of International Law

I. Introduction

A common assumption made about international law is that it is a static
system (at least in comparison with domestic law), with any changes being
gradual and considered. This impression may have been reinforced by the
first chapter of this book, which described how customary international
law tends to evolve fairly slowly, over long periods, and how treaties are
normally concluded only after prolonged consideration and negotiation.
When one also realises that a great deal of international law was formed
in the nineteenth century and earlier, then this assumption may appear to
be correct, but in fact this is not the case. There has been a remarkably
rapid development in the content of international law, especially since the
Second World War, with much of it arising from the changing nature of
three of the concepts that are central to an understanding of the subject:
sovereignty, international legal personality and the place of the individual in international law. Each of these concepts is also of relevance to the
subject matter of other chapters. In particular, the concept of sovereignty is
important in considering self-determination in international law (and also
rights over the sea and seabed), the concept of personality is important
in considering jurisdiction in international law, and the place of the individual in international law is of great importance in the burgeoning field of
human rights law.

The intention of this chapter is to introduce these three concepts, which, in
spite of being distinct, interrelate and overlap in their significance.

II. The Concept of Sovereignty and Sovereign Equality

An obvious but significant point to remember is that the concept of sovereignty in international law is intimately related to the concept of statehood. Sovereignty is what independent states are said to possess. In international law, sovereignty is the power possessed by such states and the right or ability to exercise it. Typically, such power includes the power to exercise authority over all the individuals living in the state's territory. This power, although once regarded as at least theoretically absolute (the rulers of a state could do as they wished in their own state and to their own citizens), was probably never quite as broad as this. The political reality has always exercised some constraint over the conduct of state rulers either by resistance from subjects or by 'influence' from other states. Nevertheless, such was the respect accorded to the concept of sovereignty that, as an example, when the British first learned of the atrocities being committed in Germany against Jewish people in the 1930s, the British Government declined to send even a note of protest to its German counterpart, because it was thought that such an intervention would breach German sovereignty.

As sovereignty has close links with physical territory, it is important to understand how statehood and territory are acquired. Acquisition of statehood will be considered later, when we examine the concept of self-determination in international law in the following chapter. Subject to what is said in future chapters, ordinarily, questions of a state's acquisition of territory are largely academic. The United Nations Charter, proscribing as it does 'the threat or use of force against the territorial integrity or political independence of any state' (Article 2(4)), implicitly outlaws the acquisition of territory by a state except through peaceful agreement. This position is reinforced by an important declaration of the General Assembly of the UN, known as the *Declaration of Principles of International Law Concerning Friendly Relations and Cooperation among States in Accordance with the Charter of the UN.*[1] Here, it is stated that: 'The territory of a state shall not be the object of acquisition by another state resulting from the threat or use of force', and, although the exact legal status of the declaration remains controversial, the statement was relied upon by the ICJ when, in the case of *Nicaragua v USA* (see chapter eight), it concluded that international customary law also forbade the threat or use of force.[2]

---

[1] UNGA Resolution 2625 (XXV) of 24 October 1970.

[2] *Military and Paramilitary Activities in and against Nicaragua (Nicaragua v United States of America), Merits, Judgment*, ICJ Reports 1986, 14, para 188.

This, together with the ICJ's *Palestinian Wall Advisory Opinion* of 2004, which emphasised that lawful title to territory could not be obtained by force of arms and/or effective occupation,[3] and indeed Security Council Resolution 242 of 1967, the preamble of which affirms 'the inadmissibility of the acquisition of territory by war', leads to a clear position in international law: title to territory cannot be achieved by conquest. Since the time when aggressive force became unlawful it has been impossible for a state to acquire title to territory by conquest. Given the nineteenth century's recognition of a right to colonise by conquest, this represents a remarkable change in international law.

Sovereignty has two other important aspects. The first lies in the principle of sovereign equality. This lies at the heart of the present international legal regime. The second, which is closely related, is that states have a duty of non-intervention in any area of exclusive jurisdiction of other states. Implicit in both of these is the concept of jurisdiction.

The traditional view of sovereignty is usually traced back to the Peace of Westphalia of 1648, a series of peace treaties that ended the Thirty Years' War. This is a little arbitrary, but convenient, because the Peace of Westphalia did create the foundations of a new and secular European system based on separate and equal sovereign states. This was to develop over time, and especially after the creation of the United Nations (UN) in 1945, into a world system of independent nations. In the words of one author, the Westphalian settlement may be said to have 'created the basis for a *decentralized system of sovereign and equal nation-states*'.[4] This reaction to the devastation wreaked by the Thirty Years' War was intended to enable separate states to co-exist, with a reciprocal prohibition upon intervention in the internal affairs of other states. Thus, the foundations were laid for a state to enjoy unlimited power over its own territory without interference. The agreement effectively recognised that inter-state wars could be avoided only by adhering to this principle. Needless to say, the Peace of Westphalia was not entirely effective, and there were many subsequent wars and interventions, though possibly fewer than would have occurred without it.

The acceptance, at least in theory, of sovereign equality is now enshrined in Article 2(1) of the UN Charter, which affirms that: 'The Organization is based on the principle of the sovereign equality of all its members'. However, as we shall see, the fact that the permanent members of the Security Council (the UN's most influential body, which can authorise the use of force against a state, and is able to pass legally binding resolutions) have been granted special powers over and above those of other states dramatically undercuts this supposed equality.

---

[3] *Legal Consequences of the Construction of a Wall in the Occupied Palestinian Territory, Advisory Opinion*, ICJ Reports, 2004, 136, para 87.

[4] Lynn H Miller, *Global Order: Values and Power in International Politics*, 2nd edn (Boulder, CO, Westview Press, 1990) 21 (emphasis in original).

This notion of sovereign equality is of fundamental importance in the international legal regime, because it is this that provides the system with a form of 'rule of law'. Just as, in domestic law, each individual (that is, each subject of the legal system) enjoys formal equality before the law, so, in international law, each state, as a full subject of the international legal system, is endowed with formal equality. We will see the significance (and limitations) of this proposition when we consider the methodology of the ICJ. We will also consider the opposition to the idea of sovereign equality in the final chapter.

III. The Concept of Sovereignty and Jurisdiction

Sovereignty also confers on governments complete discretion to decide matters essentially within the domestic jurisdiction of a state. Again, this is an important principle, enshrined in Article 2(7) of the UN Charter:

> Nothing contained in the present Charter shall authorize the United Nations to intervene in matters which are essentially within the domestic jurisdiction of any state or shall require the Members to submit such matters to settlement under the present Charter; but this principle shall not prejudice the application of enforcement measures under Chapter VII [detailing the powers of the Security Council to maintain peace and security in the international realm].

However, what counts as 'essentially within the domestic jurisdiction of any state' has not remained static. In the early days of the UN, some states argued that any international discussion of their internal policies amounted to a breach of this principle. Needless to say, those that adopted this view were usually pursuing policies which were anathema to the majority of the UN's membership, with states that practised apartheid being particularly prominent proponents of this interpretation of the principle. While it is still not possible to define with precision which matters will be held to fall essentially within a state's domestic jurisdiction, what is evident is that those matters have shrunk considerably.

What, however, is the meaning of 'jurisdiction'? So far we have suggested that sovereignty may be understood as 'the power possessed by states and the right or ability to exercise it'. The object now is to consider in more detail just what this power is and the limits or constraints which circumscribe it. The main focus will be on when a state may claim authority, derived from sovereignty, to act in accordance with international law. In other words, under what circumstances does a state have legal competence to make, apply and enforce rules of conduct? Clearly, this question may receive different answers in different circumstances. It might be assumed that, generally speaking, a state may do whatever it wishes in its own territory (more properly, of course, those ruling a state may do so), although there are obvious qualifications to this, arising not least from both international treaty obligations and from international human rights law.

More significantly for the purposes of international law, is the issue of when a state may exercise power *beyond* its borders and what justification can be provided for it doing so. While we will see that principles have developed that define the occasions when such an exercise of power is regarded by the international community as legitimate, it is important to remember that the reality of power imbalance between states (notwithstanding the principle of sovereign equality already discussed) means that some states will be better able to exercise power beyond their borders than others. One important preliminary distinction must be made, however – the distinction between 'jurisdiction to prescribe' and 'jurisdiction to enforce'.

Anyone who has studied public law will probably remember that, as a matter of constitutional principle, a state may enact any legislation it wishes. Many British students will recall being told that the UK Parliament could, if it so wished, pass a law banning smoking in the streets of Paris. This rather extraordinary example is intended to illustrate that the ability to legislate is not subject to any restriction. This, too, is a premise of international law, as was expressly recognised in *The Lotus Case* of 1927, one of the most famous disputes to come before the ICJ's predecessor, the Permanent Court of International Justice (PCIJ).[5] The facts of the case are quite straightforward, but exactly what propositions of international law it stands for continue to exercise legal minds. It is, however, comparatively clear as regards the jurisdiction to prescribe and the jurisdiction to enforce. The case concerned a collision on the high seas (that is, beyond the territorial jurisdiction of any state) between a French steamer, the *Lotus*, and a Turkish steamer, the *Boz-Kourt*. Eight people died in the collision, the *Boz-Kourt* sank, and, having rescued the survivors, the *Lotus* entered Constantinople (now Istanbul), where the Turkish authorities arrested and charged the officer of the watch on the *Lotus*, a Monsieur Demons. (They also arrested the captain of the *Boz-Kourt*.) Monsieur Demons was convicted of manslaughter and, after prolonged French objection to the Turkish exercise of jurisdiction over him, the Turkish Government agreed to refer the matter to the PCIJ. The Court held, in an extremely close decision determined by the casting vote of the president of the PCIJ, that Turkey had not acted contrary to the principles of international law, stating:

> Now the first and foremost restriction imposed by international law upon a State is that – failing the existence of a permissive rule to the contrary – it may not exercise its power in any form in the territory of another State. In this sense, jurisdiction is certainly territorial; it cannot be exercised by a State outside its territory except by virtue of a permissive rule derived from international custom or from a convention.

[5] *The Case of the SS 'Lotus' (France v Turkey), Judgment*, 7 September 1927, PCIJ Series A, No 10.

It does not, however, follow that international law prohibits a State from exercising jurisdiction in its own territory, in respect of any case which relates to acts which have taken place abroad, and in which it cannot rely on some permissive rule of international law. Such a view would only be tenable if international law contained a general prohibition to States to extend the application of their laws and the jurisdiction of their courts to persons, property and acts outside their territory, and if, as an exception to this general prohibition, it allowed States to do so in certain specific cases. But this is certainly not the case under international law as it stands at present. Far from laying down a general prohibition to the effect that States may not extend the application of their laws and the jurisdiction of their courts to persons, property and acts outside their territory, it leaves them in this respect a wide measure of discretion which is only limited in certain cases by prohibitive rules; as regards other cases, every State remains free to adopt the principles which it regards as best and most suitable.[6]

What this seems reasonably clearly (and, in our view, clearly reasonably) to assert is no more than that sovereignty includes the right to *prescribe* almost as a state wishes. But there is an equally plain difference between a right to prescribe jurisdiction and a right to enforce jurisdiction. While a UK Parliament may legislate to criminalise Parisian smokers, it does not have the right to enforce such legislation against French citizens, although, if such a Parisian smoker entered UK territory and was charged, the position would require further consideration (see below). Consequently, there is a crucial distinction between the almost unfettered right to prescribe and the much more limited right to enforce. In the first case, sovereignty allows the exercise of a right which comes with territory, but once action takes place beyond the borders of that territory – that is, where sovereignty no longer applies – then other rules are triggered.

There are three comparatively uncontroversial bases for international jurisdiction: territorial jurisdiction, nationality jurisdiction and what is called 'protective jurisdiction'. Many authors are adamant that territorial jurisdiction is complete and absolute. This is because sovereignty is at least co-extensive with jurisdiction: they are aspects of the same phenomenon of statehood, which implies power and authority over all persons, property and events occurring within a state's territory. The fact that a state may grant, by treaty or otherwise, limitations upon this right does not affect its absolute nature.

There is, therefore, no contentious issue of jurisdiction if an act is perpetrated within a state's territorial jurisdiction (which includes both its territorial sea and its airspace). If the act is criminal, prosecution may follow regardless of other factors, such as the nationality of the perpetrator (subject only to possible individual immunity from prosecution, particularly for diplomats). Slightly more problematic are criminal acts that are not confined to the

[6] ibid 18–19.

territory of a single state. For example, if a criminal act is planned in Pakistan and executed in India – or, to take a well-known real-life example, if a bomb is planted on an aircraft in Malta and explodes while the aircraft is in UK airspace (the Lockerbie case) – where then has the criminal act taken place and which country has jurisdiction?

In fact, two concepts have developed which have persuaded states to adopt a more flexible approach with regard to territorial jurisdiction, and which usually enable a single state to at least take the lead in the investigation and prosecution of an offence: 'subjective territorial jurisdiction' and 'objective territorial jurisdiction'.

Objective territoriality means that a state will have jurisdiction over all offences that are completed in its territory. In the Lockerbie case, for example, in which an American passenger aircraft crashed in Scotland following the explosion of a bomb on board, the UK clearly had jurisdiction over the perpetrators because this was where the act of murder was completed. (Scottish law was later used in the prosecution of the accused, although the trial actually took place in the Netherlands.)

In contrast, subjective territorial jurisdiction will allow a state to exercise jurisdiction where a crime has originated in its territory but has been completed elsewhere. The UK had not always chosen to exercise jurisdiction in such cases, but, as a result of a substantial increase in cross-border crime, elected to do so, and enacted legislation, the Criminal Justice Act 1993, which enables courts in England and Wales to exercise jurisdiction in respect of some crimes where an element of the crime has occurred on UK territory. Increasing concern at the growth of international crime in the past decade or so has also encouraged other states to assert jurisdiction in such cases.

As to 'nationality jurisdiction', this effectively holds that a national of a state is subject to that state's jurisdiction wherever in the world he or she happens to be, and a state is entitled to prosecute and punish its nationals for crimes committed anywhere in the world. This is said to be the corollary of the privilege of citizenship, which offers the diplomatic protection of the state to its nationals wherever they may be; and it is because allegiance is owed by nationals to their state that the state may in turn exercise jurisdiction over them regardless of their location.

This point is exemplified by the UK case of *Joyce v DPP*.[7] William Joyce had voluntarily made propaganda broadcasts from and for Germany during the Second World War. (He was popularly known in wartime Britain as 'Lord Haw Haw, the Humbug of Hamburg'.) After Germany's defeat, Joyce was sent back to England and charged with treason. Joyce's defence was that he had in fact been born in the US of Irish parents and, therefore, as a US citizen, owed no loyalty to the British Crown. However, Joyce had not only

[7] *Joyce v DPP* [1946] AC 347.

lived in the UK for a considerable period of time, but had also (improperly) obtained a UK passport, which was still current at the time of his broadcasts. The House of Lords held that Joyce's assertion of nationality in obtaining the passport indicated his acceptance of a duty of allegiance, as he would have been entitled to claim the protection of the Crown. Consequently, Joyce was convicted and executed.

The nationality principle obviously gives rise to important questions as to who is to be defined as a national of a state (as *Joyce v DPP* makes clear). In fact, international law does not stipulate the criteria that an individual must fulfil in order to attain the status of a national. Each state is left to determine this for itself, with the awarding of nationality a matter for a state's own internal jurisdiction. The role of international law is, however, of importance where one state objects to the grant of nationality conferred by another. For one state to be compelled to recognise the grant of nationality to an individual by another state, it has sometimes been suggested that there must exist a real link between the national and the state concerned. In fact, this is doubtful, and almost invariably the question of nationality remains at the discretion of the awarding state. The only exception would seem to be where a state has attempted to impose nationality upon an unwilling subject in order to gain nationality jurisdiction.

'Protective jurisdiction' in international law reflects and accepts the reality that states will act to punish deeds committed beyond their borders which they regard as prejudicial to their security, regardless of the nationality of the perpetrators. It is the so-called protective principle that legitimates such action. In the case of *Joyce v DPP* mentioned above, this was accepted as an alternative basis for Joyce's conviction. Whereas, in the past, the principle was most frequently applied to acts such as espionage, the counterfeiting of currency and attempts to evade immigration regulation, more recently the 'vital interests' of concern to a state have been interpreted more widely. Both acts of terrorism and international drug offences are now accepted as falling within the protective principle.

While the UK has traditionally been circumspect in its use of this principle, preferring to find other bases on which to exercise jurisdiction where possible, the Privy Council decision in *Liangsiriprasert v Government of the USA*[8] signalled that this may no longer be the case and has subsequently been accepted as good law. The defendant was a Thai national suspected of drug smuggling. A US agent lured him to Hong Kong (at that time still a British colony) on the pretext of a possible drug deal. While in Hong Kong, where he had committed no offence under Hong Kong law, the defendant was arrested, although the charges which were the basis for an extradition request involved offences committed outside the territory. Indeed, the defendant's

---

[8] *Liangsiriprasert v Government of the USA* [1991] 1 AC 225.

only connection with Hong Kong was the fact that he was temporarily present there. Notwithstanding this, the Privy Council permitted his extradition, implying that the protective principle was relevant in recognising the need for the common law to adapt to the new reality that crime is no longer largely local in its origins and effects. In that case, it was held by the Judicial Committee of the Privy Council, applying English common law, that a conspiracy to traffic in a dangerous drug in Hong Kong entered into in Thailand could be tried in Hong Kong, although no act pursuant to that conspiracy was carried out in Hong Kong. Lord Griffiths, delivering the judgment of the Board, said at p 251C–D:

> Their Lordships can find nothing in precedent, comity or good sense that should inhibit the common law from regarding as justiciable in England inchoate crimes committed abroad which are intended to result in the commission of criminal offences in England.

There is little doubt that such a view commands widespread support among the international community of states.

IV. Sovereignty and Controversial Bases of International Jurisdiction

Whereas territorial, nationality and protective jurisdiction are exercised by all states, and all are based on a clear and close connection between the state and either the person or the act giving rise to jurisdiction, other bases for international jurisdiction are not as reflective of the principle of sovereign equality. Rather, they require for their exercise a degree of power from the state claiming such jurisdiction. Some states have asserted a right to extend the principle of protective jurisdiction – intended to enable states to protect themselves from extra-territorial acts regarded as harmful to their security – by enacting legislation designed to provide them with jurisdiction over *any* matters which produce an effect in their territory. Obviously, for such legislation to be meaningful, the relevant states must possess substantial international power and/or benefit from substantial international co-operation. Hence, it is not surprising that the US has been the main proponent of such an approach. There are two main facets of such jurisdiction as claimed by the US, both of which are intended to further its economic and political interests. The first concerns US anti-trust legislation, and its detail is beyond the scope of this book. This legislation is intended to prevent anti-competitive measures in business and the abuse of monopoly/oligopoly business positions. The US has enacted legislation under which foreign companies that also operate, or have business interests, in the US may be subject to heavy penalties for business activities that take place wholly outside US territory. Such penalties could become payable even if the actions of the offending company not only take place outside of the US but are actually quite lawful in the state where they do take place. Not surprisingly, other states (and the EU in particular) have objected strenuously. If such legislation were to become widespread among states, international trade and co-operation would be greatly hampered.

The second extension of extra-territorial claims to jurisdiction has involved the US seeking to enforce trading embargoes against states of which it disapproves. The most blatant of these has been directed towards what was then Fidel Castro's Cuba. In 1996, the US Congress passed the Cuban Liberty and Democratic Solidarity (Libertad) Act (also known, after its promoters, as the Helms–Burton Act). The stated purpose of this Act was to help Cuba 'to restore its freedom', to which end it provides for unilateral measures against foreigners or foreign companies engaging in commercial activities involving assets 'confiscated' (arguably 'nationalised' is the more appropriate term) in Cuba in the early 1960s. Such attempts to prohibit trade by foreign companies with states of which the US disapproves have been bitterly resented and criticised by most other states. And here the 'effects' of the actions by other states and their companies are, of course, not to be felt in the US but only in its foreign policy objectives. Similarly, the Trump administration, after withdrawing from the multilateral nuclear pact concluded with Iran, has recently sought not only to reimpose sanctions on the country itself, but to force other states and their nationals and corporations to follow suit, including those states which remain parties to the agreement and do not wish to see it undermined (see chapter nine). According to Cassese, such jurisdictional claims are contrary to international law, particularly as they impinge upon the sovereignty of other states.[9] Nevertheless, the fact that they have been asserted by the world's most powerful state is obviously important, and may be seen as a real limitation upon even the notion of formal sovereign equality.

Whereas protective jurisdiction involves laying claim to rights in situations where acts have occurred outside a state's territory that are argued to be prejudicial to its security, the so-called 'passive personality' jurisdiction proclaims jurisdiction over non-nationals committing acts beyond the territory of the asserting state where the acts concerned do not produce an effect within the state's territory but rather on its nationals.

Usually, the passive personality principle is framed in terms of a state asserting a right to punish aliens for crimes committed abroad against its nationals. Such a jurisdictional claim is controversial and not all states regard it as compatible with international law. Traditionally, it has been opposed by common law countries, while nations such as Italy and Turkey have been supportive of the principle. Nevertheless, even in common law jurisdictions,

---

[9] Antonio Cassese, *International Law*, 2nd edn (Oxford, OUP, 2005) 50.

there have been rare occasions where the principle has formed at least an alternative basis for the assertion of jurisdiction. One such case was that of *USA v Yunis*,[10] in which a Lebanese national was prosecuted in the US for his alleged part in the hijacking of a Jordanian aircraft in the Middle East. The only connection between the US and the airliner was that there were a number of US citizens on board the hijacked aircraft. It was accepted by the court that the passive personality principle did provide an appropriate basis for jurisdiction.

Dixon explains the theoretical objections to this jurisdictional justification. In particular, as he points out, most criminal acts will give rise to liability in a state more intimately connected with the offence and clearly able to exercise jurisdiction under a non-controversial head. Secondly, the passive personality principle effectively means that all nationals carry the protection of their home state wherever they go, in that anyone who commits an offence against them anywhere in the world will then become liable under the relevant national law.[11]

These theoretical objections notwithstanding, it is arguable that at least on some occasions this basis for asserting jurisdiction is not only acceptable but desirable, but only if the defendant arrives voluntarily or lawfully (that is pursuant to extradition proceedings) in the state of the offended national. It would seem appropriate when the offence is a serious one, and when for whatever reason the state of the offender is unwilling to prosecute.

V. Sovereign Equality and the Concept of Universal Jurisdiction

Universal jurisdiction is seldom used as the basis of a prosecution, but it is nonetheless important, as it highlights once more the relationship between international law and international relations, and the interplay between international law and the ability to exercise power.

Most writers trace the origins of universal jurisdiction to the treatment meted out to pirates from the seventeenth century onwards. International law accepted that every state had jurisdiction over pirates, partly because they were to be regarded as *hostis humani generi* (enemies of all mankind) but, more practically, because, by plying their 'trade' on the high seas, pirates would, or could, have otherwise remained beyond the jurisdiction of any state, and states capturing pirates would have been unable to punish them and thereby prevent further piratical acts from taking place. In the contemporary

---

[10] *USA v Yunis*, 681 F Supp 896 (1988).
[11] Martin Dixon, *Textbook on International Law*, 7th edn (Oxford, OUP, 2013) 159.

world, the concept of universal jurisdiction has had relatively little to do with piracy – or at least this was the case until piracy re-emerged in the twenty-first century, most prominently off the coast of Somalia and around the Horn of Africa. In fact, in terms of universal jurisdiction, this resurgence in piracy has been especially notable for revealing the marked reluctance of most states to prosecute any captured pirates, owing both to the costs involved and to the human rights obligations that may then be owed to these individuals, and which might, for example, preclude any convicted pirates from being deported once their sentences have been served, because of the possible reprisals they would face if returned to Somalia.

The modern rationale for universal jurisdiction is that so-called international crimes are so heinous that each state has an interest in prosecuting the perpetrators, and a right to do so. The most important discussion of universal jurisdiction (at least, until the cases concerning General Pinochet[12]) is to be found in, and as a result of, the trial of Adolf Eichmann.[13] Eichmann had been unlawfully abducted from Argentina, where he was living, by members of the Israeli secret service. During the Second World War, Eichmann had, as a result of his post in the Third Reich, been responsible for orchestrating the deaths of many hundreds of thousands of Jewish people in concentration camps. Following Germany's defeat, he had escaped to Argentina, where he had lived with his family until his abduction. He was charged and convicted by the Israeli court on counts of war crimes and crimes against humanity under an Israeli act of 1950. In the course of Eichmann's trial, his defence counsel challenged the jurisdiction of the court, arguing that not only had Eichmann been unlawfully abducted, but that the crimes with which he was charged did not actually exist at the time he was alleged to have committed them, and, furthermore, had taken place outside of Israel, which itself did not then exist. Not surprisingly, given the enormity of Eichmann's deeds, all these arguments were rejected and the court held that the acts perpetrated by Eichmann constituted crimes known to international law, and therefore the principle of universal jurisdiction enabled the court to hear the case. In its judgment the court stated:

> The crimes defined in this [Israeli] law must be deemed to have always been international crimes, entailing individual criminal responsibility; customary international law is analogous to the common law and develops by analogy and by reference to general principles of law recognised by civilized nations, these crimes share the characteristics of crimes ... which damage vital international interests, impair the foundations and security of the international community, violate universal moral

---

[12] *R v Bow Street Metropolitan Stipendiary Magistrate, ex parte Pinochet Ugarte (No 1)* [2000] 1 AC 61; *R v Bow Street Metropolitan Stipendiary Magistrate, ex parte Pinochet Ugarte (No 3)* [2000] 1 AC 147. See section VI(B) below.

[13] *Attorney-General (Israel) v Adolf Eichmann*, Israel Supreme Court, 29 May 1962 (English translation in 36 ILR 5).

values and humanitarian principles ... and the principle of universal jurisdiction over 'crimes against humanity' ... similarly derives from a common vital interest in their suppression. The state prosecuting them acts as agent of the international community, administering international law.[14]

Since *Eichmann*, which was accepted overwhelmingly by the international community, universal jurisdiction has not been extensively used, in spite of enthusiastic support from human rights activists. However, certain states have enacted legislation to enable their domestic courts to exercise universal jurisdiction in respect of grave international crimes. Belgium in particular used such legislation as the basis upon which to prosecute (and convict) in Belgium a number of individuals who were Rwandan nationals who had significant responsibility for the massacres of Tutsi people in Rwanda in 1994. According to a 2012 report by Amnesty International, 147 out of 193 states (around 76.2 per cent) had enacted legislation that provides for universal jurisdiction over one or more of the following: war crimes, crimes against humanity, genocide and torture.[15] Notwithstanding this, there have not been many prosecutions. There are a number of reasons for this. The first is that the creation of the International Criminal Court (see chapter six) provides what many consider a more appropriate forum for such trials. Secondly, states such as Belgium that have attempted to promote universal jurisdiction have come under substantial political pressure from states that fear the possible ramifications of such a development (for example, an attempt was made in 2001 to have Ariel Sharon, then Prime Minister of Israel, prosecuted). Thirdly, questions of immunity from prosecution arise.

Rather than making use of universal jurisdiction, many states, including the UK, have elected to enact the provisions of international treaties that prohibit international crimes, thereby providing their courts with jurisdiction where appropriate. For example, the provisions of both the Convention on the Prevention and Punishment of the Crime of Genocide 1948 and the Convention against Torture and Other Cruel, Inhuman and Degrading Treatment or Punishment 1984 have been incorporated into the domestic law of the UK.

In 2002, when the ICJ had the opportunity to consider the status of universal jurisdiction, it rather ducked the issue. The *Arrest Warrant* case[16] arose as a result of a Belgian attempt to use the principle of universal jurisdiction to arrest an ex-foreign minister of the Democratic Republic of the Congo in order to charge him with grave human rights violations. (It was perhaps politically unfortunate that such a case arose between Belgium and a state that

---

[14] *Attorney-General of the Government of Israel v Eichmann* (1961) 36 ILR 5, 15 (District Court of Jerusalem).

[15] Amnesty International, *Universal Jurisdiction: A Preliminary Survey of Legislation Around the World – 2012 Update* (London, Amnesty International Publications, 2012) 2.

[16] *Arrest Warrant of 11 April 2000 (Democratic Republic of the Congo v Belgium), Judgment*, ICJ Reports 2003, 3.

it had cruelly administered as a colony.) There was strong evidence to support the Belgian allegations, but the ICJ upheld the ex-minister's claim of immunity from prosecution, and so it was not necessary to determine the validity of asserting universal jurisdiction in such a case. However, it is important to note that the majority of the Court 'assumed for the purpose of the case that universal jurisdiction was established as a principle of customary law',[17] while the minority were of the view that, while historically universal jurisdiction had been exercised where there was some positive tie between the state exercising the jurisdiction and the individuals charged, they did not conclude that this necessarily remained the case, and effectively elected to stand back and await developments.

Within the UK, individuals have tried at various times, using the principle of universal jurisdiction, to effect the arrest of a number of foreign visitors, including former US Secretary of State Henry Kissinger (for alleged breach of the Geneva Conventions during the US's war against Vietnam), then Zimbabwean President Robert Mugabe (for alleged torture carried out in Zimbabwe) and former Israeli Foreign Minister Tzipi Livni (for alleged war crimes and breach of the Geneva Conventions during the conflict in Gaza in 2008–09). Although these attempts were popular with human rights activists, they were disapproved of by various UK governments, resulting in the inclusion of a provision in the Police Reform and Social Responsibility Act 2011 (under s 153) that restricts the ability of individuals to obtain an arrest warrant against a person or persons suspected of crimes attracting universal jurisdiction; such a warrant may now be issued only with the consent of the Director of Public Prosecutions. However, although it was widely expected that the Act would bring an end to such arrests and attempted prosecutions, in January 2013 the London Metropolitan Police arrested Colonel Kumar Lama, a Nepalese national who was then living in the UK, and charged him with two counts of torture allegedly committed in the course of Nepal's civil war in 2005. He was arrested under s 134 of the Criminal Justice Act 1988, which incorporated into domestic law the relevant provisions of the UN Convention against Torture of 1984. The prosecution was approved by the Attorney-General and was pursued in spite of protests by the Nepalese Government.[18] That Nepal is an impoverished and relatively powerless state, and therefore of little consequence commercially or geopolitically to the UK, may explain why the case was allowed to proceed (it being highly unlikely, for example, that a Chinese or Indian national accused of a similar crime would have met with the same treatment). Notwithstanding the Lama case, it is improbable that prosecutions of visiting official figures (visiting in their

---

[17] Dixon, *Textbook* (2013) 154.
[18] Colonel Lama was acquitted in 2016, after the jury found him not guilty of one count of torture and failed to reach a verdict on the other (*R v Kumar Lama*, Central Criminal Court, 2016).

official capacity) would be approved. In contrast, recourse to the principle of universal jurisdiction has been much more extensive in Belgium and Spain, although both states have now opted to introduce more restrictive measures, requiring some sort of nexus to the country itself. This seems largely intended to avoid the political controversy that pursuing such cases tends to bring.[19] A similar stricter approach has been taken by US courts in relation to claims brought under its Alien Tort Statute[20] by foreign nationals.[21]

It is clear, at least in the UK, that treaties entered into by the state are binding on the state, but do not, without more, automatically become part of domestic law (as illustrated in section IX below, when we consider the place of the European Convention on Human Rights in UK domestic law). However, the position is more complicated with regard to customary international law, which many argue is part of the common law, and consequently can, and should, be applied in domestic courts without the need for implementing legislation. An example of the debate is to be found in the *Pinochet* case (discussed in the next section), which involved an attempt by a Spanish judge to extradite General Pinochet from the UK to Spain to face charges arising from his period in office as Head of State of Chile. Among the international crimes with which General Pinochet was charged was the crime of torture. Under the requirements of extradition law, extradition may only be granted where the alleged offence was, at the time of its commission, an offence under the law of both the state requesting extradition and the state to which the request is made. Thus, in Pinochet's case, it was necessary to show that, at the time of the alleged torture, it was a crime under English law to torture a non-UK citizen outside of UK territory. Ultimately, a majority of the House of Lords decided that such acts of torture only became a crime under English law following the entry into force, on 29 September 1988, of the Criminal

---

[19] Belgium enacted legislation in 1993 providing for universal jurisdiction in respect of war crimes, crimes against humanity and genocide, but this was repealed in 2003. The wide ambit of a Spanish law passed in 1985 allowing for the exercise of universal jurisdiction in relation to crimes against humanity was subject to curtailment in 2009 and 2014. In December 2018, Spain's Constitutional Court rejected an application brought by socialist members of the Spanish parliament to strike out a bill introduced by the previous ruling conservative party aimed at abolishing the 1985 law altogether. Both Belgium and Spain have attracted the ire of other states, particularly the US and Israel, for their enthusiastic embrace of universal jurisdiction.

[20] Tort Claims Statute 28 USC §1350; originally part of the Judiciary Act of 1789.

[21] The ATS grants US federal district courts jurisdiction over claims brought by non-US citizens in respect of 'a tort only, committed in violation of the law of nations or a treaty of the United States', and has in more recent years been resorted to in cases of grave human rights violations committed outside of the US – see, for example, the ultimately unsuccessful *In re South African Apartheid* litigation, culminating in *Ntsebeza et al v Ford Motor Co et al* 136 S. Ct. 2485 (2016). The scope of the ATS has been progressively whittled down in a series of judgments handed down over the past decade and a half. See in particular *Kiobel v Royal Dutch Petroleum* 133 S. Ct. 1659 (2013), holding that ATS claims must 'touch and concern the territory of the United States ... with sufficient force', and *Jesner et al v Arab Bank Plc* 138 S. Ct. 1386 (2018), in which the conservative majority on the Supreme Court (in a narrow 5–4 ruling) held that the ATS does not extend to claims against foreign corporations.

Justice Act 1988, which incorporated into English law the relevant provisions of the Torture Convention 1984 (which itself came into force in 1987).[22] A majority then went on to conclude that extradition was possible only for acts of torture for which General Pinochet was allegedly responsible that occurred after 8 December 1988, this being the date on which the UK actually ratified the Torture Convention, thus making the treaty mutually binding on the UK, Chile and Spain (the latter two countries having ratified the treaty at an earlier date).

Only Lord Millett took a significantly different view of when the acts complained of became a crime in English law. He was of the opinion that torture by public officials, carried out as an instrument of state policy, was already an international crime attracting universal jurisdiction by 1973, when General Pinochet had seized power. Writing of the events later, Lord Millett explained his position:

> On the question of jurisdiction, five of the six ruled that there was no jurisdiction over offences committed by foreigners abroad before the Criminal Justice Act 1988 conferred extraterritorial jurisdiction on the English courts. At first sight, the difference between us appears to be a technical one. We all agreed that torture by public officials carried out as an instrument of State policy was already an international crime of universal jurisdiction by 1973. The majority considered that this meant that, as a matter of international law, the United Kingdom was free to assume extraterritorial jurisdiction, which it eventually did in 1988. I considered that it meant that, as a matter of customary international law, which is part of the common law, the United Kingdom already possessed extraterritorial jurisdiction.

> But the difference really goes far deeper than that. The majority considered that torture by foreigners abroad was not a crime at all under English law before the 1988 Act made it one. I could not accept that. In my opinion torture has always been a crime under every civilised system of law. It is just that, until 1988, our courts had no jurisdiction over it if it was committed abroad.[23]

Thus, even Lord Millett, although disagreeing about when the commission of torture abroad by non-nationals became a crime in English law, recognised that domestic courts required its statutory enactment before they were able to hear cases in relation to it. A similar conclusion to that of the majority in *Pinochet* was reached in Australia, where it was held that the admittedly international crime of genocide – which, of all crimes, gives rise to universal jurisdiction – was nevertheless not a crime under Australian federal law because there was no enactment by the Australian parliament.[24]

---

[22] *R v Bow Street Metropolitan Stipendiary Magistrate, ex parte Pinochet Ugarte (No 3)* [2000] 1 AC 147.

[23] The Right Honourable Lord Millett, 'The *Pinochet* Case – Some Personal Reflections', available at http://fdslive.oup.com/www.oup.com/orc/resources/law/intl/evans4e/resources/insights/evans4e_insights_13piece2.pdf

[24] This was remedied in the Australian Criminal Code Act 1995, division 268.

The conclusion must therefore be that, at least for common law states, international crimes give rise to universal jurisdiction but domestic courts will only be able to hear such cases where the international provisions and definitions have explicitly been made a part of the domestic law of the state.

VI. Immunity from Jurisdiction

The necessary counterpart to a discussion of jurisdiction is a consideration of immunity from municipal jurisdiction. Immunity from jurisdiction provides the exception to the permissive rules of jurisdiction discussed so far. Such immunity from suit (meaning an immunity from being called upon to appear in the domestic courts of a state) is most widely and most importantly extended to all other states. Under international law, because states are equal in their sovereignty, no state is entitled to call another state before its courts. This sovereign immunity also extends to diplomatic representatives. Originally, sovereign immunity was almost always granted on an absolute basis, and this was the case in the UK. Such broad-based immunity, however, brought with it certain difficulties. The first was that, especially after the Russian revolution of 1917, and subsequently during the period of decolonisation that followed the Second World War, many activities that had been private commercial matters attracting no immunity became state enterprises, the commercial dealings of which were then immune from suit. Even states without command economies extended their commercial activities and interests. This brought problems both for those who would otherwise have been able to sue for breach of contract and for states enjoying immunity, as other parties would be unwilling to enter into contracts where there was no remedy in the event of breach. These problems led to provision for immunity being modified.

A. Sovereign Immunity

The justification for sovereign immunity is neatly summarised by a Latin maxim: *par in parem non habet imperium*, usually translated as 'one equal cannot exercise authority over another'. It was also said in earlier English cases that a sovereign was not to be 'impleaded' (meaning 'brought into litigation') in the court of another sovereign. In addition, it was accepted that where some act of a foreign sovereign fell for consideration in a domestic court, that court could not pronounce upon the legality of that act in the foreign jurisdiction. It did not have the power to make such a judgment; hence, an issue of this kind is said to be 'non-justiciable'. This extends even to matters that constitute the violation of *jus cogens* norms, as confirmed by the ICJ in *Germany v Italy*.[25] In this case, involving civil claims brought in Italian courts in respect of breaches of international humanitarian law perpetrated by the Third Reich during the Second World War,[26] the Court held that Italy had violated Germany's sovereignty by allowing the cases to proceed. The Court was at pains to emphasise that the customary law rule of state immunity was procedural in nature only, operating so as to prevent one state from exercising jurisdiction in its courts over the actions of another, and had no bearing on whether the conduct complained of was lawful or unlawful.[27] This approach had also been taken by the House of Lords in *Jones v Ministry of Interior* (*The Kingdom of Saudi Arabia*).[28] *Jones* involved allegations by UK nationals that they had been subjected to torture in a prison in Saudi Arabia by agents of the Saudi Arabian state. After returning to the UK, they brought civil proceedings in the UK against both the agents that had allegedly committed the torture and Saudi Arabia. However, the House of Lords ultimately dismissed the action, holding that a foreign state and its officials were immune from the jurisdiction of the UK courts, even in relation to torture. The claimants then filed an application with the European Court of Human Rights (ECtHR), arguing that the UK, in upholding the principle of immunity, had violated Article 6 of the European Convention on Human Rights (guaranteeing due process and the right to a fair trial) by unjustifiably restricting their right of access to a court. The ECtHR ruled[29] – in a decision that has had a very mixed reception – that granting immunity to state officials in civil proceedings in respect of torture did not amount to such a violation.

Although sovereign immunity was once absolute, as states became more and more involved in commerce, so the rule became increasingly difficult to justify. Although the precise scope of the immunity depends upon the domestic law of each state, the principle of state immunity remains. A very brief history of the change from absolute to restricted immunity may help in understanding this rather arcane (but important) area of international law, with the defence of immunity having been invoked on many occasions.

One of the earliest examples of its use, later accepted into British law, and which well illustrates the principle and the rationale of immunity, is the decision of the US Supreme Court in 1812, in *The Schooner Exchange v McFadden*.[30] The trading vessel *The Exchange* had been seized on the

---

[25] *Jurisdictional Immunities of the State (Germany v Italy: Greece Intervening), Judgment,* ICJ Reports 2012, 99.

[26] As well as the enforcement of judgments handed down by Greek civil courts in relation to claims based on similar acts.

[27] ICJ Reports 2012, 140.

[28] [2006] UKHL 26.

[29] *Jones v United Kingdom* (34356/06) (2014) 59 EHRR 1.

[30] (1812) 7 Cranch 116.

high seas by persons acting on the orders of the French Emperor, Napoleon Bonaparte, and had been taken to France, confiscated under French law, and then fitted out as a French warship. Bad weather later forced it into the port of Philadelphia. While it was there, the plaintiffs, who were the owners of the vessel at the time of its seizure on the high seas, issued a writ for the return of the schooner. Without sovereign immunity, the position at law would have been clear and the boat restored to the owners from whom it was improperly appropriated. Marshall CJ, however, giving the judgment of the Court, held that a vessel of a foreign state with which the US was at peace, and which the US Government allowed to enter its harbours, was exempt from the jurisdiction of American courts. He stated: 'The full and absolute territorial jurisdiction being alike the attribute of every sovereign, and being incapable of conferring extraterritorial power, would not seem to contemplate foreign sovereigns nor their sovereign rights as its objects.'[31] Further, he added that there was a 'perfect equality and absolute independence of sovereigns' from which it was inferable that no state could exercise territorial jurisdiction over another. (Interestingly for later developments, it was submitted in argument that if a sovereign engaged in trade he or she would enjoy no immunity in respect of those trading operations, but that question was left open in the judgment.)

Typical of the UK cases following *The Schooner Exchange* was *The Parlement Belge* of 1880,[32] another case concerning a ship. *The Parlement Belge* was a Belgian vessel which carried mail and passengers between Ostend and Dover. As a result of incompetence and negligence on the part of its crew, it collided with the British sea tug *Daring*, whose owners sought to recover damages. It was argued in defence that *The Parlement Belge* was the property of the King of the Belgians, and was therefore immune from such an action. The Court of Appeal, reversing the decision of the court below and granting immunity, stated that the court could not exercise jurisdiction if either an attempt was being made to sue a foreign sovereign in person, or an action was brought *in rem* (an expression from Latin meaning that the action is 'against or about a thing') in respect of something (in this case, the vessel) being used substantially for public purposes, as was the case with *The Parlement Belge*. Again, the question of immunity in *The Parlement Belge* had the ship been wholly or substantially involved in ordinary commerce was left open.

Nevertheless, in the UK at least, it was widely accepted that such sovereign immunity was absolute. This was not the way the law was developing in all countries. With the dramatic increase in state involvement in commercial transactions, it was difficult to defend total immunity and not helpful to trade or international contracts. Some states (particularly 'first world' or developed

---

[31] ibid 138.
[32] *The Parlement Belge* [1880] 4 PD 129.

states) moved towards a position of accepting only a restricted doctrine of immunity. They did this by providing that a state has immunity for only a limited class of acts. The distinction is between acts *jure imperii*, and acts *jure gestionis*. In Dixon's appropriate explanation, the purpose is 'to ensure that the state is treated as a normal litigant when it behaves like one, and as a sovereign when it exercises sovereign power'.[33]

Acts *jure imperii* are activities of a public nature, which continue to attract immunity; acts *jure gestionis* are commercial or private activities, to which immunity no longer applies. Some states, including the US, began to restrict immunity along these lines as early as 1950, but change came more slowly to the UK, with the concept of restrictive immunity appearing in judicial decisions only in the 1970s, eventually leading to the enactment of the State Immunity Act 1978. The cases that led to the passing of this Act were illustrative of the need for reform, and we will briefly examine two of them. The first, significantly, was a decision of the Privy Council – significant because the Privy Council could choose not to follow previous House of Lords decisions that appeared to compel adherence to the principle of absolute immunity. In *The Philippine Admiral*,[34] the Privy Council determined that a ship that had been operated throughout its life as an ordinary merchant ship, carrying cargo for normal trading purposes, did not enjoy the protection of sovereign immunity. This was consistent with decisions elsewhere and was probably informed by an appreciation that jurisdictions that did not limit immunity stood to lose business to those that did and which gave more protection to those trading with foreign governments.

Shortly after *The Philippine Admiral*, a case giving rise to the same question fell to be decided in an English court, which was of course technically still bound by House of Lords decisions thought to uphold the principle of absolute immunity. The case was *Trendtex Trading Corp v Central Bank of Nigeria*.[35] Both the facts and the decision are memorable. In the 1970s, Nigeria suffered a significant and destructive scandal concerning the importation of cement. Although there was a considerable need for cement for Nigeria's extensive building projects, orders were placed for cement delivery in 1976 of some 20 million tons: approximately 10 times the capacity of the country's ports for the entire year. The result was that many ships arrived carrying cement which could not be unloaded (and, apparently, owing to the delay in discharge and the humid conditions much of the cement 'went off' (hardened) in the ships' holds). Trendtex was one of the companies that had a contract for the delivery of cement, and was to be paid against a letter of credit, issued via a London bank, by the Central Bank of Nigeria. The Bank effectively prevented payment for the unwanted and undeliverable cement,

---

[33] Dixon (n 11) 187–88.
[34] [1977] AC 373.
[35] [1977] QB 529.

and when sued sought to rely upon state immunity. The Court of Appeal held that the Central Bank of Nigeria was a separate entity from the government of Nigeria (a rather strained interpretation) and thus was not entitled to immunity. (The effect of this decision was consistent with similar cases heard in other European jurisdictions.) Lord Denning, however, went further than was strictly required, and through remarkable judicial gymnastics, concluded that past House of Lords decisions applying international law were no longer relevant, since, he argued, international law had developed to accept restricted immunity. Precedents based on outdated principles of international law could, he said, be ignored. And he added:

> It follows, too, that a decision of this court – as to what was the ruling of international law 50 or 60 years ago – is not binding on this Court today. International law knows no rule of *stare decisis*. If this Court today is satisfied that the rule of international law on a subject has changed from what it was 50 or 60 years ago, it can give effect to that change – and apply the change in our English law – without waiting for the House of Lords to do it.[36]

Doubtful though Lord Denning's reasoning was (earlier cases had determined English law on sovereign immunity, regardless of the position in international law), the conclusion he reached was followed by the House of Lords in a case of 1983, *I Congreso del Partido*,[37] when applying the law as it stood before the enactment of legislation in the late 1970s. *Trendtex* had highlighted the need for reform, and this was contained in the State Immunity Act 1978. This effectively enacted the provisions of the European Convention on State Immunity of 1972, which had been intended to harmonise various European approaches to immunity. Like the Convention, the Act begins by providing for general sovereign immunity before proceeding to list exceptions which accord with the restrictive immunity perspective. Under the Act, a plaintiff must show that the action complained of by a foreign state comes within these exceptions. In essence, where the transaction is commercial, immunity is excluded. Nevertheless, an 'exception to the exception' is provided for, covering transactions which, although commercial in nature, are entered into 'in the exercise of sovereign authority'. As stated in *I Congreso del Partido*:

> [I]t is not just that the purpose or motive of the act is to serve the purposes of the state, but that the act is of its own character a governmental act, as opposed to an act which any private citizen can perform.[38]

The UN Convention on the Jurisdictional Immunities of States and Their Property, adopted by a General Assembly resolution in December 2004,[39]

---

[36] ibid 554.
[37] [1983] 1 AC 244.
[38] Per Lord Wilberforce, at 269, quoting from the judgment of Robert Goff J in the High Court, [1978] 1 QB 500, 528.
[39] UNGA Resolution A/59/38 of 2 December 2004.

represents a compromise between states favouring something approaching absolute immunity (primarily states of the Global South) and those favouring a more restrictive approach.[40] Existing UK legislation seems to be compatible with its provisions.

In a potentially wide-reaching development in the field of sovereign immunity, the US Congress overruled the veto of then President Barack Obama to pass the Justice Against the Sponsors of Terrorism Act (JASTA) on 28 September 2016. This was the only occasion in President Obama's presidency when the presidential veto was overruled. The effect of JASTA is to amend the US Foreign Sovereign Immunities Act 1976 (FSIA). This Act, as amended, had provided that a court could hear a case against a sovereign state if that state had been designated as a state sponsoring terrorism by the US Department of State and the claimant or victim was at the time of the act complained of a US national. The terrorism exception was introduced to FSIA by an amendment made in 1996 and then further revised in 2008. 28 USC §1605A reads:

> A foreign state shall not be immune from the jurisdiction of courts of the United States or of the States in any case [...] in which money damages are sought against a foreign state for personal injury or death that was caused by an act of torture, extrajudicial killing, aircraft sabotage, hostage taking, or the provision of material support or resources for such an act if such act or provision of material support or resources is engaged in by an official, employee, or agent of such foreign state while acting within the scope of his or her office, employment, or agency.

This law was intended to enable victims of acts of terrorism to bring actions against designated states for substantial damages in the event of harm, and to deter such states from perpetrating or sponsoring acts harmful to US citizens. As of February 2019, these 'designated states' were Iran, North Korea, Sudan and Syria.[41] Only Canada has similar legislation (Justice for Victims of Terrorism Act 2012), but with just two 'listed' states – Iran and Syria.

What makes JASTA unique is that it authorises federal courts to exercise jurisdiction over civil claims against foreign states or officials deemed to have supported an act of terrorism that results in deaths, injuries or damage in the US, regardless of whether or not the state in question is designated as a state sponsor of terrorism. The narrow intention of the legislators was to enable those who had suffered as a result of the terrorist attacks of 9/11 to

---

[40] The Convention is not yet in force, having so far failed to attract the 30 ratifications necessary. As at February 2019, there were 22 states parties to the Convention.

[41] In May 2018, Judge George B Daniels of the Southern District Court of New York issued a default judgment requiring Iran to pay a total of more than $6 billion to victims of the 11 September 2001 terrorist attacks: *Thomas Burnett, Sr et al v The Islamic Republic of Iran et al* (1:15-cv-09903) NYSD. The plaintiffs had alleged that Iran provided training and other support to the terrorist hijackers, although the 9/11 Commission investigation had unearthed no direct evidence of Iranian support: see 'US judge: Iran must pay $6bn to victims of 9/11 attacks', *Al Jazeera*, 1 May 2018. Iran has never responded to the lawsuit, which originally commenced in 2004.

bring a class action against Saudi Arabia, arguing that it had provided material support or resources to the perpetrators of those attacks. However, many
commentators have observed that, while that might have been the intention,
JASTA has the potential to significantly disrupt sovereign immunity in international law. It has been suggested that it might open the way for actions
against Israel, or indeed against states using 'drones' to attack targets on
foreign soil. The question of how any award of damages is to be satisfied
remains unclear.

B. Head of State Immunity

So far in exploring state immunity, we have considered the position of the
state itself. Indeed, historically, the state and its sovereign were regarded as
one and the same. The ruler *was* the state, in the sense that he (or, more rarely,
she) personified the territorial entity. Of course, this rather strains language,
as most of us would readily distinguish between persons and things. It is
therefore apparent that state or sovereign immunity is only meaningful if it
is extended to those people who by their actions determine the actions of the
state. For this reason, s 14(1) of the State Immunity Act 1978 explicitly sets
out what had already been accepted in both international and domestic law:
namely, that the immunities granted to a foreign state extend to

> (a) the sovereign or other head of that State in his public capacity; (b) the govern-
> ment of that State; and (c) any department of that government, but not to any
> entity … which is distinct from the executive organs of the government of the State.

The extent of the immunity granted to a head of state was at issue in the
case of General Pinochet. In brief, General Augusto Pinochet Ugarte, then
Commander-in-Chief of the Chilean army, led a violent right-wing military
coup in Chile in 1973 that overthrew the democratically elected left-wing
government of President Salvador Allende, resulting in the latter's death.
General Pinochet became head of state, a post he occupied until his resigna-
tion in 1990. In 1998, while on a private visit to the UK for medical treatment,
Pinochet was arrested pursuant to an international arrest warrant issued
by a Spanish judge requesting his extradition to Spain to face charges for
a wide range of alleged crimes, including torture and conspiracy to torture.
A first and important question for the House of Lords was whether Pinochet,
by reason of his position as Chile's head of state, enjoyed, and continued
to enjoy, immunity from English domestic courts even for acts as extreme
as torture. (As explained in the preceding section, the Court decided that
extradition would only be possible, if at all, for acts of torture committed
after the UK had incorporated the provisions of the Torture Convention into
its domestic law and had also ratified the Convention itself.) The case was
extraordinarily important, as this was the first time it had been suggested that

a domestic court could refuse head-of-state immunity on the basis that there could be no immunity against prosecution for serious international crimes.[42] There would seem to be little doubt that if Pinochet had still been Chile's head of state at the time of his arrest then he would have enjoyed immunity. Although this is manifestly harsh for those subjected to torture and other equally serious crimes, it represents the law because international relations could hardly survive otherwise. If the position was not as it is, heads of state, whether of the US, the UK, Russia, Pakistan or Zimbabwe, to name but a few, could scarcely venture beyond their borders without fear of arrest. Thus, in *R v Bow Street Metropolitan Stipendiary Magistrate ex parte Pinochet*,[43] the House of Lords (per Lord Browne-Wilkinson) stated:

> This immunity enjoyed by a head of state in power and an ambassador in post is a complete immunity attaching to the person of the head of state or ambassador and rendering him immune from all actions or prosecutions whether or not they relate to matters done for the benefit of the state. Such immunity is said to be granted ratione personae.

But what is the position of a head of state who is no longer in office? Here, the House of Lords found the position of ex-heads of state to be identical to ex-ambassadors. Lord Browne-Wilkinson said:

> The continuing partial immunity of the ambassador after leaving post is of a different kind from that enjoyed ratione personae while he was in post. Since he is no longer the representative of the foreign state he merits no particular privileges or immunities as a person. However in order to preserve the integrity of the activities of the foreign state during the period when he was ambassador, it is necessary to provide that immunity is afforded to his *official* acts during his tenure in post. If this were not done the sovereign immunity of the state could be evaded by calling in question acts done during the previous ambassador's time. Accordingly under Article 39(2) [of the Vienna Convention on Diplomatic Relations 1961] the ambassador, like any other official of the state, enjoys immunity in relation to his official acts done while he was an official. This limited immunity, ratione materiae, is to be contrasted with the former immunity ratione personae which gave complete immunity to all activities whether public or private.
>
> In my judgment at common law a former head of state enjoys similar immunities, ratione materiae, once he ceases to be head of state. He too loses immunity ratione personae on ceasing to be head of state ... [Emphasis in original.]

---

[42] Illustrative of the heightened political sensitivity surrounding this case is the fact that the first decision of the House of Lords (*R v Bow Street Metropolitan Stipendiary Magistrate, ex parte Pinochet Ugarte (No 1)* [2000] 1 AC 61), which had determined, by a three to two majority, that Pinochet should be extradited, was set aside after it was revealed that one of the judges, Lord Hoffmann, had links to the human rights organisation Amnesty International, which had intervened in the case, and has as one of its objects the procurement of the abolition of torture (see *R v Bow Street Metropolitan Stipendiary Magistrate, ex parte Pinochet Ugarte (No 2)* [2000] 1 AC 119).

[43] [2000] 1 AC 147.

It will be appreciated that there is some parallel between absolute as opposed to restricted immunity for states and the distinction between acts *ratione personae* and acts *ratione materiae* for ex-heads of state and ambassadors, in that immunity continues to attach to ex-heads of state and ambassadors for things they did in an official capacity: that is, as Lord Browne-Wilkinson put it, 'both enjoy [continuing] immunity for acts done in performance of their respective functions whilst in office'. As with absolute and restricted immunity, the test is concerned with the nature of the act performed.

In the *Pinochet* case, however, a further question arose. Could it ever be said that the alleged organisation of torture would constitute an act committed by General Pinochet as part of his official functions as head of state? The Court recognised (per Lord Browne-Wilkinson) that: 'Actions which are criminal under the local law can still have been done officially and therefore give rise to immunity ratione materiae.' However, it decided that there were strong grounds for concluding that the implementation of torture, as defined by the Torture Convention, could not be a state function and that consequently there could be no surviving immunity, because such acts were contrary to international criminal law. Following the House of Lords' judgment, a ruling was then obtained allowing the extradition of General Pinochet to Spain to face charges in respect of those alleged acts of torture that had been committed after 8 December 1988, together with further charges filed by the Spanish authorities also relating to events that occurred after 1988.

As events transpired, however, Pinochet was not extradited and never stood trial. In October 1999, the Chilean Government asked the UK to consider releasing Pinochet on the grounds of ill-health, allowing him to return to Chile. This release was ordered by the then Home Secretary in Tony Blair's administration, Jack Straw, following a medical examination, the results of which were only disclosed following a legal challenge by human rights organisations and the Belgian government (Belgium having also issued an arrest warrant against Pinochet). As the medical report indicated that Pinochet had extensive brain damage and severe memory problems, making it extremely difficult for him to participate in any trial, the Home Secretary was able, in March 2000, to release the General to Chile, bringing to an end what had been a rather delicate political situation for the UK.[44] Subsequently, there were attempts in Chile itself to prosecute Pinochet on charges relating to the infamous Caravan of Death (a military squad that had tortured and murdered political prisoners throughout Chile after the 1973 coup). However, these ultimately failed, when, following a further medical examination,

---

[44] Since Pinochet's Government had provided military and intelligence support to the UK Government of Margaret Thatcher during the 1982 war with Argentina over the Falklands/ Malvinas Islands, and hence the General enjoyed a certain amount of vocal support in the UK, most prominently from Margaret Thatcher herself.

Chile's Supreme Court ruled in 2002 that Pinochet was unfit to stand trial, albeit allowing for the possibility that he could be tried in the future if his health improved. In 2004, the Supreme Court ruled that Pinochet could indeed be tried on new charges after viewing a recording of an interview that he had given to a Miami-based television network which belied accounts of his supposed mental deterioration. However, despite further attempts to try him on multiple charges of murder and torture, Pinochet never in fact stood trial, dying under house arrest, with a number of proceedings pending, in December 2006, at the age of 91.

Following the *Pinochet* case, international criminal trials raised new questions regarding the immunity of heads of state. Courts trying the former Serbian President Slobodan Milošević and former Head of State of Liberia Charles Taylor – respectively, the International Criminal Tribunal for the Former Yugoslavia and the Special Court for Sierra Leone (sitting in the Netherlands) – refused to allow a defence of immunity to be raised, as did the Extraordinary African Chambers in Senegal (a court established by Senegal and the African Union), which tried Hissène Habré for torture, war crimes and crimes against humanity committed while he was Head of State of Chad between 1982 and 1990 (his conviction was upheld in April 2017).

Article 27(2) of the Statute of the International Criminal Court (ICC) states that: 'Immunities or special procedural rules which may attach to the official capacity of a person, whether under national or international law, shall not bar the court from exercising its jurisdiction over such a person.' However, the issuing of arrest warrants in respect of heads of state and other government officials remains controversial, as is amply illustrated by the ICC's repeated failures to secure the apprehension of Sudanese President Omar al-Bashir in relation to various alleged atrocity crimes. President al-Bashir has now visited numerous states, but even those which are members of the Court have refused to execute the warrant, with many African states, as well as the African Union, viewing the referral of the case to the ICC as inimical to their own diplomatic efforts to secure peace in Darfur, as well as redolent of hypocrisy, pointing to the Court's over-concentration on African countries and African leaders, while the crimes of Western heads of state escape scrutiny. (See chapter six for further details.)

C. Diplomatic Immunity

The previous section briefly alluded to the position of ambassadors with regard to judicial immunity. Again, the position is largely dictated by the history of international relations. This has long recognised that reciprocal respect for those representing foreign states in the territory of another is fundamental to international intercourse. In the words of the ICJ, diplomatic immunity is 'essential for the maintenance of relations between states and is accepted throughout the world by nations of all creeds, cultures and political complexions'.[45]

As with heads of state, the immunities granted to diplomatic and consular officials are personal and enjoyed by individuals, but it is of course because they are an integral part of the government of the state they represent that immunity extends to them. UK legislation protecting diplomats was first enshrined in the Diplomatic Privileges Act 1708, and is currently governed by the Diplomatic Privileges Act 1964, which is based on the Vienna Convention on Diplomatic Relations 1961. The latter has been ratified by practically all states (192 as at February 2019). Under Article 29 of the Convention, 'The person of a diplomatic agent shall be inviolable', and such persons 'shall not be liable to any form of arrest or detention'; they shall be treated 'with due respect' and the receiving state 'shall take all appropriate steps to prevent any attack' on such individuals' 'person, freedom, or dignity'. Article 30 provides that the private residence of a diplomat attracts 'the same inviolability and protection as the premises of the mission', as does his or her papers, correspondence, and property – with some exceptions in the latter case, set out in Article 31(a)–(c), relating to civil and administrative actions in respect of real property not held 'on behalf of the sending State for the purposes of the mission'; matters of succession, where the diplomat is involved as an executor or heir in a private capacity; and professional or commercial activities that do not form part of the diplomat's official functions. Apart from these exceptions, a diplomat enjoys immunity from both the civil and administrative jurisdiction and the criminal jurisdiction of the receiving state. Again, the immunity is closely related in definition to the distinction between absolute and restricted state immunity. The immunity granted to a diplomat also extends to family members that form part of the diplomat's household, provided they are not nationals of the receiving state (Article 37(1)), as well as to administrative and technical staff at the mission, together with family members forming part of their households, provided they are not nationals of, or permanently resident in, the receiving state. However, such staff will not enjoy immunity from the civil and administrative jurisdiction of the receiving state in respect of 'acts performed outside the course of their duties' (Article 37(2)).

It should be noted that, in spite of the immunity afforded to diplomats in the receiving state, they remain liable to the jurisdiction of their home state, as Article 31(4) makes clear, and so could face prosecution there for a crime committed in the receiving state, in accordance with the nationality principle of jurisdiction. The sending state may also agree to waive immunity from jurisdiction in the receiving state in respect of diplomatic agents and administrative and technical staff, as well as family members that are part of their

---

[45] *United States Diplomatic and Consular Staff in Tehran (United States of America v Iran), Judgment* ICJ Reports 1980, 3, para 24.

households (Article 32(1)). Furthermore, the receiving state retains the ultimate sanction of being able to ask, without cause, for the withdrawal of any person enjoying diplomatic privilege, rendering him or her *persona non grata*. Once a diplomat's functions have come to an end, any privileges or immunities 'shall normally cease' when the person leaves the receiving state or after a reasonable period of time in which the individual has had the opportunity to leave; 'However, with respect to acts performed by such a person in the exercise of his functions as a member of the mission, immunity shall continue to subsist' (Article 39(2)). Hence, diplomats will benefit from some residual immunity after leaving their posts, but only in relation to those actions carried out as part of their official diplomatic duties.

Immunity extends to other matters as well. In particular, diplomatic premises are inviolable and can only be entered with the permission of the head of mission (Article 22(1)). Hence, the UK could not apprehend Julian Assange – for breach of bail conditions after he was arrested pursuant to an international arrest warrant issued by Swedish prosecutors seeking his extradition to Sweden to face charges of rape and sexual assault – while he remained in the Ecuadorian embassy in London, having been granted asylum in 2012 by the then Government of Rafael Correa. He was arrested when the grant of asylum was withdrawn, in 2019.[46] Members of diplomatic missions are also assured freedom of movement in the territory of the receiving state, 'Subject to its laws and regulations concerning zones entry into which is prohibited or regulated for reasons of national security' (Article 26). Free and secret communication between the mission and the home state for all official purposes must be permitted and protected (Article 27(1); 'The official correspondence of the mission shall be inviolable' (Article 27(2)); and diplomatic bags intended for official use may not be searched (Article 27(3)). ('Bag' is a euphemism for any container, including even containers from a container ship.)

Consular premises and officials also benefit from a number of immunities and privileges (under the Vienna Convention on Consular Relations 1963), although these are narrower in scope than those conferred on embassies. The receiving state cannot generally enter consular premises without permission (Article 31). Thus, despite early indications that Saudi journalist Jamal Khashoggi had been murdered in the Saudi Arabian consulate in Istanbul in October 2018 (a murder that was later confirmed to have taken place by the Saudi Government), Turkish officials only entered the consulate to investigate after having been invited to do so by the Saudi authorities. However, consular officials that commit a 'grave crime' do not enjoy immunity from prosecution

---

[46] Assange has always maintained his innocence, and insists that, rather than simply facing possible prosecution in Sweden, he is also in danger of being extradited to the US to face espionage charges in connection with the release of diplomatic cables on his WikiLeaks website.

in the receiving state (Article 41(1)). Moreover, entering consular premises (and perhaps even an embassy) in order to avert an immediate threat to life would arguably not amount to a violation of diplomatic immunity.

The scope of the immunity granted to diplomats was considered in depth in the 2017 UK Supreme Court decision *Reyes v Al-Malki*.[47] This case involved a Philippine national (Ms Reyes) employed from January to March 2011 by a member of the diplomatic staff of the Saudi Arabian embassy in London and his wife (Mr and Mrs Al-Malki) as a domestic worker at their private residence in the capital. The Al-Malkis left the UK when Mr Al-Malki's diplomatic posting ended. Ms Reyes sought to bring a claim before an employment tribunal alleging racial discrimination, unlawful deduction from wages and failure to pay the minimum wage. She stated that the Al-Malkis had made her work excessive hours, failed to provide her with proper accommodation, confiscated her passport, prevented her from leaving the house or communicating with others, and paid her nothing until after her employment ended upon her escape from the residence. She further alleged that such treatment amounted to trafficking in persons within the meaning of the International Protocol to Prevent, Suppress and Punish Trafficking in Persons, Especially Women and Children 2000. After the Court of Appeal ruled that the employment tribunal lacked jurisdiction to hear her case, owing to the immunity enjoyed by Mr Al-Malki by virtue of his diplomatic status (with Mrs Al-Malki enjoying derivative immunity as a family member), Ms Reyes appealed to the Supreme Court.

The Court granted her appeal, on the ground that, after a diplomat leaves his or her post, he or she is entitled to immunity only in respect of those actions carried out in post that were performed in the exercise of the diplomat's official functions (as provided for under Article 39(2)). Since the employment and maltreatment of Ms Reyes did not form part of Mr Al-Malki's official duties, the Al-Malkis could no longer avail themselves of immunity in relation to these acts once Mr Al-Malki had left his position at the embassy. Consequently, the employment tribunal did possess jurisdiction and the case could be remitted back for a full hearing. The Supreme Court also rejected the Al-Malkis' argument that they had not been validly served with the claim form in regard to the employment tribunal complaint, holding that such service did not violate any of the protections afforded to diplomats and their residences under the Convention. However, the Court failed to agree on whether the Al-Malkis had lost their diplomatic immunity while Mr Al-Malki was still in post, being divided on the important question of whether or not knowingly employing a trafficked person can be characterised as a 'professional or commercial activity exercised by the diplomatic agent in the receiving State outside his official functions' (Article 31(c)), thus bringing

---

[47][2017] UKSC 61.

it within one of the exceptions to the civil immunity conferred on diplomats while in post.

VII. Legal Personality in International Law

It has often been observed that domestic legal systems are primarily concerned with the governance of individuals within their jurisdiction. Hence, the primary subjects of domestic law are individuals (ie natural persons), although created entities, such as partnerships, companies and local authorities, may also both be subject to domestic law and possess 'legal personality', allowing them to sue or be sued under defined circumstances. Even though such entities (or institutions) obviously have no *real* personality, in the sense that, unlike individuals, created organisations have no mind or consciousness of their own, they are still treated *as though* they had an existence independent of the individuals that comprise them.

In international law, the primary subjects are not individuals, but states, and traditionally international law regarded states as the *only* subjects of international law. Of course, states themselves might seem to us as no less and no more than a collectivity of individuals occupying a defined territory. However, although true in some senses, states are treated as separate entities under international law, just as corporations are regarded as discrete entities under domestic law. Actions and reactions by states are regarded as the acts of those states, and often as acts divorced from the individuals who actually carry them out.

In the nineteenth century, few would have argued that international law was about anything other than the international regulation of state conduct. Domestic law governed individuals, but the individuals of international law were states and states alone. The question of the role of individuals in international law led to rather arid discussions, which often came to the conclusion that, while only states were the subjects of international law, individuals were the objects: in other words, international law was for the benefit of individuals through the medium of the regulation of states. While such a perspective is now of little significance, it does remain the case that only states are said to be *full* subjects of international law, because only states have complete legal capacity in that regime. This complete legal capacity means that they have the power to exercise legal rights in international law and are subject to the duties prescribed by international law. This position is most easily understood by contrasting it with the position of other actors in the international law regime.

These other actors may be international organisations (ranging from the EU to the World Bank, for instance), international corporations, non-governmental organisations (NGOs) and even individuals. Each, however, will have less than complete legal capacity and will be a subject of international law for some purposes but not others. Thus, none of the above will have standing before the ICJ, but all will have some obligations under international law.

Dixon provides a very lucid account of the concept of personality in international law.[48] Most importantly, he points out that the answer to the question as to whether a particular entity is to be regarded as a subject of international law is seldom amenable to a simple positive or negative response (except in the case of states). This is because many entities may be subjects for some purposes and yet not for others. Dixon explains this by outlining the main capacities of a subject of international law. These include: the ability to make claims to directly establish rights granted under international law; the power to enter into international diplomatic relations; being subject to some or all of the obligations imposed by international law; the capacity to make binding treaties under international law; and, finally, the ability 'to enjoy some or all of the immunities from the jurisdiction of the national courts of other states'.[49] While only states possess all these capacities to the full, other entities will benefit from some of the rights or be subject to some of the duties. To be endowed with international legal personality, therefore, is to be able to participate in some ways within the system of international law.

Non-state actors within international law are basically threefold. First, there are individuals: predominantly natural persons, but also juridical entities, such as private corporations. Secondly, there are intergovernmental international organisations, and the third category consists of international NGOs.

An obvious example of the second category (which itself includes a myriad of organisations) is the UN itself. In an early case in the newly reconstituted international court, the ICJ was called upon to define the status of the UN. It did this in its Advisory Opinion on *Reparation for injuries suffered in the service of the United Nations* 1949.[50] The Opinion held that it was indispensable to attribute international personality to the UN because its Charter assigned to it specific tasks, such as international peacekeeping, together with the promotion of international economic, social, cultural and humanitarian co-operation. In concluding that the UN was an international person, the Court went on to say:

> That is not the same thing as saying that it is a State, which it certainly is not, or that its legal personality and rights and duties are the same as those of a State.

---

[48] Dixon (n 11) 115–17.
[49] ibid 116.
[50] *Reparation for injuries suffered in the service of the United Nations, Advisory Opinion*, ICJ Reports 1949, 174.

Still less is it the same thing as saying that it is a super-State, whatever that expression may mean. It does not even imply that all its rights and duties must be upon the international plane, any more than all the rights and duties of a State must be upon that plane. What it does mean is that it is a subject of international law and capable of possessing international rights and duties, and that it has capacity to maintain its rights by bringing international claims.[51]

In addition to the requirement that it is necessary to demonstrate that, when an organisation is set up, it is intended to have international functions and obligations if it is to have international personality, is the need to show that the organisation also enjoys autonomy from its member states.

In some situations, international legal personality may be explicitly provided for in the enabling document. An example is that of Article 4(1) of the statute of the ICC, which states that: 'The Court shall have international legal personality. It shall also have such legal capacity as may be necessary for the exercise of its functions and the fulfilment of its purposes.'

However, there are clear limits to the legal personality of international organisations. In particular, only states, and not international organisations, are allowed to bring (or defend) claims in the ICJ, although they may sometimes have standing before regional international courts: for example, the Council and the Commission of the European Union may appear before the European Court of Justice. Furthermore, any international agreements they conclude do not come within the definition of 'treaties' as set out in the Vienna Convention on the Law of Treaties 1969 (discussed in chapter four). Separately, the Vienna Convention on Treaties Concluded Between States and International Organizations or Between International Organizations 1986 is relevant to such agreements, but this has yet to come into force.

It should also be appreciated that not all international inter-governmental organisations have identical capacity in international law. In addition to the UN, the EU most nearly approaches the status of a state in international law, while other organisations will have much more limited capacity.

NGOs occupy a much more constrained position in international law. While they certainly have a part to play in the international legal regime, particularly in regard to standard-setting and contributing to the drafting of international documents – for example, in the creation of the ICC – they seldom enjoy rights under international law. Notwithstanding their limited capacity, such international bodies as the International Labour Organization, Amnesty International and the International Red Cross, to mention but three, influence both the creation and the administration of international law, especially in the fields of human rights and international humanitarian law.

---

[51] ibid 179.

VIII. The Place of the Individual in International Law

The notion that international organisations would ever acquire international legal personality, albeit limited, would have been quite alien to nineteenth-century writers on international law; the idea that individuals would ever possess such standing would have been simply incredible. Most obviously, the international legal regime was (at that time) concerned only with states, and related to this was the belief that states, by definition, had the right to deal with their own nationals as they wished, and an obligation to respect the right of other nations to do the same. Moreover, there were really no international organisations capable of imposing obligations on or granting rights to individuals under international law.

This does not mean that international law entirely ignored individuals. Issues that affected them were often the concern of the international regime. Questions of international commerce, marine matters and rules relating to safe conducts or passports, the rights of ambassadors and piracy were all, according to Blackstone, writing in the eighteenth century, matters for the concern of the law of nations.[52] But Blackstone also maintained that such international law was directly applicable only through municipal courts. He reasoned that, because the law of nations was (in his view) a full part of the common law and the law of England, its principles could be directly applied by English courts. Even if this were true, international law, although it could affect individuals, was still seen as a law for states alone. As such a position left the application of international law in the hands of domestic courts, it was also consistent with the Westphalian rules prohibiting interference in the affairs of one sovereign state by another.

At the same time, this view of the state as solely responsible for its nationals did give international law an indirect means of providing remedies to individuals for claims which they could not themselves enforce. In the *Mavrommatis Palestine Concessions Case*, heard by the PCIJ in 1924,[53] it was held that doctrine and procedure allowed states to protect their individual nationals in an international arena. The Court justified this position as follows:

> It is an elementary principle of international law that a State is entitled to protect its subjects, when injured by acts contrary to international law committed by

---

[52] William Blackstone, *Commentaries on the Laws of England* (1769), Book 4, ch 5.

[53] *Mavrommatis Palestine Concessions (Greece v Great Britain)*, PCIJ, 30 August 1924, Series A, No 2.

> another State, from whom they have been unable to obtain satisfaction through the ordinary channels. By taking up the case of one of its subjects and by resorting to diplomatic action or international judicial proceedings on his behalf, a State is in reality asserting its own rights – its right to ensure, in the person of its subjects, respect for the rules of international law.
>
> The question, therefore, whether the present dispute originates in an injury to a private interest, which in point of fact is the case in many international disputes, is irrelevant from this standpoint. Once a State has taken up a case on behalf of one of its subjects before an international tribunal, in the eyes of the latter the State is sole claimant.[54]

Understanding that international law could, before the Second World War, have an indirect effect upon individuals allows one to make sense of the proposition that, whereas states were the subjects of international law, individuals were its objects.

Such perceptions have undergone a dramatic transformation since (and, to a considerable extent, because of) the Second World War. Whereas, in the past, it had been accepted that it was states that waged war, the appalling loss of life that occurred in the 1939–45 conflict, coupled with the atrocities of the Holocaust, meant that attributing responsibility to individuals under international law, even for the acts of states, seemed not only appropriate but essential.

The development of an international law of human rights (discussed in chapter six) has now rendered obsolete the view that individuals have no direct place in international law. Critical to this fundamental change were the events surrounding the creation and operation of the International Military Tribunal at Nuremberg in 1945. The dilemma for the victorious Allied Powers, who wished to punish individual Nazi leaders responsible not only for waging an aggressive war but also for the mass murder of German and other nationals who were Jewish or were members of other groups unacceptable to the Reich, including homosexuals, Gypsies, communists and the disabled, was that the perpetrators of these atrocities had broken no national German laws. They had, of course, themselves actually written the laws that were intended to make legal their horrific deeds. Legal positivists (those who argued that international law was for states alone, and that for individuals there was no law above domestic law) found it difficult to identify a basis for prosecution.

Notwithstanding this, and pursuant to promises made by the Allies during the war, the US, the Soviet Union, Great Britain and France created the International Military Tribunal for Nuremberg to deal with violations of international law perpetrated by individuals. The Tribunal established irrevocably not only that rules of international law should, but in fact *did*, apply to individuals, confidently asserting that: 'Crimes against international law are

---

[54] ibid 12.

committed by men, not by abstract entities, and only by punishing individuals who commit such crimes can the provisions of international law be enforced.'

While the truth of this statement is self-evident, the legal basis for it at that time was not. However, the international assertion of control and authority over those who commit the most appalling acts has come to be regarded as permissible under contemporary international law. In the now-accepted words of the Tribunal, which have echoes in the statute of the ICC:

> The following acts, or any of them, are crimes coming within the jurisdiction of the Tribunal for which there shall be individual responsibility:
>
> (a) 'Crimes against peace': namely, planning, preparation, initiation or waging of a war of aggression, or a war in violation of international treaties, agreements or assurances, or participation in a common plan or conspiracy for the accomplishment of any of the foregoing;
> (b) 'War crimes': namely, violations of the laws or customs of war. Such violations shall include, but not be limited to, murder, ill-treatment or deportation to slave labour or for any other purpose of civilian population of or in occupied territory, murder or ill-treatment of prisoners of war or persons on the seas, killing of hostages, plunder of public or private property, wanton destruction of cities, towns or villages, or devastation not justified by military necessity;
> (c) 'Crimes against humanity': namely, murder, extermination, enslavement, deportation, and other inhumane acts committed against any civilian population, before or during the war, or persecutions on political, racial or religious grounds in execution of or in connection with any crime within the jurisdiction of the Tribunal, whether or not in violation of the domestic law of the country where perpetrated.[55]

This position has since been further developed, initially by the UN General Assembly in its Universal Declaration of Human Rights of 1948, which enumerated various rights belonging to all individuals. As noted in the last chapter, the Declaration was not itself intended to be a legal instrument, but was rather to pave the way for a later covenant that would incorporate the rights set out in the Declaration. (This is further considered in chapter six.) Also in 1948, the Convention on the Prevention and Punishment of the Crime of Genocide (commonly referred to as the Genocide Convention) was adopted. This *did* create legally binding obligations and was explicit in its attribution of international legal responsibility to individuals. Article IV states that: 'Persons committing genocide ... shall be punished, whether they are constitutionally responsible rulers, public officials or private individuals.'

Thus, by the second half of the twentieth century, it could no longer be doubted that individuals had gained a place in international law, even if that place remained confined to the realm of human rights.

[55] Article 6, Charter of the International Military Tribunal.

IX. The Individual in International Law as Exemplified by the European Convention on Human Rights

The evolution of individual rights in international law is well illustrated by the development of the European Convention on Human Rights and Fundamental Freedoms, especially as it affected individuals in the UK. It was drafted under the auspices of the Council of Europe, which at that time was an intergovernmental organisation with the object of facilitating European co-operation over a broad range of subjects. When the Convention was drafted in 1950, the Council had 25 members, and there was a requirement under the Council's statute (contained in Article 3) that each member, upon joining, 'accept the principles of the rule of law and of the enjoyment by all persons within its jurisdiction of human rights and fundamental freedoms'.

The motivation for the Convention was clear: it was to further democracy, to guard against the rise of any totalitarian regime (either Nazi or communist), and to protect human rights. Many argued that these goals were all interrelated. For our purposes, what is significant is the role assigned to the individual in all this. When drafted, provision was made within the Convention for one member state to petition against another if the petitioner considered the respondent state to be in breach of its obligations. It was probably the case that this was seen as the appropriate method under international law to achieve enforcement. Such petitions were to be judged by an adjudicatory body, and significant sanctions could be applied. A respondent state was not permitted to assert that matters complained of fell within its domestic jurisdiction and so could not be subjected to external review.

However, while it was assumed that inter-state petition would be the central mechanism of enforcement, this has proved not to be the case. Article 25 of the Convention provided that the European Commission of Human Rights (a body created by the Convention) could receive petitions from any person, non-governmental organisation or group of individuals claiming to be the victim of a violation by one of the states parties of the rights guaranteed in the Convention. However, it was left to each state to decide whether or not to grant this right of individual petition to those within its jurisdiction. As time passed, more and more states opted to do so. Some initially conferred the right for just a limited period, but most finally chose to do so irrevocably. The UK granted the right of individual petition only in 1966. Even then, however, the country's position was curious to those not familiar with international law. An individual in the UK was entitled to make an application to Strasbourg, where the Commission and the European Court of Human Rights resided, having exhausted the possibility of a domestic remedy.

Such an applicant could not, however, invoke the guarantees of the Convention before UK courts because, although the UK was a party to the Convention, the provisions of the Convention had not been made a part of the country's domestic law. Furthermore, having taken a case to Strasbourg and won, the successful applicant had no way of enforcing the judgment in a UK court. Rather, he or she had to rely on the UK fulfilling its international obligations under the Convention to provide the remedy ordered, and only other parties to the Convention (ie other states) could insist upon the UK doing so.

The UK did, in fact, give effect to judgments against it, but this was the rather curious legal position. It was only with the passage of the UK Human Rights Act in 1998, which effectively incorporated the provisions of the Convention into domestic law, that UK courts were able to give effect to the Convention's provisions.

This digression into the status of the individual under the European Convention highlights the relationship between the citizen and his or her state on the one hand – a direct relationship within which rights are directly provided – and, on the other, the relationship between a citizen and other states and international bodies with which his or her own state has entered into international legal relations. This is to be contrasted with those international legal documents which provide for direct individual responsibility (as opposed to rights) for international crimes. The Genocide Convention, together with the statute of the ICC, both provide for such responsibility unmediated by the state.

The conclusion to be drawn, therefore, regarding the status of the individual in the international legal regime is that an individual may be given rights in international law with the acquiescence of his or her state, but responsibilities may be imposed on such individuals irrespective of the position adopted by their national state.

X. Conclusion: The Interrelationship between Sovereignty, Personality and the Individual in International Law

One obvious point about the concepts we have considered in this chapter is that they are all in the process of changing, or have in fact changed. What we will consider here is whether this is simply coincidental or whether it illustrates some general phenomenon of relevance to the study of international law. The argument proposed is that, by studying these transformations, we can gain some idea of the relationship between the social and political world and the world of international law. What major political and social developments from the nineteenth to the twenty-first century necessitated fundamental changes in the international legal regime? On one level, this question is too broad to be sensible, but some generalisations can be useful.

The nineteenth century was one dominated by European states, and it was from these that nineteenth-century international law emanated. Not surprisingly, therefore, international law reflected the interests and needs of these states as perceived by those who ruled them. In turn, these interests and needs reflected a very idiosyncratic perception of the world. Colonialism was accepted as unproblematic, and sovereignty was defined accordingly. Colonialism also entailed the right to use what we would now call 'gun-boat diplomacy' (or unrestricted force) as a means of acquiring territory. The ideology that accompanied colonialism could be described as social-Darwinism: an unwavering conviction in the superiority of European thought and culture, and a resolute belief that colonial societies would not only benefit greatly by developing in the same direction, but could do so only with the help of their colonial masters. In fact, for many Europeans of the time, there was no possibility of 'primitive' peoples ever reaching a stage when they would be capable of running their own affairs. Deeply offensive as these views are, it is important to realise that they underpinned much international law. European empires and their preservation lay at its very heart.

The concept of sovereignty began to change during the era of decolonisation that followed the Second World War, as the newly independent states began to exert their influence over the international legal regime. In place of its comfortable accommodation with empire, sovereignty was redefined to legitimate and sustain anti-colonial freedom movements. As the power of empire waned, so sovereignty as the guarantor of state independence grew. At the same time, however, the very essence of sovereignty itself began to change, qualified by the increasing emphasis placed on individual human rights. No longer would states be quite as free to act as they wished within the confines of their own territories.

The nineteenth century also saw the beginnings of a system of intergovernmental organisations that foreshadowed a much greater role for such bodies in international law. Improvements in transport, communication and trade led, in the second half of the nineteenth century, to a spate of such organisations being set up, beginning with the founding of the International Telegraphic Union in 1865 and the establishment of the Universal Postal Union in 1874. This precursor of 'globalisation' made it inevitable that such bodies, created with the express consent of states and yet possessing an independent existence, would acquire at least limited international legal personality.

As for individuals, as long as one attribute of sovereignty was complete and exclusive control over those within a state's jurisdiction, there could be no place for the individual in international law. Such an attribute, however, rendered the international community legally impotent in the face of atrocities committed by a government against its own people (or in occupied territories). Whereas this had been accepted with something approaching equanimity in colonial legal circles, popular pressure that arose following the revelation of the Nazi obscenities, in particular, dictated reconsideration, manifested both at Nuremberg and in the Universal Declaration.

What should be clear, then, is that, in spite of there being no central mechanism for enacting new legal rules in the international sphere, it is possible for international law, through the medium of treaties, and through the development of customary international law, to reflect changing times, changing power structures and changing international public opinion.

In the following chapter we will explore some of these fundamental changes, particularly in relation to sovereignty, by considering the development of self-determination in international law.

3

Self-determination and Territory in International Law

I. Introduction

When, in chapter two, we considered the nature of sovereignty, we did not say a great deal about the relationship between persons and territory except in terms of jurisdiction. Probably for most of us, most of the time, the concept of identity as a national of a state is commonsensical and straightforward. We simply know and accept that we are, for example, Pakistani, or Singaporean, or Chinese. In Europe, in particular, few people question their national identity even if they recognise that they are, in addition to being French, Polish and so on, European by residence, regardless of ethnicity. Of course, it is also possible for individuals to have more than one national identity, but what is significant for present purposes is that for most inhabitants of most long-established states, the link between identity and state, captured in nationality, is unproblematic. This is not necessarily so in every part of the world. Within Europe, the fact that territory, especially at the margins or borders, has belonged to different states at different times over the last century indicates that an easy identification of an individual with a state, as opposed to identification with territory, is not always simply a matter of common sense.

In much of the world beyond Europe, 'natural' identification of person with state often has no great history. Decolonisation brought with it state independence, but, of course, almost invariably within the pre-existing colonial borders. It was the state that achieved independence rather than the state's inhabitants, an important point that we will explore further below. It is sufficient here to observe that in such states it is not unusual for persons to regard their nationality as much less significant than their ethnic, religious or tribal allegiance.

II. The Concept of Self-determination in International Law before the Creation of the United Nations

It is difficult now to imagine a time in which the ordinary population was regarded as of no consequence in determining the state to which the territory it inhabited should belong. Yet for much of history this was overwhelmingly the case. The disposition of territorial sovereignty was within the exclusive power of those who ruled – often royalty but always aristocrats in the widest sense. Frequently, the sovereignty of territory was disposed of after, or as the result of, war in which territory was conquered, and this was indeed the most common method by which territory was acquired. The wishes of the inhabitants of such territory, even if known, were deemed irrelevant and ignored. These 'rules' of territorial acquisition (they were accepted as rules in international law) were extended to facilitate and legitimate colonisation. States with sufficient power, or by agreement, asserted title over what became colonial possessions, and this ownership came to be recognised both in law and in fact by other independent states.

But the seeds of the concept of self-determination were sown in the eighteenth century, particularly through the media of the French Revolution and the American War of Independence, with the latter asserting that rulers were effectively legitimated by the 'consent of the governed'. These developments built on a renewed interest in the classical heritage and 'Athenian democracy', the writings of political philosophers, and a tradition, at least in the UK, of a limited role for parliament, all of which favoured some role for the populace – or, at least, some part of it – in government.

That few thought to apply this concept to colonised peoples reflected a European attitude to race that remained largely unchallenged until the twentieth century, notwithstanding the abolition of slavery. Such a disposition was well expressed in the Treaty of Berlin of 1885, allocating the rights and responsibilities of the European powers (including King Leopold II of Belgium) in Central Africa. Article VI of the Treaty stated:

> All the Powers exercising sovereign rights or influence in the aforesaid territories bind themselves to watch over the preservation of the native tribes, and to care for the improvement of the conditions of their moral and material well-being, and to help in suppressing slavery, and especially the slave trade. They shall, without distinction of creed or nation, protect and favour all religious, scientific or charitable institutions and undertakings created and organized for the above ends, or which aim at instructing the natives and bringing home to them the blessings of civilization.

Patronising and hypocritical though these sentiments undoubtedly were, paving the way for the famous three 'Cs' of commerce, Christianity and civilisation, they yet, as Pakenham points out, amounted to a humanitarian commitment of sorts.[1]

More immediately, the idea of self-determination did play a part in the creation of European nation states in the nineteenth century, and in the First World War it fell to President Wilson of the US to extol its virtues. (In fact, it seems that initially his purpose in doing so was, at least in the understanding of his allies, to make propaganda points against an enemy that contained within its empires many disparate minority peoples who wished for nothing less than autonomy, if not self-government. This was thought to be true especially of the Ottoman and Austro–Hungarian empires, with the latter encompassing – in addition to Germans and Hungarians – Poles, Croats, Bosnians, Serbians, Italians, Czechs, Ruthenes, Slovenes, Slovaks and Romanians, with 15 different languages spoken in total.) The fifth point of Wilson's famous 'Fourteen Points Address' to Congress in January 1918 spoke of the need for:

> A free, open-minded, and absolutely impartial adjustment of all colonial claims, based upon a strict observance of the principle that in determining all such questions of sovereignty the interests of the populations concerned must have equal weight with the equitable claims of the government whose title is to be determined.

There were, however, two significant qualifications: first, the colonial claims Wilson referred to did not include the colonies of the Allies; and, secondly, the principle of self-determination is not absolute but merely one factor of importance.

The conclusion of the First World War brought no right of self-determination to colonial peoples, and, while the map of Europe and the Middle East was redrawn, no great effort was made to consult with the inhabitants of affected regions. Rather than provide plebiscites or even consultation with such people generally, the Treaty of Versailles of 1919 only prescribed this process for those living in disputed areas. In other cases, minorities were to be protected through 'minority treaties', under which states were required to enter into agreements to guard and protect minority rights, a process of limited effect.

Colonial peoples were not granted any right of self-determination, but those that lived in what were defined as colonies of the defeated states were brought within the 'mandate system', whereby territories that were not self-governing were allocated to one of the victorious powers. This, it was stated, was to provide 'tutelage', so that such territories might 'advance' to a stage where independence was appropriate. In full, Article 22 of the Covenant of the League of Nations stated:

> To those colonies and territories which as a consequence of the late war have ceased to be under the sovereignty of the States which formerly governed them

[1] Thomas Pakenham, *The Scramble for Africa* (London, Weidenfeld & Nicolson, 1991) 254.

and which are inhabited by peoples not yet able to stand by themselves under the strenuous conditions of the modern world, there should be applied the principle that the well-being and development of such peoples form a sacred trust of civilisation and that securities for the performance of this trust should be embodied in this Covenant.

The best method of giving practical effect to this principle is that the tutelage of such peoples should be entrusted to advanced nations who by reason of their resources, their experience or their geographical position can best undertake this responsibility, and who are willing to accept it, and that this tutelage should be exercised by them as Mandatories on behalf of the League.

The character of the mandate must differ according to the stage of the development of the people, the geographical situation of the territory, its economic conditions and other similar circumstances.

Certain communities formerly belonging to the Turkish Empire have reached a stage of development where their existence as independent nations can be provisionally recognized subject to the rendering of administrative advice and assistance by a Mandatory until such time as they are able to stand alone. The wishes of these communities must be a principal consideration in the selection of the Mandatory.

Other peoples, especially those of Central Africa, are at such a stage that the Mandatory must be responsible for the administration of the territory under conditions which will guarantee freedom of conscience and religion, subject only to the maintenance of public order and morals, the prohibition of abuses such as the slave trade, the arms traffic and the liquor traffic, and the prevention of the establishment of fortifications or military and naval bases and of military training of the natives for other than police purposes and the defence of territory, and will also secure equal opportunities for the trade and commerce of other Members of the League.

There are territories, such as South-West Africa and certain of the South Pacific Islands, which, owing to the sparseness of their population, or their small size, or their remoteness from the centres of civilisation, or their geographical contiguity to the territory of the Mandatory, and other circumstances, can be best administered under the laws of the Mandatory as integral portions of its territory, subject to the safeguards above mentioned in the interests of the indigenous population.

In every case of mandate, the Mandatory shall render to the Council an annual report in reference to the territory committed to its charge.

The degree of authority, control, or administration to be exercised by the Mandatory shall, if not previously agreed upon by the Members of the League, be explicitly defined in each case by the Council.

A permanent Commission shall be constituted to receive and examine the annual reports of the Mandatories and to advise the Council on all matters relating to the observance of the mandates.

As the Article indicates, there were three categories of mandate. The first comprised those territories believed to be almost ready for independence, all of which did in fact attain self-government between 1932 and 1947. Such states, the boundaries of which were redrawn without plebiscite – primarily by France and the UK – included Syria and Lebanon (under French mandate) and Iraq, Trans-Jordan and Palestine (under British mandate). The second category consisted of German colonies in central Africa. These were considered to be at a further remove from possible independence, and were allocated to the UK, France or Belgium. The third category, thought by the Council of the League of Nations to be incapable of independence and self-government in the foreseeable future, included the former German colonies of South-West Africa, mandated to South Africa, and Pacific and other colonies in the Southern hemisphere mandated to Japan, Australia and New Zealand. With the exception of South-West Africa (now Namibia), all mandated territories of the second and third categories became 'trust territories' under the Charter of the United Nations.

The mandates were important because they provided, probably inadvertently, the basis for the subsequent movement for decolonisation. If independence was to be the goal for the mandated territories, then it was difficult to argue that it should not also be the objective for all colonies, including those of the victors of the First World War.

A. The Åland Islands Case

In the aftermath of the creation of the League of Nations, a case arose that has continuing significance. It concerned the sovereignty of the Åland Islands, which occupy a site in the Gulf of Bothnia, between Finland and Sweden. There is one main island and an archipelago of small islands and skerries (small rocky islands usually too small for habitation). Ninety per cent of the population, which in total amounts to only 27,000, lives on the main island and is overwhelmingly Swedish-speaking. In 1809 the Islands were ceded by Sweden to Russia and became part of the semi-autonomous Grand Duchy of Finland. In 1832, the Russians began to fortify the Islands, but these fortifications were destroyed by the British and French in 1854 as part of the campaign relating to the Crimean War. In the Finnish Civil War of 1918, Swedish troops briefly intervened as a peacekeeping force but were quickly replaced by German troops on behalf of the Finnish 'White' Government. The inhabitants of the Islands wished for them to be returned to Swedish sovereignty. Indeed, in a petition, it was said that more than 95 per cent of the adult population supported this change. Finland resisted such a cession but did offer autonomy. The dispute was referred to the Council of the League of Nations for resolution. In essence, the question was whether in such circumstances the wishes of the inhabitants of a territory overcame the territorial rights of the sovereign state of which it was a part.

The Swedish Government responded to the decision of the Council by stating that:

> [I]n supporting the cause of the people of the Aaland Islands before Europe and the League of nations, Sweden was not influenced by the desire to increase her

territory. She only wished to support noble and just aspirations and to defend the right of an absolutely homogenous island population to reunite itself to its mother-country, from which it had been detached by force, but to which it is still united by the ties of a common origin, a common history, and a common national spirit. This population has declared to the whole world its unanimous wish not to be bound to a country to which it had been joined by force of arms alone. The Swedish Government had hoped that an institution, which was established to assist in the realisation of right in international relationships, would have favoured a solution of the Aaland question in conformity with the principle of self-determination, which, although not recognised as a part of international law, has received so wide an application in the formation of the New Europe.[2]

The decision itself had stated unequivocally:

1. The sovereignty of the Aaland Islands is recognised to belong to Finland;
2. Nevertheless, the interests of the world, the future of cordial relations between Finland and Sweden, the prosperity and happiness of the Islands themselves cannot be ensured unless (a) certain further guarantees are given for the protection of the Islanders; and unless (b) arrangements are concluded for the non-fortification and neutralisation of the Archipelago.
3. The new guarantees to be inserted in the autonomy law should specially aim at the preservation of the Swedish language in the schools, at the maintenance of the landed property in the hands of the Islanders, at the restriction, within reasonable limits, of the exercise of the franchise by new comers, and at ensuring the appointment of a Governor who will possess the confidence of the population.
4. The Council has requested that the guarantees will be more likely to achieve their purpose, if they are discussed and agreed to by the Representatives of Finland with those of Sweden, if necessary with the assistance of the Council of the League of Nations, and, in accordance with the Council's desire, the two parties have decided to seek out an agreement. Should their efforts fail, the Council would itself fix the guarantees which, in its opinion, should be inserted, by means of an amendment, in the autonomy law of May 7th, 1920. In any case, the Council of the League of Nations will see to the enforcement of these guarantees.[3]

In effect, then, the Council of the League elevated existing territorial sovereignty above the wishes of a people even where their physical location and ethnic and linguistic identity were undeniably distinct. Sovereignty originally acquired by force remained sacrosanct. (It is, however, important to observe that, through the goodwill of the Finnish and Swedish Governments, the guarantees which provided for the autonomous rights of the population have been maintained in an unobjectionable manner.) The decision has been accepted as being of relevance in all contemporary cases of attempted or projected secession.

---

[2] Decision of the Council of the League of Nations on the Åland Islands including Sweden's Protest, September 1921. Available at www.kulturstiftelsen.ax/traktater/eng_fr/1921a_en.htm.
  [3] ibid.

B. Decolonisation and the Indian Sub-continent

One other development concerning self-determination that occurred before the UN Charter was adopted is of particular importance. Although the Indian subcontinent did not achieve independence until 1947, its struggle to that end was well established by the 1930s. This movement enjoyed overwhelming support on the sub-continent and not inconsiderable support in the colonial power itself, the UK. Independence and self-government was the inevitable result, and it is clear that the wishes of the people were irresistible. This example demonstrated that if a people had sufficient power and unity, a colonial state would have no alternative but to grant that which was demanded. Here, it was less the exercise of a right than an exercise of power which developed into a right after the creation of the UN.

III. The United Nations Charter, Self-determination and Decolonisation

The UN Charter contained nothing to suggest that the concept of self-determination would ever be conceived of as a right, let alone a *human* right, and certainly not as a peremptory norm of international law. Nevertheless, such a development was to some extent foreshadowed by the Atlantic Charter of 1941, in which Roosevelt and Churchill enumerated the principles on which their respective nations 'base[d] their hopes for a better future for the world', and which included the following:

> Second, they desire to see no territorial changes that do not accord with the freely expressed wishes of the peoples concerned;
>
> Third, they respect the right of all peoples to choose the form of government under which they will live; and they wish to see sovereign rights and self government restored to those who have been forcibly deprived of them.

The principle of self-determination was acknowledged in the UN Charter, but not as a legal right. It is first mentioned in Article 1(2), where it is stated that one of the purposes of the UN is 'to develop friendly relations among nations based on the respect for the principle of equal rights and self-determination of peoples'. There is a similarly oblique reference in Article 55, while Chapter XII of the Charter, devoted to the trusteeship system, explicitly requires that action be taken by those states charged with administering trust territories to promote the welfare of the native inhabitants and to develop them toward self-government. (The trust territories included those previously mandated but not yet independent, with the exception of South-West Africa, together with dependent territories previously held by the defeated states of the Second World War. All territories in this system had either achieved independence or had chosen otherwise by 1995. South-West Africa remained under mandate and became independent in 1990.)

From the earliest days of the UN, two issues preoccupied both the Non-Aligned Movement of states (see below) and the newly independent nations: decolonisation and apartheid. Much energy was directed to ensuring that these topics remained at the forefront of all UN concerns. Indeed, the reason for the very long delay (18 years) between the adoption of the Universal Declaration of Human Rights (UDHR) of 1948 and the signing of the two International Covenants on Human Rights of 1966 (see chapter six) arose from what was seen as persistence in concentrating on these issues on the part of non-aligned and newly independent states, and viewed as 'bloody-mindedness' by many Western nations.

A. The Process of Decolonisation

While Chapter XII of the Charter dealt with the mandated territories and territories detached from those states defeated in the Second World War, Chapter XI was concerned with other non-self-governing territories, which remained outside the trusteeship system. Small and medium-sized states had made an important contribution to the drafting of this section, which was intended to deal with colonial territories. Article 73 provided as follows:

> Members of the United Nations which have or assume responsibilities for the administration of territories whose peoples have not yet attained a full measure of self-government recognize the principle that the interests of the inhabitants of these territories are paramount, and accept as a sacred trust the obligation to promote to the utmost, within the system of international peace and security established by the present Charter, the well-being of the inhabitants of these territories, and, to this end:
>
> a.   to ensure, with due respect for the culture of the peoples concerned, their political, economic, social, and educational advancement, their just treatment, and their protection against abuses;
> b.   to develop self-government, to take due account of the political aspirations of the peoples, and to assist them in the progressive development of their free political institutions, according to the particular circumstances of each territory and its peoples and their varying stages of advancement;
> c.   to further international peace and security;
> d.   to promote constructive measures of development, to encourage research, and to co-operate with one another and, when and where appropriate, with specialized international bodies with a view to the practical achievement of the social, economic, and scientific purposes set forth in this Article; and
> e.   to transmit regularly to the Secretary-General for information purposes, subject to such limitation as security and constitutional considerations may require, statistical and other information of a technical nature relating to

economic, social, and educational conditions in the territories for which they are respectively responsible other than those territories to which Chapters XII and XIII apply.

While the requirements placed upon the colonial powers were scarcely onerous, the mere fact that they encapsulated a rudimentary form of accountability provided a substantial impetus for decolonisation. Crucial in this respect was the role played by liberation movements in the colonies themselves and the support these movements derived from non-aligned and newly independent states within the UN. At the Bandung Conference of 1955, 29 African and Asian countries met (with China, India and Indonesia playing a prominent role) and agreed to resist colonialism. This conference led to the formation of the Non-Aligned Movement in 1961, also dedicated to decolonisation. Other factors – the support of the 'Second World' (that is the USSR and its allies) for decolonisation, the economic and social cost to colonial states, the waning support of the US for European colonial empires and the rise to power of European parties that favoured decolonisation – were also important, but less so than the resistance of indigenous populations. And Article 73 certainly played its part.

But while decolonisation was one of the great triumphs of the United Nations (UN), with the process largely completed by 1975, self-determination also entailed a number of problems, to which we will turn shortly. Firstly, however, it is necessary to consider the role of the UN in this remarkable process.

Even the mild obligations imposed by Article 73 were unacceptable to some colonial states, which attempted, by means of various rationalisations, to avoid the reporting requirement imposed on them. Portugal and Spain claimed that they had no colonies, as their 'overseas territories' were in fact an integral part of the states themselves (thus Mozambique and Angola were argued to be a part of Portugal). France argued that, as its overseas territories were a part of the French Union, they too were beyond the scope of Article 73, while the UK contended that the article did not apply to territories that had local autonomy. The issue was really whether the power to define territories as colonies was to lie with the colonial powers themselves or with an external body.

By 1960, the newly independent and non-aligned states were in the majority in the UN General Assembly, and promoted a Declaration on the Granting of Independence to Colonial Countries and Peoples that was passed as Resolution 1514 by a vote of 89 in favour and none against.[4] There were, however, nine significant abstentions, including the US, the UK, Portugal, Spain and Belgium. This Resolution, together with the subsequent Resolution 1541,[5]

---

[4] UNGA Resolution 1514 (XV) of 14 December 1960.
[5] UNGA Resolution 1541 (XV) of 15 December 1960.

greatly altered and advanced the cause of decolonisation. Resolution 1514 provided:

1. The subjection of peoples to alien subjugation, domination and exploitation constitutes a denial of fundamental human rights, is contrary to the Charter of the United Nations and is an impediment to the promotion of world peace and co-operation.

2. All peoples have the right to self-determination; by virtue of that right they freely determine their political status and freely pursue their economic, social and cultural development.

3. Inadequacy of political, economic, social or educational preparedness should never serve as a pretext for delaying independence.

4. All armed action or repressive measures of all kinds directed against dependent peoples shall cease in order to enable them to exercise peacefully and freely their right to complete independence, and the integrity of their national territory shall be respected.

5. Immediate steps shall be taken, in Trust and Non-Self-Governing Territories or all other territories which have not yet attained independence, to transfer all powers to the peoples of those territories, without any conditions or reservations, in accordance with their freely expressed will and desire, without any distinction as to race, creed or colour, in order to enable them to enjoy complete independence and freedom.

6. Any attempt aimed at the partial or total disruption of the national unity and the territorial integrity of a country is incompatible with the purposes and principles of the Charter of the United Nations.

7. All States shall observe faithfully and strictly the provisions of the Charter of the United Nations, the Universal Declaration of Human Rights and the present Declaration on the basis of equality, non-interference in the internal affairs of all States, and respect for the sovereign rights of all peoples and their territorial integrity.

Thus, the Resolution called for immediate decolonisation, regardless of the opinion of the colonial power as to whether the requisite 'readiness' or 'maturity' had been achieved. At the same time, it reinforced the view discussed below that territorial integrity implied that self-determination would be exercised within colonial borders. Resolution 1541 complemented this by providing that acts of self-determination must be exercised by the people to whom it applied, by free and fair elections by which they might choose either to constitute themselves as a sovereign independent state, or to associate freely with an independent state, or to integrate with an already existing state.

Other important developments in the UN were to be found in the finally adopted two International Covenants on Human Rights of 1966, which had a common first Article, namely:

1. All peoples have the right of self-determination. By virtue of that right they freely determine their political status and freely pursue their economic, social and cultural development.

2. All peoples may, for their own ends, freely dispose of their natural wealth and resources without prejudice to any obligations arising out of international economic co-operation, based upon the principle of mutual benefit, and international law. In no case may a people be deprived of its own means of subsistence.

3. The States Parties to the present Covenant, including those having responsibility for the administration of Non-Self-Governing and Trust Territories, shall promote the realization of the right of self-determination, and shall respect that right, in conformity with the provisions of the Charter of the United Nations.

The significance of these common provisions in the Covenants, intended to give legal effect to the UDHR, cannot be over-emphasised. Not only is a right of political self-determination asserted, but it is asserted as a *human* right. Of equal importance to the right of political self-determination is that of economic self-determination, which is discussed below.

One other development is also important. As we observed earlier, the preoccupations of the newly independent states and the Non-Aligned Movement lay not only with decolonisation but also with states that practised apartheid. Consequently, there was a determination in the General Assembly that those living under racist regimes or those living in occupied territories (especially, but not exclusively, Palestinians) also had a right to self-determination, even in an established state such as South Africa.

While all these developments accelerated the process of decolonisation and kept international attention focused on the topic, they were not unproblematic. Three aspects of decolonisation presented particular difficulties: the operation of the principle of *uti possidetis*, the methods by which the wishes of people claiming the right of self-determination were to be ascertained and guaranteed, and finally the operation of a proclaimed right of economic self-determination.

B. The Principle of *uti possidetis*

Derived from Roman law, and meaning 'you will have sovereignty over those territories you possess as of law', the concept of *uti possidetis* has now been adapted and absorbed from the principles upon which Latin American states obtained independence in the early-nineteenth century. Independence was acquired within the frontiers of the pre-existing colonial territory and these could not be altered unilaterally but only in agreement with adjacent states. Following the Second World War, it was quickly accepted both by the colonial powers and by colonies seeking independence that this was an appropriate general principle, and was in turn accepted both by the Organization of African Unity and by the International Court of Justice (ICJ).[6]

As a means of promoting stability, this was no doubt sensible. It has, however, had a great number of unfortunate consequences, many of which continue to plague African states in particular. The most cursory glance at a political map of contemporary Africa reveals a number of straight and prolonged boundaries, drawn by colonial draftsmen without reference either to the physical features of the territory being bounded or to the people and their ethnicity living either side of the line. Not surprisingly, therefore, many African borders unintentionally cut through tribal territories, dividing people from their kith and kin, and resulting in disparate ethnic groups being concentrated within one nation state. This in turn has led to serious secession- ist problems, most acutely in Biafra's attempt to secede from Nigeria during the years 1967 to 1970, and Katanga's attempted secession from the Congo after the country gained its independence from Belgian rule. In fairness to those who opposed these secessions, it should be pointed out that both would have involved the breaking away of the wealthiest parts of the states in ques- tion, and in both cases the independence movements were supported by states hoping to profit from the resulting secessions.

The result of the application of *uti possidetis* has been a series of fron- tier disputes coming before the ICJ, involving the rather unedifying spectacle of border disagreements being resolved in ways thought to conform with colonial intentions and evidenced by the earliest colonialist maps or treaties. Many contemporary disputes in Africa, both internal and external, have their origins in colonial frontier-drawing, with examples ranging from the civil strife within Ivory Coast to the frontier dispute between Eritrea and Ethiopia.

Hence, the effect of *uti possidetis* has been to greatly constrain the proclaimed right of self-determination. Although value judgements may be inappropriate, some have argued that, while the concept of self-determination and the accompanying process of decolonisation were progressive, the conse- quent constraints of *uti possidetis* were distinctly conservative and prevented many peoples from breaking free from the colonial borders that had been imposed upon them. Certainly, many minority peoples in African states have remained in what they experience as subjugation. At the same time it remains obvious that statehood can never, and should never, be equated with ethnic homogeneity. Arguably, almost all states contain diverse ethnic groups, and what is important is the access such people have to government participa- tion and transparency. Nevertheless, when the factor of religious diversity is added to ethnic diversity, it is hardly surprising that for many decolonised

---

[6] *Frontier Dispute (Burkina Faso/Mali), Judgment*, ICJ Reports 1986, 554.

states, national unity is hard to achieve, and harder to maintain. In many cases, political unity has been maintained only by eschewing democratic governance in favour of autocracies or dictatorships. Examples are legion, but obviously include states such as Syria, Iraq, Libya, Sudan and many sub-Saharan countries. And, as such autocracies are challenged, or their leaders toppled in 'regime change' exercises, so these artificially created states have begun to cease to function as effective polities, fragmenting along ethnic and religious lines, becoming vulnerable to incursions by radical terrorist groups, and even morphing into 'failed' states that can no longer effectively protect the populations within their boundaries.

C. Methods of Self-determination and Consequences

Once the inevitability of decolonisation had been accepted by the colonial powers, there remained two further issues to be dealt with: the means by which the future of the decolonised territory was to be determined, and the terms on which self-government would be granted.

As to the first, it seems in retrospect obvious that the opinion of the people in the territory subject to decolonisation should have been sought, and normally such an exercise was carried out, typically by plebiscite. For African states gaining their independence, this was generally unproblematic, with the majority of inhabitants overwhelmingly preferring domestic governance to continuing colonial rule. In such cases the debate centred on the constitutions with which these states were to be provided rather than on ascertaining the wishes of the indigenous population. This was not always the case elsewhere, however, and occasionally events occurred that were difficult to reconcile with the spirit of decolonisation, and indeed its reality. Two examples indicate once more the significance of power in any analysis of international law.

The first concerns Goa, an enclave on the west coast of the Indian sub-continent. Goa was a thriving Portuguese colony for some 450 years. Portugal was arguably in breach of its UN obligations in not taking steps to ascertain the wishes of the people of the colony. In 1961 India entered and annexed Goan territory, which it claimed was an integral part of 'Mother India'. It therefore refused to hold a referendum, and the de facto result was accepted by the UN, a draft resolution condemning the annexation having been vetoed by the USSR.

The second involves what was once West New Guinea, a colony of the Dutch from 1883, and the western half of the second largest island in the world, the other half of which became independent Papua New Guinea in 1975. When, in 1949, the independent state of Indonesia was formed from the Dutch colonies known as the Dutch East Indies, West New Guinea was retained by the Netherlands with a view to preparing the territory for independence. Indonesia under President Sukarno, with the support of the

Non-Aligned Movement, in which he was influential, laid claim to all former Dutch territory. Indonesia had already successfully incorporated the Moluccas, although the Dutch decolonisation agreement had provided for the possibility of Moluccan secession – a point subsequently ignored by the United Nations. Sukarno's claim to West New Guinea was no more attractive or reasonable than Dutch colonial occupation. There was no natural link between West New Guinea and Indonesia, and the claim can be seen as an attempt at late colonisation. Nevertheless, after armed confrontation by Indonesia in 1962, the Dutch entered into negotiations that led to the transfer of the territory and its sovereignty to the United Nations Temporary Executive Authority (UNTEA) for six years, after which period it was to determine the people's preference – whether for independence or Indonesian integration. Almost immediately, Indonesia began to direct events, and finally, in 1969, a referendum of 1205 delegates was organised in a vote that was neither representative, free nor fair. This vote in favour of integration into Indonesia was accepted by the UN, despite misgivings, and the territory was unhappily transferred to Indonesia in November 1969. Needless to say, the change in sovereignty has brought no happiness to the ordinary people of West New Guinea (now known as the Indonesian provinces of West Papua and Papua, having previously been known to Indonesians as Irian Jaya) and opposition to the regime continues.

What should be appreciated, therefore, is that although self-determination is often portrayed as always beneficial to those who enjoy this right, this is not necessarily so, particularly where the intended process for attaining such self-determination is abandoned.

Very recently, in response to a request from the General Assembly, the ICJ has considered whether the UK's decolonisation of Mauritius was lawfully completed in 1968, in view of the fact that the UK had earlier separated the Chagos Archipelago from Mauritius: *Legal Consequences of the Separation of the Chagos Archipelago from Mauritius in 1965, Advisory Opinion*, ICJ Reports, 25 February 2019. (The islands were incorporated into a new colony, the British Indian Ocean Territory, in 1965, and the largest island, Diego Garcia, was leased to the US, which continues to operate a military base there.) The ICJ was also asked to specify the consequences under international law of the UK's continued administration of the Archipelago, including with regard to the inability of Mauritius to resettle its nationals on the islands, especially those of Chagossian origin (many of whom have long campaigned for the right of return following the UK's expulsion of the islanders in the late 1960s and early 1970s).

The ICJ concluded that the detachment of the Archipelago was not in accordance with international law at the time in question – having failed to respect the free and genuine will of the Mauritian people or the territorial integrity of Mauritius – thereby rendering the subsequent decolonisation unlawful. It further stated that the UK's continued administration of the islands constitutes a wrongful act entailing the international responsibility of the UK, which is under an obligation to end its administration as quickly as possible. Furthermore, although it is for the General Assembly to determine the 'modalities' by which the completion of Mauritius's decolonisation is to take place, all member states have a duty to co-operate with the UN in putting these into effect, since respect for the right to self-determination is an obligation *erga omnes*. The advisory opinion has multiple implications, but in view of what has just been said above in relation to Goa and West New Guinea, it is worth noting that certain of the judges, in separate declarations appended to the Opinion, stated that they did not consider the division of a non-self-governing territory to be contrary to the principle of territorial integrity per se, provided such an outcome reflects the true and freely expressed will of the peoples of the territory concerned.

As to the role of the colonial power in defining subsequent constitutional arrangements, we turn to two other examples that remain pertinent: Myanmar (Burma) and Indonesia.[7] Both represent attempts by a departing colonial power to leave a constitutional legacy, in the form of a written constitution, intended to constrain the sovereignty of the newly independent state. This was a common occurrence, but the two chosen illustrations took place early on during the period of decolonisation, and demonstrate the real difficulties with such imposed constitutions, even when well meant.

Burma gained independence from the UK in 1948 with a constitution that had been drafted in 1947. This provided for a parliamentary democracy, and also, in recognition of the different peoples that inhabited Burma, for different states within the country for each of the Karen, Kachin and Shan people. Although the parliamentary democracy was to be unitary, Article 201 of the Constitution stated that any of the above groups would have a right to secede after 10 years of constitutional rule. Within that 10-year period, however, the Burmese (Bamar) majority, comprising 68 per cent of the population, took power and unilaterally removed the right to secession, even though it was thought that this right had been effectively entrenched. This illustrates two points. Firstly, although constitutions usually continue to operate 'beyond the grave' (the US Constitution is an obvious example of this), where the constitution has been drawn up by the departing colonial power, it is likely that its prestige will be greatly diminished. Secondly, where a newly independent state makes changes to its constitution, the effect may well be to extinguish the very 'self-determination rights' of minority peoples that were supposedly achieved through decolonisation.

Indonesia, too, was formed from many different peoples in what had previously been the Dutch East Indies. The Dutch used many soldiers from the Moluccan islands in the struggle against decolonisation. When, in 1949,

---

[7] More detailed information can be found in Karen Parker, 'Understanding Self-Determination: The Basics', available at www.guidetoaction.org/parker/selfdet.html.

a Round Table Conference between the Netherlands, the Javanese (leaders of the Indonesian independence movement) and the United Nations agreed upon a decolonisation instrument, it also included the possibility of 'opt-outs' providing for plebiscites for territories not wishing to be a part of the 'United States of Indonesia'. Plebiscites were never in fact permitted, and when the Moluccan leadership declared independence in 1950, the islands were invaded by Indonesian forces. The matter was taken up by the United Nations Commission for Indonesia, but the UN did nothing and the Commission ceased to exist five years later, no doubt reflecting the wishes of both newly independent states and those of the Second World, which were more concerned with decolonisation than true self-determination. Parallels to these cases can also be found in the experiences of many African states with regard to decolonisation and state constitutions drafted by the departing colonial ruler.

D. Economic Self-determination

As is clear from common Article 1 of the International Covenants on Human Rights of 1966, it was recognised that political self-determination in itself was insufficient. Consequently, there was an insistence that independent states should have the right to control both their economies and their resources free from external interference. What was claimed was both the right to nationalise property within the new state regardless of ownership and title, and the right to economic development on equitable terms. (At this time, it was not expressed in such a way but it was implicit in the request of many independent but disadvantaged countries for financial and technical assistance.) Unfortunately, for many decolonised states, the achievement of formal sovereignty was not matched by the freedom to follow an economic path radically different from that which had been pursued prior to independence. The continuing domination by former colonial powers of key sectors and resources (including land-ownership), and the inevitability of having to engage with a world market that operated largely to the advantage of the Northern industrialised states, significantly limited attempts by newly independent nations to correct wealth imbalances and improve the living standards of all citizens. As Naomi Klein was to observe of South Africa after it finally achieved independence from white-minority rule in 1993, such countries were 'given the keys to the house but not the combination to the safe'.[8]

---

[8] Naomi Klein, *The Shock Doctrine* (London, Penguin, 2007) 206. Interestingly, as Quinn Slobodian's recent study of the Geneva School neoliberals demonstrates, such a hollowed-out form of sovereignty, involving a clear demarcation between the political and the economic realms – with the state responsible for the former, but supranational institutions very much in charge of the latter – was precisely what certain economists, including Hayek, were advocating from the 1920s onwards. Influenced by the way in which the old Ottoman and Austro-Hungarian Empires had functioned, the Geneva School believed that newly independent nations (and, ideally, all

Although newly independent states could opt to nationalise foreign-owned property (normally belonging to the government or to private individuals or entities of the former colonial ruler), fears about the negative consequences that could flow from this tended to reduce its attractiveness. These ranged from a possible decrease in foreign investment to, at the most extreme, military intervention by the ex-colonial power(s) aimed at restoring the status quo ante – as occurred in Egypt in 1956, when Britain and France, with the help of Israel, sought (unsuccessfully) to wrest back control of the Suez Canal after its nationalisation by President Nasser. Also relevant was the view taken by capital-exporting states that the corollary of any right of expropriation was the obligation to pay 'fair' compensation (see chapter four). Regrettably, this was rarely matched by any reparations from the ex-colonisers for the resources appropriated during the long era of colonial rule. Much of the poverty and violence that continues to plague South Africa and Zimbabwe, to take just two examples, can ultimately be traced back to the forced seizure by white settlers of prime land belonging to the indigenous populations of both countries, leaving a skewed pattern of land-ownership that persists to this day.[9]

After independence, many states also found themselves severely prejudiced by the terms of trade with which they were forced to contend. Prices for industrial and finished goods rose persistently, whereas those for primary products and raw materials – the major exports of the newly independent states – tended to remain at or below that achieved at independence, as well as being vulnerable to speculation, over-supply and adverse weather events (especially droughts and flooding) that could suddenly and dramatically depress the price of a commodity, with devastating consequences for the country concerned. A related problem for decolonised and other under-industrialised nations has been a particular susceptibility to the 'resource curse'. This is the phenomenon whereby discovery of an abundant supply of a valuable natural resource (oil, gas, diamonds, etc), rather than boosting the prosperity of the state, leads instead to economic contraction and even stagnation, as investment becomes over-concentrated in industries associated with the relevant resource, to the neglect of other sectors, making the country especially vulnerable to any downturn affecting its principal activity. It tends to be a particular problem in those

nations) should be prevented from taking economic decisions that would serve only to disrupt the smooth operation of the global economy and harm private capital rights (such as the nationalisation of key industries or the imposition of currency controls). Instead, they argued that international institutions should be entrusted with the conduct of economic policy, which should be protected against interference from national legislatures. Quinn Slobodian, *Globalists: The End of Empire and the Birth of Neoliberalism* (Cambridge, MA, Harvard University Press, 2018).

[9] See, for example, Alex T Magaisa, 'The Land Question and Transitional Justice in Zimbabwe: Law, Force and History's Multiple Victims', *Oxford Transitional Justice Working Paper Series*, 30 June 2010; and Karen S Openshaw and Patrick CR Terry, 'Zimbabwe's odious inheritance: Debt and unequal land distribution' (2015) 11 *McGill International Journal of Sustainable Development Law and Policy*, 39–86.

countries that have been unable to develop a diversified industrial sector (and which perhaps under colonial rule were actively prevented from doing so) and hence are less resilient in the face of global market upheavals. Such resources can also become a focus for corruption and even bloodshed, which again has tended to be more prevalent in poorer and decolonised nations, since they are more likely to lack strong democratic governance and rule of law.

Although newly independent states managed to ensure the passage of a General Assembly Resolution in 1974 establishing a 'New International Economic Order',[10] one of the main intentions of which was to provide a 'level playing field' for trade, this failed to bring about any significant change in global economic relations.[11] To exacerbate matters further, many decolonised states – as indeed has been the case with a great number of poorer nations in general – have been unable to access trade deals or loans without implementing policies designed to reshape their economies in favour of capital-exporting states. At times, this has occurred directly as a consequence of the terms included in bilateral commercial treaties with more powerful nations, but has more often been imposed via the 'conditionality' demanded by the Western-dominated International Monetary Fund (IMF) – that is, a set of economic conditions that a borrowing state is forced to comply with in order to access funds from the IMF.

Established during a conference at the New Hampshire mountain resort of Bretton Woods in 1944, the IMF and its sister organisation, the World Bank, were initially charged with helping to rebuild and stabilise the international economic order in the aftermath of the Second World War. The purpose of the IMF was to encourage stable exchange rates, and to provide short-term loans to states experiencing balance-of-payments difficulties, thereby avoiding the competitive currency depreciations that had helped precipitate the global depression of the 1930s. In contrast, the responsibility of the World Bank, as indicated by its official title – the International Bank for Reconstruction and Development – was to provide longer-term loans to rebuild the damaged infrastructures of the postwar European and Asian nations. However, as the economies of Europe and Japan recovered, so the remit of both organisations changed, with both focusing on providing financial assistance to poorer nations, often by means of loans dependent on the recipients agreeing to implement certain economic reforms stipulated by the IMF (what came to be referred to as 'structural adjustment policies' and, later, as 'conditionality').

The IMF's role was also affected by the shift to variable exchange rates following the US's abandonment of the gold standard in 1971. Rather than focusing on a relatively narrow set of criteria to determine whether a state's currency had maintained its par value (and hence whether the state was likely

---

[10] UNGA Resolution 3201 (S-VI) of 1 May 1974.
[11] See Wade Mansell and Joanne Scott 'Why Bother About a Right to Development?' (1994) 21 *Journal of Law and Society* 171.

to meet its balance-of-payments target), the IMF instead became involved in scrutinising an ever-widening range of policy areas, extending to 'military expenditures, environmental issues, governance issues and social safety nets (which amount to welfare, housing, and unemployment policies)',[12] with the result that its area of operations 'now encompasses virtually anything and everything with implications for economic and financial stability'.[13] Thus, the IMF's greatly expanded sphere of influence has arguably blurred any meaningful distinction between the economic and political (assuming the two are ever truly separable), which has had significant implications for the political independence of states subject to one of its lending programmes.

This transformation of the IMF's role was accompanied (and some would say caused) by a dramatic shift in the Fund's underlying philosophy in the late 1970s and early 1980s that coincided with the rise to power of the Reagan and Thatcher administrations in the US and UK respectively. This saw the IMF abandon its Keynesian roots (exemplified by a willingness to support interventionist policies where necessary to encourage expansion and maintain employment levels) and instead oblige borrowing countries to adopt a range of fiscal and monetary policies in line with the so-called Washington Consensus favoured by US governments: in particular, increasing exports, privatising state-owned assets, dismantling trade barriers, curtailing public expenditure, minimising inflation, and liberalising capital and financial accounts. The avowed aim was to enable these countries to reduce budget deficits and build up government revenues, thereby encouraging economic growth in the long term through increased foreign investment and inter-state trading, albeit at the short-term cost of higher unemployment and lower wages.[14]

However, for many analysts, including Joseph Stiglitz (an economics Nobel laureate and a former Chief Economist of the World Bank), the policy prescriptions of the IMF are misconceived and, far from producing prosperity in the longer term, have in fact led to a deterioration in the economic and social life of the countries to which they have been applied. Reflecting, for example, on the East Asian financial crisis of the late 1990s, Stiglitz describes how the IMF's policies worsened and even partly precipitated the economic downturn which occurred in the region, most notably through the Fund's

---

[12] Daniel D Bradlow, 'The World Bank, the IMF, and Human Rights' (1996) 6 *Transnational Law and Contemporary Problems* 67–70, 70.

[13] Barry Eichengreen and Ngaire Woods, 'The IMF's Unmet Challenges' (2016) 30 *Journal of Economic Perspectives* 29–51, 30.

[14] The US has been able to refrain from taking its own medicine (not least owing to the privileges flowing from the US dollar's status as the global reserve currency), as John Gray makes clear: 'The [Washington] consensus prescribed sound money and balanced budgets as touchstones of economic virtue – not of course for America, which has rarely submitted itself to any economic orthodoxy, running up massive federal deficits year after year – but for everyone else and especially poor countries. The consensus also dictated free trade, another injunction that applied mainly to the developing world.' John Gray, *False Dawn: The Delusions of Global Capitalism* (London, Granta, 2009) xviii.

insistence on over-rapid financial and capital market liberalisation, which increased currency speculation and capital flight from the affected countries.[15] He also notes how the Fund's insistence on the maintenance of high interest rates led, as a result of the severe indebtedness of many companies in the region, to large numbers of insolvencies and high levels of unemployment.[16] Meanwhile, a requirement to cut public expenditure resulted in cutbacks in education and health programmes, and a reduction in food and fuel subsidies, which ultimately led to rioting in Indonesia.[17] The imposition of such programmes not only severely limits the ability of recipient states to fashion their own economic destinies, but can also have, as will be explained in chapter six, devastating effects on the human rights of their citizens, especially economic and social rights.

Indeed, for many critics of IMF 'conditionality', the Fund, far from being a neutral, 'technocratic' adviser on economic matters, is in fact beholden to its major contributors. The IMF makes use of a weighted voting system, under which the more resources a state makes available to the Fund – referred to as its 'quota', and calculated using a weighted average of a state's GDP, openness to trade and financial flows, economic variability and international reserves – the more voting rights it is allocated. Since the US has for many years held the largest quota at the IMF, it also exercises the greatest control over the Fund's decision-making. (As at February 2019, the US's quota expressed as a percentage of the total was 17.46, followed by Japan (6.48), China (6.41), Germany (5.60), and France and the UK (each with 4.24). In return, the US enjoys 16.52 per cent of voting rights on the IMF's governing board, compared with 6.15 for Japan, 6.09 for China, 5.32 for Germany and 4.03 for each of France and the UK.)[18] This in turn explains why the mandates of the neoliberalist Washington Consensus have figured so heavily in the Fund's policy prescriptions, and why, according to certain research studies, countries whose voting patterns match those of the US in the UN General Assembly, or which owe large amounts to US commercial banks, tend to receive IMF loans with fewer conditions attached.[19]

Similarly, the IMF has been accused of being overly influenced by the wishes of its European members, who together account for a large share of the Fund's resources and hence voting rights. Following the global financial crisis,

[15] Joseph E Stiglitz, *Globalization and its Discontents* (London, Penguin Books, 2002) 89–90.
[16] ibid, 97 and 112.
[17] ibid, 119–20.
[18] 'IMF Members' Quotas and Voting Power, and IMF Board of Governors', available at www.imf.org/external/np/sec/memdir/members.aspx.
[19] Carmen M Reinhart and Christoph Trebesch, 'The International Monetary Fund: 70 Years of Reinvention' (2016) 30 *Journal of Economic Perspectives* 3–27, 21; Stephanie J Rickard and Teri L Caraway, 'International Negotiations in the Shadow of National Elections' (2014) 68 *International Organization* 701–20, 710.

for example, the IMF was widely criticised for providing funds to Greece (in a joint programme with the European Commission and the European Central Bank) without first insisting on a restructuring of the country's extremely high debt burden: a move opposed by France and Germany for fear of the harm it would wreak on a number of French and German banks that had lent heavily to Greece.[20] (Debt which Greece owed to private creditors was finally restructured in 2012, by which point the country had suffered a severe recession.) The Fund is also in something of an invidious position in regard to calling for debt restructurings, since it has traditionally stipulated that its own loans be discharged in full, as well as repaid before loans provided from other sources, exposing it to accusations of double-standards when it attempts to lecture fellow creditors about the necessity of write-offs.

Moreover, since a great number of IMF decisions need to be approved by an 85 per cent majority, the US, which for years has held just under 17 per cent of voting rights, has been free to block any decision with which it disagrees. The US Congress has therefore been able to thwart attempts to reform the way in which the IMF is governed, including plans to double contributions to the Fund and to award greater voting rights, and hence a greater say in the running of the organisation, to nations such as China, Brazil, India and Russia. Consequently, such states have begun to develop alternative strategies and lending structures, including a $240 billion multilateral currency swap arrangement established by the Association of South East Asian Nations (ASEAN), together with China, Japan and South Korea, and the $100 billion Contingent Reserve Arrangement, set up by Brazil, Russia, India, China and South Africa (BRICS), both of which are designed to provide loans to participant states faced with short-term liquidity problems – a clear encroachment on IMF territory.[21]

Loans accompanied by IMF conditionality in turn form a subset of a more general scourge afflicting decolonised and poorer states – and, since the financial crisis, some Western European nations, most notably Greece – that of unsustainable sovereign debt. Such debt (contracted by the government of a nation and hence binding on subsequent governments and the state as a whole) originates both from official sources – country-to-country lending and loans provided by inter-governmental institutions, such as the IMF, World Bank and regional development banks – and from private institutions and individuals (foreign and domestic banks and bondholders). Poorer nations, whose debts will overwhelmingly be denominated in foreign currencies (often the US dollar, but also the yen, the euro and, increasingly, the renminbi)

---

[20] Eichengreen and Woods, 'Unmet Challenges' (2016) 43 and 45; Reinhart and Trebesch (ibid) 19–20.

[21] For a discussion of these initiatives (including their weaknesses), see John D Ciorciari, 'China's Structural Power Deficit and Influence Gap in the Monetary Policy Arena' (2014) 54 *Asian Survey* 869–93; see also Eichengreen and Woods (n 13) 48–49.

encounter particular problems when there is an interest-rate rise, making the debt more expensive, and/or they suffer a severe curtailment of export income, reducing the amount of foreign currency earned, and so making the debt harder to pay back. The 'solution' is frequently to incur a further loan or loans to pay back the original sum borrowed (often on more onerous terms), thereby increasing the overall debt burden.

In certain cases, a country will be able to agree a restructuring of the debt with its creditors. The options include extending the date on which the loan matures, reducing the principal owed or the amount of interest to be paid, a combination of the foregoing, or even writing off the loan in its entirety. However, as there is as yet no sovereign bankruptcy mechanism in place providing for an orderly rescheduling or cancellation of state debt (a supra-national version of the insolvency procedures that exist in most jurisdictions for bankrupt individuals, companies and even local authorities),[22] those that do occur do so on an ad hoc basis, and typically only after a great deal of economic damage has been done to the state concerned, usually at the expense of its most vulnerable citizens. Complicating matters further, especially in the context of sovereign bond issues, is the fact that a small number of creditors may be able to jeopardise the success of a restructuring plan by insisting that they are paid in full – a fate that has recently befallen Argentina.

After defaulting on nearly $100 billion-worth of debt in 2001, Argentina reached restructuring agreements with the vast majority of its bondholders (93 per cent) in 2005 and 2010. However, a number of investments funds that had bought up deeply discounted Argentinian bonds on the secondary debt market were able, with the backing of a US federal court in 2012, to stop Argentina from using the US banking system to make interest payments to the majority bondholders until it had agreed to pay these minority 'holdouts' the full face value of their bonds. This resulted in the country defaulting on its sovereign debt in 2014. For many commentators, such behavior fully justified the moniker that is routinely applied to such investment vehicles – 'vulture funds' – and many deplored the fact that an economic initiative of fundamental importance to a sovereign state (reducing its debt load) could ultimately be held hostage to the demands of a few wealthy individuals. And, although states are now modifying the contracts governing new bond issues to ensure

[22] In September 2015, the UN General Assembly adopted a draft resolution on 'Basic Principles on Sovereign Debt Restructuring Processes' designed to provide guidance for sovereign debt workouts (UNGA A/69/L.84, 29 July 2015). The nine principles seek, inter alia, to protect indebted states from abusive action by minority creditors (see the comments that follow on Argentina) but also to preserve the rights of creditors, with restructuring envisaged only as a last resort. The Global South largely voted in favour of the resolution and the Global North largely voted against. UNCTAD (the UN Commission on Trade and Development), which is supportive of the principles, has also published its own proposals on the matter: 'Sovereign Debt Workouts: Going Forward Roadmap and Guide', April 2015, available at https://debt-and-finance.unctad. org/Documents/SDW_roadmap.pdf.

that debt restructurings agreed to by the majority of bondholders will be binding on all, there are still many bonds in existence to which the old rules apply, making it possible that the situation will arise again. Nor, ultimately, did the decision of President Mauricio Macri's administration in 2016 to accede to the demands of the investment funds and settle with them in full help to restore confidence in Argentina's economy. Capital flight, a sharp depreciation of the peso against the dollar and rampant inflation have raised fears that the government may not be able to meet future interest payments, which will necessitate further cuts in public expenditure. It has also prompted the Macri Government to seek a $50 billion bailout from the IMF, eliciting angry denunciations from those Argentinians who blame IMF-imposed austerity measures for the deep recession that Argentina experienced in 2001–02 and which caused the country to default on its debt originally.[23]

Adding insult to injury, the original sums borrowed by impoverished nations have often done little, if anything, to improve the lives of the citizens responsible for paying them back, and have frequently been of active harm to them, if only in terms of the reductions in health, education and welfare budgets that discharging such debt normally entails. According to some legal commentators and debt activists, such loans merit non-repayment on the ground that they amount to 'odious debt' – that is, debt which has been contracted without the consent of the citizens concerned (normally by non-democratic governments), has failed to benefit those citizens, and has been provided by creditors who were aware of both this lack of consent and lack of benefit when they advanced the loan monies.[24]

China's increasing importance as a provider of funds to African states, as well as to other nations – notably as part of its 'Belt and Road' and 'String of Pearls' initiatives – is also provoking disquiet. A number of states, including the Democratic Republic of the Congo, Zambia, Djibouti, Malaysia, Pakistan, Nepal, Montenegro, Myanmar, Cambodia, Laos, Papua New Guinea and Tonga, have borrowed heavily from China to finance large infrastructure projects, involving the building of ports, highways, airports and hydroelectric dams, and now face severe difficulties paying back these loans. Nor is much of this construction of obvious benefit to the populations of the borrowing states, some of it instead recalling the debt-fuelled 'vanity projects' carried out throughout much of Africa and Latin America in the 1970s. The Zambian Government, for example, has borrowed funds from China to build two new

---

[23] See 'Argentina agrees to $50bn loan from IMF amid national protests', *Guardian*, 8 June 2018; and Larry Elliott, 'Markets are all about the timing – and Argentina got clocked', *Guardian*, 30 August 2018.

[24] See especially Patricia Adams, *Odious Debts: Loose Lending, Corruption, and the Third World's Environmental Legacy* (Earthscan, London and Toronto, 1991); and Jeff King, *The Doctrine of Odious Debt in International Law: A Restatement*, Cambridge Studies in International and Comparative Law (Cambridge, CUP, 2016).

airports that critics argue the country simply does not need and is serving only to divert funds away from more important sectors, such as education. And, after having most of its loans written off in the early years of the new millennium as part of the World Bank's Heavily Indebted Poor Countries Initiative, Zambia has experienced a tripling of its debt as a share of national income in the past five years, with the need to repay this being linked to the imposition of new charges on Zambian citizens, such as taxes on water bore holes and speeding-camera fines.[25]

There have even been suggestions that China is using the extreme indebtedness of certain states as leverage to gain control of important resources or strategic locations in the states affected. For example, Sri Lanka has granted a 99-year lease of its deep-sea port at Hambantota on the Indian Ocean to a state-controlled Chinese company in return for funds to enable it to pay off Chinese loans, exciting fears that China may ultimately wish to use the port as a naval outpost.[26] Similarly, Ecuador is reported to be paying back in oil the approximately $19 billion it has borrowed from China for various infrastructure projects (including around $2.25 billion owed to the Chinese Export–Import Bank for the construction of a controversial dam near the site of an active volcano), with repayment of such loans now absorbing most of the country's petroleum resources.[27] Coupled with unease about the levels of indebtedness resulting from such loans is the fact that China, in keeping with its policy of non-interference in the political affairs of other states, does not link the provision of funds with improvements in the human rights or democratic governance records of recipient countries.

Consequently, as the above has tried to indicate, attempts to reduce the wealth disparity between the North and the South have made little headway, notwithstanding the concept of 'the common heritage of mankind' being adopted in the Law of the Sea Convention of 1982 (see section VI), and in spite of the adoption of a UN General Assembly Declaration recognising a

[25] The Inquiry, 'Is the China–Africa Love Affair Over?', BBC World Service, 5 November 2018, available at www.bbc.co.uk/programmes/w3cswqv4.

[26] See, for example, 'Sri Lanka Dismisses Concerns About China's Control of Hambantota', *The Maritime Executive*, 11 October 2018; and 'China is doing the same things to Sri Lanka that Great Britain did to China after the Opium Wars', Panos Mourdoukoutas, *Forbes*, 28 June 2018. Both Sri Lanka and China have denied that the port will ever be used for military purposes.

[27] Nicholas Casey and Clifford Krauss, 'It Doesn't Matter if Ecuador Can Afford This Dam. China Still Gets Paid.', *New York Times*, 24 December 2018; and 'Coca Codo Sinclair: Pérdida de $27 millones', *El Universo*, 15 November 2018. The Coca Codo Sinclair dam, built near the Reventador Volcano, around 100km east of Quito, by the then Government of Rafael Correa, is controversial not only for its location, provoking anxiety about possible earthquakes and landslides, but also for its poor construction and for allegations that bribes were paid to politicians and officials involved with the project. According to the *New York Times*, about 80% of Ecuador's petroleum resources are currently dedicated to paying back the country's loans to China, with the high level of debt incurred prompting the current government of Lenín Moreno both to drill further into the Amazon Rain Forest and to cut public spending, including fuel subsidies.

'human right to development'.[28] All these attempts to argue for economic redress for the debilitating effects of colonialism by way of fair trade and development, while very successful in obtaining widespread support in the UN, have had little practical impact. Indeed, it is possible to argue that, while self-determination brought political control, at least to parts of the indigenous population, one of its major effects was to remove the administrative burden and cost of colonialism from the colonial states and to place it directly upon the ex-colonies. Having said this, it should still be acknowledged that many states which have achieved independence since 1945 have made much greater strides towards economic independence and prosperity than would have been the case had their colonial status persisted.

IV. Self-determination after the Cold War

By the end of the Cold War in 1991, the concept of self-determination was widely regarded as of historical interest only, its relevance confined to colonial or occupied peoples, the vast majority of whom had gained their independence by this point. One obvious remaining exception concerned the Palestinian situation, particularly following the Arab–Israeli war of 1967, in which Israel captured the West Bank and Gaza. Despite many UN resolutions recognising the right of Palestinian self-determination, unwavering support from the US has allowed successive Israeli governments to continue to occupy these areas and indeed strengthen Israel's control over them by permitting the widespread building of Israeli settlements.

As has been noted, any right of self-determination was subordinate to the principle of the territorial integrity of a state, and hence there was no automatic entitlement to secede. Many jurists have argued that where secession is sought, this is justifiable only if those wishing to secede have been deprived of their civic rights within the state in question. A right of internal self-determination meant that all peoples within a state should have equal rights of access to the means of government, but not a right to their own government. In some ways, this emphasis upon territorial integrity was understandable, since, if distinct ethnic groups, religious groups or language groups were all to be granted their independence, the resulting fragmentation of states would have no end. It was also recognised that if secession was tolerated, most secessions would themselves lead to the creation of a new minority within the seceding state.

Notwithstanding this, the events that occurred following the end of the Cold War forced a reconsideration of the right of self-determination. That the

---

[28] UNGA Resolution 41/128 of 4 December 1986.

dissolution of the Soviet Union into 15 independent states was accomplished with so little violence was little short of astounding. The disintegration not only meant new institutions of government had to be established, but also that agreement had to be reached as to the division of the Soviet Union's assets and debts. Again, the principle of *uti possidetis* was applied, with the new states becoming established within their erstwhile federal frontiers. Eleven of the states that replaced the Soviet Union remained in loose alliance with Russia, in a Commonwealth of Independent States (CIS), while the Baltic states (Latvia, Estonia and Lithuania), together with Georgia, rejected such a link.

Immediately following the break-up of the Soviet Union came the disintegration of Yugoslavia. In the early stages of the crisis, the international emphasis was upon maintaining the territorial integrity of Yugoslavia, and it is still widely argued that the recognition of the independent states of Croatia and Slovenia occurred only when the dissolution of the country was acknowledged to be a fait accompli. (While there can be no right to secession, sufficient power to assert the fact of secession may suffice for recognition. This is discussed further below.)

The cases of South Sudan and Kosovo highlight the fact that secession in international law cannot be divorced from the wider political context and the support (or lack thereof) that the would-be seceding state receives from the parent state, as well as from powerful actors in the international community. As the independence of South Sudan was granted after a negotiated agreement between those seeking independence and the Government of Sudan in Khartoum, the new state immediately received widespread recognition, and shortly after celebrating independence was granted admission as a member of the UN. The position with regard to Kosovo was very different.

Kosovo's Unilateral Declaration of Independence was made in February 2008, in the face of strong opposition from Serbia, from which Kosovans had voted to secede in a referendum held in 1991. On a turnout of 87 per cent, 99 per cent voted in favour of independence, while Kosovan Serbs, amounting to 10 per cent of the population, boycotted the referendum. Although the Declaration quickly led to Kosovo being recognised as an independent state by 69 countries, a significant number of states opposed the move. Many of these states are contending with their own secessionist movements, and therefore disapprove of the precedent set by Kosovo, while others have traditional religious or political ties to Serbia. Those states that recognised Kosovo's independence stressed that this should be seen as a *sui generis* case, while those that refused to do so argued that the Declaration was illegal and would also encourage other secessionist movements. Consequently, the General Assembly requested an advisory opinion from the ICJ:

> In the present case, the question posed by the General Assembly is clearly formulated. The question is narrow and specific; it asks for the Court's opinion on whether or not the declaration of independence is in accordance with international

law. It does not ask about the legal consequences of that declaration. In particular, it does not ask whether or not Kosovo has achieved statehood. Nor does it ask about the validity or legal effects of the recognition of Kosovo by those States which have recognized it as an independent State.[29]

To this narrow question the Court (understandably perhaps) gave a narrow and specific answer, holding that a declaration of independence was not a violation of international law: it was neither prohibited by general international law, nor yet by any specific source of international law. Most importantly for our purposes, the Court, in deciding that there was no obligation in international law to refrain from attempting to secede, stated:

> During the eighteenth, nineteenth and early twentieth centuries, there were numerous instances of declarations of independence, often strenuously opposed by the State from which independence was being declared. Sometimes a declaration resulted in the creation of a new State, at others it did not. In no case, however, does the practice of States as a whole suggest that the act of promulgating the declaration was regarded as contrary to international law. On the contrary, State practice during this period points clearly to the conclusion that international law contained no prohibition of declarations of independence.[30]

What this is saying in effect is that such a declaration, while not forbidden, carries with it no other implication. This is a question not of law but of power. As long as veto-power states, such as China and Russia, remain opposed to secession in principle (not wishing to encourage the various independence movements within their own borders), the legal position is unlikely to change.

A. Contemporary Independence Movements and Rules on Secession

While there has been a myriad of secessionist movements since the Cold War, these have tended to be distinct in their natures, causes and hopes. They have included attempts by Tamils to create an independent state in Sri Lanka, Somali efforts to establish a state of Somaliland, the struggle to achieve independence for Western Sahara, Chechnyans fighting for independence from Russia, and Québécois wishing to separate from Canada. The past few years have also witnessed the holding of referendums by peoples determined to forge their own independent nations, both with and without the blessing of the parent state.

In September 2014, Scotland, one of the constituent nations of the UK, held an independence referendum, the terms of which had previously been

---

[29] *Accordance with International Law of the Unilateral Declaration of Independence in Respect of Kosovo, Advisory Opinion*, ICJ Reports 2010, 403, para 51.
[30] ibid para 79.

agreed with the UK Government of David Cameron.[31] The population voted to remain part of the UK,[32] and it seems that the outcome of the vote was influenced both by economic concerns (fear of reduced income levels and of disruption to trade; loss of control over monetary policy in relation to the shared currency) and by a desire not to fall out of the EU (in itself an important economic factor), since officials from the EU Commission indicated that Scotland would be treated as having left the EU if it became independent from the UK, and would therefore have to formally reapply for membership, with all the uncertainty that this would entail. Ironically, Scotland now faces ejection from the EU as a result of the outcome of the June 2016 referendum in which the UK as a whole voted to leave the Union, of which it has been a member since 1973. (The majority of the populations of both Scotland and Northern Ireland actually voted to remain in the EU, but a majority of the peoples of England and Wales voted to leave, with the English vote determining the matter, since the population of England is far greater than that of the other three nations combined.) At the moment, there appears to be little appetite among the Scottish population for a second independence referendum, but this could change after the UK has left the EU, especially if this leads to worsening economic conditions in Scotland.

Another European country, Spain, was also the site of an independence referendum, which took place in the autonomous province of Catalonia. In this case, the Catalonian Government (controlled by various pro-independence parties) held a referendum in October 2017; however, unlike the Scottish one, this was most definitely not conducted with the approval of the parent state. Such an action is in fact unlawful under the current Spanish Constitution – drawn up in 1978 when the country was transitioning to democracy after nearly 40 years of the Franco dictatorship – since this proscribes any threat to the political integrity of Spain. Consequently, the referendum, in which 90 per cent of those who voted (on a turnout of around 43 per cent) opted to secede from Spain, was bitterly opposed by the central government in Madrid, then led by Mariano Rajoy of the conservative Partido Popular.[33] It also led to some violence, as members of the national police force and Guardia Civil forcibly tried to prevent people from voting. The outcome was the dissolving

---

[31] Although agreeing that the referendum could take place, the Cameron Government actively campaigned for Scotland to remain part of the UK, as did Labour, the main UK opposition party.

[32] The result was just over 55% against independence, and just under 45% in favour, on a turnout of over 84%.

[33] The main Spanish opposition party, PSOE, was also opposed to the referendum, as was the right-of-centre Ciudadanos party, which enjoys a relatively high level of support in Catalonia. The low turnout can be attributed largely to the boycotting of the referendum by anti-separatist Catalans, especially in view of its 'unofficial' nature and government warnings not to participate.

of the Catalan Parliament, the imposition of direct rule from Madrid, and the holding of new elections in December 2017 (although these again resulted in the pro-independence parties holding the balance of power). The Catalan leaders responsible for organising the referendum are now either in exile in Belgium or on trial at Spain's Supreme Court, facing sentences ranging from seven to 25 years.[34] Nor has the coming to power of a new government under Pedro Sánchez (of the Partido Socialista Obrero Español) resolved the stand-off. Despite gaining the initial support of the pro-independence parties, the Sánchez administration's refusal to agree to talks on self-determination for Catalonia resulted in the separatists joining with opposition parties to vote down the Government's proposed budget, prompting Sánchez to call an early election in April 2019 (Spain's third general election in four years). Although PSOE gained the most votes in the election, it failed to attain a governing majority (winning 123 out of a possible 350 seats).[35] At present, it seems that Sánchez's best hopes of forming a government lie in securing the support of the leftwing Unidas-Podemos party and certain of Spain's smaller, regional groupings – including, possibly, those committed to Catalan independence. Future relations between Madrid and Barcelona therefore remain uncertain, complicated by the fact that Catalonia is one of the wealthiest regions of Spain (unlike Scotland in relation to the rest of the UK), and hence any attempt at secession is always likely to meet with opposition from the parent state, regardless of the constitutional position.

At the supranational level, the attempted Catalan secession was, unsurprisingly, opposed by the EU Commission, which stated that, were Catalonia to become an independent state, it would automatically fall out of the EU, and would be very unlikely to be readmitted in view of both Spain's veto of any such proposal and the opposition forthcoming from other member states fearful of encouraging separatist movements within their own borders. Indeed, even in the case of the Scottish referendum, the Commission was at best lukewarm at the prospect of an independent Scotland, even where such an outcome was sanctioned (if not exactly welcomed) by the parent state. Territorial integrity was prioritised over self-determination. Again, this illustrates that a would-be independent state, if it is to be accepted as such and is going to be able to function effectively on the international stage, will have to take into account not only the attitude of the state from which it is separating but also the interests and beliefs of more powerful nations and the international institutions of which they form part. It is possible, of course,

---

[34] The defendants are charged with having committed a number of alleged crimes, including rebellion, sedition and misuse of public funds. See, for example, 'Doce dirigentes del "procés" secesionista, ante el Supremo', *El País*, 12 February 2019, 1; and Sam Jones, 'Catalan leaders' lawyer attacks "vaudeville" case as trial begins', *Guardian*, 12 February 2019.

[35] This, and the collapse of the PP's vote (it won 66 seats – its worst-ever result), is indicative of the fragmentation of Spain's political landscape, in which a far-right party, Vox, won representation in the national parliament for the first time since the end of the Franco era.

that the EU's attitude to the admission of an independent Scotland in the future would be much more accommodating, once the UK itself has left the bloc. In fact, the UK, now fast approaching its own 'secession' date from the EU (currently postponed from 29 March to 31 October 2019), is finding that attempting to negotiate a productive future relationship with what will remain by far its most important trading partner, while at the same time 'taking back control', allowing it to forge completely independent economic, trade and migration policies, is akin to squaring the circle. Some continued pooling/loss of sovereignty (on the UK's part) seems almost inevitable, given the disparity in economic terms between the country and the organisation from which it is departing.

The Kurdish population in northern Iraq also voted for independence, in a referendum conducted by the Kurdish Regional Government (KRG) of Masoud Barzani in September 2017, with over 92 per cent of the votes cast (on a turnout of over 72 per cent) favouring the creation of an independent Kurdish state. Although Barzani chose not to issue a declaration of independence, speaking instead of the result giving the KRG a mandate to negotiate independence with the then central government of Haider al-Abadi, as well as with neighbouring states (which have their own sizeable Kurdish populations), the referendum served only to heighten tensions between the KRG and Baghdad. Especially devastating for the KRG was the loss of Kirkuk, which the Kurds had held since expelling ISIS forces in 2014, and which was retaken by the Iraqi army, supported by Iranian militias, in the wake of the referendum. Harbouring Iraq's third-largest oil reserves, Kirkuk is seen as vital to the prosperity of an independent Kurdistan, and is also, of course, unlikely to be relinquished by the Iraqi state. The KRG's decision to hold a referendum also, predictably, drew the wrath of Turkey and Iran, which object to any action likely to encourage the separatist demands of their own Kurdish populations, and hence remain implacably opposed to the establishment of an independent Kurdish state on their doorsteps. The UN and US also condemned the holding of the referendum for its potentially destabilising effect on the region.

From an international law perspective, when considering any of these cases, it is useful to refer to the conclusions reached by the Canadian Supreme Court when asked by Canada's federal government to rule on the legitimacy of any Québécois declaration of independence if Québec obtained a positive vote for independence in a referendum.[36] (When the question was put to the Court there had already been two such referenda, in 1980 and 1995, and, although independence was rejected, the second vote was very close, with a majority of only one per cent.)

The most important point made by the Supreme Court is consistent with the Åland Islands decision of 1923 (see section II A above). The Court

---

[36] [1998] 2 SCR 217.

had been asked to consider both whether such a declaration of independence would be legal under the Canadian Constitution and whether it would be consistent with international law. Its response was that such unilateral secession was not consistent with either, and it emphasised that territorial integrity prevails over any right of external self-determination. In particular, the Court stated that, where rights of internal self-determination were protected, so that the state's

> government represents the whole of the people or peoples resident within its territory, on a basis of equality and without discrimination, and respects the principles of self-determination in its own internal arrangements, [the state] is entitled to maintain its territorial integrity under international law and to have that territorial integrity recognized by other states.[37]

In other words, as noted above, a right of external self-determination can exist only where a people or peoples are denied equal access to the machinery of government and civil rights.

Québec's situation is, of course, in some ways unique. It is not a case where a territory at the extremity of a state might seek to detach itself. The geographical position of Québec, in the centre of Canada, means that were it to achieve independence, this would have a severe impact on the rest of the country. In addition, as with the Åland Islanders, not only were the inhabitants not discriminated against but their language and culture received real protection.

The contemporary position is accurately stated (though with a caveat we shall add at the end) in the summary of legal advice given by Professor James Crawford of Cambridge University (now a Judge at the ICJ) in answer to a request from the Canadian Department of Justice in 1997. These were his conclusions:

(a) In international practice there is no recognition of a unilateral right to secede based on a majority vote of the population of a sub-division or territory, whether or not that population constitutes one or more 'peoples' in the ordinary sense of the word. In international law, self-determination for peoples or groups within an independent state is achieved by participation in the political system of the state, on the basis of respect for its territorial integrity.

(b) Even where there is a strong and sustained call for independence (measured, for example, by referenda results showing substantial support for independence), it is a matter for the government of the state concerned to consider how to respond. It is not required to concede independence in such a case, but may take into account the national interest and the interests of all those concerned.

(c) Even in the context of separate colonial territories, unilateral secession was the exception. Self-determination was in the first instance a matter for the

---

[37] ibid para 154.

colonial government to implement; only if it was blocked by that government did the United Nations support unilateral secession. *Outside the colonial context, the United Nations is extremely reluctant to admit a seceding entity to membership against the wishes of the government of the state from which it has purported to secede. There is no case since 1945 where it has done so.* Where the parent state agrees to allow a territory to separate and become independent, the terms on which separation is agreed between the parties concerned will be respected, and if independence is achieved under such an agreement, rapid admission to the United Nations will follow. But where the government of the state concerned has maintained its opposition to unilateral secession, such secession has attracted virtually no international support or recognition.

(d) This pattern is reflected in the so-called 'safeguard' clause in the United Nations General Assembly Resolution 2625 (XXV), the Friendly Relations Declaration of 1970. In accordance with this clause, a state whose government represents the whole people on a basis of equality complies with the principle of self-determination in respect of all of its people and is entitled to the protection of its territorial integrity. The people of such a state exercise the right of self-determination through their equal participation in its system of government.[38] [Emphasis added.]

In spite of these conclusions, it is possible to infer, from the first and fourth paragraphs above, that a right of external self-determination may exist where a people or peoples enjoy no participation in the political system and/ or are subject to discrimination. Such examples could arguably be found in Chechnya or Tibet. However, these two examples make a different but familiar point: no secession will ever be permitted from a strong state regardless of the political conditions obtaining. Of the three 'referendum cases' described above, the Iraqi Kurds would seem to have the greatest claim to external self-determination, in that, certainly under the regime of Saddam Hussein, they suffered severe repression at the hands of the parent state.[39] Following the fall of that regime and the confirmation of Kurdistan's autonomous status by Iraq's central Government, it remains to be seen whether the Kurds will be accorded sufficient rights and safeguards to be able to achieve meaningful self-determination within the Iraqi state.

Finally, notwithstanding the conclusions reached by Professor Crawford, the example of Eritrea's independence should be mentioned. At the end of the Second World War, Eritrea became a trust territory administered by the UK. In 1952, control of the territory was transferred by the UN to Ethiopia, with Eritrea retaining full autonomy until annexed by Ethiopia in 1962. With the acquiescence of the UN, Eritrea remained an Ethiopian province,

---

[38] James Crawford, *State Practice and International Law in Relation to Unilateral Secession: Report to Government of Canada Concerning Unilateral Secession by Québec*, 19 February 1997.

[39] Most infamously during the al-Anfal (spoils of war) campaign, conducted from 1987 to 1988, aimed at reasserting Baghdad's control over Kurdistan. Chemical weapons were widely employed, culminating in the notorious attack on Halabja on 16 March 1988, which killed around 5,000. See Charles Tripp, *A History of Iraq*, 3rd edn (Cambridge, CUP, 2007) 235–36.

prompting it to fight a prolonged war of resistance/independence, in which it finally achieved victory in 1993 with the downfall of the Ethiopian dictator Haile Mariam Mengistu. An Eritrean plebiscite under the supervision of the UN was held, as a result of which independence was declared and the new state was recognised by Ethiopia. What this case demonstrates is that where a territory is physically able to insist upon its demands for secession the de facto position will gain recognition. The state from which the secession has taken place will have no realistic alternative to acceptance and recognition.

V. States, Territory and Recognition

There are two further areas that are crucial for a full understanding of territory and international law: first, the principle of *uti possidetis* and the question of how a state acquires or disposes of territory; and, secondly, the recognition of a state's claim to territory.

A. State Acquisition or Disposal of Territory in International Law

Before the adoption of the UN Charter, how states acquired and disposed of territory was a complex topic with abstruse rules. A world in which territory was won by conquest, or by the planting of a flag, or by international agreements concluded between European colonial powers, or by purchase regardless of the wishes of the indigenous population, or simply by occupying territory previously uninhabited – at least by 'civilised' people – called for rules of an elaborate kind. Those that existed were based initially upon Roman law. On occasions, they remain relevant, even post-Charter – as, for example, where frontier disputes arise between decolonised states, leading to uncertainty as to where the borders are to which *uti possidetis* applies, or should have applied upon independence.

Article 2(4) of the UN Charter states: 'All Members shall refrain in their international relations from the threat or use of force against the territorial integrity or political independence of any state, or in any other manner inconsistent with the Purposes of the United Nations'. Having recalled this provision, the ICJ, in its 2004 advisory opinion *Legal Consequences of the Construction of a Wall in the Occupied Palestinian Territories*, stated:

> On 24 October 1970, the General Assembly adopted resolution 2625 (XXV), entitled 'Declaration on Principles of International Law concerning Friendly Relations and Co-operation among States' (hereinafter 'resolution 2625 (XXV)'), in which it emphasized that 'No territorial acquisition resulting from the threat or use of force shall be recognized as legal.' As the Court stated in its Judgment in

the case concerning Military and Paramilitary Activities in and against Nicaragua (Nicaragua v. United States of America), the principles as to the use of force incorporated in the Charter reflect customary international law (see I.C.J. Reports 1986, pp. 98–101, paras. 187–190); the same is true of its corollary entailing the illegality of territorial acquisition resulting from the threat or use of force.[40]

This unequivocally states the law of territorial transfer as it exists at present. The transfer of territory is lawful only if carried out with the agreement of the sovereign parties concerned. Such a conclusion has manifest consequences for the future of Israeli settlements in the Occupied Territories, and only Israel and the US have argued that 'facts on the ground' might displace the position in international law. It is also relevant that Israel's purported annexation of the Syrian Golan Heights and all of Jerusalem has received no external support or recognition – at least, not until the coming to power of the Trump administration (for further details, see chapter nine). Russia's use of its troops to help wrest control of Crimea from Ukraine in 2014 also amounted to a violation of Article 2(4), as well as constituting a territorial acquisition prohibited under UNGA 2625, notwithstanding the fact that Russia did not formally annex the territory until after the holding of a referendum in which almost 97 per cent of voters were reported to have opted for reunification with Russia. However, despite widespread condemnation, including from the General Assembly, which exhorted members not to recognise any change in Crimea's status, Russia's acquisition of the territory is now a *fait accompli* and is extremely unlikely to be reversed.[41]

B. Recognition in International Law

The emergence of new states, and of new configurations of old states, has been a constant feature of international relations. As we have seen, in the second half of the twentieth century, new states arose not only from the process of decolonisation, but also from the dissolutions of the Soviet Union and the

---

[40] *Legal Consequences of the Construction of a Wall in the Occupied Palestinian Territories, Advisory Opinion*, ICJ Reports 2004, 136, para 87.

[41] For further details, see Christine Gray, *International Law and the Use of Force* 4th edn (Oxford, OUP, 2018), 32–33, 112–13. Russia has always denied forcibly intervening in Crimea or sending troops into eastern Ukraine in support of Russian separatists. It has emphasised its historic claims to the Crimea, since the peninsula formed part of Russia until it was transferred to Ukraine in 1954, when both formed part of the Soviet Union. It has also claimed that Crimea's transfer to Ukraine was unlawful under the Soviet constitution; that the transfer was in any event premised on the continuing existence of the Soviet Union; and that Crimea's separation from Ukraine and reabsorption by Russia represented a species of 'remedial secession': that is, oppression of Crimea's Russian population by the Ukrainian state justified it seceding from Ukraine. Dubious legal rationalisations aside, the Crimean peninsula is obviously of crucial geostrategic importance to Russia; and some argue that NATO's eastwards expansion after the end of the Cold War has provoked Russia's incursions into Ukraine and Georgia.

former Yugoslavia, not to mention the amicable division of Czechoslovakia into the Czech Republic and Slovakia. Such geopolitical changes necessitate a response from other states, and it is here that the issue of recognition becomes important. Recognition signals that the recognising state is willing to enter into relations with the entity that is being recognised, whether this is another state or the government of a state. Where it is the state that is being recognised, recognition implies that the recognising state accepts that the recognised state has the attributes of a state and is prepared to treat it as such. The recognition of a government means that the recognising state accepts that the regime in question is the effective government of the state concerned and is willing to deal with it on that basis. Such recognition may be express – with, for example, the recognising state issuing a formal announcement of its decision to recognise the other state – or it may be implied through an act which of itself indicates recognition *unequivocally*, particularly the conclusion of a bilateral treaty with the state concerned.

Very often the act of recognition will be a collective one, as when a state is newly admitted to membership of the UN under the procedure provided for under Article 4 of the Charter. Once a state has been admitted to the UN, it becomes subject to, and has the benefit of, sovereign equality (Article 2(1)). Indeed, it was the fact of Kuwait's membership of the UN that made Iraq's purported annexation before the first Gulf War subject to almost unanimous condemnation.

There is an academic debate as to whether recognition is 'declaratory' or 'constitutive'. In other words, does recognition simply recognise an existing reality or is it the act(s) of recognition that creates the reality of statehood? When the Montevideo Convention on the Rights and Duties of States of 1933 stated the generally accepted criteria for statehood as requiring: a) a permanent population; b) a defined territory; c) a government; and d) capacity to enter into relations with other states, it added, in Article 3: 'The political existence of a state is independent of recognition by the other states.' This is clearly an expression of the declaratory thesis, but it is equally clearly largely obsolete. Those who argue that recognition amounts to something more than this, point, first, to Article 4 of the UN Charter that provides for admission only to those states willing to accept the Charter's obligations. This position is reinforced by the events that led to the recognition of those states that emerged out of the disintegrations of the Soviet Union and the former Yugoslav Republic. In these cases, the EU was determined that recognition would be granted only if specified conditions were met by the states in question. To this end, the foreign ministers of the Member States of the EU adopted the following 'Guidelines on the Recognition of New States in Eastern Europe and in the Soviet Union' in 1991:

> In compliance with the European Council's request, Ministers have assessed developments in Eastern Europe and the Soviet Union with a view to elaborating an approach regarding relations with new states.

In this connection they have adopted the following guidelines on the formal recognition of new states in Eastern Europe and in the Soviet Union:

The Community and its Member States confirm their attachment to the principles of the Helsinki Final Act and the Charter of Paris, in particular the principle of self-determination. They affirm their readiness to recognize, subject to the normal standards of international practice and the political realities in each case, those new States which, following the historic changes in the region, have constituted themselves on a democratic basis, have accepted the appropriate international obligations and have committed themselves in good faith to a peaceful process and to negotiations.

Therefore, they adopt a common position on the process of recognition of these new States, which requires:

- respect for the provisions of the Charter of the United Nations and the commitments subscribed to in the Final Act of Helsinki and in the Charter of Paris, especially with regard to the rule of law, democracy and human rights;
- guarantees for the rights of ethnic and national groups and minorities in accordance with the commitments subscribed to in the framework of the CSCE;
- respect for the inviolability of all frontiers which can only be changed by peaceful means and by common agreement;
- acceptance of all relevant commitments with regard to disarmament and nuclear non-proliferation as well as to security and regional stability;
- commitment to settle by agreement, including where appropriate by recourse to arbitration, all questions concerning State succession and regional disputes.

The Community and its Member States will not recognize entities which are the result of aggression. They would take account of the effects of recognition on neighbouring States.

The position would therefore seem to be that states are not under an obligation to recognise a state merely because of a political reality. East Germany, for example, was not recognised as a state by the West until 1973, and the Turkish Republic of Northern Cyprus has been recognised only by Turkey.

Finally, there remains one anomalous territory: that of Palestine. A state of Palestine was proclaimed in November 1988, establishing the state of Palestine in the land of Palestine, with a capital at Jerusalem (Al-Quds Ash-Sharif), though of course it is difficult to reconcile this with the Montevideo criteria for statehood. Nevertheless, the state has been recognised by almost half of the nations of the world and all of the Arab League. Obviously, such recognition is a politically motivated act reflecting the frustration of many states at the Middle Eastern impasse.

In 2011, Palestine tried again to obtain full membership of the UN – an attempt that was bound to be thwarted by the opposition of the US, as indeed it was, in the Security Council. Palestine did, however, gain full membership of UNESCO, although this prompted the US to withhold its UNESCO budget contribution, and in fact the US has now left the organisation (see chapter five).

On 29 November 2012, the UN General Assembly voted overwhelmingly (138 votes were cast in favour, nine voted against while 41 states abstained) to grant Palestine the status of non-member state observer that it had requested, in place of the observer 'entity' status that it had previously enjoyed. Finally, in 2015, Palestine became party to the Rome Statute of the International Criminal Court, and has asked the Court to investigate alleged international crimes committed by Israeli officials and forces in occupied Palestinian territory since June 2014. This too has provoked an angry response from the US, both against Palestine and the ICC (see chapter six).

VI. Territorial and Other Rights Over the Sea and its Bed

So far, the discussion of self-determination and the acquisition and disposal of territory has focused on land alone. Until well into the twentieth century, this would have been sufficient. Whereas territorial rights over land were highly developed, questions of ownership and rights over the sea and its bed remained largely unasked. This was for a number of reasons. The first concerned the rights of passage of ships. So important was merchant shipping, that all powerful trading nations had an interest in protecting the rights of ships to the freedom of the seas. The only real limitation lay over the territorial sea, where it was generally accepted that states could claim three nautical miles from their respective coastlines as part of national territory. As a result, these states enjoyed full sovereignty over the territorial sea, the airspace above it, the seabed, and all that lay beneath it. Even then, however, this sovereignty was subject to the right of innocent passage that was granted to all foreign merchant shipping and warships. 'Innocent passage' meant that the right could be exercised if passage was not prejudicial 'to the peace, good order or security of the coastal state'. While the right has sometimes been contested, usually the power of states in whose interests the rule operates has been sufficient to ensure that it is respected.

The 1982 Convention on the Law of the Sea determined that coastal states should be able to claim up to 12 nautical miles of territorial sea (one nautical mile being 1.852 kilometres, or 1.508 miles). This development was very much a part of the process by which property rights were being asserted over what had previously been available to all. Typically, property claims are made over resources that have scarcity value. As long as the sea was perceived as primarily being of use as a route for shipping and as a source of fish, with enough fish for all, there was no need to make property claims. By the end of the Second World War, coastal states had come to realise that the seabed and what lay beneath it could be extraordinarily valuable. There then followed a 'property grab' unseen since the scramble for colonies in the late-nineteenth century. It began with President Truman's Proclamation 2667 of September 1945, which stated:

> Having concern for the urgency of conserving and prudently utilizing its natural resources, the Government of the United States regards the natural resources of the subsoil and sea bed of the continental shelf beneath the high seas but contiguous to the coasts of the United States as appertaining to the United states, subject to its jurisdiction and control. In cases where the continental shelf extends to the shores of another States, or is shared with an adjacent State, the boundary shall be determined by the United States and the State concerned in accordance with equitable principles. The character as high seas of the waters above the continental shelf and the right to their free and unimpeded navigation are in no way thus affected.

Customary international law quickly followed suit, to the great benefit of all coastal states fortunate enough to have a continental shelf. In turn, the Geneva Convention on the Continental Shelf (1958) (and the later 1982 Convention on the Law of the Sea) regularised the position, and, as a result, states are able to claim up to 200 nautical miles of continental shelf, not as sovereign territory but as territory that the coastal state has exclusive right to explore and exploit. Such rights do not affect the status of the high seas nor the airspace above the continental shelf.

Initially, coastal states without a significant continental shelf appeared to be prejudiced by this fact, in that their ability to exploit the sea was not immediately extended in the same way. This disadvantage was removed with the creation of an 'exclusive economic zone' (EEZ). The 1982 Convention defined this EEZ as 'an area beyond and adjacent to the territorial sea' which was not to extend 'beyond 200 nautical miles'. Again, sovereignty is limited: in this case, to rights 'for the purpose of exploring and exploiting, conserving and managing the natural resources, whether living or non-living, of the seabed and subsoil and the superjacent waters'. Most importantly, even if there is no continental shelf, the rights include the right to regulate fishing within the EEZ.

What will be apparent, then, is that within 30 years of the adoption of the UN Charter, the law of the sea had undergone immense change to the considerable benefit of most coastal states (although, not all, because some that had been involved in distance fishing found their rights restricted). Particularly as a result of off-shore oil exploitation, many coastal states had title to resources to which a claim was recognised only in the second half of the twentieth century. Landlocked states received no such benefits, of course, and it was this that persuaded many of the delegations at the Law of the Sea conferences to attempt to distribute at least the proceeds of the exploitation of the deep seabed in a way dictated more by need than luck. While this was the view of developing states, which argued that the benefits of deep-sea exploitation should be recognised as 'the common heritage of mankind', the developed states (not altogether coincidentally the states with the ability to exploit the deep seabed) argued merely for regulation and licensing. The 1982 Convention provided that all deep seabed exploration should be carried out and controlled by an 'International Sea Bed Authority'. But, whereas the Convention paved the way for the deep seabed to be used 'in the interest of mankind', this was firmly rejected by industrialised countries. Such was the opposition that the Convention did not enter into force until 1994, after considerable concessions were made to the developed nations.

VII. Conclusion

The development of the right of self-determination in international law has throughout been imbued with politics and power. While Professor Crawford's advice to the Canadian Government accurately describes the legal position, such advice might be impractical in application. For example, should Québec ever vote decisively in a referendum for independence, it is unlikely that the Canadian Government could resist such a demand, or would attempt to preserve the status quo by force. In the case of the Scottish referendum of 2014, the UK Government committed beforehand to respecting a vote for independence, even though this would have undoubtedly left the rest of the UK weaker. However, territories wishing to secede must always reckon not only with the parent state but with other important actors in the international community. Secession as a successful policy therefore remains a question of power, as the ICJ recognised, and as the Tamils of Sri Lanka and the separatists of Biafra discovered.

4

The International Obligations of States: Treaties and State Responsibility

I. Introduction

This chapter introduces readers to two important areas of international law: the acceptance of international obligations by a state (by entering into treaties); and the obligations thrust upon them by virtue of their statehood (state responsibility). As will become apparent, the rules relating to these topics are to be found both in customary international law and in treaties or proposed treaties. Rules relating to treaties are to be found in the 1969 Vienna Convention on the Law of Treaties, the precise status of which is explained below, while those relating to state responsibility are contained in the International Law Commission's Draft Articles on Responsibility of States for Internationally Wrongful Acts, adopted in 2001. While the Draft Articles clearly do not have the status of a treaty, they were to a considerable extent intended to codify existing customary international law and are therefore highly relevant. The intention is to do no more than introduce the topic, but in so doing to illustrate once more the relationship between international law and power. Again, it will be argued that underlying the asserted neutrality of international law are barely disguised protected interests.

II. The Law of Treaties

In chapter one we briefly considered treaties as a major source of international law, and indeed observed that treaties are now the most important of

these sources. Whereas much customary international law remains contentious (and contended), treaties are supposed to be explicit and unambiguous,
expressing the will of the parties who wish to be bound by agreement to the
negotiated terms stated in the document. (Although, of course, it should be
remembered that agreements not reduced to writing may still be binding.)
That at least is the theory: states voluntarily commit themselves to act in
accordance with the negotiated terms, and underlying this is the principle of
pacta sunt servanda, which takes such obligations beyond the realm of 'mere'
international relations and makes them legally binding.

Needless to say, in practice the situation is much less clear and remains
controversial. Indeed, such is the potential for dispute that the International
Law Commission (ILC) spent 20 years codifying and drafting rules that
finally received significant international approval in the form of the Vienna
Convention on the Law of Treaties 1969 (VCLT), which came into force in
January 1980.[1] The Convention is intended to clarify rules both of interpretation and definition, and to ensure a uniform approach is adopted in dealing
with problems relating to treaties, whether concerned with their formation,
content or termination. The majority of the world's states are now parties to
the VCLT (116 as at February 2019), although not the US, which has signed
the treaty, but has yet to receive the 'advice and consent' necessary from
Congress for ratification. The US's position, however, is that it considers many
of the provisions of the VCLT to constitute customary international law on
the law of treaties. The *pacta sunt servanda* principle is incorporated into the
Convention in Article 26, which states: 'Every treaty in force is binding upon
the parties to it and must be performed by them in good faith.'

The law of treaties might seem a rather dull topic; however, crucially
important questions of policy and politics arise in cases concerned with the
interpretation of treaties. To illustrate the point, we will consider in some
depth the ICJ's 1997 decision in the case of the *Gabčíkovo–Nagymaros Project*,
involving a treaty concluded between Hungary and what was then the state
of Czechoslovakia to build and operate a system of dams and locks on the
river Danube.[2]

Furthermore, as Cassese points out, political positions and considerations
had much to do with the eventual form that the VCLT took, and the Convention ultimately represented a shift in the thinking about treaties. Whereas,
traditionally, the emphasis in treaty law was upon the equivalent of 'freedom
of contract', in that states could enter into any treaty on any terms under any
circumstances in the expectation that it would be upheld, the VCLT introduced constraints and controls that had not previously existed. Of course,
just as in freedom of contract theory, so too in the freedom to enter into

---

[1] Vienna Convention on the Law of Treaties 1969.
[2] *Gabčíkovo-Nagymaros Project (Hungary/Slovakia), Judgment*, ICJ Reports 1997, 7.

international treaties, the 'freedom' was not always what it seemed, and the effect of upholding such treaties was often to wilfully refuse to see the unequal bargaining power that had led to those treaties being concluded. In colonial times particularly, strong states were able to impose 'agreements' upon weaker nations. The spirit of the VCLT is very much opposed to validating such coercion, although this remains controversial.

The Convention also limited the terms a treaty might contain by proscribing the inclusion of provisions in contravention of the 'central core of international values' from which no country, however great its economic and military strength, may deviate. Article 53 of the VCLT provides that:

> A treaty is void if, at the time of its conclusion, it conflicts with a peremptory norm of general international law. For the purposes of the present Convention, a peremptory norm of general international law is a norm accepted and recognized by the international community of States as a whole as a norm from which no derogation is permitted and which can be modified only by a subsequent norm of general international law having the same character.

The status of *jus cogens* (peremptory norms) in treaty interpretation was unclear until the Convention was concluded. There is no fixed or agreed list of peremptory norms, although the prohibition on the threat or use of force as it appears in Article 2(4) of the UN Charter is clearly one; so, too, are the prohibitions upon slavery, genocide and torture. A treaty in conflict with such a norm or norms is necessarily void in its entirety. The indeterminacy of such a list is recognised in Article 64 of the VCLT, which states that, should a new peremptory norm emerge in international law, then this too will render void and terminate any existing treaty in conflict with it. Of relevance here is the *Gabčíkovo-Nagymaros Project* case discussed below, in which the ICJ, in its judgment, noted that neither of the parties contended that new peremptory norms of environmental law had emerged since the conclusion of the 1977 treaty between them, and that consequently the Court need not examine the scope of Article 64.

It is important to note that the VCLT both codifies existing customary law and also contains some innovative provisions (such as Article 53). Obviously, codification of existing law introduces no changes, and ordinarily all states will be bound as they were before. Where, however, the provision is new, it will, under the terms of the Convention, apply only in relation to a treaty concluded after the VCLT entered into force (on 27 January 1980), and only where the parties to such a treaty are also parties to the Convention. As observed above, the US is not a party to the VCLT, although it has signed the Convention, and therefore, as with all signatories to a treaty, is under an obligation to refrain from any act that would defeat the object and purpose of it. (By inference the US seems to have accepted that this is the case, since, when it wished to avoid such an obligation in respect of the Rome Statute of the International Criminal Court, which the US had signed but not ratified, it took steps to 'unsign' the Statute, by sending a letter to the UN Secretary-General explaining it no longer intended to become a party to the instrument.) The only exception to this is where an innovative provision of the VCLT can itself be shown to have developed into customary international law, and thus come to bind even those states that are not party to the Convention.

There is one further significant difference between treaties and contracts. It is possible in international law for a unilateral statement made by one state in the expectation that another state or states will rely upon it to have legal effect as if it were a treaty. Thus, in the *Nuclear Tests* cases between Australia and France, and New Zealand and France,[3] the ICJ held that when France, acting through its President and Foreign Minister, issued a statement to the effect that France's current round of atmospheric nuclear tests would be its last, this was a statement upon which the international community could rely. Here, unlike contract (at least in the common-law system), there is no need for reciprocity or even acceptance by other states.

Yet another difference between a treaty and a contract concerns interpretation. Whereas contracts tend to be interpreted by considering the meaning of the text and the text alone, treaties are interpreted both with the help of 'context' and by taking into account the subsequent practice of the parties (as provided for under Article 31(3) of the VCLT). In addition, in order to confirm the interpretation, recourse may be had, under Article 32, to *travaux préparatoires* (the preparatory work leading up to the conclusion of the treaty, including documents detailing the negotiation and drafting of the instrument). Subsequent practice may even have the effect of modifying a treaty if the common consent of the parties can be shown. An example of this concerns the requirements for voting procedures in the Security Council. Article 27(3) of the UN Charter provides that decisions of the Security Council on matters other than procedural ones 'shall be made by an affirmative vote of nine members including the concurring votes of the permanent members'. As mentioned in chapters five and eight, following the Council's resolutions to intervene in Korea in 1950, notwithstanding the absence of a Soviet vote, Article 27(3) has come to be interpreted as meaning that a decision must be made 'without veto' on the part of a permanent member, rather than, as is clearly stated in the Article, with the affirmative vote of all permanent members.

The art of treaty interpretation is not dissimilar from that of statutory interpretation in domestic law. Problems arise where treaty provisions are ambiguous, uncertain or contested. Historically, different rules of interpretation were applied depending on the circumstances. That said, the first and most common principle was that the words of a treaty should be given their common meaning, and if this was clear, that should be determinative of the

---

[3] *Nuclear Tests (Australia v France), Judgment,* ICJ Reports 1974, 253; *Nuclear Tests (New Zealand v France), Judgment,* ICJ Reports 1974, 457.

matter. Thus, in the *Interpretation of the Peace Treaties* case,[4] the ICJ decided that the matter was at an end if the language of the text was clear. Nevertheless, other considerations might be relevant, especially if the aim is to give effect to the obligations the parties intended when concluding their agreement. It has also been suggested that a 'teleological' approach might on occasions be helpful. This concentrates on the objectives of a treaty and what interpretation or construction of the treaty would best satisfy those objectives.

Article 31 of the VCLT adopts a sensible and modified 'ordinary meaning' approach. It states that a treaty 'shall be interpreted in good faith in accordance with the ordinary meaning to be given to the terms of the treaty in their context and in the light of its object and purpose'. Consequently, object and purpose will not be irrelevant. The Article also states that context means not only the text of the treaty and its preamble and annexes, but also any other agreement made between the parties relating to the conclusion of the treaty or any instrument made by a party (these would be letters or declarations) in connection with the conclusion of the treaty and accepted by the other parties as relating to the treaty. In addition, as a further aid to interpretation, any subsequent agreements or practice between the parties concerning the interpretation or application of the treaty can be taken into account, and if the parties intended any special meaning to attach to a particular term, then this, too, will be applied. As a supplementary means to interpretation, recourse may be had to other sources, including the *travaux préparatoires*, but only to confirm the meaning or to resolve ambiguity (as provided in Article 32).

A. The Formation and Formalities of Treaties

The ways in which treaties may be concluded and their formal requirements are both remarkably few and extraordinarily flexible. Article 2(1)(a) of the VCLT defines a treaty to which the Convention applies as 'an international agreement concluded between States in written form and governed by international law, whether embodied in a single instrument or in two or more related instruments, and whatever its particular designation'. It also provides, however, that this does not affect the legal force of other agreements between states and other bodies having international legal personality, or agreements between states not in written form. For our purposes, we will concentrate only on agreements between states and only those reduced to writing. (Since Article 102 of the UN Charter provides for all treaties to be registered with the UN Secretariat – without which a treaty may not be invoked before any organ, including the ICJ – it is plain that this requirement can be met only if the agreement has been written down, and hence there are very few treaties not in written form.)

---

[4] *Interpretation of Peace Treaties (second phase), Advisory Opinion,* ICJ Reports 1950, 221.

As the Convention refers to agreements 'governed by international law', it is possible to infer the requirement that the parties must have intended to create legal relations (and thus legal obligations). Agreements that do not meet this requirement are not without effect but have no legal content. An example of such an agreement, already referred to in chapter one, is the Final Act of the Helsinki Conference on Security and Co-operation of 1975. This was described as 'not eligible for registration under art 102 of the Charter of the United Nations', which was understood to mean that the Act was not legally enforceable. Nonetheless, it proved to be a document of immense political significance, and has had an influential effect on the development of international law.

The making of a treaty is usually a three-stage process, involving the negotiation of the treaty, the authentication of the drafted document (usually by signature or initialing) and then ratification. Article 12(1) of the VCLT nevertheless provides that if a treaty does not require ratification, and the signature was intended to express the consent of a state to be bound, then the signature shall have that effect. Much more commonly, the signature represents a step along the way of treaty creation and the treaty will require ratification.

Ratification has two important aspects: one international and the other domestic. For domestic law purposes, ratification in the UK is effected by the Crown. How this is achieved in other states depends upon the domestic legislation of the state concerned. When ratification has taken place in the UK, the treaty exists in domestic law as an international treaty to which the UK is bound. Without more, however, it will not be part of the domestic law of the country, and thus will not be enforceable in municipal courts. The precise status of a ratified treaty in each state's domestic law will depend upon that state's constitution. The second aspect of ratification involves ratification in international law. This procedure, which brings the treaty into force, usually requires the deposit of ratification documents or their exchange. This common, two-stage process of signature and then ratification provides time for the signed treaty to be scrutinised at the domestic level. The only obligation of a signatory before ratification (where this is required) is not to do anything to undermine the signed but unratified treaty.

The position in the US is a little different, and not least because of the attitude of the current Trump administration to treaties,[5] as discussed in chapter nine. According to constitutional law and the doctrine of separation of powers, foreign policy is the prerogative of the executive branch of government (that is, the administration). As such, the president is able to enter into 'international agreements' that will be binding in international law. This will not, however, affect domestic law. For an agreement to become a treaty,

---

[5] An attitude which might be characterised as abiding by *pacta sunt servanda* only in so far as this does not conflict with the principle of 'America First'.

and thus also create domestic law, it must (by Article II, section 2(2) of the US Constitution) be made with the 'Advice and Consent' of the US Senate (that is, the legislative branch of government), and this requires approval in the Senate, by a two-thirds majority. Thus, while the negotiation and signing of treaties and international agreements is the responsibility of the executive branch, such agreements may only become a treaty when, upon presentation to the Senate by the President, a two-thirds majority is obtained. Thus, clearly a president will be able to deal with a 'mere' international agreement (such as the agreement concerning Iran and its nuclear policy – see chapter nine) in a way that he or she could not if the treaty had been passed by the Senate.

Certain states whose national constitutions do not require the treaty to be ratified by a head of state use acceptance and approval instead. 'Acceptance' or 'approval' of a treaty has the same legal effect as ratification: ie it expresses the consent of a state to be bound by the treaty (Article 14(2)) of the VCLT). 'Accession' refers to a state becoming party to a treaty already negotiated and signed by other states (Article 15). This normally occurs after the treaty has entered into force, and, again, expresses the consent of the state to be bound by the instrument in question.

Finally, it should be noted that the question of when a treaty enters into force is normally resolved by a provision in the treaty document itself. Such a provision will often explicitly state, for example, that the treaty will come into force upon the deposit of the sixtieth (or whatever number is specified) instrument of ratification, or upon a date some time after such ratification has been received. If the treaty is silent as to when it is to enter into force, this will be inferred from the context.

B. Reservations to Treaties

Reservations, which we briefly discussed in chapter one, are obviously relevant only to multilateral treaties; in a bilateral treaty, each party will be bound to the same terms. Where there are more than two parties, however, there are many occasions when not all the parties will be prepared to accept all the provisions of a treaty as drafted. The VCLT codifies customary law in defining a reservation to a treaty, in Article 2(1)(d), as:

> a unilateral statement, however phrased or named, made by a State, when signing, ratifying, accepting, approving or acceding to a treaty, whereby it purports to modify the legal effect of certain provisions of the treaty in their application to that State.

The status and effect of a reservation is not exactly the same in customary international law as it is under the Convention. The traditional approach to reservations was that they would be valid only if permitted by the treaty's terms, and only if all other parties to the treaty accepted the reservation.

Such an approach, although consistent with principle, was not well suited to multilateral treaties with large numbers of states parties, since obtaining the agreement of all parties to a reservation would be difficult. The approach was reviewed in an important ICJ advisory decision of 1951, *Reservations to the Convention on Genocide.*[6] In 1948, the UN General Assembly had adopted the Convention on the Prevention and Punishment of the Crime of Genocide, and a dispute arose over whether reservations to the Convention were permitted, there being no provision for reservations in the instrument itself. The majority of the Court held that a state could be regarded as a party to a treaty, even if its reservation had not been accepted by all other parties, so long as that reservation [was] compatible with the object and purpose of the Convention. Where, however, another state would not accept such a reservation, the refusing state would be entitled to regard the reserving state as not being in a treaty relationship with itself. Although the ILC thought the compatibility test too subjective, the VCLT, in Articles 19–23, followed the principles of the *Reservations* opinion, but with a slight modification, in that it accepts that every reservation will be incompatible with some types of treaties unless the treaty parties unanimously agree otherwise.

The effect of a valid reservation on a multilateral convention is important. Not only does it restrict the obligations of the reserving state in accordance with the terms of the reservation, but it also, in effect, redrafts the treaty as between the reserving state and all others, so all are affected by the same reservation. In other words, no party can rely upon a reservation to give it an advantage against a state that has not made a similar reservation. This principle is set out in Article 21 of the VCLT, already quoted in chapter one.

There are occasions where a state does not want to make a formal reservation but does want to make explicit its interpretation of a provision. These so-called 'interpretive declarations' may, on occasion, be deemed to be reservations if that is the true effect of the words.

C. The Validity of Treaties

Article 26 of the VCLT formally recites the principle of *pacta sunt servanda*, providing that every treaty in force is binding upon the parties to it and must be performed by them in good faith. This is reinforced by the following article, Article 27, which forbids any state from relying on the provisions of its domestic law as justification for failing to perform its obligations under a treaty.

Questions as to the validity of a treaty may again resonate with considerations as to when a contract is valid under domestic law. Unfortunately, the parallels are not exact, and it is better to consider the validity of a treaty

---

[6] *Reservations to the Convention on Genocide, Advisory Opinion*, ICJ Reports 1951, 15.

as a quite separate matter. Under the VCLT, the validity of a treaty can be challenged only by the ways provided for in that instrument. Similarly, the termination of a treaty, its denunciation (the announcement of termination) or the withdrawal of a party will be valid only if it is consistent with the provisions of the treaty itself, or the provisions of the Convention. The application of this principle is illustrated in our case study below on the *Gabčíkovo–Nagymaros* judgment.

The VCLT states the reasons and causes that may justify a treaty being held invalid. Under Article 48, error may be invoked if it 'relates to a fact or situation which was assumed by that state to exist at the time when the treaty was concluded and formed an essential basis of its consent to be bound by the treaty', but this will not apply if the state in error 'contributed by its own conduct to the error' or should have been aware of the mistake. Article 49 allows for the invalidation of an expressed consent to be bound by a treaty, if the consenting state was induced to conclude the treaty by the fraudulent conduct of another negotiating party, while Article 50 permits such invalidation if a state's consent has been procured by the corruption of its representative.

Much more significant are the provisions of Articles 51 and 52 concerning the coercion of a state or its representative. Article 51 provides that, where a state's consent to be bound by a treaty has been procured by the coercion of its representative through acts or threats directed against him or her, that expression of consent shall be without any legal effect. Article 52 states that a treaty is void if its conclusion has been procured by the threat or use of force 'in violation of the principles of international law embodied in the Charter of the United Nations'. What amounts to such coercion has been the subject of much discussion.

As the ILC observed, prior to the conclusion of the Covenant of the League of Nations, it had not been thought that the validity of a treaty would be affected 'merely' because one party had been induced to enter into it under threat from the other.[7] Many treaties had resulted from weaker states being forced to acquiesce to the demands of more powerful nations, and this had simply been accepted as the way in which international relations was conducted. However, this was to change dramatically with the adoption of the UN Charter, with its proscription of the threat or use of force (under Article 2(4)) and its emphasis on sovereignty and sovereign equality. Moreover, the VCLT was negotiated during the era of decolonisation, and the newly independent states wanted their independence to be more than purely nominal. Within the ILC there was disagreement as to what sort of coercion should be proscribed. Pressure to define coercion beyond 'threat or use of force in violation of the principles of the Charter' was resisted. Soviet jurists often argued that, for a treaty to be binding, it must have been concluded on the

---

[7] Anthony Aust, *Modern Treaty Law and Practice* (Cambridge, CUP, 2000) 256.

basis of the equality of the parties, and that unequal treaties were therefore not legally enforceable.

As is plain from Article 52, not all threats of force will invalidate a treaty. Anthony Aust gives the example of the restoration of the Haitian Government of President Jean-Bertrand Aristide in 1994 pursuant to an agreement between the provisional President of Haiti, General Raoul Cédras, and the US. The agreement was concluded while US bombers were on their way to Haiti, but, because the Security Council had adopted a resolution authorising the use of force to restore the legitimate government,[8] this instance of coercion constituted a lawful use of force.

At the Vienna Treaty Conference, a compromise was reached as to the sorts of coercion that would be deemed to invalidate a treaty. The provision limiting the coercion to the threat or use of force was supplemented by a Declaration on the Prohibition of Military, Political or Economic Coercion in the Conclusion of Treaties, adopted by the Conference and stating that the Conference, while 'Deploring the fact that in the past States have sometimes been forced to conclude treaties under pressure exerted in various forms by other States' and 'Desiring to ensure that in future no such pressure will be exerted in any form by any State in connexion with the conclusion of a treaty':

> Solemnly condemns the threat or use of pressure in any form, whether military, political or economic, by any state in order to coerce another State to perform any act relating to the conclusions of a treaty in violation of the principles of the sovereign equality of States and freedom of consent.[9]

Notwithstanding this, the exact scope of the provisions remains uncertain. Many states have been forced to conclude treaties with other states or with international bodies such as the International Monetary Fund or the World Bank because their parlous financial position has left them with little alternative. There is no indication that the ICJ will accept that such economic pressure qualifies as a form of coercion allowing the state concerned to avoid its obligations under the agreement.

A further example concerns so-called 'Article 98 Agreements' and the Rome Statute of the International Criminal Court (ICC). Article 98 provides as follows:

> 1. The Court may not proceed with a request for surrender or assistance which would require the requested State to act inconsistently with its obligations under international law with respect to the State or diplomatic immunity of a person or property of a third State, unless the Court can first obtain the cooperation of that third State for the waiver of the immunity.

---

[8] UNSC Resolution 875 of 16 October 1993.

[9] Mark E Villiger, *Commentary on the 1969 Vienna Convention on the Law of Treaties* (Leiden, Martinus Nijhoff, 2008) Art 52, 651.

2. The Court may not proceed with a request for surrender which would require the requested State to act inconsistently with its obligations under international agreements pursuant to which the consent of a sending State is required to surrender a person of that State to the Court, unless the Court can first obtain the cooperation of the sending State for the giving of consent for the surrender.

The US, in addition to deciding not to become a party to the Rome Statute, wished to ensure that none of its citizens would be subject to the jurisdiction of the ICC. Consequently, it has 'persuaded' a substantial number of other states to enter into bilateral immunity agreements in order to ensure that these states are under an obligation in international law not to comply with any ICC request to transfer a US citizen into the custody of the Court. The method of persuasion was the threatened withdrawal of military or other US aid to the state concerned. In 2002, the US Congress passed the American Service-Members' Protection Act. Section 2007(a) of the Act included a prohibition of military assistance to the governments of countries that were parties to the ICC, although section 2007(c) included an 'Article 98 waiver', which allowed the President to waive the prohibition of military assistance provided for in section 2007(a). As a consequence, almost 100 states have opted to enter into bilateral immunity agreements with the US, promising not to deliver up US service personnel to the jurisdiction of the Court,[10] and it is unlikely that the Declaration on the Prohibition of Military, Political or Economic Coercion in the Conclusion of Treaties will affect their validity.

D. The Amendment and Termination of Treaties

In view of the fact that all treaty law is based upon the consent of the parties, it is not surprising that such consent is the main method by which treaties may be amended, suspended or terminated. Broadly speaking, the parties to a treaty may agree between or among themselves to regard a treaty as at an end or to modify or suspend it. Often, too, the treaty itself will provide either for its termination or will define the circumstances that will bring it to an end. It may also provide for the withdrawal of one or more parties. Difficulties arise when all parties are not in agreement, and it is here that rules become important. Most of these are customary international law rules that have been codified in the VCLT. Again, the case study in the next section will help illustrate the relevant law.

What reasons, then, may be advanced to justify the termination of a treaty? The three main non-consensual grounds are material breach, supervening impossibility of performance and fundamental change of circumstances.

---

[10] The Georgetown Law Library lists 96 Art 98 Agreements in force between the US and other states: http://guides.ll.georgetown.edu/c.php?g=363527&p=2456099.

i. Material Breach

Article 60 of the VCLT defines a material breach as 'a repudiation not sanctioned by the present Convention' or 'the violation of a provision essential to the accomplishment of the object or purpose of the treaty'. A material breach committed in relation to a bilateral treaty entitles the party not in violation to 'invoke the breach as a ground for terminating the treaty or suspending its operation in whole or in part'. Where one party to a multilateral treaty is in material breach, this allows all the other parties by unanimous agreement to suspend the treaty in whole or in part, or to terminate it either as between themselves and the defaulting party, or as between all parties. A single state especially affected by material breach may invoke it as a ground for suspending the operation of the treaty in whole or in part in the relations between it and the defaulting state; and otherwise allows any party not in breach

> to invoke the breach as a ground for suspending the operation of the treaty in whole or in part with respect to itself if the treaty is of such a character that a material breach of its provisions by one party radically changes the position of every party with respect to the further performance of its obligations under the treaty.

As we will see in the case study, the ICJ is reluctant to accept that a breach is sufficiently material to permit termination. There seems to be no objective definition of 'material breach', and the circumstances in which a breach may be deemed to be material have not been defined. The emphasis is on the performance of treaty obligations wherever possible.

ii. Supervening Impossibility of Performance

Article 61 of the VCLT has also been interpreted in such a way as to ensure performance except in the most extraordinary of circumstances. While it provides that there is a right to terminate where there is impossibility of performance resulting from 'the permanent disappearance or destruction of an object indispensable for the execution of the treaty', this ground may not be invoked if the impossibility results from a breach by the party wishing to terminate either an obligation under the treaty or any other international obligation owed to any other party to the treaty.

Again, the case study below will demonstrate just how high the ICJ will set the bar before permitting termination. The fact that performance has become extraordinarily more difficult than could have been (or was) foreseen by the parties at the time the treaty was negotiated and agreed has been held to be insufficient.

iii. Fundamental Change of Circumstances (Rebus sic stantibus)

Termination in the event of a fundamental change of circumstances, provided for in Article 62 of the VCLT, is also expected to occur relatively rarely.

The wording of the Article emphasises this point, stating that an unforeseen (by the parties) change of circumstances may be invoked as a ground for terminating or withdrawing from a treaty only if the existence of those circumstances constituted an essential basis of the consent of the parties to be bound, and only if the effect of the change is to radically transform the extent of obligations still to be performed under the treaty.

As an additional qualification, under Article 62(2), fundamental change of circumstances cannot be invoked to challenge the validity of a treaty establishing a boundary, or if the change results from the breach of the party that is seeking relief. Once more, therefore, Article 62 and the customary international law it codifies stress the performance of treaty obligations wherever possible. The perils of this course of action are all too apparent in the case study that follows.

E. *Gabčíkovo–Nagymaros Project (Hungary/Slovakia)* 1997[11]

In September 1977, Hungary and what was then the state of Czechoslovakia entered into a major and significant treaty providing for the construction and operation of the Gabčíkovo–Nagymaros system of locks on part of the river Danube. The agreement was for the creation of a typically 'communist' Eastern European 'modernist' project, never known for their environmental or social sensitivity. According to the treaty's preamble, the barrage system was designed to attain 'the broad utilization of the natural resources of the Bratislava–Budapest section of the Danube river for the development of water resources, energy, transport, agriculture and other sectors of the national economy of the Contracting Parties'.[12] The project was intended to generate hydro-electric power and also to improve navigation and flood defences on the relevant part of the river.

The two states agreed that the development was to be a joint investment and 'a single and indivisible operational system of works'.[13] The intended control of this section of the Danube was to be achieved by damming the river at Dunakiliti on Hungarian territory, with the majority of the river-flow diverted through a constructed asphalt-lined bypass canal to Gabčíkovo in Czechoslovakia, where electricity was to be generated twice daily (peak power generation). The intended intermittent damming and releasing of water in this way necessitated a further dam downstream of Gabčíkovo to regulate flow. This was to be built at Nagymaros in Hungary, where electricity was also to be generated, though on a smaller (non-peak power) scale.

---

[11] *Gabčíkovo-Nagymaros Project (Hungary/Slovakia), Judgment*, ICJ Reports 1997, 7.
[12] ibid para 15.
[13] ibid para 18.

Although environmental protection was hardly central to the scheme, the treaty did nevertheless provide that the development was not to compromise water quality in the Danube (Article 15) and that it should 'ensure compliance with the obligations for the protection of nature' (Article 19), and that the parties should protect fishing interests in conformity with a 1958 Convention concerning fishing in the waters of the Danube.[14] Whether, however, the project could ever have been completed while giving effect to these provisions is highly doubtful.

Work on the project began in 1978, but while Czechoslovakia made rapid progress, the Hungarians began work at Nagymaros only in 1986. By this time, reservations had been expressed, especially in Hungary, about the potentially damaging effect of the project on the environment. In addition to the direct environmental impact of the construction, concerns centred on the reduction in quantity and quality of surface and ground waters and the repercussions of this. Decreasing the flow in the Danube by 95 per cent by the use of the asphalt-lined bypass canal threatened to dry up the last inland delta in Europe, comprising the islands of Szigetköz (in Hungary) and Žitný Ostrov (in Slovakia) and hosting unique wetland ecosystems. Eutrophication (an excess of nutrients), leading to changes in the nature of surface water quality, was also feared. It was also argued that damming the river would lead to a slow but certain deterioration in water quality in the aquifer under the inland delta (one of Europe's largest, and used to supply Budapest), owing to the accumulation of pollutants, with the result that the water would be either undrinkable, or drinkable only after prohibitively expensive treatment. Moreover, damage to biodiversity in the delta wetlands, owing to the lowering of the water table and the lack of floods, also appeared likely. These wetlands have been referred to as the 'fish-crib of the Danube', and are of exceptional importance for biodiversity. There were also fears of risks to fisheries and the loss of recreational amenities.

These concerns finally gave rise to large-scale public demonstrations in Budapest against the scheme. The Hungarian Government, despite having agreed in February 1989 to accelerate the project, decided in May of that year to suspend work at Nagymaros and then extended the suspension of operations to all works on Hungarian territory until the completion of a full investigation into the environmental consequences of the scheme.

Despite ongoing negotiations between Czechoslovakia and Hungary, in September 1991, the Czechoslovakian Government decided to adopt its own 'provisional solution' in response to Hungary's failure to proceed with the project. It did so notwithstanding considerable opposition to the scheme within Czechoslovakia itself, and also at a time of unprecedented political upheaval for both countries, with 1991 witnessing the disbanding of

[14] ibid.

COMECON (the East European economic organisation), the dissolution of the Warsaw Pact, and the disintegration of the Soviet Union, which had greatly encouraged the original project with an eye to the increased integration of Eastern European economies.

The 'provisional solution' came to be known as 'Variant C', and involved the Czechoslovakian Government doing as much as it could to maximise the benefits of the scheme given Hungary's inactivity. Variant C provided for the completion of the Gabčíkovo reservoir and all works on Czechoslovakian territory originally envisaged downstream, together with the construction of a dam at Čunovo, where the Danube would be diverted into the headrace canal leading to Gabčíkovo. As work at Nagymaros had ceased, peak power production had to be abandoned. Although further negotiations were held, in May 1992 the Hungarian Government issued a written communication terminating the 1977 treaty.

On 24 October 1992, despite the involvement of the European Commission as mediator, the damming of the Danube at the diversion weir at Čunovo began and the vast majority of flow was directed through the artificial bypass canal to Gabčíkovo. Thereafter, a temporary water management plan was put in place pending final reference to the ICJ. Under this plan, Slovakia (which peacefully separated from the Czech Republic on 1 January 1993) was committed to maintaining 95 per cent of the flow in the Danube and was to refrain from operating the power plant, yet it continued to divert more than 80 per cent of the flow to Gabčíkovo for power production. The environmental consequences were stark. In November 1992, the Danube floodplain dried out completely. From 1993, both countries instigated artificial floodplain water supply systems, as well as joint monitoring of environmental impact, and in 1995 Slovakia guaranteed a minimum flow into the original Danube bed below Čunovo. Together with construction of a new Hungarian weir near Dunakiliti, this would allow water supply into the side-arms of the Danube at Szigetköz. However, there is evidence of considerable drought stress to large forest areas as a result of the two- to four-metre drop of river and ground water levels in the Danube floodplains after diversion.

Unsurprisingly, therefore, the dispute that the ICJ was called upon to resolve was one of immense complexity. A construction treaty had been entered into by two Eastern bloc communist states, both of whose governments had given way to democratically elected regimes by the time the case fell for judgment. In addition, Czechoslovakia had separated into two new states: the Czech and Slovak Republics. Czechoslovakia had expended large sums of money in respect of its obligations, Hungary very much less. Evidence was increasingly available to suggest that if construction were to be completed the resulting environmental damage might well be catastrophic. There were also social considerations involving the people who would be adversely affected by the project. In fairness to the parties and the ICJ, there was no obvious and just solution. Nevertheless, subsequent events do much to highlight the

shortcomings of legal dispute resolution in the context of a possible termination of a treaty.

The very questions agreed by the parties (obviously on the advice of
their lawyers) illustrate just what was gained and lost by translating this
complicated matter into one that the ICJ could be called upon to decide.
The questions referred to the Court on 2 July 1993 by the agreement of the
parties were as follows:

1.   Was Hungary entitled to suspend and subsequently abandon, in 1989,
      the work on the Nagymaros Project and on its part of the Gabčíkovo
      Project?
2.   Was Czechoslovakia entitled to proceed, in November 1991, to the 'provi-
      sional solution' and to put this system into operation from October 1992
      (that is by the damming of the Danube at Cunovo on Slovak territory)?
3.   What were the legal effects of the notification of the termination of the
      treaty by Hungary?

The parties also requested the Court to rule on their respective legal obligations arising from its answers to these three questions.

It will immediately be apparent how restricted these questions are and how
they could not be dealt with satisfactorily without some contemplation of the
social issues involved. In particular, the first question could really be answered
only after an in-depth consideration of the environmental risks posed by
the completed (or even incomplete) project. In the main, however, the ICJ
confined its deliberations to the law relating to treaties. The Court considered
the status of the contract (treaty) and delivered a judgment as narrow as the
questions it had been asked.

If a wider perspective than the purely legal is adopted, it can be seen that
the Court's decision suffers from two significant defects. The first arises from
the application of the law itself; the second from an inability to determine environmental issues concerned with water. As to the first, the questions posed by
the parties seemed far removed from the pressing problems relating to health
and the environment, commerce and development, and political and social
transformation confronting two post-communist Eastern European nations.
The questions asked focused solely on treaty law, and were thus couched in
such a way that it would have been difficult for the Court to devote adequate
attention even to the fundamentally important environmental concerns that
the case raised.

Difficult, but not impossible. In the four-and-a-half years that elapsed
between the joint submission of the legal questions and the delivery of the
judgment, 10,000 pages of supporting evidence were provided, much of
which the Court considered superfluous to its needs and did not consider.
Even though the questions put to the Court were narrowly framed, the Court
should have asked itself whether it was in fact impossible for the parties to
perform their obligations as set out in the treaty while also complying with

the treaty's environmental protection provisions. These provisions are not straightforward, for they provide that the states parties 'shall ensure, *by the means specified in the joint contractual plan*, that the quality of the water in the Danube is not impaired as a result of the construction and operation of the System of Locks' (Article 15) and 'shall, *through the means specified in the joint contractual plan*, ensure compliance with the obligations for the protection of nature arising in connection [with such construction and operation]' (Article 19) (emphases added).[15] The underlying assumption of the treaty, therefore, is that it will be possible to build the locks and dams – if necessary, after research and negotiation – in such a way that neither water resources nor conservation are compromised. Evidence was, however, submitted which suggested that it was simply not possible to comply with the provisions set out in these Articles. This evidence, although not incontrovertible, was fairly formidable. Given the serious threats posed to the environment, it might have been thought appropriate to call for evidence from neutral experts in order to determine whether there would be a detrimental effect on water quality, conservation or fisheries that amounted to a breach of these provisions. However, the Court took no such step.

Hungary's contention that the treaty had become impossible to perform, because 'the essential object of the Treaty – an economic instrument which was consistent with environmental protection and which was operated by the two contracting parties jointly – had permanently disappeared',[16] met with a dismissive response from the Court, which stated that the treaty articles concerned with environmental protection 'actually made available to the parties the necessary means to proceed at any time, by negotiation, to the required readjustments between economic imperatives and ecological imperatives'.[17] Thus, the Court suggested, these two imperatives are always amenable to compromise and 'adjustment', ignoring the possibility that they may sometimes prove irreconcilable. Hungary had put forward evidence, which the Court found unnecessary to consider, indicating that the inevitable result of the constructions proposed was a risk of irreversible ecological and environmental damage, no matter how the 'economic imperatives' were adjusted.

Not surprisingly, then, the Court's responses to the three questions asked were narrow and applied the relevant provisions of the VCLT. It held that Hungary was not entitled to terminate the 1977 treaty, there being found no sufficient legal grounds for termination. It also held that the purported termination could not justify Czechoslovakia's 'provisional solution', which was a clear violation of the express provisions of the treaty and thus an internationally wrongful act. Having answered the first two questions, the Court avoided detailed findings as to the respective future obligations of the parties.

---

[15] ibid para 18.
[16] ibid para 103.
[17] ibid.

It did stress the need, unless the parties agreed otherwise, for the joint regime to be restored, taking into account 'essential environmental concerns'. As to the basis upon which any compensation should be payable, the Court decided that, given the intersecting wrongs of both parties, the issue of compensation could be resolved if each of the parties was to renounce or cancel all financial claims and counterclaims. However, in relation to the settlement of accounts for the construction of the works, this was to be resolved in accordance with the 1977 treaty and related instruments, with the Court holding: 'If Hungary is to share in the operation and benefits of the Cunovo complex, it must pay a proportionate share of the building and running costs'.[18]

As for settling the dispute itself, in essence the ICJ instructed the parties to negotiate an agreement in the light of the Court's findings, but gave little indication as to how such an agreement could be reached. Thus, the legal questions were answered but the dispute's resolution remained elusive, if not illusory.

A final parenthetic point can be made. An additional argument put forward by Hungary was that it was entitled to invoke the legal concept of fundamental change of circumstances to justify termination. One of the fundamental changes referred to related to advances in scientific understanding suggesting it was impossible to implement the treaty in a way that complied with environmental protection standards. Another was that the object of 'socialist integration' which the treaty sought to foster disappeared when the governmental system in both Hungary and Slovakia changed from 'communist' dictatorship to democracy. In addition, Hungary contended, 'the basis of the planned joint investment had been overturned' once both states had been transformed into market economies.[19] These arguments were rejected by the Court, however, which continued to lay primary emphasis upon the fundamental principle underpinning international law: *pacta sunt servanda*. Few international lawyers would question that rejection, but such an emphasis does perpetuate, via the concept of international legal personality, the injustice by which newly democratic governments and the people they represent remain bound by contracts and treaties entered into by dictatorial or non-representative predecessor regimes (as in the case of apartheid South Africa), even when the other party to such a treaty or contract was fully aware of the unrepresentative nature of the regime it was dealing with, and hence knew, or should have known, that the agreement being concluded was unlikely to enjoy the support of the population of the state concerned.

The consequence of such strict adherence to *pacta sunt servanda* is summed up well by Eyal Benvenisti:

> In reaching [its] conclusion the Court deliberately emphasised international undertakings at the expense of domestic pressures. It rejected Hungary's claim

[18] ibid para 154.
[19] ibid para 95.

that a 'state of ecological necessity', if it existed, precluded the wrongfulness of the unilateral suspension of the project, and did so because Hungary could instead have recourse to negotiations to reduce the environmental risks. It similarly rejected Hungary's claim to impossibility of performance, fundamental change of circumstance, and of a lawful response to Czechoslovakia's earlier material breach (namely, Slovakia's construction of the provisional diversion project). The ICJ also found that Slovakia's diversion of the Danube waters breached its obligation towards Hungary to respect the right to an equitable and reasonable share of the river. Despite its findings to the effect that both sides failed to comply with their obligations under the treaty, the ICJ concluded that 'this reciprocal wrongful conduct did not bring the Treaty to an end nor justify its termination'. Finding the agreement flexible and therefore renegotiable, the ICJ held that the 1977 treaty continued to apply, requiring both sides to negotiate its implementation, taking into account current standards on environmental protection and sustainable development, and to regard Slovakia's diversion dam and canal as a 'jointly operated unit' under the treaty regime.

Without entering into the doctrinal aspects of the judgment, it is revealing to examine its implications for the interface between domestic and international politics. The judgment clearly seeks to insulate international politics from the influence of domestic politics. Notwithstanding momentous internal political, economic and social changes affecting both countries, and despite strong public pressure and even parliamentary resolutions, domestic options remain constrained by an international agreement entered into during a past era. Even when one government breaches its obligations to renegotiate in good faith, the other government cannot bow to internal public pressure and take unilateral action.[20]

Readers will probably be unsurprised to learn that negotiations between the Slovak and Hungarian Governments over the carrying out of the ICJ's decision have yet to be concluded. In 2017, Slovakia – in a step unopposed by Hungary – discontinued proceedings it had initiated with the ICJ requesting it to issue a further judgment, Slovakia having claimed that Hungary was unwilling to implement the Court's original ruling. However, both parties reserved the right to request from the ICJ 'an additional judgment to determine the modalities for executing its Judgment of 25 September 1997'.[21]

III. State Responsibility in International Law

When we considered the concept of sovereignty, we observed that its meaning has become more restricted over time. Whereas, theoretically at least,

---

[20] Eyal Benvenisti, 'Domestic Politics and International Resources: What Role for International Law?' in Michael Byers (ed), *The Role of Law in International Politics* (Oxford, OUP, 2001) 121.
[21] ICJ Press Release No 2017/31 of 21 July 2017.

sovereignty once meant that rulers enjoyed absolute power within their respective realms, we saw that in practice this was never completely the case, simply because each state's sovereignty will have been limited by the reality of the world in which the state existed: only the most powerful states and rulers could do exactly as they wished, because other states could and would object if the conduct of a sovereign was deemed unacceptable. Furthermore, as we have seen with treaties, sovereignty is limited by the voluntary agreements that states choose to enter into. Nonetheless, the concept of sovereignty did allow rulers considerable latitude. From the Second World War onwards, however, further explicit constraints, most notably relating to the protection of human rights, have been placed upon state conduct. This is so in spite of the principle enshrined in Article 2(7) of the UN Charter – generally preventing the UN from intervening in matters falling within the domestic jurisdiction of a state – which has come to be construed more narrowly than some states would have liked.

More generally, this book suggests that there are many situations involving international law in which poor or weak states find themselves in a position where they as a group believe their interests to be opposed to those of rich and powerful states. In this respect, the concept of state responsibility is of considerable relevance. Very often these situations of interest–conflict relate to the ability, justified by international law, of one state to intrude into what might be considered the sovereign preserve of another state. Powerful states have an interest in making such intrusions lawful, while the weak states have an interest in preserving their existence from the predations of others.

A. What is the Meaning of State Responsibility?

Like so much of international law, the topic of state responsibility seems (at least initially) to be imbued with common sense. In the words of Article 1 of the ILC's Draft Articles on Responsibility of States for Internationally Wrongful Acts:[22] 'Every internationally wrongful act of a State entails the international responsibility of that State'.[23] The purpose of state responsibility is to render states in breach of international obligations liable in international law for such breach or breaches, and there will be a consequent obligation to make reparation. When put in such terms, the position probably seems unexceptionable. In the oft-quoted words of Judge Huber in relation to the *Spanish Zone of Morocco Claims*:[24] 'Responsibility is the necessary

---

[22] Report of the 53rd Sess, ILC (2001). The General Assembly of the UN recommended the text of the Draft Articles to governments in UNGA Resolution 56/83.

[23] The Articles and Commentaries of the ILC are to be found in James Crawford, *The International Law Commission's Articles on State Responsibility: Introduction, Text and Commentaries* (Cambridge, CUP, 2001).

[24] *Spanish Zone of Morocco Claims (Great Britain v Spain)* (1925) 2 RIAA 615.

corollary of a right. All rights of an international character involve international responsibility. If the obligation in question is not met, responsibility entails the duty to make reparation.'[25]

Hence, all that is being recognised (apparently) is that a failure to meet international obligations will lead to reparations. Before considering why this topic is in fact so controversial, a little more of the law needs to be sketched out. A first point to be observed is that the responsibility referred to in the Draft Articles is concerned with civil, and not criminal, liability. The decision of the ILC was that earlier attempts to provide responsibility for criminal actions were misconceived, and the Articles effectively reinforce the conclusions of the International Military Tribunal for Nuremberg in 1946 to the effect that crimes against international law are 'committed by men, not by abstract entities'. Of course, this does not mean that there is no state responsibility for crimes against international law, rather that the liability is civil, not criminal, and the intention is to provide reparation rather than punishment. Indeed, Chapter three of Part two of the Draft Articles specifically provides for (civil) responsibility in such cases, as is noted below.

The Draft Articles are divided into four parts. Part one, 'The Internationally Wrongful Act of a State', sets out, in 27 Articles, the principles of state responsibility and the requirements that must be met for it to be incurred. Part two, 'Content of the International Responsibility of a State', considers the legal consequences for a state responsible for any internationally wrongful acts and includes provision (in Chapter III) for reparations in the event of 'Serious breaches of obligations under peremptory norms of general international law'. Part three is concerned with the implementation of international responsibility, including countermeasures, while Part four consists of general provisions applicable to the Articles, with Articles 57 and 58 providing that the Draft Articles are without prejudice to any question of the responsibility of any international organisation, or individual responsibility, for a breach or breaches of international law.

Although these Draft Articles attempt to address comprehensively the question of state responsibility, they do so by seeking 'to formulate, by way of codification and progressive development, the basic rules of international law concerning the responsibility of States for their internationally wrongful acts'.[26] Thus, because the Articles have not been incorporated in a convention, their status is not entirely clear. In the words of the UK's representative at the General Assembly's Sixth Committee, sixty-second session, held on 23 October 2007:

[R]eaching agreement on the text of the Articles was not easy, and required intense negotiation and compromise. Consequently the text ... in its entirety is not wholly

---

[25] ibid 641.
[26] Crawford, *International Law Commission's Articles* (2001) 74.

satisfactory to any state. Nevertheless states generally have accepted the Articles in their current form. At present many of the Articles represent an authoritative statement of international law and have been referred to by international courts and tribunals, writers and ... domestic courts ... there is a real risk that in moving towards the adoption of a convention ... old issue[s] may be re-opened ... If few states were to ratify a Convention, that instrument would have less legal force than the Articles ... and [would] stifle the process of development and consolidation of the law that the Articles ... have set in train.[27]

While this is an accurate statement, it does acknowledge that there remain important disagreements between states over particular issues, and it is to these that we will in due course turn. However, a number of preliminary points first need to be made.

The ILC's Commentary on the Draft Articles fairly makes the point that the Articles are concerned with the *secondary* and not the *primary* rules of state responsibility. What this means is that the Articles do not attempt to define *under what circumstances* a state will be held to have committed an internationally wrongful act (this requires primary rules) but rather they seek to define 'the general conditions under international law for the State to be considered responsible for wrongful actions or omissions, and the legal consequences which flow therefrom'.[28] The issues that the Articles seek to address are well summarised in the Commentaries, as follows:

> Given the existence of a primary rule establishing an obligation under international law for a State, and assuming that a question has arisen as to whether that State has complied with the obligation, a number of further issues of a general character arise. These include:
>
> (a) the role of international law as distinct from the internal law of the State concerned in characterising conduct as unlawful;
> (b) determining in what circumstances conduct is to be attributed to the State as a subject of international law;
> (c) specifying when and for what period of time there is or has been a breach of an international obligation by a State;
> (d) determining in what circumstances a State may be responsible for the conduct of another State which is incompatible with an international obligation of the latter;
> (e) defining the circumstances in which the wrongfulness of conduct under international law may be precluded;
> (f) specifying the content of State responsibility, i.e. the new legal relations that arise from the commission by a State of an internationally wrongful act, in terms of cessation of the wrongful act, and reparation for any injury done;

---

[27] Cited in David Harris, *Cases and Materials on International Law*, 7th edn (London, Sweet & Maxwell, 2010) 422.
[28] Crawford (n 23) 74.

(g)   determining any procedural or substantive preconditions for one State to invoke the responsibility of another State, and the circumstances in which the right to invoke responsibility may be lost;

(h)   laying down the conditions under which a State may be entitled to respond to a breach of an international obligation by taking countermeasures designed to ensure the fulfilment of the obligations of the responsible State under these articles.[29]

This is the province of the secondary rules of state responsibility.

A further question then arises, and this is concerned with 'imputability' or 'attribution'. When is a state to be held liable for the actions of entities other than itself? Clearly, this question will not always arise. In a situation where a state is in breach of its obligations under a ratified treaty the responsibility will be direct. Where, however, the acts for which it is sought to make a state responsible have been committed by state officials, or even private individuals, the position is a little more complex. As a state is 'merely' a legal entity, it can do nothing except through the activities of its organs and representatives, and there are rules for determining under what circumstances such activities will be imputed or attributed to the state, whether the actions are those of state officials or private individuals. If attribution is to be made, it must be the case that the representatives or individuals were acting on behalf of the state. The general rule is to be found in Draft Article 4, which provides:

1.   The conduct of any State organ shall be considered an act of that State under international law, whether the organ exercises legislative, executive, judicial or any other functions, whatever position it holds in the organization of the State, and whatever its character as an organ of the central Government or of a territorial unit of the State.

2.   An organ includes any person or entity which has that status in accordance with the internal law of the State.

Draft Articles 5 to 11 further clarify when attribution is to be made, and are thought to broadly reflect customary international law, although this may not be the case in respect of Draft Article 7, which provides for attribution of responsibility even where the organ of the state has acted ultra vires, and even if that fact is known or it is manifest that the organ is in fact acting beyond the powers given to it by domestic law. This position is consistent with the principle that liability in international law cannot be negatived by domestic law provisions. Acts of a private person or persons may lead to state responsibility if the conduct in question is directed or controlled by the state (Draft Article 8) or if the conduct is acknowledged and adopted by a state as its own. The latter position is illustrated by the ICJ case

[29] ibid 74–75.

United States Diplomatic and Consular Staff in Tehran,[30] in which staff at the US embassy in Tehran were taken and held hostage by militants. This became a matter of state responsibility only when a decree of the Iranian state expressly approved and maintained this situation.

A state may even be held responsible for the actions of individuals or groups acting beyond the state's borders. In the case of the *Rainbow Warrior* 'incident', which took place in New Zealand waters, the French Government admitted responsibility for the criminal acts of agents of its Ministry of Defence in deliberately sinking the Greenpeace ship and killing one of its crew.[31] The ICJ was also called upon to determine state responsibility in the Merits phase of the *Nicaragua* case,[32] where it held that the US would be responsible for activities that it promoted in Nicaragua intended to destabilise that state and its government. The criteria for such responsibility required more than 'mere' financing, organising, training, supplying equipping and encouraging, and in that case it was held that responsibility would arise only where there was some real control by the US Government or its officials over the activities of the US-sponsored 'Contras' (as, for example, in the mining of Nicaraguan harbours). As explained by the ICJ in its judgment:

> The Court has taken the view ... that United States participation, even if preponderant or decisive, in the financing, organizing, training, supplying and equipping of the *contras,* the selection of its military or paramilitary targets, and the planning of the whole of its operation, is still insufficient in itself, on the basis of the evidence in the possession of the Court, for the purpose of attributing to the United States the acts committed by the *contras* in the course of their military or paramilitary operations in Nicaragua. All the forms of United States participation mentioned above, and even the general control by the respondent State over a force with a high degree of dependency on it, would not in themselves mean, without further evidence, that the United States directed or enforced the perpetration of the acts contrary to human rights and humanitarian law alleged by the applicant State. Such acts could well be committed by members of the *contras* without the control of the United States. For this conduct to give rise to legal responsibility of the United States, it would in principle have to be proved that that State had effective control of the military or paramilitary operations in the course of which the alleged violations were committed.

> The Court does not consider that the assistance given by the United States to the *contras* warrants the conclusion that these forces are subject to the United States to such an extent that any acts they have committed are imputable to that State.[33]

---

[30] *United States Diplomatic and Consular Staff in Tehran (United States of America v Iran), Judgment,* ICJ Reports 1980, 3.

[31] The *Rainbow Warrior* had been taking part in protests at continuing French nuclear tests in the Pacific. After mediation by the UN Secretary-General, compensation was awarded for the breach of New Zealand's territorial sovereignty.

[32] *Military and Paramilitary Activities in and against Nicaragua (Nicaragua v United States of America), Merits, Judgment,* ICJ Reports 1986, 14.

[33] ibid paras 115–16.

The application of such 'generous' criteria to the activities of the US is probably partly owing to the fact that the US was unrepresented at the Merits phase of the case, having refused to participate (see chapter seven). Even so, the ICJ has reaffirmed its decision on this point.[34] These criteria have been called into question, particularly in the Appeals Chamber of the International Criminal Tribunal for the Former Yugoslavia, where, in considering the degree of control required for attribution, it was said that this might vary according to the factual circumstances of each case.[35] The significance of these criteria is obviously great, as are their consequences. Should the US have been able, using these criteria, to impute the conduct of Al Qaeda in attacking the US on 11 September 2001 to the state of Afghanistan with its Taliban Government? Was Israel able to impute to the state of Lebanon the actions of Hezbollah in 2006 (or, even more ominously, to Iran)? The conclusion reached may well determine which, if any, forceful response may be justified in international law.

B. State Responsibility and the Expropriation of Foreign-owned Property

One of the most contentious areas of state responsibility concerning the treatment of aliens (that is, those who are not nationals of the state in question) involves the expropriation of property owned by foreign nationals. The controversy has been provoked not so much by the act of expropriation itself as with the obligations that flow from that decision. In the decades following the Second World War, when the process of decolonisation was at its most pronounced, many newly independent states argued that political self-determination did not of itself bring economic self-determination (see chapter three), and feared that if their natural resources remained under the ownership and control of foreigners (often the old colonial powers from which they had gained their independence) then little progress could be made in developing their nations' economies.

Even capital-exporting states (generally the developed states but not always) concede that sovereignty includes a right to expropriate property within a state's territorial jurisdiction. Expropriation comes in many forms, but what it always involves in relation to state responsibility is a taking away of some or all of the property rights enjoyed by foreign nationals or entities, whether as individuals, shareholders, or companies. It can range from total expropriation of property or nationalisation of an industry, through the compulsory acquisition of shares (often a majority shareholding) and/or

---

[34] *Application of the Convention on the Prevention and Punishment of the Crime of Genocide (Bosnia and Herzegovina v Serbia and Montenegro), Judgment,* ICJ Reports 2007, 43, para 406.

[35] Case IT-94-1, *Prosecutor v Tadić* (1999) ILM, vol 38, 1518, at 1541, para 11. As this case concerned individual criminal responsibility rather than state responsibility, it is not directly relevant, but the Appeals Chamber did explicitly disapprove of the approach taken by the ICJ.

insistence upon new management of foreign corporations, to something much less drastic that nevertheless results in a diminution in the worth of the property to the foreign owner. Furthermore, the property expropriated need not be tangible property: it can, for example, be intellectual property, or even contractual rights. Finally, of course, because this is public international law, any liability that results will be incurred in respect of the state of the injured property owner rather than the owner itself.

As mentioned above, there is now little debate over whether a state has the right to expropriate foreign-owned property. Indeed, it is now difficult to imagine a time when it was believed that natural resources such as oil belonged to those states and companies which had discovered and exploited the resource rather than to those who inhabited the land in which the resource was located, although this was in fact an argument made for many years against nationalisation.[36] In the era of decolonisation, such a position became untenable, but the result was that disagreement instead arose over the obligations owed by an expropriating state to provide compensation for the losses incurred. In 1962, in the early days of decolonisation and before many emerging states had gained independence and joined the United Nations, the last General Assembly resolution to win a consensus on this matter – Resolution 1803, 'Permanent sovereignty over natural resources'[37] – declared that:

> Nationalization, expropriation or requisitioning shall be based on grounds or reasons of public utility, security or the national interest which are recognized as overriding purely individual or private interests, both domestic and foreign. In such cases the owner shall be paid appropriate compensation, in accordance with the rules in force in the State taking such measures in the exercise of its sovereignty and in accordance with international law. In any case where the question of compensation gives rise to a controversy, the national jurisdiction of the State taking such measures shall be exhausted. However, upon agreement by sovereign States and other parties concerned, settlement of the dispute should be made through arbitration or international adjudication.[38]

What was most significant about Resolution 1803 as a whole was its complete acceptance of a right of expropriation but requiring 'appropriate' compensation 'in accordance with international law'. But what was the position in international law? According to the US and other capital-exporting states, what this demanded was compensation that was 'prompt, adequate and effective': the so-called 'Hull formula', named after its originator, US Secretary of State Cordell Hull. This, it was argued, meant that payment should be made

---

[36] An excellent example of such thinking concerned Britain's reaction to Iranian attempts to nationalise the British-owned Anglo–Iranian Oil Company in 1951. See Stephen Kinzer, *All the Shah's Men: An American Coup and the Roots of Middle East Terror* (Hoboken, NJ, John Wiley & Sons, 2003).

[37] UNGA Resolution 1803 (XVII) of 14 December 1962.

[38] ibid, operative para 4.

in hard currency, and, if not made immediately, a realistic rate of compound interest had to be added. Before the Second World War, such a view was probably unremarkable, and had in fact been confirmed in 1928 by the Permanent Court of International Justice.[39]

Even within its own terms, however, Resolution 1803 gave rise to more questions than it answered. How was 'appropriateness' to be defined? Newly decolonised states were unlikely to agree that anything approaching full value of the asset expropriated could be justified, particularly if the foreign owners had already reaped profits in the past – a stance that was unlikely to commend itself to capital-exporting countries. There was also a further problem of interpretation. The 'appropriate' compensation was to be paid 'in accordance with the rules in force' in the expropriating state but also in accordance with international law, which, as we have seen, was understood by states at risk of having their nationals' property appropriated as meaning 'prompt, adequate and effective'.

The post-war influx of newly independent states into the UN, coupled with increasing criticism of the status quo from the Soviet bloc and the Non-Aligned Movement, resulted in a significant change in the nature of General Assembly resolutions, and also highlighted the lack of consensus in relation to economic issues between these two groups of states and the industrialised nations. The most visible manifestation of this dispute involved the 'Charter of Economic Rights and Duties of States', adopted by the General Assembly in Resolution 3281.[40] The Charter received enthusiastic support from a substantial majority of UN member states, but failed to secure the backing of the industrialised states, all of which either voted against its adoption or abstained. Article 2(c) of the Charter provided that each state has the right:

To nationalize, expropriate or transfer ownership of foreign property, in which case appropriate compensation should be paid by the State adopting such measures, taking into account its relevant laws and regulations and all circumstances that the State considers pertinent. In any case where the question of compensation gives rise to a controversy, it shall be settled under the domestic law of the nationalizing State and by its tribunals, unless it is freely and mutually agreed by all States concerned that other peaceful means be sought on the basis of the sovereign equality of States and in accordance with the principle of free choice of means.

---

[39] *Chorzów Factory Case (Germany v Poland) (Merits)*, PCIJ, 13 September 1928, Series A, No 17.

[40] UNGA Resolution 3281 (XXIX) of 12 December 1974. This Resolution followed UNGA Resolution 3201, in which the majority of UN members (led by the OPEC cartel) supported a 'Declaration on the Establishment of a New International Economic Order' – a resolution that was, of course, strongly opposed by states with an interest in the 'old economic order', particularly the industrialised states. For a broader discussion of these events, see Balakrishnan Rajagopal, *International Law from Below: Development, Social Movements and Third World Resistance* (Cambridge, CUP, 2003).

Gone was all reference to international law and its criteria for 'appropriate-ness'. Nevertheless, if the law to be applied has remained problematic, many cases of nationalisation or expropriation have in fact been decided by refer-ence to the politics of the situation rather than the law, with the amount to be paid a matter for negotiation between the parties, each of whose long-term interests will have to be considered. Expropriation for less than full value will bring the danger of future investors being unwilling to invest without substantial guarantees and security. However, if expropriation were only to be possible upon payment of 'market value', it is scarcely any sovereign right at all. As Alan Story has pointed out, although no one would now argue that vested rights are inviolable, if they are to be 'divested' only upon payment of full value, all that has happened is that the vested right continues in money form as opposed to inhering in some other kind of property.[41]

The differences between these two perspectives is well exemplified by contrasting the approach adopted in the Iran–United States Claims Tribunal with that advocated by those who dispute a US right to recover compensation from Cuba for US-owned property confiscated around 60 years ago. There are, of course, substantial differences between the two factual situations, but the contrast highlights both the possibilities and the problems. Although the facts are well known, it is worth briefly rehearsing those of most relevance. As the Iran–United States Tribunal made use of the earlier 'prompt, adequate and effective', or full reparation, standard, we will consider this case first.

The Shah of Iran was forced to leave the country in January 1979. His departure was a triumph for the Islamic revolution and a disaster for US foreign policy, which had developed and cultivated very close trade and 'defence' links with the Iranian Imperial Government over the previous quarter of a century. From 1970 to 1978, annual trade between Iran and the US rose from $400 million to $6.5 billion. In 1978, there were some 45,000 American military advisers and other personnel, together with their families, living in Iran. By January 1979, as a result of growing civil unrest in the country, much of it directed against US citizens, this number had fallen to only 2,000, with many Americans feeling forced to abandon property in order to return home safely.[42] On 11 February 1979, crowds invaded the imperial

---

[41] Alan Story, 'Property in International Law: Need Cuba Compensate US Titleholders for Nationalising Their Property?' (1998) *Journal of Political Philosophy* 306. This is the implica-tion of O'Connell's observation that the well-established respect in international law for acquired rights 'does not protect the titleholders from expropriation, [but] it at least guarantees them resti-tution'. DP O'Connell, *The Law of State Succession* (Cambridge, CUP, 1956) 102.

[42] On the background to the Shah's departure, see in particular Wayne Mapp, *The Iran–United States Claims Tribunal: The First Ten Years, 1981–91* (Manchester, Manchester University Press, 1993). See also Allahyar Mouri, *The International Law of Expropriation as Reflected in the Work of the Iran–US Claims Tribunal* (Leiden, Martinus Nijhoff, 1994); and Rahmatullah Khan, *The Iran–United States Claims Tribunal: Controversies, Cases and Contribution* (Dordrecht, The Netherlands, Kluwer, 1990).

palace, and the Shah's Prime Minister had no alternative but to resign, with the Iranian military forced to accept the reality of the Islamic revolution.

At first, the new Government attempted to reconcile Islamic traditions with the state's mixed economy, but this proved unpopular, and the ascendance of the newly returned (and enthusiastically received) Ayatollah Khomeini and his 'revolutionary guards' prompted a transition to a considerably less tolerant regime. Although many defence and other contracts between the US and Iran were cancelled immediately, economic reorganisation began in earnest only in June 1979, with a programme of nationalisation that affected both foreign and domestically owned banks and insurance companies, followed by major manufacturing industries. US citizens were at the forefront of those whose property was expropriated, although sometimes this was carried out without any explicit change in ownership, by giving government appointees management control of a company. Not only was there a loss of control over assets, but contracts with US corporations were repudiated as well.

Predictably, those who had suffered losses brought actions against Iran and its government agencies in US courts. The results were initially mixed. Sovereign immunity in one case was held to prevent the attachment of US–Iranian property and deposits, while in two other cases the courts held that there could be pre-judgment attachments.[43] No cases were finally decided before the Algiers Declarations of January 1981 (see below), and thus the question of sovereign immunity was never actually resolved, although, at least in terms of international legal theory, Iran's position would seem to have been strong.

On 4 November 1979, the situation was further complicated when Iranian militants (or 'university students' depending on the perspective adopted) stormed (or 'invaded') the US embassy in Tehran and took more than 60 US diplomats hostage. The following day, Ayatollah Khomeini endorsed these actions, and on 14 November Mr Bani Sadr (a minister in the Government of the Islamic Republic of Iran with responsibility for both Finance and Foreign Affairs) issued a statement which aired the possibility of Iran withdrawing its multi-billion-dollar deposits from US banks – a statement that one author fairly describes as 'somewhat provocative and unnecessary'.[44] The US's response was immediate. The Carter administration issued an executive order on the same day,[45] supposedly in order to protect the dollar, but its effect was to freeze all Iranian assets and property in the US, including everything held in the name of Iran or its organisations and entities, including the Iranian Central Bank. The order applied not only to the US, but anywhere

---

[43] Mapp (ibid) 5.

[44] Mouri, *Expropriation* (1994) 1.

[45] The breathtaking speed with which Executive Order 12170 was produced strongly suggests that it had been drafted before Mr Bani Sadr made his statement. Since it purported to rely on the International Emergency Economic Powers Act and the National Emergencies Act, intended to protect the 'national security, foreign policy, and economy of the United States', some have questioned its legality, although the point is a purely academic one.

in the world where Iranian assets were controlled by US nationals or banks – amounting in total to some $12 billion-worth of money and property.

April 1980 brought both an abortive (and illegal) mission from the US to free the hostages by the use of force, and also further executive orders to block all commerce and travel between the US and Iran, with the exception of journalists and the export of medical supplies. Furthermore, the US Treasury had, in late November and on 19 December 1979, issued, under delegated powers, regulations permitting judicial proceedings against Iranian assets held in the US.[46]

Legality aside, the fact that Iranian assets had been placed under US control acted as a strong incentive for the Iranian Government to settle the hostage question, even if this meant reaching an accommodation with the US for compensation for the harms that the country claimed to have suffered. Yet further pressure was placed on Iran when Iraqi forces invaded the country in September 1980, instigating a war of attrition that was to last for eight years. Consequently, with Algeria acting as mediator, an agreement was reached, embodied in the Algiers Declarations, to which both Iran and the US adhered (in effect making themselves party to the Declarations).[47]

We need not consider the Declarations in detail. Suffice to say, they provided for the return of the hostages, the unfreezing of Iranian assets held in the US (subject to a substantial sum to be held in escrow for the settlement of claims), a stay of proceedings involving claims against Iranian assets held in the US, and, most importantly, provision for the settlement of claims by either state or their nationals against each other through the Iran–US Claims Tribunal.[48]

The Tribunal, which continues its work to this day,[49] was charged with deciding claims 'on the basis of respect for law, applying such choice of law rules and principles of commercial and international law as the Tribunal determines to be applicable'.[50] What is of interest are the criteria chosen by the Tribunal to determine the level of compensation payable: was it to be as

[46] Again, the legal authority for this measure is difficult to establish.

[47] The 'Algiers Declarations' or 'Algiers Accords' were adhered to by Iran and the US on 19 January 1981. Internal ratification by the US and Iran was not required by the Declarations, which gave rise to some doubt as to their legality; however, the authority of the executive branch of the US Government to adhere to the accords was upheld by the US Supreme Court in *Dames and Moore v Regan* 453 US 654 (1981). The position in Iran, the constitution of which requires all treaties to be ratified by the Majlis (the Iranian Parliament), remains unclear, but has not been tested.

[48] Interestingly, Article 1 of the General Declaration states that: 'The United States pledges that it is and from now on will be the policy of the United States not to intervene, directly or indirectly, politically or militarily, in Iran's internal affairs.'

[49] In March 2018, Sir Christopher Greenwood was appointed by the US to be a Member of the Tribunal. Sir Christopher was formerly the UK's judge on the International Court of Justice, but failed to garner sufficient support in the General Assembly in 2017 to be re-elected for a second term (see chapter seven).

[50] Article V of the Claims Settlement Declaration.

traditional international law seemed to suggest – ie the 'prompt, adequate and effective' formula – or could and should the Tribunal take account of the very different views expressed by developing countries? According to Nico Schrijver, writing from a more general viewpoint in 1997: 'With few exceptions there have been no decisions of international courts and tribunals which have straightforwardly adopted and applied the "prompt, adequate and effective" compensation rule',[51] notwithstanding the arguments of capital-exporting states. Indeed, Schrijver argued that there is much to be said for the argument of the then Chair of the Iran–US Claims Tribunal, Judge Lagergren, who said, when determining the *INA Corporation v Iran Award*[52] (in terms strongly disputed by the US judge in the Chamber), that:

> [I]n the event of large scale nationalizations of a lawful character, international law has undergone a gradual appraisal, the effect of which may be to undermine the doctrinal value of any 'full' or 'adequate' (when used as identical to full) compensation standard as proposed in this case.[53]

Perhaps the high-water mark of this approach is to be found in *Shahin Ebrahimi v Iran*,[54] where the Tribunal once more refused to accept that the Hull formula, demanding 'prompt, adequate and effective' compensation for expropriation, finally determined the position:

> Rather, customary international law favors an 'appropriate' compensation standard ... The gradual emergence of this rule aims at ensuring that the amount of compensation is determined in a flexible manner, that is, taking into account the specific circumstances of each case ... the Tribunal finds that once the full value of the property has been properly evaluated, the compensation must be appropriate to reflect the pertinent facts and circumstances of each case.[55]

It is, of course, the case that what counts as 'appropriate' is open to a great deal of interpretation. It is also the case that the tribunal arbitrator in this instance, Arbitrator Allison, argued in a separate opinion that there was almost total uniformity in tribunal decisions awarding compensation that equalled the full value of the expropriated property as it stood on the date of taking – a conclusion that is difficult to oppose in law if not otherwise. Certainly, it is consistent with the 1987 *Restatement (Third) of the Foreign Relations Law of the United States*, section 712, and with the conclusions of Brice Clagett in his article 'Just Compensation in International Law: The Issues Before the Iran–United States Claims Tribunal'.[56] Indeed, in a later

---

[51] Nico Schrijver, *Sovereignty Over Natural Resources: Balancing Rights and Duties* (Cambridge, CUP, 1997) 294.

[52] *INA Corporation v Iran Award* (1985) 8 Iran–US CTR 373.

[53] ibid 385.

[54] *Shahin Ebrahimi v Iran* (1994) Iran–US CTR 38.

[55] ibid para 88.

[56] This article appears as ch II in Richard B Lillich (ed), *Valuation of Nationalized Property in International Law* (Charlottesville, VA, University of Virginia Press, 1987).

article, Clagett expressed his resistance to an argument some had made that, in the case of a widespread nationalisation programme, perhaps only 'partial compensation' should be payable:

> I call this [the partial compensation theory] the 'partial confiscation' theory. If a man steals $10 from me and gives me back $4 he has still stolen $6. I am not able to understand why similar conduct by governments should be viewed any differently. And I have never seen any suggestion of a principled – or even an unprincipled – basis on which 'partial' compensation might be measured or calculated.[57]

Finally, this approach is fully consistent with the views to be found in *Protecting Foreign Investment Under International Law.*[58]

Many readers might find such an attitude entirely reasonable, particularly as set out in the rather simplistic formulation above, but in fact it deserves much greater scrutiny. International disputes are never as straightforward as the example suggests, but even in this instance we might wish to ask more questions. 'Where and how did the holder obtain the $10?' would be an obvious starting point. In real life, matters are certainly more complicated. What of the situation, for example, where the expropriating state comes to an arguably not unreasonable view that the appropriate level of compensation is nothing. One such case involves Chile under President Salvador Allende. Elected on a socialist platform in 1970,[59] Allende determined to move forward with the land reforms and nationalisations that had begun under his predecessor, Eduardo Frei. (When Frei's term of office concluded, '40% of the economy was already state-owned, 30% depended on state funding and only 30% was entirely in private hands'.[60]) The question of compensation was most acute when Allende purported to expropriate what remained in non-government hands of the copper companies – a very popular move with the electorate. The two largest US companies that retained an interest in copper mining, Anaconda and Kennecott, were informed that their holdings had been expropriated and, in view of the fact that they had already received excess profits that exceeded the book value of their investment, no compensation would be payable.[61]

---

[57] Cited in Paul Comeaux and Stephen Kinsella, *Protecting Foreign Investment Under International Law: Legal Aspects of Political Risk* (New York, Oceana Publications, 1997) 84.

[58] Comeaux and Kinsella (ibid).

[59] Allende was elected with 35% of the vote in coalition with a number of left-wing parties, the remainder of the vote being split among a divided opposition. In the following year, however, his Unidad Popular (Popular Unity) Party won almost 50% of the vote in local elections.

[60] John Hickman, *News From the End of the Earth: A Portrait of Chile* (London, Hurst & Co, 1998) 75.

[61] As to the figures involved, Eduardo Galeano suggests that, in half a century, these companies made $4 billion dollars after tax while investing no more than $800 million, most of that coming from the profits made. Eduardo Galeano, *Open Veins of Latin America* (New York, Monthly Review Press, 1997) 144.

As is well known, the overthrow of Allende in a CIA-aided coup led by General Augusto Pinochet in September 1973 was the forcible response to expropriation without compensation, together with a determination to prevent Chile pursuing socialist policies. Unsurprisingly, the US has never accepted state responsibility for the promotion of the coup, or for the violence that subsequently occurred.

It is, however, the case of Cuba that most suggests the inadequacy of the stolen $10 example. Many readers will be aware that, for nearly 60 years, the US has maintained an economic and trade embargo against the island. When Castro's revolutionary movement overthrew the government of the dictator Fulgencio Batista in 1959 – a dictator who had enjoyed full US backing – the US responded by reducing importation of Cuba's crucial sugar exports by 700,000 tons (only for the Soviet Union to agree to purchase the sugar instead). As a step on the path to building a socialist economy, Castro began to nationalise the property of US citizens and corporations. Before any negotiations regarding compensation could be held, the ill-fated US-backed Bay of Pigs invasion was launched in April 1961. When this failed, the embargo was further strengthened, ostensibly in order to secure compensation for expropriated property. What was demanded was Brice Clagett's $10 in full.

Alan Story, however, adopts a rather different perspective.[62] His argument is that when one considers the circumstances under which US property was acquired, the poverty of the Cuban people and the exploitation and oppression to which they had been subjected, appropriate compensation should amount to very little indeed. While he does not dispute the acceptance of the 'Hull formula', it is his contention that it is manifestly ill-founded, and in essence represents, quite unjustly, the interests of those who live in capital-exporting states against the interests of those who live in states where the exported capital has maintained and reinforced oppressive and harsh regimes. Moreover, while it was obvious that Cuba was an impoverished state (not least because of the Batista dictatorship), the value of US-owned property was estimated as amounting to some $1.8 billion: a sum that has now, with compound interest, risen to a variously estimated $7–12 billion, supposedly owed to almost 6,000 US corporations and individuals.

Story's argument is that, if Cuba is to be expected to make good the losses suffered by expropriation, then, in assessing the appropriate reparation, factors other than simple property rights need to be considered. Unfortunately, there is little evidence of a change in US governmental thinking at present. The thaw in US–Cuba relations pioneered by President Barack Obama has been dramatically reversed under the Trump administration, which threatened in

---

[62] Story, Property in International Law (1998).

January 2019 to activate Title III of the Helms–Burton Act 1996,[63] to allow US citizens (including Cuban immigrants who later became US nationals) to sue US and foreign companies that 'traffick' in property expropriated from them following the 1959 revolution ('trafficking' being rather nebulously defined and covering a wide range of economic transactions). Doing so would depart from the practice of all previous administrations since the Act was passed, and would likely deter foreign investment in Cuba (clearly intended in order to place political pressure on the Cuban Government), as well as giving rise to a multitude of lawsuits.[64]

IV. Conclusion

The aspects of treaty law and state responsibility we have chosen to focus on are those which most obviously demonstrate that even apparently politically neutral areas of international law conceal issues of power. In treaty law, unequal bargaining power is unlikely to invalidate a concluded agreement – even one reached between undemocratic states. In the case of state responsibility, we have observed the tension between the right to economic self-determination and the recognised right to nationalise foreign-owned property on the one hand, and arguments for full compensation for such appropriation on the other.

---

[63] Cuban Liberty and Democratic Solidarity (Libertad) Act of 1996, 22 USC 6021–6091. It is popularly known as the Helms–Burton Act after the last names of its original sponsors, Senator Jesse Helms and Representative Dan Burton.

[64] The Trump administration initially delayed the implementation of Title III for 45 days from 1 February 2019, rather than suspending its operation for the normal six months, in line with all previously issued waivers. On 19 March 2019, a further waiver was applied, due to last just 30 days, which does not extend to Cuban entities on the US State Department's Cuba Restricted List. See 'U.S. considering allowing lawsuits over Cuba-confiscated properties', *Reuters*, 16 January 2019; 'US warns Cuba, considers allowing suits over property', *France 24*, 16 January 2019; and 'Trump grants 30-day waiver for companies doing business in Cuba', *Fortune*, 4 March 2019.

5

The United Nations, the UN Charter and International Law

I. Introduction

The United Nations (UN) lies at the heart of the contemporary global legal regime. Not only is it the world's pre-eminent international organisation, counting practically all states among its membership, but the activities of various UN institutions and agencies have contributed greatly to the development of international law in the more than seven decades since the UN was established, giving rise to an international legal landscape vastly different from that which existed before its creation. Moreover, the formal document that created the organisation and sets out its fundamental aims and principles – the UN Charter – remains the closest thing to a constitution that the world community possesses. Practically all subsequent international legal developments of note have been built on its edifice, and it is possible to discern from the Charter's contents the trajectory that international law would trace in the post-Second World War era: progressing from a preoccupation solely with the rights and duties of states (traditionally regarded as the only possible subjects of international law) to an increasing concern with the rights and interests of the peoples and individuals who make up those states.

Any attempt to understand modern international law therefore calls for some appreciation of the UN: its provenance, structure, aims and activities, including the extent to which *realpolitik* – notwithstanding the noble sentiments expressed in the UN Charter – continues to inform the organisation's operations, especially where the use of force is concerned. The UN, in fact, exemplifies the problem of attempting to formulate, and then secure adherence to, legal rules in an anarchical system of sovereign states, where the temptation to 'defect', at least by the dominant members of the international community, is always present. Indeed, it was this need to accommodate the wishes of the then most influential states in order to bring the UN into being in the first place that accounts for the way in which power is distributed in the organisation – a distribution that remains largely undisturbed to this day. This in turn explains why, although the UN's membership is now overwhelmingly drawn from states of the global South, the organisation is still accused of being a predominantly Western institution, and one that continues to reflect and promote the interests of a small subset of nations rather than being truly representative of the global community. It also explains why the formal equality of the sovereign states that are members of the UN remains in many ways just that: a formality, with some states still definitely more equal than others. On the other hand, it is also the case that, without this unequal allocation of power, it is extremely unlikely that the UN would have been brought into existence at all.

II. The Origins of the UN

Formally established at the end of 1945, the UN was intended to prevent a recurrence of the instability and nationalist aggression that had plagued the first half of the twentieth century. The result had been two bloody and prolonged world wars conducted within the span of just over 30 years, with the latter conflict involving both the genocidal horrors of the Holocaust and the devastation wreaked on the civilian populations of Hiroshima and Nagasaki by the first-ever deployment of atomic weapons. Unsurprisingly, therefore, the primary aim of the new organisation was to be the maintenance of peace and security. This was to be achieved in two principal ways: by instituting a system of collective security under the auspices of the great powers that would deal with future threats to global peace and safety (thereby severely curtailing the use of force by individual nations); and by encouraging the peaceful settlement of inter-state disputes, mainly by providing a forum for their adjudication in the form of an International Court of Justice (ICJ) (see chapter seven).

Originally, in fact, the term 'United Nations' referred not to the organisation itself but to those states that were instrumental in its creation: the Allied powers of the Second World War. As the war progressed, and particularly as the defeat of the Axis powers (Germany, Italy and Japan) edged ever closer, it was the most powerful of the Allied states – the US, USSR, Britain and China – that took the initiative in constructing a framework for the post-war international order. As early as August 1941, before the US had formally entered the war, US President Franklin Roosevelt and UK Prime Minister Winston Churchill issued the Atlantic Charter: a declaration of shared principles, setting out the two leaders' vision for 'a better future for the world', including 'the establishment of a wider and permanent system of general security'.

The Charter was duly signed and issued as a 'Declaration of the United Nations' by the US, USSR, Britain and 23 of their allies on 1 January 1942 (within a month of the US declaring war first on Japan and then on the other Axis states). This was followed by the Moscow Declaration of 30 October 1943, in which the USSR, the US, Britain and China noted

> the necessity of establishing at the earliest practicable date a general international organisation, based on the principle of the sovereign equality of all peace-loving states, and open to membership by all such states, large and small, for the maintenance of international peace and security.

Representatives from each of these four powers then met to discuss draft proposals for what was to become the charter of the UN at Dumbarton Oaks, near Washington, DC, from August to October 1944, and subsequently at the Black Sea resort of Yalta in February 1945. It was at the Yalta Conference, in fact, that many of the most important provisions of the UN Charter were hammered out, including, most significantly, the preferential voting procedure within the Security Council that would ensure that real power within the new organisation remained concentrated in the hands of the four main Allied states.

The Yalta summit ended with an agreement to convene a general conference at San Francisco in April 1945, at which the Charter would be finalised and adopted by the international community. After much discussion and negotiation, the Charter was eventually signed by representatives of 50 nations at San Francisco on 26 June 1945, and came into force on 24 October 1945, having been ratified by the requisite number of states. The first meeting of the newly created organisation took place early the following year, once the war had finally ended, with representatives of the member states gathering in London for the opening session of the General Assembly on 10 January 1946. Later that year, the UN took the first step towards securing a permanent home for itself when the oil and banking magnate John D Rockefeller, Jr donated to the organisation an 18-acre plot alongside the East River in mid-town Manhattan. It is here that the UN's headquarters were constructed in 1948–52, and here that the UN continues to be based, although its subsequent growth means that it now has a permanent presence in many other parts of the globe, including regional offices in Geneva, Nairobi and Vienna.

The UN was not the first attempt made to curb inter-state conflict. As might be expected, previous wars involving multiple state actors had prompted their own efforts to prevent further outbreaks of violence. Thus, the French Revolutionary and Napoleonic Wars of the late-eighteenth and early-nineteenth centuries gave rise to the 'Concert of Europe' following the defeat in 1814 of Napoleon Bonaparte, an arrangement that sought to maintain peace principally by providing for regular meetings between representatives of the great European powers at which mutual interests could be discussed and potential threats defused. The Concert even gave rise to an early collective security system of sorts, the Holy Alliance, in which Austria, Prussia, Russia (and later France) pledged to intervene militarily in order to crush any further revolutionary outbursts – initially in France, but subsequently elsewhere on the continent too. Although the Concert and Holy Alliance were eventually superseded by more traditional forms of 'balance of power' diplomacy, the summit meetings that had been instigated with the Congress of Vienna of 1815 continued to play an important role in international diplomacy ('international' at this point really being limited to the major European powers and America) up until the outbreak of the First World War.

The UN's immediate predecessor, the League of Nations, established by the victorious powers under the Treaty of Versailles of 1919, also sought to dissuade individual states from resorting to war. A product of the Great War, the League embodied the popular sentiment of the time: that the immense loss of life and terrible injuries inflicted during the conflict of 1914–18, and largely attributable to the increasing mechanisation of warfare, meant that this surely had to be 'the war to end all wars'. Based in Geneva, the League consisted of a General Assembly, made up of representatives of all its member nations; a Council comprised of the most powerful of the Allied states that opted to join the organisation (initially, just Britain, France, Italy and Japan) and four non-permanent members, elected for a period of three years by the General Assembly; plus a Secretariat to carry out the work of the League under the stewardship of a Secretary-General. The General Assembly met annually and was responsible for formulating the general policy of the League, while the Council, which met four times a year and could also convene for emergency sessions, was entrusted with the task of settling disputes between member states, including imposing sanctions on members that flouted the principles of the League or failed to comply with its decisions. Provision was also made for the establishment of an international court to decide inter-state disputes: the Permanent Court of International Justice, located at the Hague, which began hearing its first cases in 1922.

The League's Covenant – its founding principles or constitution – encouraged member states to resolve their differences by pacific means, submitting any dispute to arbitration or judicial settlement or, if preferred, to the Council, which would then conduct an inquiry into the matter. It also obliged member states to reduce their stocks of weaponry 'to the lowest point consistent with national safety and the enforcement by common action of international obligations' and 'to interchange full and frank information as to the scale of their armaments, their military, naval and air programmes and the condition of such of their industries as are adaptable to war-like purposes' (Article 8). This emphasis on disarmament reflected the widely held belief that an arms race between the major powers, spurred on by private weapons manufacturers driven by a relentless thirst for profit, had been a significant contributing factor to the outbreak of war.

Long before the commencement of the Second World War dealt a fatal blow to the League of Nations, its weaknesses were apparent. Ironically, given the fact that the organisation was predominantly the brainchild of President Woodrow Wilson, the United States Senate refused to ratify the League's Covenant, primarily because of the opposition of Republican Senators, who maintained that membership of the League would serve only to embroil the US in further European conflicts: a re-emergence of the isolationist strain that had seen many Americans oppose their country's involvement in the Old World's first war. As a consequence, the League was deprived of what was, by 1919, the world's most powerful state, damaging its credibility, robbing it of the US's much-needed economic and naval power, and also, perhaps, draining it of much of the inspirational idealism that had been central to the Wilsonian project. Furthermore, two other important global players, the Soviet Union and Germany, were not initially admitted to the League, the former's Bolshevik Government not yet recognised by the Western powers following the Russian Revolution of 1917, and the latter still categorised as an aggressor state that had yet to atone for its sins and prove itself worthy of membership. In spite of its universalist aspirations, therefore, the League was never a truly 'international' organisation, even by the limited Euro–American conception of international community prevalent at the time. In fact, many came to view the organisation as little more than a projection of Anglo–French power. As a result, the League's ability to impose its will on various nations to curb aggression was severely hampered from the outset.

Nor did it help that Britain and France, the two most influential members of the League, had radically different ideas about how the organisation should operate, including how best to deal with an increasingly recalcitrant Germany, chafing against what it regarded as its unjust treatment at the hands of the Allied powers, particularly in relation to the level of war reparations demanded and the disarmament obligations with which it was expected to comply. Britain's response to German grievances was much more accommodating, favouring a relaxation of the terms of the Versailles settlement and Germany's admission to the League as soon as possible as a means of averting future conflict, reflecting in large part its belief that it would not be possible to combat German aggression militarily without the input of the US. France, however, lacking any guarantee of American assistance should its borders again be threatened, and unable to extract a concrete offer of help from the British, came to exactly the opposite conclusion: that German territorial ambitions could be contained only through strict adherence to the terms of the peace treaties and the continuing exclusion of Germany from League membership.

These irreconcilable views were also apparent in the two countries' attitudes to the League itself. Given the absence of the US, Britain came to believe that it would be difficult to impose effective economic or military sanctions on states that failed to abide by the League's decisions, and so placed more emphasis on the dispute-settlement provisions of the League's covenant as a means of defusing inter-state tensions, if only as a means of buying time in which to allow dust to settle and reason to prevail. France, however, remained sceptical about the efficacy of the League's dispute-resolution mechanisms, convinced that they would have little deterrent effect on a determined aggressor. As a consequence, France fell back on traditional diplomatic methods, building alliances with Eastern European states, in which each agreed to come to the defence of the others in the event of an attack. This conviction that it would remain necessary to resort to the use of force in order to repel a future attack inevitably impacted on the willingness of many League members to comply with the Covenant's disarmament obligations. Alarmed at the expansionist ambitions of a reinvigorated Germany and an increasingly powerful Soviet Union, France and its Eastern European allies baulked at impairing their own defensive capacity by cutting armament levels and divulging sensitive information about their military capability to other League members. This in turn allowed Germany to argue that, since the other Great Powers had signally failed to abide by their promise to reduce their levels of armaments as agreed in 1919, it too should no longer be bound by the terms of Versailles and should be permitted to rearm.

A further significant obstacle to the League's effectiveness was the fact that it lacked the means to enforce compliance with its decisions. No provision was made for any forces to be placed at the League's disposal, and hence it remained reliant on the willingness of its members to come to the aid of one another in the event of an attack. This points to one of the inherent problems with any scheme for collective security: one that would later afflict the League's successor, the UN. To be successful, such a policy demands that sovereign states relinquish some of their sovereignty, and in an area conventionally regarded as vital to the national interest: state security. That is, states must be willing to compromise their ability to pursue an independent policy in respect of the use of force in order to participate in the greater good of a collaborative peacekeeping enterprise. In practice, however, all but the weakest states tend to be wary of such schemes, preferring to retain control of their troops and weaponry, and reluctant to risks lives or money unless national interests are obviously implicated.

Another difficulty was that the League's powers, such as they were, extended only to its own members. No attempt was made, therefore, to exert control over the actions of the international community as a whole. Furthermore, even states that joined the League were free to withdraw on giving two years' notice, and, although such flexibility may have encouraged some states to become members in the first place, it was also the case that providing such a clearly marked exit sign had the unfortunate effect of reminding states that they could always walk away from their commitments under the Covenant or disregard the League's decisions if it proved more convenient to do so.

Muddying the waters still further was the fact that the League initially had to contend with a 'rival': a Supreme Council set up to ensure compliance with the Treaty of Versailles. Although some believed that such an arrangement would be beneficial for the League, allowing it to concentrate on broader issues, rather than becoming bogged down in the minutiae of enforcing the terms of the peace settlement, in reality it served only to confuse matters. Although the Supreme Council eventually faded away, many believed that it had served to undermine the League's authority during the organisation's first years of operation.

All of these difficulties meant that the League, in spite of some early successes in resolving inter-state conflicts (tellingly, not involving the interests of any of the Great Powers) was fundamentally ill-equipped to deal with the various blatant acts of nationalist aggression that began to occur from the early 1930s onwards, and which, even more disconcertingly, were perpetrated by the organisation's own members. These involved, most prominently, Japan's invasion of Manchuria in 1931, Italy's annexation of Abyssinia (present-day Ethiopia) in 1935, and the Soviet Union's seizure of Finland in 1939.[1] Each of these powers, in fact, ceased to be a member of the League by the end of the 1930s. The Soviet Union enjoyed the dubious distinction of being the only state to be expelled from the League, as punishment for its invasion of Finland, while Japan and Italy left the League of their own accord in 1933 and 1937 respectively. Most ominously of all, the League was unable to offer any effective resistance to the growing belligerence of a remilitarised and Nazi-led Germany, which in 1933 also withdrew from the League (Germany having eventually been admitted to the organisation in 1926). Thus was the way cleared for Hitler's reoccupation of the Rhineland in 1936, the absorption of Austria through the *Anschluss* and the annexation of Czechoslovakia's Sudetenland in 1938, and, finally, the invasion of Poland in 1939, igniting a second global conflict just over 20 years after the First World War – 'the war to end all wars' – had been concluded.

The architects of the UN therefore had the flaws of the League very much in mind when drawing up the blueprint for its successor during the course of the Second World War. They did not, however, totally reinvent the wheel, and in some significant respects the UN's structure is modelled on that of its predecessor, making it a 'new and improved version' of the League rather than an outright replacement.

---

[1] The Soviet Government, which had gradually (and grudgingly) won recognition from the other major powers as the legitimate representative of the Russian state, agreed to join the League in 1934, despite having for many years derided the organisation as nothing more than a vehicle of Western imperialism.

III. The Structure of the UN

As set out in Chapter III of the UN Charter, the UN consists of the following main bodies or organs: the General Assembly, the Security Council, the Economic and Social Council, the International Court of Justice and the Secretariat (Article 7(1)). (Officially, there is one further principal UN organ: the Trusteeship Council. This assumed responsibility both for the colonial territories of the defeated Axis powers and for those territories which had, at the end of the First World War, been 'mandated' or assigned to various Allied powers under the aegis of the League of Nations, its object being in both cases to prepare these territories for eventual independence or self-government. The Trusteeship Council effectively completed its mission in October 1994, when the last 'trust territory', the western Pacific island of Palau, gained its independence. As a result, the Council voted the following month to suspend its operations.) Each of these principal organs is described briefly in the next section, with the exception of the ICJ, which is discussed in chapter seven.

It is important to note, however, that the UN system or 'family' is in fact much wider, having proliferated since the organisation's inception to encompass a dizzying array of bodies, programmes and activities. The principal organs themselves have established a number of subsidiary bodies (as they are allowed to do under Article 7(2)), which are entrusted with carrying out particular aspects of the UN's work. The General Assembly, for example, has, among numerous other bodies, created the Human Rights Council (which replaced the UN Commission on Human Rights) to promote and protect human rights internationally, as well as the UN Commission on International Trade Law (UNCITRAL), to help reform and harmonise rules and regulations relating to international commercial transactions. The Security Council, meanwhile, has established various peacekeeping missions throughout the globe and also set up the two ad hoc international criminal tribunals to investigate war crimes and other crimes against humanity that occurred in the former Yugoslavia and Rwanda.

At a further remove are the specialised agencies: independent bodies with their own charters, budgets, staff and separate state membership, which are established by individual treaties in accordance with Article 57 of the Charter and operate 'in economic, social, cultural, educational, health, and related fields'. These agencies (currently 15 in total) are then 'brought into relationship with the United Nations' via agreements concluded with the Economic and Social Council and approved by the General Assembly (Article 63(1)). Some of the specialised agencies actually pre-date the formation of the UN itself, such as the International Telecommunication Union, which traces its origins back to 1865, and is responsible for promoting the development of, and improving access to, information and communication technologies, and the International Labour Organization, set up as part of the 1919 peace settlement, with the object of fostering social justice and peace by encouraging the adoption of more humane working conditions. In addition, and much less obviously perhaps, both the International Monetary Fund and the World Bank[2] are specialised agencies of the UN, having been founded in 1944 with the object of helping to rebuild and stabilise the international economic order in the aftermath of the Second World War.

The General Assembly has also been responsible for establishing a large number of programmes and entities (as permitted under Article 22 of the Charter), including UNICEF (the United Nations Children's Fund), UNDP (the United Nations Development Programme) and UN Environment (the United Nations Environmental Programme).

A. General Assembly

The General Assembly (UNGA), the powers and duties of which are set out in Chapter IV of the Charter, is the UN's 'main deliberative, policymaking and representative organ'. It meets annually from September to December, although emergency sessions can be convened at other times of the year, if necessary. Each of the UN's 193 member states is represented at the UNGA, with each state allocated one vote, regardless of the size of its population or the amount that its government contributes to the financing of the organisation. Consequently, ignoring the difference in size of constituencies, it is the most democratic of the UN's main bodies (if each sovereign state is formally equal). Decisions on 'important questions' can be made only if they attract the support of at least two-thirds of the states present and voting; other decisions require just a simple majority. Questions are 'important' if they relate to the following topics:

> [T]he maintenance of international peace and security, the election of the non-permanent members of the Security Council, the election of the members of the Economic and Social Council, the election of members of the Trusteeship Council [now of little importance following the Council's suspension of its activities] ... the admission of new Members to the United Nations, the suspension of the rights and privileges of membership, the expulsion of Members, questions relating to the operation of the trusteeship system [again, of no real significance now there are no trust territories left], and budgetary questions.[3]

---

[2] Originally known as the International Bank for Reconstruction and Development (IBRD), the World Bank now consists of two institutions: the IBRD, the remit of which is to provide assistance to middle-income poorer countries; and the International Development Association, which is responsible for aiding the world's most indigent nations. The World Bank is in turn part of the World Bank Group, which also includes the International Finance Corporation, the Multilateral Guarantee Agency and the International Centre for the Settlement of Investment Disputes.

[3] Article 18(2).

The UNGA is empowered to discuss, and make recommendations on, any matter that falls within the purview of the Charter or which relates to the powers and functions of any UN organ (Article 10). It can therefore consider issues relating to the all-important aim of maintaining international peace and security, including drawing the attention of the Security Council to anything that may jeopardise such peace and security (Article 11); recommend measures to deal with situations that threaten to disrupt relations between states, including those that involve a violation of the purposes and principles of the Charter (Article 14); inaugurate studies and make recommendations to nurture international cooperation on political, economic, social, cultural and health matters, and assist in realising human rights and fundamental freedoms (Article 13(1)(b)).

The UNGA also has an important role to play in promoting and strengthening international law. In practice, it has delegated this task to a subsidiary organ, the International Law Commission (ILC). Established by the UNGA in 1947, the ILC is tasked with 'the promotion of the progressive development of international law and its codification'.[4] The ILC's remit, therefore, extends both to the formulation of new legal rules in areas that are not yet covered, or not adequately covered, by international law, and to the articulation, in a more precise and systematic format, of customary legal rules and doctrines that have not yet been formally enshrined.

In matters of international peace and security, however, it is the Security Council that takes precedence. In cases where the Council is carrying out any of its functions under the Charter in relation to a particular dispute or situation, the UNGA is not permitted to make any recommendations concerning that matter unless invited to do so by the Council (Article 12(1)).

During the Cold War, when the actions of the Council were effectively paralysed by the permanent members' use of the veto power (see below), the UNGA did adopt a more prominent role in relation to peace and security. In 1950, it adopted the 'Uniting for Peace' Resolution,[5] which stated that:

> [I]f the Security Council, because of lack of unanimity of the permanent members, fails to exercise its primary responsibility for the maintenance of international peace and security in any case where there appears to be a threat to the peace, breach of the peace, or act of aggression, the General Assembly shall consider the matter immediately with a view to making appropriate recommendations to Members for collective measures.[6]

This led to the development of the first UN peacekeeping forces, although, after the end of the Cold War, the Security Council again reasserted its

---

[4] Article 1(1) of the Statute of the International Law Commission 1947, which in turn echoes Article 13(1)(a) of the UN Charter.
[5] UNGA Resolution 377 (V) of 3 November 1950.
[6] ibid para 1.

authority, and is now largely responsible for these operations. Classic peace-keeping exercises were aimed only at deterring further hostilities, with UN forces acting as a physical barrier between warring states, and, in deference to the principle of non-interference, being deployed only with the consent of the parties concerned. The UN's peacekeeping remit has expanded consider-ably over time, in spite of the lack of any clear mandate for such operations in the Charter itself. It now extends not only to situations involving intra-state hostilities, but also encompasses so-called 'peacebuilding' operations, aimed at helping to resolve the conflict itself, and 'peace-enforcement' exer-cises, which, as the name suggests, involve some kind of enforcement action in order to keep the peace.

One significant weakness of UNGA decisions or resolutions is the fact that they are not binding on states (the only binding decisions the Assem-bly can make relate to internal administrative matters). Notwithstanding this, many UNGA resolutions have had an influential effect on the development of international law, not least because they can be said to embody the opin-ion of the majority of the world's states. Thus, where the UNGA has issued declarations purporting to explain what is meant by certain provisions of the UN Charter, or clarifying other issues that relate to international law, these pronouncements have come to be regarded as authoritative interpretations of these matters.

B. Security Council

If the present-day UNGA is the most democratic of the UN's main organs, then the Security Council (UNSC) remains its most powerful, and the one whose structure was most obviously designed to cure the defects that had prevented the League of Nations from functioning effectively. Established under Chapter V of the Charter, the UNSC consists of 15 member states, five of which – China, France, Russia, the UK and the US – are permanent (often referred to as 'the P5'), with the other ten being elected for a two-year term from among the five regional groups of states in the UNGA, with five of the 10 replaced each year. Of these 10 non-permanent seats, three are reserved for Africa, two each are allocated to the following regions: Asia; Latin America and the Caribbean; and Western Europe and Other States (which includes Australia, Canada and New Zealand), with the remaining seat awarded to an Eastern European nation. To secure one of these seats, a country must attract at least two-thirds of the votes cast for that seat, irrespective of whether or not it faces any competition. The P5 remains virtually unchanged since 1945, the only exceptions being the allocation of China's seat on the Council to the Government of the People's Republic of China in 1971 (up until that point China had been represented on the Council by the Taiwan-based Nationalist government of Chiang Kai-shek), and the succession of the

Russian Federation to the USSR's seat on the Council following the dissolution of the Soviet Union in 1991.

The UNSC is primarily responsible for the maintenance of peace and security in the international realm (Article 24). This includes determining 'the existence of any threat to the peace, breach of the peace, or act of aggression', and then making recommendations or deciding what measures shall be taken 'to maintain or restore international peace and security' (Article 39). Such measures can encompass the use of force (Article 42) or may fall short of this, involving, for example, the interruption of economic relations or communications, or the severing of diplomatic ties (Article 41). Member states are bound to carry out the decisions of the UNSC (Article 25). Under Chapter VI of the Charter, the UNSC's role in maintaining peace and security extends to the pacific settlement of disputes. In particular, it can call upon the parties to a dispute likely to threaten international peace and security to resolve their disagreement peacefully, employing means ranging from negotiation to judicial settlement (Article 33) and can investigate any dispute or situation in order to determine whether it is likely to disrupt international peace and security (Article 34). With regard to such disputes, it may 'recommend appropriate procedures or methods of adjustment', taking into consideration any settlement procedures already adopted by the parties and also the fact 'that legal disputes should as a general rule be referred by the parties to the ICJ in accordance with the provisions of the Statute of the Court' (Article 36). It can also, 'if all the parties to any dispute so request, make recommendations to the parties with a view to a pacific settlement of the dispute' (Article 38). (For more information on the UNSC's role in maintaining peace and security, see chapter eight.)

With the exception of decisions that relate to purely procedural matters (in which case the affirmative vote of nine of the Council's members will suffice), UNSC resolutions are adopted only if they both attract the support of at least nine Council members and – crucially, in a move designed to protect the interests of the major powers in 1945 – if every member of the P5 consents to the resolution being passed (Article 27). Consequently, each of the P5 has the power to block a UNSC resolution with which it disagrees. Oddly, and in defiance of the strict wording of Article 27, which specifies that a resolution can be adopted only with 'the concurring votes of the permanent members', a convention has now been established that a resolution will be deemed to have passed even if one or more of the P5 abstains in the vote. In other words, if a member of the P5 wishes to prevent the adoption of a UNSC resolution, then it must actively veto it, by voting against the measure in question.

It is this aspect of the UN system more than any other – the power of veto wielded by the P5 in respect of UNSC decisions, together with the unchanging composition of the permanent membership – that has attracted the most criticism over the years and demands for reform. Changing global fortunes since the end of the Second World War have left many wondering why certain nations whose military and economic powers have dwindled considerably since 1945 (the UK and France) nevertheless remain a fixture of one of the world's most influential institutions, while other, apparently more credible, candidates, including India, Brazil, Japan and Germany (the latter two states being significant financial contributors to the UN) continue to be excluded.

In 2003, the UN's then Secretary-General, Kofi Annan, unveiled two alternative proposals for a revamped UNSC, both of which would have added a further nine seats, bringing the total number of Council members to 24. Under the first model, a further six permanent members would have been created (albeit without the veto power enjoyed by the current membership), along with three extra non-permanent members. Under the second, one non-permanent seat would have been added, together with eight semi-permanent seats: that is, seats that would be held for four years rather than the normal two, and that could also be renewed for further terms. The fact that the status quo has persisted for so long is attributable not only to the determination of the present members of the P5 to hold on to their seats at the table of power, but also to regional tensions and rivalries, which have ensured that, for every country for which permanent membership of the UNSC has been mooted, there are one or more others prepared to raise an objection. For example, although India – in terms of sheer population alone – appears an obvious choice for any new permanent position created, its candidacy is vociferously opposed by Pakistan. Similarly, when South Africa or Nigeria asserts a claim to an African seat on the UNSC, Egypt counters that they are incapable of representing the interests of African nations north of the Sahara, which must therefore be awarded their own seat. In turn, Mexico sees no reason why Brazil should take precedence in the Americas.

Efforts at UNSC reform therefore remain stalled. The Group of Four – consisting of Brazil, Germany, India and Japan – argues for an expansion in the number of permanent seats on the Council (with four such seats being taken by themselves), together with an increase in seats for non-permanent members. In contrast, the Uniting for Consensus group, which includes Argentina, Italy, Pakistan and South Korea, maintains that only non-permanent seats should be added, albeit for longer terms than the current two years. Meanwhile, the African and Arab regional UN groupings continue to argue the case for representation for their respective members. And, although the granting of permanent seats to other powerful nations would better reflect current geopolitical reality, it is also the case, as smaller states and those supportive of a more democratic UNSC contend, that this carries the risk of further entrenching privilege on the Council. There is no guarantee that newly created permanent members would be any less likely than the P5 to promote their own interests rather than act as representatives of the wider UN membership, nor, given the likelihood of states' fortunes fluctuating over time, that the situation of a state awarded a permanent seat today would not, with the passage of enough years, appear as incongruous as the privileged positions now enjoyed by the UK and France.

It is unlikely that any change to the Council's membership will take place in the near future, since this would require the UN Charter itself to be amended, with any such amendment needing to secure (by virtue of Article 108) the vote of two-thirds of UNGA members, followed by ratification by two-thirds of UN member states (including all of the P5), who would thus be able to veto, either collectively or individually, any reform with which they disagreed.

C. Secretariat

The Secretariat, largely modelled on its predecessor in the League of Nations, performs the role of an international civil service, and its composition and operation is governed by Chapter XV of the Charter. It serves the other main bodies of the UN, with the exception of the ICJ, and is responsible for implementing the UN's policies and programmes around the globe. The Secretariat draws its personnel from state members throughout the world, with Article 101 specifying that 'Due regard shall be paid to the importance of recruiting the staff on as wide a geographical basis as possible'. Such staff pledge their loyalty to the UN rather than to their respective home countries, being instructed by Article 100(1) 'not [to] seek or receive instructions from any Government or from any other authority external to the Organization'. Reinforcing this neutrality, UN member states themselves agree, under Article 100(2), 'to respect the exclusively international character of the responsibilities of the Secretary-General and the staff and not seek to influence them in the discharge of their responsibilities'.

The Secretariat is headed by a Secretary-General (S-G) appointed for a five-year term that has, in practice, almost always been renewed for a further five years. Appointments are made by the UNGA on the recommendation of the UNSC (Article 97), with any permanent member of the UNSC able to block the appointment (or reappointment) of an S-G to whom it objects.[7] The process by which an S-G is selected has traditionally been rather opaque, and there have been calls to rectify this.[8]

---

[7] China exercised its veto to prevent the fourth S-G, the Austrian Kurt Waldheim, from serving a third term in 1981, on the ground that it was time that a European appointee made way for a candidate from the global South. Waldheim was succeeded by Peru's Javier Pérez de Cuéllar. Since then, S-Gs have served only a maximum of two terms. In 1996, the US vetoed the sixth S-G, Egypt's Boutros Boutros-Ghali, being granted a second term, apparently owing to Boutros-Ghali's reluctance at the time to endorse NATO airstrikes against Serbian forces in Bosnia. Ghana's Kofi Annan took over in Boutros-Ghali's place.

[8] See UNGA Resolution 69/321 of 22 September 2015, operative para 34, which 'emphasizes in particular that the process of selection of the Secretary-General shall be guided by the principles of transparency and inclusiveness, building on best practices and the participation of all Member States'.

The S-G is 'the chief administrative officer of the Organization' (Article 97), must report annually to the General Assembly on the work of the UN (in accordance with Article 98), and can also alert the Security Council to any matter which he or she believes 'may threaten the maintenance of international peace and security' (Article 99). The S-G has come to play an important part in the peaceful resolution of disputes, with the mediation and good offices aspect of the role having expanded considerably over the years. The position of S-G is a high-profile one, since the S-G is effectively the head of the UN and acts as its public face and advocate. As a result of this, and owing to the highly political nature of the organisation and its work, it is almost impossible for an S-G to avoid controversy altogether, as many UN decisions and actions are likely to upset one or more states. That the role was perceived as an influential one from the outset certainly explains why an S-G can serve only with the approval of all the permanent members of the UNSC. Nor is the role without its dangers. The UN's second S-G, the Swede Dag Hammarskjöld, was killed in an air crash over Northern Rhodesia (modern-day Zambia) in 1961 while on his way to help broker a ceasefire in the civil war that had broken out in the newly liberated Congo (now Democratic Republic of the Congo), following the withdrawal of the former colonial power, Belgium, the year before.[9] The organisation is now on its ninth S-G: former Portuguese Prime Minister António Guterres, who assumed office at the beginning of 2017, succeeding Ban Ki-moon of South Korea, who served two terms, from 2009 to the end of 2016. Although, of the S-Gs that have served to date, several have been nationals of states of the global South, a woman has yet to be appointed to the role. It would appear that both the General Assembly and the Security Council are now more mindful of this omission, having urged state members, at the start of the selection procedure for the last S-G, 'to consider presenting women as candidates'.[10]

D. Economic and Social Council

As its name indicates, the Economic and Social Council (ECOSOC) coordinates the UN's vast panoply of economic and social programmes, as well as being responsible for environmental issues and the implementation of

---

[9] Researchers for a documentary on the case have recently claimed to unearth further evidence that a Belgian pilot who trained and flew with the British Air Force during the Second World War, and who was contracted to work for the Katangese separatist group seeking independence from the Congo, shot down Hammarskjöld's plane on the group's orders. See 'RAF veteran "admitted" 1961 killing of UN secretary general', *The Observer*, 12 January 2019, available at www.theguardian.com/world/2019/jan/12/raf-veteran-admitted-killing-un-secretary-general-dag-hammarskjold-in-1961.

[10] UNGA Resolution 69/321 (n 8), operative para 38. See also the joint letter from the Presidents of the UNGA and UNSC (A/70623–S/2015/988 of 15 December 2015) inviting states to put forward candidates for the post of S-G, in which 'Member States are encouraged to consider presenting women, as well as men, as candidates for the position of Secretary-General.'

internationally agreed development objectives, such as the Millennium Development Goals. Governed by Chapter X of the Charter, ECOSOC presides over a complex structure that consists of numerous subsidiary organs – including five regional commissions; eight 'functional' commissions (that is, bodies set up to deal with a particular subject area, such as improving the status of women worldwide or tackling the problem of the global traffic in narcotic drugs); several expert bodies focusing on various technical fields, such as the transportation of dangerous goods and the classification and labelling of hazardous chemicals – as well as coordinating the work of the UN's 15 specialised agencies. ECOSOC is made up of 54 member states (Article 61(1)), with the seats distributed among the UNGA's five regional groups as follows: 14 are allocated to Africa, 11 to Asia–Pacific, six to Eastern Europe, 10 to Latin America and the Caribbean, and 13 to Western Europe and Other States. Members are elected by the UNGA for three-year terms, with 18 of these (or a third of the membership) being elected each year (Article 61(2)). A retiring member can be elected for a further term.

ECOSOC's status as one of the primary institutions of the UN is testament to the emphasis that the UN's founders placed on economic stability and the improvement of living standards as a means of preventing further conflict between states. The outbreak of the Second World War, and the rise of Nazism in Germany that preceded this, was seen as largely attributable to the disastrous economic policies pursued throughout Europe in the 1930s, and hence ameliorating hardship and providing a secure economic environment were considered crucial to maintaining international peace and security.

IV. How the UN is Financed

The UN is funded by contributions from all its member states, with the UNGA responsible for approving the organisation's budget and for apportioning costs among the members (Article 17). It was initially suggested that a weighted voted system apply to the UN, so that the more money a country contributed to the organisation's coffers the more votes it should have, both in the UNGA and UNSC. The plan was eventually rejected, although a system of weighted voting rights does apply to both the International Monetary Fund (IMF) and the World Bank, as explained in chapter three. At the other end of the scale, it has been accepted that not even the most indigent of nations should be exempt from contributing to the running costs of the UN, since 'collective financial responsibility implies that all Member States pay at least a minimum percentage of the expenses of the Organization'.[11]

---

[11] UNGA, 'Scale of Assessments', A/RES/31/95/A, 14 December 1976, preambular para 5.

The contributions made by member states fall into one of three main categories: assessed; peacekeeping; and voluntary. Assessed contributions are those payments that each state is obliged to pay towards the regular budget of the UN, and are 'intended to cover core costs arising from the work of the UN's principal organs and main offices, as well as some programme costs'.[12] These contributions are primarily determined by a country's gross national income (GNI), worked out over a six-year base period, with the most recent three years in the period given greater weighting in the calculation. However, other factors are also taken into account, with a state's contribution reduced if it has a high level of external debt (loans that must be repaid to foreign creditors) or a less-than-average per-capita income (because the country is especially populous and hence not as wealthy as the GNI figure taken on its own might suggest).[13] Assessed contributions to the UN budget are subject to a maximum rate for the richest countries and a minimum one for the poorest, set at 22 per cent and 0.001 per cent of the total respectively. Additionally, no state classified as a Least Developed Country (LDC) contributes more than 0.01 per cent.[14] The US is the only country subject to the maximum levy of 22 per cent[15] and is thus by far the largest contributor to the UN's budget. Peacekeeping contributions are also compulsory and, as the name indicates, help cover the cost of the UN's peacekeeping missions. Again, these are calculated according to the capacity of a state to pay, but the formula used is more protective of poor countries, allowing them a more generous discount than is the case with the assessed contributions; the P5 are then responsible for making up the shortfall, the justification being that 'permanent members of the Security Council are responsible for authorising peacekeeping missions'.[16]

As the UN Committee on Contributions reminds those who visit its website, member states that fail to make their compulsory payments to the UN, and whose arrears equal at least two years' worth of contributions, forfeit their right to vote in the General Assembly (under Article 19 of the Charter). The Assembly can, however, exercise its discretion to allow the state to continue to vote 'if it is satisfied that the failure to pay is due to conditions

[12] United Nations Association–UK (UNA–UK) briefing document 'The UN's Finances', 17 July 2017, available at www.una.org.uk/news/un-briefings-uns-finances.

[13] For a detailed explanation of how the calculation is made, see UN Statistics Division, 'The methodology used for the preparation of the United Nations scale of assessments for the period 2016–2018', 78th Session of the UNGA Committee on Contributions, 4–29 June 2018, available at www.un.org/en/ga/contributions.

[14] Created as a category by the UNGA in 1971, LDCs are the world's most impoverished states, with 47 countries currently accorded this status (as at 2018). For more information, see the website of the UN Office of the High Representative for the Least Developed Countries, Landlocked Developing Countries and Small Island Developing States at http://unohrlls.org/about-ldcs.

[15] The maximum rate used to be 25%, but the US successfully negotiated a reduction of 3% that has applied from the year 2000 onwards.

[16] 'The UN's Finances' (n 12).

beyond the control of the Member'. Hence, if a state is having difficulty paying its membership dues because it genuinely lacks the funds to do so, then this would not be a reason to deprive it of its say in Assembly matters. Despite having accumulated significant arrears, the following states are still permitted to vote: Comoros; São Tomé and Principe; and Somalia.[17]

In addition to the mandatory assessed and peacekeeping contributions, UN member states can opt to make voluntary payments to the UN, and many of the organisation's agencies and programmes would not survive without this additional source of finance: the World Food Programme, for example, is currently wholly dependent on voluntary funding.[18] Furthermore, since such funding may vary dramatically from year to year (normally being dependent on the approval of domestic legislatures), it can make it extremely difficult for these agencies to plan ahead. The two exceptions are the IMF and the World Bank: these have their own systems of contribution, which, as noted above, determine the number of votes allocated to each of these organisations' members.

The most recent scale of assessments approved by the General Assembly, determining the contributions to be paid by each member state towards the regular and peacekeeping budgets, covers the period 2019–21. It is particularly notable for marking the debut of China as the second-largest contributor to the regular budget, displacing Japan, which has occupied this position since the 1980s. Of the 2019 regular budget, set at $3.06 billion, the US is expected to contribute 22 per cent, with the next five major contributors, in descending order, being China (12.005 per cent); Japan (8.564 per cent); Germany (6.090 per cent); the UK (4.567 per cent); and France (4.427 per cent).[19] The peacekeeping budget for 2018–19 (peacekeeping budgets straddle calendar years, running from 1 July to 30 June) was set at $6.7 billion.[20] For 2019, the US's contribution was set at 27.89 per cent; followed by China (15.22 per cent); Japan (8.56 per cent); Germany (6.09 per cent); the UK (5.79 per cent); and France (5.61 per cent).[21]

These sums are not negligible, but it is worth bearing in mind that they represent a tiny percentage of the richer countries' GNI and only a modest amount

---

[17] UNGA, 'Scale of assessments for the apportionment of the expenses of the United Nations: requests under Article 19 of the Charter', A/RES/73/4, 15 October 2018.

[18] 'The UN's Finances' (n 12).

[19] United Nations Secretariat, 'Assessment of Member States' contributions to the United Nations regular budget for the year 2019', ST/ADM/SER.B/992, 24 December 2018, available at www.un.org/en/ga/contributions/current.shtml. At the other end of the scale, a total of 30 states, many of which are small island states or are located in Sub-Saharan Africa, have been assessed at the minimum rate of 0.001%, which, for the 2019 budget, equates to a payment of $30,646.

[20] UNGA, 'Approved resources for peacekeeping operations for the period from 1 July 2018 to 30 June 2019', A/C.5/72/25, 5 July 2018.

[21] UN Peacekeeping, 'How We Are Funded', available at https://peacekeeping.un.org/en/how-we-are-funded, and UNGA, 'Implementation of General Assembly resolutions 55/235 and 55/236', A/73/350/Add.1, 24 December 2018.

of their expenditure. Notwithstanding this, UN contributions are frequently not made on time, causing severe cash-flow difficulties that have led the current S-G, António Guterres, to write to member states with increasing urgency to point out the gravity of the UN's financial straits. At the end of 2018, 41 of the UN's member states had yet to pay their contributions to the regular budget, resulting in a shortfall of $323 million. Even worse, at the beginning of 2019, the peacekeeping budget faced a shortfall of nearly $2 billion, partly caused by the fact that the US Congress has, for the past two years, reverted to its previous practice of capping the US's contribution at 25 per cent, rather than pay the full assessment of around 28 per cent. The situation prompted Guterres to warn that current cash balances would cover less than two months' worth of peacekeeping operations.[22] Six months earlier, in July 2018, the S-G had issued a blunt health check in respect of the UN's funding as a whole: 'we are running out of cash sooner and staying in the red longer'.[23]

Occasionally, assessed payments may also be withheld from a UN body as a form of political protest. In October 2011, the US Congress voted to withhold the US's 22 per cent contribution to the budget of the United Nations Educational, Scientific and Cultural Organization (UNESCO) in retaliation for the agency's decision to admit Palestine as a full member in defiance of American wishes. According to UNESCO's director general, interviewed a year after the cut-off had been implemented, the loss of US funding had led to a shortfall of approximately $144 million in the agency's budget, and had, in spite of help received from other sources, forced UNESCO to freeze or cancel many of its programmes.[24] Since 2011, the US's unpaid contributions have mounted up to an estimated $600 million, and relations have deteriorated to the point where the US and Israel have left UNESCO, both having objected to Palestine's admission and both alleging anti-Israel bias on the part of the organisation.[25]

In a similar fashion, in August 2018, the Trump administration cancelled its contribution to the UN Relief and Works Agency (UNRWA), the body that aids Palestinian refugees, citing disagreements with the way in which UNRWA defines refugees for the purposes of its programmes, anger at what it characterises as unjust criticism of the US by Palestinians, and dissatisfaction with the levels of funding provided to UNRWA by other states, referencing

[22] 'UN peacekeeping missions at risk over $2 bln budget gap', *France 24*, 15 January 2019, available at www.france24.com/en/20190115-un-peacekeeping-missions-risk-over-2-bln-budget-gap.

[23] 'UN "running out of cash" and facing urgent cuts, warns chief', *Guardian*, 27 July 2018, available at www.theguardian.com/global-development/2018/jul/27/un-running-out-of-cash-and-facing-urgent-cuts-warns-chief-antonio-guterres.

[24] 'Cutoff of U.S. Money Leads UNESCO to Slash Programs and Seek Emergency Aid', *New York Times*, 12 October 2012, A6.

[25] 'U.S. and Israel officially withdraw from UNESCO', *PBS*, 1 January 2019, available at www. pbs.org/newshour/politics/u-s-and-israel-officially-withdraw-from-unesco.

in particular Saudi Arabia, the United Arab Emirates and Kuwait.[26] Since the US was by far the largest donor to UNRWA – contributing around $350 million a year, over a quarter of its annual budget[27] – this represents a considerable blow, and has attracted criticism from a wide range of sources for increasing hardship in the region and potentially bringing more instability. It appears that the cut-off in funding is aimed both at discouraging an eventual return of Palestinians to Israel, and pressuring the Palestinian leadership to re-engage with the Trump administration's peace plans for the Middle East, discussions having been broken off following the administration's relocation of the US embassy in Israel from Tel Aviv to Jerusalem.[28]

Arguably, the UN as a whole has been vulnerable to being undermined by its largest financial sponsor since Donald Trump assumed the US presidency at the beginning of 2017, consistent with the administration's general retreat from multilateralism in pursuit of its 'America First' strategy (see chapter nine). However, an enhanced belligerence towards the UN has been evident since the appointment in April 2018 of John Bolton to the post of US National Security Adviser. A former US ambassador to the UN (from 2005–06, during the tenure of George W Bush), Bolton has long been contemptuous of the organisation. Along with the International Criminal Court (see chapter six), the UN is viewed by Bolton as a potential threat to US sovereignty and he has frequently railed against what he characterises as both its over-intrusiveness into national affairs and its inefficiency, having once infamously remarked that if the UN's headquarters in New York 'lost 10 stories, it wouldn't make a bit of difference'.[29] In addition to the defunding of UNRWA and UNESCO, and the US's withdrawal from the latter agency, this more hostile attitude has led the country to withdraw from the UN Human Rights Council (see chapter six). There have also been suggestions that the Trump administration is seeking to downgrade the role of UN ambassador (the new proposed appointee being Kelly Knight Craft) and bring it more under the control of Bolton and US Secretary of State Mike Pompeo.[30]

[26] 'Trump administration to end U.S. funding to U.N. program for Palestinian refugees', *Washington Post*, 30 August 2018, available at www.washingtonpost.com/world/national-security/trump-administration-to-end-us-funding-to-un-program-for-palestinian-refugees/2018/08/30/009d9bc6-ac64-11e8-b1da-ff7faa680710_story.html?utm_term=.05f09df1470b.

[27] 'U.S. to End All Funding to U.N. Agency That Aids Palestinian Refugees', *Foreign Policy*, 28 August 2018, available at https://foreignpolicy.com/2018/08/28/middle-east-palestinian-israel-pompeo-trump-kushner-u-s-to-end-all-funding-to-u-n-agency-that-aids-palestinian-refugees.

[28] ibid.

[29] Cited in, for example, 'A Short Guide to John Bolton's Government Career', *The Atlantic*, 23 March 2018, available at www.theatlantic.com/international/archive/2018/03/john-bolton/556346.

[30] See, for example, 'Trump's New Pick for UN Ambassador Has Zero Foreign-Policy Credentials', *The Nation*, 10 December 2018, available at www.thenation.com/article/heather-nauert-united-nations-ambassador-trump, and 'Trump picks US ambassador to Canada for UN ambassador', *CNN*, 23 February 2019, available at https://edition.cnn.com/2019/02/22/politics/trump-nomination-un-ambassador-kelly-knight-craft/index.html.

All of this serves to demonstrate the political constraints within which the UN is inevitably forced to operate, and the precariousness of its situation (especially from the viewpoint of financial viability) when it attracts the wrath of the government of its most powerful member.

V. The UN Charter: A Constitution for the World?

The entry into force of the UN Charter in 1945 marked a watershed in the development of international law, so that it is not too fanciful to speak of an era BC (before the Charter had been adopted) and the period that came after. Although, on one level, the Charter is simply another treaty,[31] one of the thousands that have now been concluded between various states parties, its special status and contents, and the way in which it has subsequently been viewed and interpreted, set it apart from these other instruments. As a result, the Charter is best viewed as a sort of 'uber' treaty, unusual in terms of the sheer number of states that have ratified it (there are now 193 state parties to the Charter, the vast majority of the world's nations[32]), and also because of the purposes and principles it enshrines, which have led many to characterise it as a supranational constitution.

The Charter can be said to resemble a constitution in two senses of the word: in the narrow sense of representing the constituting document of the UN organisation itself (establishing the UN's various bodies and setting out their roles and responsibilities), but also in the wider sense of incorporating the fundamental principles by which the international community is to govern itself. Moreover, just as, at the domestic level, a state's constitution is likely to evolve and find itself subject to qualification and differing interpretations over time, so the UN Charter has developed in a number of significant ways since

[31] A treaty, as defined by Art 2 of the Vienna Convention on the Law of Treaties 1969, is 'an international agreement concluded between States in written form and governed by international law, whether embodied in a single instrument or in two or more related instruments and whatever its particular designation'.

[32] South Sudan was the last state to join the UN, after it seceded from Sudan in July 2011. In addition to states that have been granted full membership of the UN, the UNGA can, by means of a resolution, grant observer status to other states and organisations. As the 'observer' tag indicates, such states or entities are not permitted to participate fully in the activities of the Assembly – in particular, they are not allowed a vote on substantive issues – but they have a limited right to speak in debates and to sponsor and sign resolutions and table amendments. There are currently two non-member states with permanent observer status in the GA: the Holy See and Palestine (such status having been conferred on the latter by a General Assembly vote in November 2012). There are also a number of intergovernmental organisations and other non-state entities that have been awarded observer status by both the UNGA and ECOSOC, such as the EU.

it first came into existence almost 75 years ago, and not always in directions foreseen or approved of by its framers.

In terms of structure, the UN Charter consists of 111 articles divided into 19 chapters.[33] Chapter I records the purposes and principles of the organisation; Chapter II notes the criteria for membership; Chapter III lists the principal organs of the UN; Chapters IV and V describe the powers and functions of the UN's two most important organs – the UNGA and the UNSC; Chapter VI deals with the peaceful settlement of disputes; Chapter VII (probably the most important part of the Charter) details the powers of the UNSC in relation to combating threats to the peace, breaches of the peace and acts of aggression; Chapter VIII deals with regional security arrangements; Chapters IX and X are devoted to economic and social matters, including the establishment of the Economic and Social Council; Chapters XI to XIII set out the arrangements for non-self-governing territories (ie those territories that had not yet achieved either self-governance or full independence, and which, as a result of decolonisation, would more than double the number of UN state members over the course of the next two decades); Chapters XIV and XV provide for, respectively, the establishment of the ICJ and the Secretariat; and Chapters XVI to XIX deal with a number of miscellaneous and other matters, including the procedure for making amendments to the Charter. Appended to the Charter, and consisting of a further 70 articles, is the statute of the ICJ.

The purposes of the UN, as set out in Article 1 of the Charter, include the maintenance of peace; the development of friendly relations based on the principle of equal rights and self-determination; the achievement of international cooperation in the resolution of international problems, together with the promotion of human rights and fundamental freedoms; and functioning as a centre for harmonising international action to attain these goals.

The overriding objective of the UN, therefore, enshrined in the very first line of the very first article of the Charter, is the maintenance of international peace and security. The other main purposes may at first seem tangential to this central mission of preventing further war and bloodshed, but were actually deemed by many to be vital to its success. And, in the years since the Charter was adopted, all other goals that the organisation has pursued, from attempts to improve the living standards of the poorest citizens of the global South, to efforts to persuade the rich, industrialised northern states to reduce their carbon emission levels so as to combat the problem of global warming, have arguably been intended to contribute to this overarching aim: the creation of a more peaceful and stable world.

The UN and its members also promise, under Article 2 of the Charter, to abide by certain fundamental principles in attempting to fulfil the purposes

---

[33] A full copy of the Charter can be viewed on the UN's website at www.un.org/en/sections/un-charter/un-charter-full-text.

of the organisation. Here, a great deal of emphasis is placed on the equality of member states and, as a corollary of this, the importance of respecting one another's autonomy and not attempting to compromise the independence of another nation. Consequently, it is affirmed that the UN 'is based on the principle of the sovereign equality of all its Members' (Article 2(1)), and that state members are to desist from employing 'the threat or use of force against the territorial integrity or political independence of any State' (Article 2(4)). With the exception of measures taken to enforce the peace under Chapter VII of the Charter, the UN is not 'to intervene in matters which are essentially within the domestic jurisdiction of any state', nor can it compel states 'to submit such matters to settlement' (Article 2(7)). In addition, states pledge to carry out their obligations under the Charter in good faith (Article 2(2)) and to settle their disputes in a peaceful and just manner (Article 2(3)). Furthermore, states are to assist the UN with any action it takes under the Charter and, conversely, are to refrain from helping any state against which the organisation 'is taking preventive or enforcement action' (Article 2(5)). Finally, the UN is to be responsible for ensuring that states which do not belong to the organisation nevertheless comply with its principles 'so far as may be necessary for the maintenance of international peace and security' (Article 2(6)).

The Charter has several features that have led to its being hailed as a global constitution. Most obviously, it sets out the basic purposes and principles that states are to comply with, particularly in relation to matters of peace and security. To a certain extent, therefore, it embodies a rudimentary form of governance for the international community, much as a state's constitution incorporates guiding principles that the nation's inhabitants and institutions are to respect for the good of the community as a whole. It is even possible to map out, if somewhat sketchily, the ways in which certain of the UN's principal organs correspond to major constitutional bodies commonly found at the domestic level. Thus, the UNSC is described as having both a legislative function (albeit limited to matters of peace and security) and an executive role, being responsible for the enforcement of measures designed to maintain peace and stability in the international realm. Meanwhile, the adjudicative function naturally falls (however imperfectly in comparison with national and regional courts) to the ICJ.

In common with a domestic constitution, the Charter also lays claim to being a superior source of law. Under Article 103, member states' obligations under the Charter are to take precedence over their obligations under any other international agreement. It is also, as with a state's constitution, difficult to make any changes to the Charter, since Article 108 provides that any amendments must be approved by two-thirds of the members of the UNGA, and then ratified by two-thirds of the members of the UN, including all the permanent members of the UNSC.

Unusually, the Charter also purports to exercise governmental functions in respect of all nations, at least as far as matters of peace and security are concerned. Hence, under Article 2(6), even those states that have not rati-fied the Charter and are not members of the UN are nevertheless obliged to comply with the principles of the Charter to the extent that this is neces-sary for the preservation of international peace and security. This is in stark contrast to its predecessor, the Covenant of the League of Nations, which purported to bind only those states that were members of the organisation. Furthermore, where a non-member state has concluded an agreement with a member state, it may find that, by virtue of Article 103, the latter is compelled to disregard that agreement in so far as it conflicts with an obligation imposed under the Charter. Again, this contrasts markedly with the comparable provi-sion of the League's Covenant, which required members simply to use their best efforts to extricate themselves from any treaty provisions concluded with a non-member that conflicted with an obligation under the Covenant. On the other hand, and more positively from a non-member state's point of view, all member states are prohibited, by Article 2(4), from using force against any other nation, whether that nation belongs to the UN or not. Although, in practice, these provisions of the Charter are of diminishing importance as more and more states have ratified the document and become part of the UN system, it still serves to highlight the unusual and constitutional-like nature of the Charter when compared with a conventional treaty. Similarly, the process for amending the treaty also represents a constraint on state sovereignty: although treaties can normally be altered only if all relevant parties consent, an amendment to the Charter would, under Article 108, be valid even if one-third of the UN membership (minus one) objected to the proposed change.

Even the choice of the word 'Charter' itself, as in the case of Roosevelt and Churchill's Atlantic Charter, seems intended to signal that this was no ordinary international agreement, but one that was intended to have particu-lar significance for the global community. More striking still, perhaps, is the language employed in the document's preamble. Eschewing the conventional phrasing employed to introduce a treaty ('The High Contracting Parties'), the drafters instead opted for 'We the peoples' in conscious imitation of the opening of the US Constitution.[34] The effect was to shift the spotlight from the states themselves onto their citizens, heralding the transformation that was to take place in the international legal regime in the post-war world, in which individuals and peoples would begin to take their place alongside states as fitting subjects of international law, and the notion of state sovereignty, in spite of the due deference accorded to it in the Charter (Article 2(7)), would increasingly find itself subject to qualification.

---

[34] On the constitutional significance of the word 'charter' and the resemblance between the UN Charter's introductory words and those of the US Constitution, see Bardo Fassbender, 'The United Nations Charter as Constitution of the International Community' (1998) 36 *Columbia Journal of Transnational Law* 529, 579–80.

The principle of self-determination embodied in Article 1(2) of the Charter was to have particular resonance in the decades following 1945. Inserted at the behest of the US and the USSR, and resisted by the old colonial empires of Britain and France, this principle was to be seized on by independence movements in the global South, and proclaimed as a right – which indeed it did become.

The deliberately vaguely worded 'respect for human rights and for fundamental freedoms' eventually included in Article 1(3) was also to have a profound effect on the international legal landscape in the years that followed the signing of the Charter, notwithstanding the inability of the great powers to agree on exactly what those rights should be, or whether economic and social rights should, or even could, be granted the same status as civil and political rights. This seemingly innocuous phrase marked the first step on the road towards the creation of the so-called International Bill of Rights, comprising the Universal Declaration of Human Rights of 1948 and the two International Covenants on Human Rights of 1966 (discussed in chapter six). Together, these three instruments have done much to promote the notion of the increasing 'constitutionalisation' of the international legal regime, in the sense of establishing many fundamental norms that are now deemed to be binding on states. They have also had the effect of greatly widening the ambit of international law, opening up the 'black box' of individual states in order to pay attention to the rights and interests of their citizens, a process that has also helped undermine traditional notions of state sovereignty. Although this view is not accepted by all (see chapter nine), it is important to remember the words of the Charter's preamble, where one of the preliminary assertions that is made about the UN is that it is intended: 'to establish conditions under which justice *and respect for the obligations arising from treaties and other sources of international law can be maintained'* (emphasis added).

VI. Conclusion

This chapter has presented a brief overview of the essential elements of the UN, primarily to enable readers to place in context references to the organisation and certain of its agencies that occur throughout the rest of the book.

The UN is such an enormous and complex institution that it is difficult to offer a succinct summary of its achievements and failures. Whereas most of us are only too aware of its weaknesses – principally its inability to prevent or resolve violent conflict between states, which has continued unabated despite the UN Charter's qualified prohibition on the use of force[35] – its successes are much less evident or celebrated. It has certainly played a role in promoting a more just and peaceful world, notwithstanding the inherent instability of a body made up of 193 member states, each supposedly sovereign, and each with its own agenda to pursue. That the outcome has been somewhat mixed, to put it mildly, should come as no surprise. As former UN Secretary-General Dag Hammarskjöld reportedly said, the UN 'was not created to take mankind to heaven, but to save humanity from hell'.[36]

---

[35] See Patrick CR Terry, 'The Return of Gunboat Diplomacy: How the West has Undermined the Ban on the Use of Force' (2019) 10 *Harvard National Security Journal* 75–147.

[36] UN Secretary-General, 'Remarks at Dag Hammarskjöld lecture: "Evolving Threats, Timeless Values: The United Nations in a Changing Global Landscape"', 30 March 2016, available at www.un.org/sg/en/content/sg/statement/2016-03-30/secretary-generals-remarks-dag-hammarskjöld-lecture-"evolving.

6

Human Rights in International Law

I. Introduction

This chapter must begin with a caveat. The human rights regime is immensely difficult to assess sensibly. If it is to be judged by the number of charters, covenants, treaties and conventions; the number of related institutions; the quantity of documentation and the amount of academic outpouring, then the regime is unbelievably impressive. Regrettably, the correlation between such evidence and the reality of human rights promotion and protection remains opaque. The human rights industry is highly productive, but to what extent the product secures individual human rights and ameliorates the unnecessary suffering of humankind is unknown and probably unknowable. Indeed, the fear might be that some of the product is actually dysfunctional in apparently guaranteeing rights which in fact remain elusive or even entirely unprotected. It remains true that it is almost impossible to judge the effect (if any) of the work and effort manifested in many human rights documents, particularly those emanating from the United Nations (UN). This should alert us to the fact that the concept of human rights is something more than an agreed means by which individuals' quality of life is to be improved. Underlying the apparently neutral and uncontroversial phrase 'human rights' is a maelstrom of philosophical and political ideas and disagreements that makes it remarkable that any consensus has ever been reached on the issue.

The chapter begins with a discussion as to what is meant by the phrase 'human rights': how such rights might be defined, by whom and with what significance. Initially, this may seem irrelevant to a discussion of human rights in international law, but, as we shall see, one of the primary difficulties in enforcing human rights at the international level arises precisely from this lack of consensus as to what such rights are and how far they extend. We will then consider the politics of human rights, since the way in which different states, different governments and different peoples and religions seek to define human rights depends upon their political perspectives. It will be suggested that the end of the Cold War, and the proclaimed triumph of liberal capitalism, has directly affected the way in which human rights are viewed, with much greater emphasis being placed upon civil and political rights, at the expense of economic, social and cultural rights. In fact, this distinction between the two sets of rights is itself reflective of different political ideologies.

Having provided the background to the international law of human rights, we will then examine the role of the UN in the protection of human rights through the 'International Bill of Human Rights': that is, the Universal Declaration of Human Rights 1948 (UDHR), and the two covenants of 1966 – the International Covenant on Civil and Political Rights (ICCPR) and the International Covenant on Economic, Social and Cultural Rights (ICESCR) – both of which entered into force in 1976. We will also discuss a number of other important human rights conventions adopted under the UN's auspices, as well as briefly considering the development of regional rights protection. Finally, we will conclude with a discussion of the International Criminal Court (ICC), founded as a permanent forum in order to try individuals accused of the most serious human rights violations.

Whatever conclusions we reach on the international law of human rights, one point at least should be clear. The 'rise and rise of human rights', to borrow the title of Kirsten Sellars's book on the subject,[1] represented probably the most startling development in international law since the Second World War. In placing the protection of individuals at the heart of the international legal regime, the old 'state-centric' model of international law was seemingly changed forever. Perhaps the most remarkable effect of this was on the fundamental concept of sovereignty: by the twenty-first century, no state would have argued that how it treats its nationals was completely its own business. It is here that the work of non-governmental organisations (NGOs) has been particularly important in publicising human rights abuses and seeking to hold states accountable for these abuses. Nevertheless, it must be acknowledged that over the last few years more and more states have begun to treat 'human rights' as something of an optional extra in matters of domestic governance. Even more worryingly, this trend has not met with the universal opprobrium that might have been expected; rather, it has even led to serious discussion as to whether we are heading towards a 'post-human rights world'. The number of states now refusing to accept criticism of domestic human rights abuses has grown steadily, as evidenced

---

[1] Kirsten Sellars, *The Rise and Rise of Human Rights* (Stroud, Sutton Publishing, 2002).

by those states that either refuse to accept the jurisdiction of the ICC or have chosen to withdraw from it. This has been true both of states within which armed conflict has or is taking place, such as Syria, Yemen and the Democratic Republic of the Congo, and of states supporting such conflicts, either directly – such as Russia, Iran and Saudi Arabia – or indirectly, through the sale of arms and provision of logistical aid. Beyond this, some states are simply refusing to accept that their internal policies warrant international concern for the human rights of their citizens or residents, with China, Egypt, Israel, the Philippines, Turkey and Zimbabwe standing as clear examples.

Similarly, those provisions of the Geneva Conventions of 1949 (adopted the year after the Universal Declaration of Human Rights) that were intended to protect civilians in war and to guarantee the right of medical staff to work freely and safely in war zones have recently been widely ignored, on the supposed justification that hospitals may harbour enemy fighters. Even torture, clearly internationally proscribed, and equally clearly a peremptory norm of international law not subject to modification, has been touted as a necessary military option by some of the world's most powerful leaders.[2] Of course, the prohibition on torture was not always respected by states, but none had dared to openly praise it as a legitimate course of action.

Further evidence of a human rights regime in retreat is the dramatic decline in protection provided for refugees. Although space does not permit extensive discussion of international refugee law, it is clear that the rights guaranteed to those seeking political asylum, which originated in Article 14 of the Universal Declaration of Human Rights, have recently been ignored or abused, particularly by affluent states in Western Europe, North America and Australia. European nations, when faced with hundreds of thousands of asylum seekers and migrants, have refused entry – erecting physical barriers in the case of Hungary, and in other cases refusing to allow the docking of boats in which people are travelling. The conditions in which those who have entered Europe and are awaiting asylum decisions are kept is often deplorable, and the burden has fallen very unevenly, with Greece and Italy most adversely affected. These observations are not about refugee policy per se but rather point to a further decline in human rights protection.

---

[2] Shortly before assuming office in January 2017, President Trump, when asked whether he would sanction 'water-boarding', replied: 'I'd do much worse ... Don't tell me it doesn't work, torture works ... believe me, it works.' Cited in Imogen Foulkes, 'Are we heading towards a "post human rights world"?', *BBC News*, 30 December 2016. In similar fashion, Jair Bolsonaro, elected president of Brazil in October 2018, has made clear his belief in the acceptability of torture as a tool of governance, dedicating his vote to impeach former president Dilma Rouseff to the army chief who oversaw the programme under which she was tortured during Brazil's military dictatorship, and having stated in a television interview in 1999 that 'I am in favour of torture – you know that. And the people are in favour of it, too.' Cited in 'Jair Bolsonaro: Brazil's firebrand leader dubbed the Trump of the Tropics', *BBC News*, 31 December 2018.

Thus, it is difficult not to sympathise with a typographical error in a recent student essay referencing not the Universal Declaration but the Universal *Deceleration* of Human Rights.

II. What are Human Rights?

Practical lawyers might question the need for this section, and the next. However, unless an attempt is made to understand what is meant by human rights any appraisal of the role and effect of the international law of human rights is impossible. It is, of course, very difficult to isolate the concept of human rights from international law in general, and it will be argued that the two are not really separable. The political and ideological world that dictates international law also defines the reality of human rights. In this section, there are two separate but related questions that need to be raised. The first requires us to understand what is meant by 'human rights', and the second considers whether such rights must be seen as time- and culture-specific, or whether they are, as is generally asserted, universal. The answers to these questions have significant implications.

The term 'human rights' is normally used to refer to certain fundamental rights with which, it is argued, all human beings are, or should be, endowed. Consequently, the concept of human rights has close links with natural law: that is, the theory that, beyond the laws enacted by people, there are natural or divine laws with which these created laws must conform. On this view, human rights are either God-given or are something that human beings possess *qua* human beings: ie, simply by virtue of their humanity.

With a divine explanation, there can be no rational debate. Religion is about faith, not susceptible either to proof or disproof through reason. The preamble to the US Declaration of Independence of 1776 asserts that: 'We hold these truths to be self-evident: That all men are created equal; that they are endowed by their Creator with certain unalienable rights; that among these are life, liberty, and the pursuit of happiness.' Such an appeal to the divine origins of human rights is, however, possible only when the constituency to which it is addressed is less than religiously diverse. When the UDHR was in the process of being drafted, not all participants accepted this as the correct philosophical basis on which the rights were to be premised, and certainly not the USSR, with its state commitment to atheism. As a result, the words chosen to introduce the UDHR articulate a secular version of natural rights: 'Whereas recognition of the inherent dignity and of the equal and inalienable rights of all members of the human family is the foundation of freedom, justice and peace in the world.'

This approach entails some difficulties. On the one hand, the first line of the UDHR amounts to nothing more than an assertion, which is no more amenable to proof than the opening words of the Declaration of Independence. On the other hand, it may be argued that the authority of the UDHR derives not from any appeal to natural law but from the consensus of the international community (although this was not absolute, since eight states abstained in the vote to adopt the Declaration). Moreover, there can be no doubt that 'human rights' exist as a social fact. In other words, although quite *how* anything may be proved to be a human right remains unresolved, the reality is that such concepts acquire their meaning from the fact that they receive constant recognition in the language and effect of international diplomacy and relations.

The second issue is related to the first. The UDHR describes itself as universal, and yet almost everyone would agree that, as drafted, it is clearly time- and place-specific, embodying a determination to prevent a recurrence of the horrific abuses to which Nazism had led. Furthermore, although its provisions may seem largely unexceptionable, some, especially those concerned with economic and social rights, would certainly not have found favour with many post-Cold War governments in the West. And, as Cassese observes:

> On the whole, the view of human rights expressed in it [the UDHR] is Western. More space and importance are allotted to civil and political rights than to economic, social, and cultural rights, and no mention at all is made of the rights of peoples. The position taken with regard to colonized peoples, who had been partially or completely denied their right to freedom, was purely formal. Nor did the Declaration say anything specific about economic inequalities between States (although today many commentators cite with increasing frequency Article 28 whereby 'Everyone is entitled to an international and social order in which the rights and freedoms set forth in the Declaration can be fully realized'). In addition one could note that the Declaration did not consider the fact that some States, being underdeveloped, faced special problems when trying to guarantee certain basic rights, such as those to work, to education, to suitable housing etc.[3]

Consequently, there has been a continuing debate between so-called 'cultural relativists' and 'universalists', with the former arguing that the concept of human rights must necessarily vary from culture to culture (hence nothing can be written in stone as irrevocably permanent), while, for the latter, the concept of *human* rights makes sense only if they are granted to all individuals, regardless of culture, solely on the basis of their membership of the human race. The former seems reasonable but the latter desirable.

We would argue that this debate is less important than it might seem. It will be significant only if one believes that the concept of human rights carries with it some 'magical' quality over and beyond its existence as a social fact. In our view, the significance of the concept lies in the weight implied by international acceptance of the appellation, and much of the struggle for

---

[3] Antonio Cassese, *International Law*, 2nd edn (Oxford, OUP, 2005) 381.

human rights is about seeking this acceptance. This seems particularly clear in relation to so-called 'third-generation' rights (the first-generation rights being civil and political, and those of the second generation being economic, social and cultural – although such a hierarchical ordering is itself reflective of political preferences). Third-generation rights are said to include group rights as opposed to individual rights, exemplified by the claimed right to development and the right to self-determination. Whatever objections there may be to these rights being described as 'human rights' (and there are many), once there is overwhelming acceptance among the international community that they are to be regarded as human rights, it makes little sense to oppose the categorisation.[4]

The philosophical meaning to be ascribed to human rights has preoccupied many, while others have attempted to use the term in order to lend weight to their demands. Some have argued that 'human rights' must be clearly definable, and specify both the holders of the rights and those having reciprocal duties to provide them. This reasonable but narrow view, much favoured by Western governments and legal philosophers, has not found favour in the global South, where states have invoked the concept of human rights in order to emphasise that their economic demands are made as of right and are not merely requests for charity.

The problem of what meaning is to be attributed to 'human rights' can (at least to some extent) be avoided by accepting that such rights are social constructs, and exist as human rights because of the international community's belief in them as such. They are no less real because of this.

III. The Politics of Human Rights

The protection of human rights is conventionally portrayed as an objectively desirable, and politically neutral, goal. In reality, however, the whole area is imbued with politics and ideology. Human rights are also often depicted (in the West, at least) as a gift that democratic states bestow on those nations less fortunate than themselves. However, as was observed in the last section, the history of human rights is in fact much shorter than is often appreciated, with the contemporary incarnation of the concept scarcely predating the Second World War. Indeed, it was revulsion and incredulity at the fact that a second global conflict could have followed the first so quickly, and a consequent desire to construct a new world order in which the atrocities of the war and the Holocaust could not be repeated, that helps explain the

---

[4] For further argument on this point, see Wade Mansell and Joanne Scott, 'Why Bother about a Right to Development?' (1994) 21 *Journal of Law and Society* 171.

post-war enthusiasm for deploying a new type of vocabulary, in which the rights of individuals, not states, would take pride of place.

The UDHR was very largely the handiwork of the victorious allies, especially the US. However, it was not an isolated project. At the end of the war, the US laid out its plans for the brave new world it hoped to bring forth. This was a world of economic liberalism, in which new international financial institutions would be created to encourage free trade, and a 'United Nations' (originally to have been called 'Associated Powers') would provide global security and stability. Human rights was but one aspect of this overall plan, even if it did provide the moral foundation. The preparation of the UDHR was not, even then, an easy matter. There were three obvious problems, and many more less obvious ones. The first main difficulty centred on the disparity in ideological outlook between the first world and the second (including the so-called socialist states of the Soviet bloc) in terms of the centrality of the individual and the pre-eminence to be accorded to civil and political rights. The second was that, for states with an Islamic population (in this case, Saudi Arabia), the notion of enshrining a right to change one's religion was completely unacceptable, and indeed the very concept of a Universal Declaration seemed incompatible with the supremacy of the Koran. The third involved a right of participation in government and the free movement of people, which was complete anathema to apartheid South Africa (let alone the prohibition on discrimination). Notwithstanding this, the Declaration was accepted by the General Assembly in Paris in 1948 by a vote of 48 in favour, none against and eight abstentions (the Soviet bloc, Saudi Arabia and South Africa).

In retrospect, however, what seems most remarkable about the document is the inclusion of what would come to be known as economic and social rights. Amazingly, these provisions received the support of, as Sellars puts it, 'everyone from Soviet Stalinists and Latin American socialists to British Keynesians and American Democrats'.[5] These provisions would, towards the end of the twentieth century and into the twenty-first, command less and less support from the governments of states pursuing a liberal economic agenda. Their very presence had repercussions that were unforeseen.

Almost immediately, however, the objectivity of the human rights concept was called into question, as the Declaration began to be deployed to serve political ends. With the onset of the Cold War, human rights discourse became largely determined by the propaganda advantages the opposing sides could derive from it.

The UN's earliest days were dominated by the Allied Powers, whose status lent them a moral superiority which they exploited in the organisation. Even at this period, however, the first ideological battles took place between the US

---

[5] Sellars, *Rise of Human Rights* (2002) 21.

and its allies and the Soviet Union and its. Perhaps to the surprise of Western delegates, they found it difficult to occupy the moral high ground in arguing for the protection of civil and political rights in the face of concerted opposition from both the 'second' socialist world and the 'third' (poor) world. As the proclaimed right to self-determination gained increasing prominence, so colonialism came to be vilified and also identified with something approaching racism – white colonial masters subjugating non-white colonial peoples. Nor was it solely the 'Old World' European powers that were vulnerable to such attacks: the US, too, began to take its first steps towards the abolition of segregation in response to international criticism. Hence, in the 1950s and 1960s, the West faced accusations of double standards in relation to the granting of civil and political rights, as well as condemnation for failing to pay sufficient attention to economic and social rights, including the ability of individuals to access basic food and shelter.

The demise of the USSR in 1991, coupled with the completion of the decolonisation process some years earlier, had a decisive impact on human rights rhetoric in the corridors of power. As a neoliberalist economic orthodoxy gained ascendancy, so the importance accorded to economic and social rights declined, at least in so far as they were incompatible with the policies sanctioned and often insisted upon by the international financial institutions. Adopted in 1981, the African Charter on Human and Peoples' Rights, with its inclusion of economic, social and cultural rights, its emphasis on social obligations, and its incorporation of peoples' rights based upon collective community interest, quickly seemed out of date in comparison with the new orthodoxy, and was certainly barely compatible with it.

A first conclusion, therefore, about the politics of human rights must be that the subjects of popularity are negotiable depending upon competing or dominant ideologies. The popularity of economic rights represented in a claimed right to a New International Economic Order, as expressed in a General Assembly resolution[6] (or even a *human* right to development), now seem hopelessly unfashionable. Need has not changed but the way in which it is talked about certainly has.

What can also be inferred from the above is that a state's rhetoric (the way it talks) about human rights will reflect its own political ideology. This is an obvious but important point. There is an evident tension between the proclaimed universality of human rights and the particularity with which they are chosen. Liberal democratic states, including the US and many Western European nations, laid stress upon civil and political rights (as evidenced in the drafting of the European Convention on Human Rights (ECHR)), while regarding the social provisions of the UDHR as inappropriate for comparable protection or even substantive recognition. This led to the abandonment of a holistic approach to rights protection, as Western states insisted that there

---

[6] UNGA Resolution 3201 (S-VI) of 1 May 1974.

were simply fundamental differences between what came to be portrayed as two types of rights. Civil and political rights, it was argued, are clearly defined concepts, susceptible to adjudication and enforcement, and can be implemented immediately, since they cost little or nothing to provide. In contrast, social and economic rights were said to be capable only of gradual realisation, to be very much dependent on the wealth of the state concerned, and to involve decisions about resource allocation that are inherently political and therefore not amenable to judicial enforcement.

In reality, we would argue that there is no sharp distinction between the two sets of rights. Courts have shown themselves perfectly willing to hand down judgments in relation to education, housing, health and other economic and social issues (this has been particularly true in post-apartheid South Africa, where courts have taken their cue from the country's remarkably progressive constitution), while the right to a fair trial – a classic civil and political right – is dependent upon the existence of an effective and independent judicial system, including the appropriate infrastructure to support this, which can be time-consuming and costly to establish. Nevertheless, the dichotomy persists, and, in the West at least, the view increasingly promulgated was that economic, social and cultural rights are at best desirable and at worst Utopian or even counterproductive because of their threat to the perceived benefits of a free-market economy.

In fact, when economic and social rights have been referenced in a Western context, this has frequently involved advocating a number of entitlements that prop up the free market (often across national frontiers), with the overriding issue being framed as one of safeguarding the autonomy of the individual against the unwarranted interference of the state. Hence, the emphasis has been on opposing the expropriation of property and investments (especially that which is foreign-owned), supporting free movement of labour, and seeking the abolition of capital controls that prevent the unrestricted flow of currencies across borders. This entails not so much a repudiation or downplaying of economic and social rights as their reorientation in order to serve the needs of the market. As Quinn Slobodian has pointed out:

> Rather than reject human rights outright, the neoliberal tendency has been to undermine social democratic interpretations of human rights and international law while simultaneously co-opting them to cover clearly capitalist prerogatives. To say this was (or is) a critique of 'social and economic rights' would be misleading, because the free movement of capital, goods, and labor was just as much a social and economic right as the demand for social security, employment, or nourishment.[7]

Even the recipients of economic and social rights are subject to mutation in a market-oriented context, so that, in effect, certain human rights have

---

[7] Quinn Slobodian, *Globalists: The End of Empire and the Birth of Neoliberalism* (Cambridge, MA, Harvard University Press, 2018) 136.

now been bestowed on companies and other entities,[8] recalling former US presidential candidate Mitt Romney's *cri de cœur* during the 2012 election campaign: 'Corporations are people, my friend.'

The Western, individualistic approach to human rights was, of course, countered by collectivist states, which asserted the importance of distributive justice and the need to ensure the participation of individuals in the collective life of the state. (This tension between the rights belonging to citizens collectively and those enjoyed by the individual, and which is superior or deserving of priority, forms part of a long-standing debate in human rights discourse; in 'On the Jewish Question', Marx, in discussing the Declaration of the Rights of Man of 1793, drew a distinction between those rights he viewed as exercisable by people in their role as citizens – that is, rights held in common with others, such as the right to hold public officials to account – and those he saw as exercisable only in an individual capacity (such as the right to own property), which he believed fostered isolation and selfishness, and served only to weaken the bonds of society.[9]) Regrettably, and in spite of the fact that a level of economic and social security was enjoyed by the inhabitants of many of these collectivist states (something which came to be accepted only with the dramatic decline in the living standards of the poorest people living in the former USSR), their governments refused to provide any meaningful civil and political rights, which were depicted as incompatible with a 'socialist' property regime.

Meanwhile, the rise of the 'tiger economies' of south-east Asia led to the formation of a third perspective on human rights protection, according to which the safeguarding of individual civil liberties was not necessarily compatible with the needs of development. Malaysian Prime Minister Mahathir Mohamad, in particular, has in the past expressed the view that 'the Asian tradition' gave rise to relativist positions on human rights that are irreconcilable even with the UDHR. If such arguments seem manifestly specious, and designed only to justify wilful human rights abuses, this is less important (in the sense of comprehending the human rights world) than recognising that adopting such a position reflects a particular power structure with particular goals: one dedicated to economic 'progress' (that is, increased economic growth) both for its own sake and for the sake of national pride. Whether or not such 'progress' is ever adversely affected by protecting such rights as those concerned with freedom of speech or freedom from arbitrary detention remains highly questionable.

---

[8] ibid 142–43, describing how bilateral investment treaties, drawing on earlier proposals for an international code aimed at protecting foreign investors, defined 'nationals' entitled to compensation in the event of expropriation as including 'any other company or association, with or without legal personality'.

[9] See Jeremy Waldron's discussion of Marx's attitude to rights in 'On the Jewish Question' in Jeremy Waldron (ed) *Nonsense upon Stilts: Bentham, Burke and Marx on the Rights of Man* (London and New York, Methuen, 1987) 119–50.

Furthermore, prioritising one kind of right while downgrading or denigrating the other is to ignore the fact that they are interdependent and, ultimately, indivisible. This was recognised by those members of the UN General Assembly who argued that both sets of rights should be enshrined in a single covenant rather than in the two separate instruments that were eventually adopted: 'Without economic, social and cultural rights, civil and political rights might be purely nominal in character; without civil and political rights, economic, social and cultural rights could not be long ensured.'[10]

Another factor in the politics of human rights concerns the distinction between those international institutions that operate under the principle of sovereign equality, and hence each nation is allocated one vote (such as the General Assembly), and those where the power of each voting state affects the strength of its vote (the Security Council, where the permanent five members possess the power of veto, and the International Monetary Fund and the World Bank, in which votes are weighted in accordance with the financial contributions made by member states). As the numbers in the General Assembly grew, so the Assembly's resolutions became increasingly independent of the wishes of the great powers. Interests diverged, with the concerns and preoccupations of the 'underdeveloped' newly admitted states very much at odds with those of the majority of the UN's founder members. This in turn affected the status of General Assembly resolutions. As Edward McWhinney, writing just as the Cold War came to an end, pertinently observed:

> The Third World majority in the United Nations, and their supporting jurists, argued that the General Assembly resolutions – adopted, as they invariably were, by overwhelming majorities, with only a few Western states holding out in the form of negative votes or abstention – effectively made new law. UN General Assembly resolutions would qualify, thereby, as new sources of international law, side by side with traditional or classical sources. As an abstract, *a priori*, legal issue, this debate over the new sources remains unsolved. Western and Soviet jurists have conceded, equally, that resolutions of the General Assembly, if adopted unanimously or at least with substantial intersystemic consensus – Western bloc, Soviet bloc and Third World [McWhinney was writing before the demise of the Soviet Union] – may acquire normative legal quality in their own right. This has clearly become the case by now, with most of the General Assembly resolutions on decolonisation, and self-determination of peoples, sovereignty over natural resources, and nuclear and general disarmament, however intransigent the last-ditch resistance of predominantly Western members may have been at the actual time of their adoption.[11]

---

[10] 'Annotations on the Text of the Draft International Convention on Human Rights', UN Doc A/2929 (1955), 7, para 8. Cited in Henry J Steiner, Philip Alston and Ryan Goodman, *International Human Rights in Context: Law, Politics, Morals* (Oxford, OUP, 2008) 272.

[11] Edward McWhinney, 'International Law' in Mary Hawkesworth and Maurice Hogan (eds), *Encyclopaedia of Government and Politics* (London, Routledge, 1992) 864.

These remarks now need to be approached with some caution. Although partially true, the failure (as regards their effect) of the resolutions concerning the 'New International Economic Order' and the 'human right to development', each of which received overwhelming assent in the General Assembly, indicates the continuing ability of the West generally, and the US in particular, to deny the status of law to unwelcome initiatives. It has certainly been the case that mere numerical superiority in terms of votes cast has brought little law-making power to the majority. Rather, true authority still lies with the Security Council, where democracy is subordinated to power, or at least power as it existed in 1945. The role of the General Assembly remains as defined in the Charter, to make recommendations to state members or to the Security Council (Article 11(1)). Article 12 provides that, while the Security Council is exercising 'in respect of any dispute or situation the functions assigned to it' by the Charter, the General Assembly shall not make any recommendations with regard to that dispute or situation unless the Security Council asks it to do so. The power to recommend rather than to decide is that of the General Assembly. Thus, the final ability to define human rights content does not lie with the majority of states.

What, however, of the effect of the international financial institutions themselves on the politics of human rights? In chapter three, we considered the role of the IMF in constraining any real exercise of self-determination, but it also has a part to play in restricting the ability of states (especially poorer ones) to fulfil human rights obligations – particularly those concerning economic, social and cultural rights. The most obvious ways in which this has been effected has been through the terms and conditions attached to IMF loans granted to states in order 'to correct maladjustments in their balance of payments', as per Article 1 of the IMF's Articles of Agreement, which sets out the purposes of the organisation. Obviously, the borrowing states were those whose debt burden had become unsustainable. Again, according to the IMF's Articles, such loans were to be made 'under adequate safeguards' so as to ensure that states were not forced to resort to 'measures destructive of national or international prosperity'. As was observed in chapter three, since the 1980s, these 'safeguards' have taken the form of 'structural adjustment lending' or 'conditionality', in which states are obliged to introduce policies that conform to the IMF's fiscal and macroeconomic mandate, which in turn is heavily shaped by its most powerful contributors.

There is little consensus on the effectiveness of the prescribed measures, which are informed by an economic ideology that eschews state intervention. Consequently, many policies aimed at making life possible for the most indigent of the population, such as subsidised food, health care, and transport, have been anathema to the IMF, which generally requires their elimination as part of the economic policy reforms it insists indebted countries implement in return for its loans. (Observers of the recent European 'bail-out' funds provided to such indebted European countries as Greece and Cyprus may recognise this 'standard-indebtedness-medicine'.) Structural adjustment has just one central goal: the eradication of unsustainable indebtedness. According to IMF orthodoxy, this can be achieved only by recognising the superiority of the market over central economic planning. Evidence for this is, in the view of most structural adjustment sceptics (ourselves included), very difficult to discover. The so-called Asian tigers, which are often hailed as exemplars of the success of IMF policy prescriptions, opted to pursue, at least initially, state-led forms of development.

But even were it to be satisfactorily demonstrated that these policies had achieved their limited objectives, many might still reasonably conclude that the human cost of their implementation is unacceptably high, since the wrong people (the most impoverished section of the nations in question) are effectively being called upon to repay loans that have brought them no advantage whatsoever.

What is incontrovertible is the effect that they have had upon states' obligations to nurture their citizens' economic, social and cultural well-being. This has given rise to the paradoxical situation in which, while certain organs of the UN – principally the General Assembly and the Economic and Social Council (ECOSOC) – have sought to promote a conception of human rights broad enough to encompass economic, social and cultural rights, the IMF and the World Bank (also agencies of the UN) have become devotees of an approach which, whether wittingly or not, has undermined those very rights. Indeed, faithful adherence to IMF conditionality by states that are parties to UN human rights instruments, especially the International Covenant on Economic, Social and Cultural Rights (ICESCR; discussed below), will almost certainly entail the states in question violating their obligations under such instruments. For example, implementing IMF-mandated programmes that lead to higher unemployment will lead to non-compliance with Article 6 of the ICESCR, which guarantees the right to work – and, in a domino effect illustrative of the interdependence of many rights, if a person cannot work, or can work only intermittently or for a very low wage (in violation of Article 7 of the ICESCR), this is likely to impair his or her ability to access food, housing and a 'continuous improvement in living conditions' (guaranteed under Article 11(1)), especially in those states where there is little in the way of state-subsidised welfare provision, or such provision is heavily curtailed at the insistence of the IMF. This in turn means that it is unlikely that the individual affected will enjoy 'the highest standard of mental and physical health' (enshrined in Article 12(1)), with any deterioration in health making it more difficult to work, and hence more likely that the person concerned and his or her family will suffer hunger (violating Article 11(2)), and so entering a downward spiral from which it is difficult to escape. Impoverished families are also much less likely to educate their children (in contravention of Article 13(1)), owing either to a lack of affordability where free education is not provided by the state and/or to the fact that children are required to work in order to support the family (falling foul, in the vast majority of cases, of Article 10(3), which protects children and young persons from economic and social exploitation: a right also enshrined in Article 32(1) of the Convention on the Rights of the Child). The withdrawal of children from formal education in turn impacts disproportionately on women, with male children generally given priority if any schooling is available (thus infringing Article 10 of the Convention on the Elimination of all Forms of Discrimination against Women), which in due course leads to greater poverty for women, malnutrition, and an increase in deaths in childbirth, stillbirths and child mortality rates (violating Article 12(2)). As Anne Orford has pointed out, women tend to bear the brunt of IMF policy prescriptions:

> Women ... have been described as the 'shock absorbers' of shock therapy and structural adjustment programmes, often the first to face the loss of employment security when the IMF or the World Bank require the public sector to reduce the number of employees, or when the workforce is casualized. Women are likely to be requested to pick up the burden of caring for sick, homeless or mentally ill family or community members when the state divests itself of those responsibiliites.[12]

Nor have economic, social and cultural rights as promulgated in the ICESCR and later conventions been the only casualties of IMF conditionality. Arguably, civil and political rights, and what Rodwan Abouharb and David Cingranelli have termed 'physical integrity rights'[13] – defined as 'rights not to be tortured, imprisoned for political reasons, disappeared, or murdered by one's government' – have also suffered. Hence, studying data from 131 developing countries for the period 1981 to 2003, Abouharb and Cingranelli note that:

> World Bank and IMF structural adjustment programs usually cause increased hardship for the poor, greater civil conflict, and more repression of human rights, resulting in a lower rate of economic development. ... The poor, organized labor, and other civil society groups protest these outcomes. Governments respond to challenges to their authority by murdering, imprisoning, torturing and disappearing more of their citizens.[14]

In more recent years, both the IMF and World Bank have expressed a willingness to modify their stances in response to criticism that their policies have an overly injurious effect on human rights. However, the aftermath of the global financial crisis saw standard IMF policy prescriptions again being applied

---

[12] Anne Orford, 'Globalization and the Right to Development' in Philip Alston (ed) *Peoples' Rights* (Oxford, OUP, 2005) 155.
[13] M. Rodwan Abouharb and David Cingranelli, *Human Rights and Structural Adjustment* (Cambridge, CUP, 2007) 30.
[14] ibid 4.

to the Western world, and to certain Eurozone members in particular. In return for providing bail-outs to certain states – most prominently, Greece, Ireland, Portugal and Cyprus – the Fund imposed conditions almost identical to those previously demanded of countries of the global South experiencing balance-of-payment difficulties. The same is now true in relation to Argentina and Pakistan. Whether or not such 'conditionality' ultimately achieves the desired outcome – improving a state's competitiveness to the point where it can borrow at relatively affordable rates from the private market once again – there is no doubt that its imposition conflicts with the social welfare economic policies traditionally pursued throughout much of continental Europe. Again, demands are being made that will necessarily result in a transfer of resources away from those most dependent on social spending, and, as explained above, this inevitably impacts on a state's ability to respect and nurture the economic, social and cultural rights of its citizens.

The point of this discussion is to demonstrate that 'human rights' is not, and never can be, a politically neutral concept. What dictates the terms of any debate about human rights is very often the political and economic interests and ideology of those making or rejecting demands in connection with such rights. We can also observe the division that has been created between civil and political rights and economic and social rights, notwithstanding the fact that these rights are in many ways interdependent. The West has been much more concerned with promoting the former, while often making the protection of the latter exceedingly difficult.

IV. The International Bill of Human Rights

The instruments that are together known as the International Bill of Human Rights trace their origins to the UN Charter. Although the references in the Charter to human rights are limited, they are nevertheless significant, and formed the basis for what followed. The Charter's preamble reaffirmed the 'faith in fundamental human rights, in the dignity and worth of the human person, in the equal rights of men and women', while one of the purposes of the UN Charter (set out in Article 1(3)) is:

> [T]o achieve international co-operation in solving international problems of an economic, social, cultural, or humanitarian character, and in promoting and encouraging respect for human rights and for fundamental freedoms for all without distinction as to race, sex, language, or religion.

This in turn is reinforced by Articles 55 and 56. Article 55 states that:

> With a view to the creation of conditions of stability and well-being which are necessary for peaceful and friendly relations among nations based on respect for

the principle of equal rights and self-determination of peoples, the United Nations shall promote:

a.   higher standards of living, full employment, and conditions of economic and social progress and development;

b.   solutions of international economic, social, health, and related problems; and international cultural and educational co-operation; and

c.   universal respect for, and observance of, human rights and fundamental freedoms for all without distinction as to race, sex, language, or religion.

Article 56 provides that:

All Members pledge themselves to take joint and separate action in co-operation with the Organization for the achievement of the purposes set forth in Article 55.

Article 55 is noteworthy for the way in which it combines the promotion of human rights and fundamental freedoms with economic and social goals. Article 68, one of the provisions of Chapter X of the Charter, dealing with the establishment of ECOSOC, gives this new body the task of setting up 'commissions in economic and social fields and for the promotion of human rights'. Initially, it was intended that the International Bill of Human Rights should consist of three documents: a declaration, a convention and a document concerned with implementation. On 10 December 1948, the General Assembly, sitting in Paris, adopted the UDHR and also asked the Commission on Human Rights (a body created by ECOSOC in 1946) to prepare drafts of the other two documents. From the outset, there was much discussion about the relationship between proclaimed civil and political human rights on the one hand, and economic, social and cultural rights on the other. As we saw in the last section, the debate was to a large extent ideological. All agreed that the rights were interrelated but quite how that relationship was to be encapsulated in legal instruments was the matter of fierce debate. In the sixth session of the General Assembly (1951/52), it was resolved to request that two separate covenants be prepared, one concentrating on civil and political rights and the other dealing with economic, social and cultural rights, but with as much duplication as possible. It then took until 1966 before the drafting of both covenants was completed and the instruments adopted, and a further 10 years, to 1976, before both covenants were able to attract enough ratifications to enter into force.

A.   The Universal Declaration of Human Rights

The UDHR was not intended to be a legal document. Nevertheless, owing to the disparate ideological outlooks of the member states that initially made up the UN (much less heterogeneous than now, but diverse enough, with democratic states, communist states, Islamic states and an apartheid state), it was extremely difficult to devise a wording on which all nations could agree. Of course, since it was merely a declaration, legal precision was not required: these were not articles that a court would have to interpret. Cassese suggests that the task involved finding the lowest common denominator of all states[15] (that is, the minimum to which all would be prepared to subscribe), but the eight abstentions in the final vote on the document demonstrates a significant amount of discontent with the final product. Nonetheless, the UDHR remains a remarkable document, and almost all states would now accept that its contents reflect their aims and aspirations. In retrospect, what seems most surprising, perhaps, is not that the 'communist' states merely abstained from, as opposed to voting against, a declaration that included numerous civil and political rights that they had no intention of accepting, but rather that the radical economic, social and cultural rights were acceptable to the US in particular. Such has been the widespread acceptance of the UDHR, that many of its provisions are now deemed to form part of customary international law, although this was never the aim. In the Proclamation of the Tehran International Conference on Human Rights of 1968, it was unanimously accepted that 'the Universal Declaration ... states a common understanding of the peoples of the world concerning the inalienable and inviolable rights of all members of the human family and constitutes an obligation for the members of the international community'. The Tehran Conference was followed by a further global conference on human rights held in Vienna in 1993. This resulted in the adoption of the Vienna Declaration and Programme of Action to further promote human rights worldwide, including the protection of the rights of women, children and indigenous peoples. The conference also led to the creation of the post of UN High Commissioner for Human Rights.

The UN Centre for Human Rights usefully summarises the provisions of the UDHR as follows:

Article 1   All human beings are born free and equal;
Article 2   Everyone is entitled to the same rights without discrimination of any kind;
Article 3   Everyone has the right to life, liberty, and security;
Article 4   No one shall be held in slavery or servitude;
Article 5   No one shall be subjected to torture or cruel or degrading treatment or punishment;
Article 6   Everyone has the right to be recognized everywhere as a person before the law;
Article 7   Everyone is equal before the law and has the right to equal protection of the law;
Article 8   Everyone has the right to justice [ie to an effective remedy for the violation of any fundamental right];

[15] Cassese, *International Law* (2005) 381.

Article 9   No one shall be arrested, detained, or exiled arbitrarily;

Article 10   Everyone has the right to a fair trial;

Article 11   Everyone has the right to be presumed innocent until proven guilty [and no-one to be held guilty of a penal offence for an act or omission that was not a penal offence at the time it was committed];

Article 12   Everyone has the right to privacy;

Article 13   Everyone has the right to freedom of movement and to leave and return to one's country;

Article 14   Everyone has the right to seek asylum from persecution;

Article 15   Everyone has the right to a nationality;

Article 16   All adults have the right to marry and found a family. Women and men have equal rights to marry, within marriage, and at its dissolution;

Article 17   Everyone has the right to own property [and not to be arbitrarily deprived of it];

Article 18   Everyone has the right to freedom of thought, conscience and religion;

Article 19   Everyone has the right to freedom of opinion and expression;

Article 20   Everyone has the right to peaceful assembly and association;

Article 21   Everyone has the right to take part in the government of one's country;

Article 22   Everyone has the right to social security and to the realization of the economic, social and cultural rights indispensable for dignity;

Article 23   Everyone has the right to work, to just conditions of work, to protection against unemployment, to equal pay for equal work, to sufficient pay to ensure a dignified existence for one's self and one's family, and the right to join a trade union;

Article 24   Everyone has the right to rest and leisure [including reasonable limits on hours worked and 'periodic holidays with pay'];

Article 25   Everyone has the right to a standard of living adequate for health and well-being, including food, clothing, housing, medical care and necessary social services;

Article 26   Everyone has the right to education [which shall include at least free and compulsory elementary education];

Article 27   Everyone has the right to participate freely in the cultural life of the community;

Article 28   Everyone is entitled to a social and international order in which these rights can be realized fully;

Article 29   Everyone has duties to the community;

Article 30   No person, group or government has the right to destroy any of these rights.

It is significant that the International Bill of Human Rights does not form part of the UN Charter. The Charter incorporated a commitment to the promotion and protection of human rights, but most of the work was left to the Third Committee (the Social, Humanitarian and Cultural Affairs Committee) of the General Assembly and ECOSOC. The UDHR has received a remarkable level of support, but with different states emphasising the centrality of different provisions. The intended convention on enforcement was never drafted, and such enforcement provisions as there are were incorporated in the two International Covenants.

B. The International Covenants on Human Rights

The International Covenants were drawn up to give legal effect to the principles contained in the UDHR. The difference in priorities between those who drafted the Covenants and those responsible for the formulation of the UDHR is immediately apparent in the wording of Article 1, which is common to both Covenants, and which asserts a legal human right to self-determination – a right that does not even appear, let alone take pride of place, in the UDHR. Its primacy reflects the drafting committee's determination that decolonisation and anti-racism (and newly won sovereignty) (Article 1(2)) be at the forefront of any international human rights concern, and is in turn indicative of the profound changes that occurred in the composition of the UN as a large number of newly independent states gained admission to the organisation in the 1950s and 1960s.

i. The International Covenant on Civil and Political Rights

As might be expected, the ICCPR essentially grants the civil and political rights contained in the UDHR, with a few variations. It has been ratified by 172 states (as at February 2019). States are obliged to introduce legal or other measures within their domestic jurisdictions to give effect to the rights set out in the ICCPR (Article 2(2)) and also to provide 'an effective remedy' for those whose rights under the Covenant are violated (Article 2(3)). It is possible for a state to derogate from some of its obligations if there is an emergency threatening the life of the nation (Article 4), but not from those provisions regarded as fundamental: ie the right to life, to be recognised before the law, and to freedom of thought, conscience and religion (Articles 6, 16 and 18); the right not to be subjected to torture or to cruel, inhuman or degrading treatment or punishment, or to slavery or servitude (Articles 7 and 8); and the right not to be imprisoned for non-fulfilment of a contractual obligation or to suffer a criminal penalty for an act or omission that was not a criminal offence at the time it was committed (Articles 11 and 15).

What is of most interest, however, are the means chosen to give legal effect to the provisions. Part IV of the Covenant created the Human

Rights Committee, consisting of 18 elected independent experts (Article 28). Article 40 gave the Committee the primary task of reviewing state reports (which states parties to the ICCPR are obliged to submit every five years) 'on the measures they have adopted which give effect to the rights' of the Covenant. This review provides for the public questioning of state representatives on the content of their reports. Fairly obviously, such a procedure leaves itself open to abuse from governments wishing to conceal the true state of affairs within their nations. The Committee has, however, developed a practice that allows individual members to receive reports from human rights NGOs and to ask questions based upon that information. After such questioning, the Committee will issue concluding observations which may well be critical. Having said that, there is little further 'enforcement', and states are expected to listen to criticisms and to correct the situation before the next five-yearly report.

Under Article 41, there is a further optional procedure, under which the Committee can receive and consider complaints from one state party against another state party alleging that the state complained of is not fulfilling its obligations under the Covenant. Both the alleging party and the alleged violator must have declared acceptance of this optional process.

More important is the procedure under the First Optional Protocol to the ICCPR, which also came into force in 1976 and, as at February 2019, has been ratified by 116 states (not including China, the UK or the US). The Protocol allows individual communications (complaints) with regard to alleged violations of the Covenant to be made to the Committee where the victim is a national of a state party to the Protocol, subject to certain restrictions, such as all domestic remedies having first been exhausted. If the Committee decides the communication is admissible, it requests comments from the state concerned and, if it finds that a state has violated an obligation under the ICCPR, will require the situation to be remedied. States are not bound to implement these findings, but can be asked by the Committee to provide information within a set time limit on the steps they have taken to comply with its decisions. There is also a Second Optional Protocol, which came into force in 1991, and provides for the abolition of the death penalty on the territory of ratifying states. As at February 2019, it had been ratified by 86 states.

Those new to international law may well be astounded at just how 'unenforceable' the ICCPR is, despite its ratification by so many states. Such a reaction, while understandable, ignores the political realities of international agreements. The use of international force against a state not fulfilling its treaty obligations is generally unthinkable. This may be less true of economic sanctions, although even these are unlikely to be adopted by the international community save where the most extraordinary and egregious breaches of the Covenant have occurred (perhaps as exemplified by apartheid South Africa). All of this, of course, re-emphasises the points made at the outset of this book: that international law is a system based on the consent and coordination of participating nations.

ii. The International Covenant on Economic, Social and Cultural Rights

The ICESCR contains the following economic, social and cultural rights: the right to work (Article 6); 'the enjoyment of just and favourable conditions of work', which includes fair wages and equal pay for work of equal value, 'a decent living for [workers] and their families', 'safe and healthy working conditions', equal opportunity with respect to promotion, and a reasonable limitation on hours of work, together with paid holidays (Article 7); the right to form or join a trade union (Article 8); the right to 'social security, including social insurance' (Article 9); assistance and protection for the family, including paid leave or 'leave with adequate social security benefits' for women at the time of childbirth, and protection for children against 'economic and social exploitation' (Article 10); the right to 'an adequate standard of living' for oneself and one's family, 'including adequate food, clothing and housing', and 'the continuous improvement of living conditions', with particular emphasis on freedom from hunger (Article 11); the right to enjoy 'the highest attainable standard of physical and mental health' (Article 12); the right to receive an education, which, at a minimum, means free and compulsory primary education (Article 13); and the right to participate in cultural life, including 'enjoy[ing] the benefits of scientific progress and its applications' (Article 15). As at February 2019, the Covenant had been ratified by 169 states.

As was noted in the previous section, the assumption underlying the ICESCR is that the granting of these rights is very much dependent on the resources of the state in question, making immediate implementation impossible in many cases, and also rendering these rights non-justiciable, since, it is argued, decisions as to how a state's resources are used fall within the realm of politics rather than law. Unsurprisingly, therefore, the rights provided under the ICESCR are framed in much weaker terms than their counterparts in the ICCPR. In particular, a state need implement the rights detailed in the covenant only 'to the maximum of its available resources' and 'with a view to achieving progressively [their] full realization' (Article 2(1)). This does indeed seem to confirm that economic, social and cultural rights really are 'children of a lesser God'.

In a procedure similar to that which applies to the ICCPR, states parties are required to submit five-yearly reports to the Committee on Economic, Social and Cultural Rights (a body of 18 elected experts set up by the Economic and Social Council to monitor the implementation of the ICESCR) detailing the steps they have taken to comply with their obligations under the Covenant (Articles 16 and 17). The Committee then makes observations on the progress (or not) that a state is making in this regard and issues recommendations. The Committee also accepts reports from civil society groups as part of the review process, and can, if a state fails to issue a report, conduct its review using alternative sources of information.

Under an Optional Protocol to the ICESCR, which came into force in May 2013 after receiving the 10 ratifications necessary, the Committee can hear complaints from individuals or groups of individuals claiming to be a victim of the violation of a right set out in the Covenant. If the Committee decides that a breach has occurred, it will make recommendations to the state concerned as to how to remedy the situation. The Protocol also allows one or more states parties to complain that another state party is in breach of its obligations under the ICESCR, but only if the relevant states have previously entered into a declaration confirming such complaints can be made against them. States can also choose to enter into a further declaration allowing the Committee to examine any 'reliable information' it receives 'indicating grave or systematic violations' of any of the rights set out in the ICESCR in the state in question, and to conduct an inquiry into the matter if the Committee believes this is warranted. The Committee will then transmit its conclusions, along with any comments and recommendations, to the state concerned, which is expected to reply within six months. The state may also be asked to inform the Committee of the steps it has taken in response to the inquiry. As at February 2019, the Optional Protocol had received 45 signatures and 24 ratifications (the most recent ratification coming from Venezuela).

Some had anticipated that the effect of the Protocol would be to bring enforcement of the rights provided for under the ICESCR into line with those contained in the ICCPR. However, the 'progressive realisation' of the rights enumerated in the ICESCR is not a concept that easily translates into the sort of questions which a legal regime is equipped to answer. Furthermore, there is a lack of clear indicators and reliable data to enable an assessment of such 'progressive realisation'. This is so, even though the World Bank estimates that, as of 2015, there were still 736 million people worldwide living in extreme poverty,[16] while, according to a joint report prepared by the World Health Organization and UNICEF, as of 2017, 4.5 billion people on the planet (six out of 10) lacked access to safe sanitation.[17]

---

[16] Defined as living on less than $1.95 a day. According to World Bank data, extreme global poverty fell to a new low of 10% in 2015, down from 11% in 2013 and from nearly 36% in 1990. However, although the first Millenium Development Goal of cutting the 1990 extreme poverty rate in half by 2015 was reached five years early (in 2010), it is doubtful whether the target of ending extreme global poverty by 2030 is now achievable. Moreover, Sub-Saharan Africa remains by far the most impoverished part of the world: 'In fact, the number of poor in the region increased by 9 million, with 413 million people living on less than US$1.90 a day in 2015, more than all the other regions combined. If the trend continues, by 2030, nearly 9 out of 10 [of the] extreme poor will be in Sub-Saharan Africa.' See the World Bank website at www.worldbank.org/en/topic/poverty/overview.

[17] In addition, 2.1 billion (three in 10 people worldwide) did not have access to safe, readily available drinking water. World Health Organization (WHO) and the United Nations Children's Fund (UNICEF), *Progress on drinking water, sanitation and hygiene: 2017 update and SDG baselines* (Geneva, 2017), available at www.unicef.org/publications/index_96611.html.

Perhaps what the two International Covenants illustrate most starkly is that the range of ideological positions exhibited by states within the UN is so broad that, difficult though it was to draft the UDHR, it has proved almost impossible to devise legally binding provisions that will be acceptable to all members. It is this that has encouraged the development of regional protection mechanisms, to which we will turn after a brief consideration of the other main UN human rights treaties, together with the Human Rights Council and the Office of the UN High Commissioner for Human Rights.

V. Other Principal UN Human Rights Conventions and Bodies

In addition to the International Covenants, there are a number of other UN international human rights treaties. Once again, while the texts of the treaties are clear, their effectiveness is difficult to assess. In this section, we will list the main conventions and will then look in a little more detail at one of them, the Convention on the Elimination of All Forms of Discrimination Against Women, in order to demonstrate the extent to which the rights enshrined in an instrument can be severely undermined by state reservations.

The other principal UN human rights conventions (not including their protocols) are as follows:

1. Convention for the Prevention and Punishment of the Crime of Genocide 1948.
2. Convention for the Suppression of Traffic in Persons and of the Exploitation of the Prostitution of Others 1950.
3. Convention Relating to the Status of Refugees 1951.
4. International Convention on the Elimination of All Forms of Racial Discrimination 1965.
5. International Convention on the Suppression and Punishment of the Crime of Apartheid 1973.
6. Convention on the Elimination of All Forms of Discrimination Against Women 1979.
7. Convention against Torture and Other Cruel, Inhuman or Degrading Treatment or Punishment 1984.
8. Convention on the Rights of the Child 1989.
9. International Convention on the Protection of the Rights of All Migrant Workers and Members of Their Families 1990.
10. Convention on the Rights of Persons with Disabilities 2006.
11. International Convention for the Protection of All Persons from Enforced Disappearance 2006.

In the words of the relevant UN website:[18]

> The Convention on the Elimination of All Forms of Discrimination Against Women (CEDAW), adopted in 1979 by the UN General Assembly, is often described as an international bill of rights for women. Consisting of a preamble and 30 articles, it defines what constitutes discrimination against women and sets up an agenda for national action to end such discrimination.
>
> The Convention defines discrimination against women as '... any distinction, exclusion or restriction made on the basis of sex which has the effect or purpose of impairing or nullifying the recognition, enjoyment or exercise by women, irrespective of their marital status, on a basis of equality of men and women, of human rights and fundamental freedoms in the political, economic, social, cultural, civil or any other field.'
>
> By accepting the Convention, States commit themselves to undertake a series of measures to end discrimination against women in all forms, including:
>
> - to incorporate the principle of equality of men and women in their legal system, abolish all discriminatory laws and adopt appropriate ones prohibiting discrimination against women;
> - to establish tribunals and other public institutions to ensure the effective protection of women against discrimination; and
> - to ensure elimination of all acts of discrimination against women by persons, organizations or enterprises.
>
> The Convention provides the basis for realizing equality between women and men through ensuring women's equal access to, and equal opportunities in, political and public life – including the right to vote and to stand for election – as well as education, health and employment. States parties agree to take all appropriate measures, including legislation and temporary special measures, so that women can enjoy all their human rights and fundamental freedoms.
>
> The Convention is the only human rights treaty which affirms the reproductive rights of women and targets culture and tradition as influential forces shaping gender roles and family relations. It affirms women's rights to acquire, change or retain their nationality and the nationality of their children. States parties also agree to take appropriate measures against all forms of traffic in women and exploitation of women.
>
> Countries that have ratified or acceded to the Convention are legally bound to put its provisions into practice. They are also committed to submit national reports, at least every four years, on measures they have taken to comply with their treaty obligations.

CEDAW, which entered into force in 1981, has now been ratified by 189 nations (as at February 2019). Initially, this appears a remarkable feat, suggesting that rapid progress is being made in eradicating discrimination against women worldwide. Things are not, however, quite what they seem. Not only is the

---

[18] www.un.org/womenwatch/daw/cedaw.

list of reservations that states parties to CEDAW have entered remarkably extensive, but many of these reservations seem scarcely compatible with the purposes of the Convention.[19] This worrying state of affairs is described by the UN body charged with administering CEDAW, the Committee on the Elimination of Discrimination against Women:

> The Convention permits ratification subject to reservations, provided that the reservations are not incompatible with the object and purpose of the Convention. Some States parties that enter reservations to the Convention do not enter reservations to analogous provisions in other human rights treaties. A number of States enter reservations to particular articles on the ground that national law, tradition, religion or culture are not congruent with Convention principles, and purport to justify the reservation on that basis. Some States enter a reservation to article 2, although their national constitutions or laws prohibit discrimination. [Article 2 condemns discrimination against women 'in all its forms' and obliges states parties to pursue its elimination through various means, including the adoption of constitutional and legislative measures.] There is therefore an inherent conflict between the provisions of the State's constitution and its reservation to the Convention. Some reservations are drawn so widely that their effect cannot be limited to specific provisions in the Convention. ...
>
> Impermissible reservations
>
> Article 28, paragraph 2, of the Convention adopts the impermissibility principle contained in the Vienna Convention on the Law of Treaties. It states that a reservation incompatible with the object and purpose of the present Convention shall not be permitted.
>
> Although the Convention does not prohibit the entering of reservations, those which challenge the central principles of the Convention are contrary to the provisions of the Convention and to general international law. As such they may be challenged by other States parties.
>
> Articles 2 and 16 are considered by the Committee to be core provisions of the Convention. [Article 16 commits parties to taking appropriate steps to eliminate discrimination against women 'in all matters' that relate to marriage, including its dissolution, and family relations.] Although some States parties have withdrawn reservations to those articles, the Committee is particularly concerned at the number and extent of reservations entered to those articles.
>
> The Committee holds the view that article 2 is central to the objects and purpose of the Convention. States parties which ratify the Convention do so because they agree that discrimination against women in all its forms should be condemned and that the strategies set out in article 2, subparagraphs (a) to (g), should be implemented by States parties to eliminate it.
>
> Neither traditional, religious or cultural practice nor incompatible domestic laws and policies can justify violations of the Convention. The Committee also remains convinced that reservations to article 16, whether lodged for national, traditional,

---

[19] A full list of these reservations can be viewed at www.un.org/womenwatch/daw/cedaw/reservations-country.htm.

religious or cultural reasons, are incompatible with the Convention and therefore impermissible and should be reviewed and modified or withdrawn.

Such a situation effectively illustrates both the strength and weakness of such a treaty. The strength is that CEDAW is an international statement that clearly sets out a goal and defines discrimination against women as unacceptable and increasingly incompatible with international law (treaty law for those states that are party to the Convention, and customary international law for others, since CEDAW has been so comprehensively accepted). The weakness once more concerns the problems of enforcement (states must submit reports every four years describing the progress they have made), particularly in view of the number of reservations of doubtful compatibility with the treaty that have been made. States with a substantial Muslim population, in particular, have entered reservations against either or both Article 2 and Article 16 to the effect that, where an obligation under these provisions conflicts with a tenet of sharia law, then the latter must prevail. This is notwithstanding the fact, as the Committee has observed, that 'religious or cultural reasons' cannot be allowed to eviscerate the Convention.

In summary, it can be said that the UN has been highly successful in both drawing up and securing the acceptance of international human rights treaties. Genocide, torture, slavery, racism and apartheid are all now clearly proscribed in international law. In other areas, however, it is harder to assess the contribution that human rights treaties are making to the protection of human rights. In the case of CEDAW, while almost all states have ratified the Convention and are apparently prepared to work towards eradicating discrimination against women, the reservations entered by many of them reveal a substantially different, and altogether more depressing, picture.

In terms of the global protection of human rights, there are two UN organisations that are particularly involved in this area: the Human Rights Council and the Office of the UN High Commissioner for Human Rights.

A. The Human Rights Council

The Human Rights Council, based in Geneva, was established in 2006 as a subsidiary body of the General Assembly, and is the UN's main intergovernmental body responsible for human rights issues. It consists of representatives of 47 UN member states elected by a simple majority in the Assembly for a three-year term, a third of which are renewed each year. The Council is responsible for encouraging the promotion and protection of human rights worldwide, and seats are allocated according to the following UN geographical groupings: 13 each for the African States and the Asia–Pacific States; eight for the Latin American and Caribbean States; seven for the Western European and other States; and six for the Eastern European States.

The Council replaced the UN Commission on Human Rights (created in 1946) after that body became increasingly discredited as a result of the overt politicisation of its proceedings (especially during the Cold War era), as well as the election of a number of states to the Commission with extremely poor human rights records. In addition, a number of states, led by the US, objected to what they argued was a disproportionate amount of attention paid by the Commission to the human rights record of Israel. Although the intention was that the new Council should begin with a clean state, unfortunately past problems have resurfaced, and in June 2018 the US withdrew from the Council, with the then US Ambassador to the UN, Nikki Hayley, describing the Council as a 'hypocritical and self-serving organisation' and a 'protector of human rights abusers and cesspool of political bias', guilty of displaying 'unending hostility towards Israel'.[20] The withdrawal occurred shortly after the then UN Human Rights Commissioner, Zeid Ra'ad Al Hussein, had, in his opening address to the 38th session of the Human Rights Council, castigated the Trump administration for forcibly separating child migrants from their parents at the Mexico–US border, describing the policy as 'unconscionable'.[21]

When the Council was created, an attempt was made to avoid the problems that had plagued the Commission it replaced. Each candidate is required to demonstrate a good record on human rights, and each elected member can be expelled for transgressions. The expectation was that states with abysmal human rights records (Saudi Arabia being a notorious example) would no longer be able to secure a seat. Regrettably, the expected improvement has not materialised, and the politicisation of the process, whereby regional neighbours or regimes with equally appalling human rights records support one another's candidacy has not changed. The position is aggravated by the slates put forward by the state groups, which, in all cases in 2018, were no more than the number of places to which the relevant group was entitled. The limited number of nominations may be owing to regional solidarity, or is perhaps attributable to the expense of maintaining a delegation in Geneva. Whatever the reason, the October 2018 elections resulted in, among others, Bahrain, Cameroon, Eritrea, the Philippines and Somalia gaining seats on the Human Rights Council, joining existing members such as Egypt, Iraq, Pakistan and Saudi Arabia – all of which enjoy the distinction of possessing utterly deplorable human rights records.

As to Israel, it is true that Israel alone has been subject to regular examination because of its actions in Gaza and the Occupied Territories, which is regarded as unfair by the US, Israel and some few allies, but these are greatly outnumbered by those states that are strongly of the view that Israel must be permanently held to account.

---

[20] 'US quits "biased" UN human rights council', *BBC News*, 20 June 2018.
[21] 'UN rights chief slams "unconscionable" US border policy of separating migrant children from parents', *UN News*, 18 June 2018, available at https://news.un.org/en/story/2018/06/1012382.

Despite its obvious defects, the Human Rights Council has done some important work, sending independent experts and setting up commissions of inquiry to report on human rights violations occurring in various states, including Burundi, Myanmar, North Korea, South Sudan and Syria. And, perhaps equally importantly, the Council monitors the human rights situation in all UN member states via the Universal Periodic Review procedure to check what action states have taken to improve human rights conditions and meet their human rights obligations. This a unique process by which the human rights records of all 193 UN member states are regularly reviewed on the basis of equal treatment for each country. More than 40 states are reviewed each year in a process that relies on initial state reports which then form the basis for discussion. The process is intended to be collaborative rather than accusatory, and if the paperwork that results may be relied upon it does seem that the process has not been without positive results. (It is difficult to be more robust than this.)

There is also a complaints procedure, under which individuals, groups and NGOs can complain to the Council about human rights violations, as well as 'special procedures', under which human rights experts are mandated to investigate and report on the human rights situation in a particular country or in respect of a specific issue, such as the problem of arbitrary detention or of the right to education. Nor is it only poorer countries that fare badly in such reports. In 2017 and 2018, the UN Special Rapporteur on Extreme Poverty and Human Rights, Philip Alston, visited impoverished communities in the US and UK respectively, and produced damning critiques of the levels of deprivation he found, castigating the governments of both states – among the wealthiest in the world – for introducing policies that had caused poverty and misery for millions of their citizens.[22]

B. Office of the UN High Commissioner for Human Rights

Set up in 1993, the Office of the UN High Commissioner for Human Rights (OHCHR) forms part of the UN Secretariat, and is the principal UN organ-isation charged with promoting and protecting human rights. It is headed up by the High Commissioner for Human Rights, who is responsible for the activities and administration of the OHCHR, and is accountable to the UN Secretary-General. The current High Commissioner is former Chilean president Michelle Bachelet, who assumed the role on 1 September 2018.

---

[22] UN OHCHR, 'Statement on Visit to the USA, by Professor Philip Alston, United Nations Special Rapporteur on extreme poverty and human rights', 15 December 2017, available at www. ohchr.org/EN/NewsEvents/Pages/DisplayNews.aspx?NewsID=22533; and 'Statement on Visit to the United Kingdom, by Professor Philip Alston, United Nations Special Rapporteur on extreme poverty and human rights', 16 November 2018, available at www.ohchr.org/en/NewsEvents/Pages/DisplayNews.aspx?NewsID=23881&LangID=E.

Among other activities, the OHCHR provides support to the Human Rights Council and other UN human rights bodies, assists governments in implementing their human rights obligations by offering advice and technical training in particular areas, promotes the ratification and implementation of international human rights treaties, and is the main focus of human rights research and education within the UN.

VI. Regional Protection of Human Rights

As we have already observed, it is difficult to evaluate the contribution made by human rights conventions to the protection of human rights. A cost–benefit analysis would be highly useful but almost impossible to carry out. Henry Ford is supposed once to have observed that he knew 90 per cent of his advertising budget was wasted, but the problem was that he was unable to discover which 10 per cent was effective. When it comes to the international protection of human rights, the situation is even more uncertain. Conventions do at least encourage a standard-setting process, with some provisions having achieved a *jus cogens* status in international law, but the effect of this standard-setting is difficult to quantify.

Problems of enforcement at the global level prompted the implementation of regional protection mechanisms. As we have seen, the drawing up of the International Covenants hardly proceeded at a rapid pace, and this provided one incentive for the development of systems of regional rights protection. In addition, it was thought that a higher degree of homogeneity among the participating states would make compliance more likely. It was in Europe that the impetus for such regional protection was at its greatest, primarily in reaction to the war that had been fought against fascism. In the words of the most famous historian of the development of post-war human rights, AWB Simpson:

> The idea that there was a link between the protection of human rights and the preservation of peace was to become a common feature of post-war thinking. ... Thus it came about that whereas before the Second World War there was virtually no public interest in the international protection of human rights, except in relation to European minority protection, by 1944, and even earlier, there was a widespread interest in the subject, and a growing belief that the protection of human rights against oppressive governments should be embodied in a new world order which needed to be established to ensure not only security through a lasting peace, but also a just world in which governmental misconduct would be brought under the control of the international community. ... The idea that the war had been about the protection of the rights of individuals, originally little more than a rhetorical adornment, was coming home to roost.[23]

---

[23] AWB Simpson, *Human Rights and the End of Empire* (Oxford, OUP, 2001) 219–20.

Regional regimes of human rights protection have also developed in the Americas and Africa, under the auspices of, respectively, the Organization of American States and the Organization of African Unity (now the African Union). There has been no comparable Asian development. For reasons of brevity, and because the European system is the most highly developed of the regional protection regimes (in terms of allowing individuals to complain of human rights violations), we will outline its main features below.

The ECHR was drafted by the Council of Europe, an organisation established in 1949 to promote democracy, the rule of law and human rights protection on the continent.[24] It was opened for signature in November 1950, and entered into force after 10 ratifications in 1953. The provisions of the ECHR are largely based upon the civil and political rights contained in the UDHR, and reflect the Western view that such rights are justiciable in a way that social, economic and cultural rights are not. However, as the Convention is a legal document, it is necessarily much more guarded in its wording, with almost every right heavily qualified and expressed in significantly less absolute terms than its counterpart in the Declaration. It is also possible for states to derogate from their obligations under the ECHR 'In time of war or other public emergency threatening the life of the nation ... to the extent strictly required by the exigencies of the situation' (Article 15). However, this power to derogate does not apply to certain fundamental provisions of the ECHR, which must be maintained at all times: namely, the right to life, 'except in respect of deaths resulting from lawful acts of war', and the right not to suffer retrospective punishment (Articles 2 and 7), and the prohibitions on torture and inhuman or degrading punishment or treatment, and on slavery and servitude (Articles 3 and 4(1)).

In order to enforce the rights set out in the Convention, three bodies were established: the European Commission on Human Rights, the European Court of Human Rights (ECtHR), based at Strasbourg, and the Committee of Ministers of the Council of Europe (consisting of the foreign ministers of states parties or their representatives). However, Protocol No 11 to the Convention, which came into force on 1 November 1998, abolished the judicial function of the Committee of Ministers, and replaced the Commission and part-time Court with a single, full-time Court, which now deals with all complaints alleging breaches of the ECHR. As mentioned in chapter two, originally such complaints could be brought only by one state party against another, unless the state in question was also willing to grant the right to bring individual complaints to its nationals. This, too, however, was changed by Protocol 11, which required all states parties to the ECHR to allow individual

---

[24] For more information about the Council, which should not be confused with the European Council – one of the main institutions of the European Union – see http://hub.coe.int.

applicants (including groups of individuals and NGOs) the right to petition the Court in respect of harm suffered as a result of a violation of the Convention.

This right of individual petition, coupled with the fact that there are now 47 states parties to the ECHR with a combined population of 800 million, has increased the workload of the ECtHR enormously. Many of these cases have been brought by nationals of Eastern European states that joined the Council of Europe at the end of the Cold War. As a result, steps have been taken to streamline the Court's operations and reduce the number of cases brought. Protocol 14 has been designed to tackle the problem of the ECtHR's excessive workload. It provides that, first, a single judge can decide on a case's admissibility (there are the same number of judges as states, ie 47), in place of the three judges that were formerly required. Secondly, it provides that where a case is broadly similar to one previously brought before the Court, and is filed essentially because of the failure of a member state to change its domestic law to comply with a previous judgment, admissibility can be decided by three judges rather than the seven-judge Chamber. Thirdly, a case may not be admissible if it is considered that the applicant has not suffered 'significant disadvantage', although this is not a 'hard and fast' rule. Fourthly, a member state can be brought before the Court by the Committee of Ministers if that state refuses to abide by a judgment against it. Finally, the Committee of Ministers can ask the Court for an 'interpretation' of a judgment to help determine the best way for a member state to comply with it. And, of course, as the ECHR is an inter-state convention, the obligation remains upon states to give effect to the Court's judgments.

The ECHR has been remarkably successful in effectively guaranteeing fundamental civil and political rights, and is the foundation of what is undoubtedly still the most successful of the regional systems for the protection of human rights. Until the 1990s, the role of the ECtHR approached that of a supreme constitutional court for the interpretation of civil liberties protection throughout Europe. However, the accession of a number of Eastern European states with histories and ideological outlooks very different from those of the original members necessarily changed this, and also resulted in an unmanageable caseload for the Court.

The ambivalent attitude of British governments towards the ECHR is not without interest. Although the UK was a party to the ECHR from the outset, for many years its provisions did not form part of domestic law, and consequently the UK faced a significant number of cases brought by its citizens to the ECtHR in Strasbourg. If a complainant was successful, he or she had to rely upon the UK Government to provide the redress awarded. Enforcement of an order was possible only in the unlikely event of an action by another party to the treaty. Finally, in 1998, the UK Government decided to effectively incorporate the provisions of the ECHR into domestic law through the Human Rights Act, which came into force in October 2000, allowing remedies to be awarded by UK courts. The Act was not universally welcomed, since many felt that its effect was to award the judiciary a power that properly belonged to Parliament. However, the Human Rights Act in fact preserves the doctrine of parliamentary supremacy by directing judges, in cases where they deem domestic legislation to be incompatible with the ECHR, to issue a declaration to this effect. Such a 'declaration of incompatibility' informs the legislature that, in judicial opinion, the legislation in question would be found to be in breach of ECHR treaty obligations by the Strasbourg Court, but leaves it to Parliament to remedy the situation. Nevertheless, it has been a manifesto commitment of the current UK Government to repeal the Human Rights Act and replace it with a 'British Bill of Rights'. In the past, there have even been calls, including by the current Prime Minister, Theresa May, for the country to withdraw from the ECHR itself. Such attitudes and statements are reflective of a hostility, particularly prevalent among some UK Conservative politicians, to human rights legislation, especially where this is perceived to have emanated from European rather than 'home-grown' sources.

As a result of the June 2016 referendum, and the UK Government's formal notification under Article 50 of the Lisbon Treaty of the country's intention to withdraw from EU membership, the UK is due to leave the EU in 2019. At present, it is still unclear on what terms the UK will leave and what aspects of EU law (if any) may continue to apply for a period after the formal withdrawal date or will be replicated in domestic law. The UK's exit from the EU has, however, raised fears among human rights specialists and activists that this will weaken the country's human rights regime. This is primarily because, once the UK leaves the EU, it will no longer be bound by the Charter of Fundamental Rights of the European Union, which applies to the interpretation and enforcement of European law throughout the EU, and has been binding on member states since December 2009, when the Treaty of Lisbon entered into force. The Charter incorporates the rights set out in the ECHR, but also encompasses additional civil, political, economic and social rights, drawn from, among other sources, the constitutional traditions of its EU member states and other international conventions to which the EU or its members are a party (although the UK, along with Poland, negotiated an opt-out to the economic and social rights). The Government has refused to incorporate the provisions of the Charter into its EU (Withdrawal) Bill, and it appears that the effect of this will almost inevitably be an erosion in the human rights of UK citizens, most notably because some of the substantive rights set out in the Charter, and some of the mechanisms by which its rights are protected, do not have direct equivalents in UK domestic law.[25]

---

[25] See the concerns expressed by the British Equality and Human Rights Commission, available at www.equalityhumanrights.com/en/what-are-human-rights/how-are-your-rights-protected/what-charter-fundamental-rights-european-union-0.

VII. The International Criminal Court

The most recent major development in the protection of human rights has been the establishment of the International Criminal Court (ICC), set up to try individuals accused of committing the most heinous crimes under international law. Created under the Rome Statute of the International Criminal Court of 1998, the ICC came into existence in July 2002, after the Statute received the 60 ratifications necessary to bring it into force. The ICC's first judges and first prosecutor were appointed in 2003, and the Court has therefore been operating for over 15 years. There are currently 123 states that are party to the Rome Statute (as at February 2019) and thus subject to the Court's jurisdiction. These do not include P5 members China, Russia and the US. Palestine was the last state to ratify the Statute, in 2015.

In common with the International Court of Justice, the ICC is based at the Hague in the Netherlands, although the Rome Statute does permit it to sit elsewhere if the Court's judges deem it desirable to do so. The Court is funded by contributions from states parties to the Statute and also by voluntary donations from a number of sources, including governments, international organisations, individuals and corporations. The Court's budget for 2019 has been set at €148.14 million.[26] This has disappointed some smaller and medium-sized states parties, who say that the modest increase on the 2018 budget (which amounted to €143.85 million[27]) represents a reduction in real terms (ie after inflation is taken into account), although it is reflective of the wishes of larger contributors, who believe that the Court's burgeoning costs need to be reined in.[28] The ICC does not form part of the UN system, although the Court and the UN did enter into an agreement in 2004 governing the relationship between their two organisations, and confirming their agreement to consult with each other and to co-operate on matters of mutual interest.[29]

---

[26] ICC Press Release 'Assembly of States Parties concludes its seventeenth session', 12 December 2018, available at https://asp.icc-cpi.int/en_menus/asp/press%20releases/Pages/PR1426.aspx.

[27] ICC, 'Proposed Programme Budget for 2019 of the International Criminal Court', ICC-ASP/17/INF.4, 23 July 2018, available at https://asp.icc-cpi.int/iccdocs/asp_docs/ASP17/ICC-ASP-17-INF4-ENG.pdf.

[28] See Journalists for Justice, '"Small 10" protest as states leave ICC with a reduced budget', 19 December 2018, available at www.jfjustice.net/en/asp/a-small-10a-protest-as-states-leave-icc-with-a-reduced-budget.

[29] Negotiated Relationship Agreement between the International Criminal Court and the United Nations, available at www.icc-cpi.int/NR/rdonlyres/916FC6A2-7846-4177-A5EA-5AA9B6D1E96C/0/ICCASP3Res1_English.pdf.

A. Background to the Establishment of the ICC

The founding of the ICC marked the culmination of a series of attempts, dating back to immediately after the First World War, to find some means of holding individuals to account for the perpetration of war crimes and other grave crimes under international law. The Treaty of Versailles of 1919 had provided not only for senior German military personnel to be prosecuted for committing war crimes, but also for Kaiser Wilhelm II to be brought before a special tribunal in order to answer 'for a supreme offence against international morality and the sanctity of treaties'.[30] As matters transpired, however, only a very few, relatively minor, individuals eventually stood trial (and then, not before an international court, but the German Supreme Court at Leipzig), and even fewer were convicted.[31] Nor was a proposal for the creation of a High Court of International Justice, mooted at the time plans were being drawn up for the establishment of the Permanent Court of International Justice in 1920, greeted with much enthusiasm or taken any further.[32]

It was only at the end of the Second World War that individuals accused of war crimes and other serious violations of international law were tried before an international court. In 1945, the Allied Powers (Britain, France, the Soviet Union and the US) set up the International Military Tribunal for Nuremberg to try senior German military leaders, government officials, industrialists and financiers with crimes against the peace, war crimes and crimes against humanity (see chapter two). This was followed, in 1946, by the establishment of the International Military Tribunal for the Far East to try high-ranking Japanese officials charged with similar offences. Although the two sets of trials heralded the first real beginnings of international criminal law, and undoubtedly resulted in some well-deserved convictions, they have not been immune from criticism.

Given the fact that both Tribunals were instituted by the winning side, it was inevitable that the outcome was a selective or victors' justice: one that focused exclusively on crimes committed by nationals of the defeated Axis powers while ignoring certain culpable acts perpetrated by the Allies. Moreover, there was some disquiet at the fact that the crimes with which the defendants were charged had arguably not actually existed when the alleged acts which constituted those crimes had taken place, thereby contravening the fundamental principle that there should be no retrospective application of criminal law. Both these points were raised by Radhabinod Pal, an Indian judge appointed to the Tribunal for the Far East, in his dissenting opinion from the majority's

---

[30] Article 227 of the Treaty of Versailles. However, the Dutch authorities (Wilhelm having fled to the Netherlands) refused to surrender him, on the ground that the offence with which he was charged had no basis in Dutch law, as well as the fact that there was no treaty in place permitting his extradition. See Antonio Cassese et al, *Cassese's International Criminal Law*, 3rd edn (Oxford, OUP, 2013) 242; William A Schabas, *An Introduction to the International Criminal Court*, 5th edn (Cambridge, CUP, 2017) 3.

[31] Cassese et al (ibid) 254.

[32] ibid 254–55; Schabas, *An Introduction to the ICC* (2017) 5.

verdict. A staunch anti-colonialist, Pal offered a stinging rebuke to the premises on which the Tokyo trial had been based, asserting that the Western colonial powers had no right to sit in judgment on an Asian government, especially when they themselves were guilty of committing war crimes, and that, in defining new crimes with which to punish individuals, their actions represented a dangerous contravention of international law.[33] On the plus side, the accused had at least received the benefit of a trial, whatever its flaws. Both the then British Prime Minister, Winston Churchill, and Cordell Hull, Secretary of State in Franklin D Roosevelt's administration until November 1944, had favoured summary justice, at least for those individuals regarded as major war criminals, whom, they believed, should simply have been shot.[34]

More immediate precursors for the ICC can be found in the ad hoc tribunals set up by the Security Council under its Chapter VII powers in response to the atrocities committed in the former Yugoslavia and Rwanda in the early 1990s. The International Criminal Tribunal for the Former Yugoslavia (ICTY) was established in 1993,[35] with jurisdiction over individuals accused of perpetrating the following crimes on the territory of the former Yugoslavia from 1 January 1991 onwards: grave breaches of the Geneva Conventions for the Protection of War Victims, violations of the laws and customs of war, genocide, and crimes against humanity.[36] The following year saw the creation of the International Criminal Tribunal for Rwanda (ICTR)[37] to try individuals alleged to have committed genocide, crimes against humanity, and serious violations of Common Article 3 of the Geneva Conventions and Additional Protocol II (governing the treatment of victims of war in the context of an internal conflict) on the territory of Rwanda from 1 January to 31 December 1994, together with Rwandan citizens accused of committing any of these crimes in neighbouring states over the same period.[38] Both the ICTY and ICTR shared the same Appeals Court, in order to ensure some consistency of jurisprudence, and both have now ceased to operate (the ICTR in December 2015 and the ICTY in December 2017). Their remaining functions are now performed by the International Residual Mechanism for Criminal Tribunals, created by the Security Council for this purpose in 2010.[39] Divided into two branches, one for the ICTR, based in Arusha, Tanzania, and the other for the ICTY, located in The Hague in the Netherlands, the Mechanism is responsible for finishing off the tasks inherited from the ICTY and ICTR, having been endowed for this purpose with 'the jurisdiction, rights, obligations and essential functions' of the two Tribunals.

---

[33] See Sellars (n 1) 62–63.
[34] ibid 26 and 28.
[35] Under UNSC Resolution 827 of 25 May 1993.
[36] Statute of the International Criminal Court for the Former Yugoslavia, Arts 1–5.
[37] Under UNSC Resolution 955 of 8 November 1994.
[38] Statute of the International Criminal Court for Rwanda, Arts 1–4.
[39] UNSC Resolution 1966 of 22 December 2010.

B. Structure and Composition of the ICC

The Court consists of four main organs: Judicial Divisions; Office of the Prosecutor; a Presidency, composed of three judges of the Court elected by their peers for a three-year renewable term, and responsible for the overall administration of the ICC (apart from the Office of the Prosecutor); and a Registry, responsible for the non-judicial aspects of the Court's adminis- tration. Governing the Court as a whole is the Assembly of States Parties (ASP), a management oversight and legislative body that consists of one representative from each state that is party to the Rome statute. The ASP's responsibilities include electing the ICC's judges and its Prosecutor, as well as approving the Court's budget. The ASP has also established, in accord- ance with Article 79 of the Rome Statute, a Trust Fund for Victims (TFV) to counteract harms arising from the crimes over which the Court has juris- diction. The TFV is responsible for implementing Court-ordered reparations (the Court can order that money and other property collected through fines and forfeiture be transferred to the TFV) and for providing support funded by voluntary donor contributions to victims and their families.

The Court has 18 full-time judges allocated to one of three Divisions: Pre- trial, Trial and Appeals. Judges are elected by representatives to the ASP and serve nine-year terms. Unlike their counterparts on the ICJ, they are not eligible for re-election. Candidates for election are put forward either by the relevant national group of the Permanent Court of Arbitration, as with the ICJ nomi- nation process (see chapter seven), or by a state party following the procedure it uses to appoint individuals to high judicial office in the state in question. As with the ICJ, elections are staggered in order to achieve a measure of continu- ity, with a third of the ICC, or six judges, being elected every three years.

Compared with the Statute of the ICJ, the Rome Statute prescribes in much greater detail the criteria to be met by candidates for ICC judgeships.[40] In addition to requiring the Court's judges to be 'of high moral character, impartiality and integrity', and qualified 'in their respective States for appoint- ment to the highest judicial offices' (Article 36(3)(a)), the Rome Statute also seeks to ensure that the Court as a whole possesses expertise in both criminal and international law. States parties are also directed to 'take into account the need to include judges with legal expertise on specific issues including, but not limited to, violence against women or children' (Article 36(8)(b)).

As with the Statute of the ICJ, the Rome Statute also directs states parties to ensure that the Court as a whole is representative 'of the principal legal systems of the world' and also reflects 'Equitable geographical representation' (under Article 36(8)(a)). In fulfilment of this requirement, the ASP has

---

[40] The relative terseness of the ICJ Statute on this point can be attributed to the fact that it was formulated in a very different, and much earlier, era; its wording actually following that of the Statute of the Permanent Court of International Justice, which was drafted as far back as 1920.

resolved that states parties must elect at least three judges from each of the following UN regional groupings: Africa, Latin America and the Caribbean, and Western Europe and Other States (which includes Australia, Canada and New Zealand); and two from each of Asia and Eastern Europe. This leaves a further five 'floating' seats to be allocated among the groups. No two judges may be of the same nationality. Additionally, the Rome Statute seeks to promote gender balance on the Court. States parties are required to also take into account the need for 'A fair representation of female and male judges' (Article 36(8)(a)(iii)), and the ASP has stipulated that at least six judges, or a third of the Court, must be female. At present (February 2019), the ICC is composed of six female and 12 male judges. This level of female representation compares extremely favourably with that of the ICJ, where at present only one-fifth of the judges are female (see chapter seven).

In spite of the efforts made to encourage inclusivity on the Court (particularly in relation to the number of women judges appointed) and also to specify with much greater precision the professional qualifications and experience which ICC judges are expected to possess, the selection process is as subject to political influence as that for the ICJ. Again, this is perhaps only to be expected when both the nomination and election procedures remain effectively in the hands of states.

Headed by a Prosecutor elected by representatives of the states parties for a nine-year term, the Office of the Prosecutor is responsible for investigating and prosecuting crimes that fall within the jurisdiction of the ICC. The Court's current Prosecutor is Fatou Bensouda of The Gambia. She assumed office in June 2012, having previously acted as a deputy to the Court's first Prosecutor, Luis Moreno-Ocampo of Argentina.

C. Crimes Over Which the ICC has Jurisdiction

Under the Rome Statute, the ICC's jurisdiction is 'limited to the most serious crimes of concern to the international community as a whole': genocide, war crimes, crimes against humanity, and the crime of aggression (Article 5(1)). Until recently, the ICC was empowered to act only in respect of the first three crimes, with its jurisdiction over the crime of aggression not activated until July 2018. This long delay regarding the fourth 'core' crime is attributable both to the difficulty that states parties had in defining the crime and also to disagreements about the extent of the Court's powers in relation to it.[41] As a consequence, the jurisdictional regime applicable to the crime of aggression differs from that already in place for crimes falling under the first

---

[41] For a detailed and insightful summary of the relevant negotiations between the states parties, see Roger S Clark, 'Exercise of jurisdiction over the crime of aggression', *Max Planck Encylopedia of International Procedural Law* (forthcoming).

three heads – genocide, crimes against humanity, and war crimes – and, as will be explained below, the scope of the Court's powers in relation to this crime remains ambiguous.

Defined in Article 6 of the Statute, genocide covers a number of acts 'committed with intent to destroy, in whole or in part, a national, ethnic, racial or religious group': killing members of such a group, causing serious bodily or mental harm to them, imposing conditions on the group calculated to destroy it in whole or in part, imposing measures designed to prevent births within the group, and forcibly transferring children from the group to another group. Crimes against humanity, the meaning of which is described in Article 7, refers to actions 'committed as part of a widespread or systematic attack directed against any civilian population, with knowledge of the attack', and includes acts such as murder, enslavement, deportation, torture, rape and the enforced disappearance of persons. War crimes, defined in Article 8, encompasses grave violations of the Geneva Conventions and other serious breaches of the laws and customs applicable to international armed conflicts (ie conflicts between states), and also serious violations of Common Article 3 of the Geneva Conventions (applicable to non-international armed conflicts, such as those between a state and an organised armed group or which are fought between two or more of such groups.)

The crime of aggression is now defined in Article 8*bis*(1) of the Statute as

> the planning, preparation, initiation or execution, by a person in a position effectively to exercise control over or to direct the political or military action of a State, of an act of aggression which, by its character, gravity and scale, constitutes a manifest violation of the Charter of the United Nations.

An 'act of aggression' is defined under Article 8*bis*(2) as 'the use of armed force by a State against the sovereignty, territorial integrity or political independence of another State, or in any other manner inconsistent with the Charter of the United Nations.' Some examples are then given of what counts as an act of aggression, including 'The invasion or attack by the armed forces of a State of the territory of another State, or any military occupation, however temporary, resulting from such invasion or attack, or any annexation by the use of force of the territory of another State or part thereof'; the bombardment or use of weapons by the armed forces of one state against the territory of another; the blockade of the ports or coasts of a state by the armed forces of another; an attack by the armed forces of one state on another's 'land, sea or air forces, or marine and air fleets'; the use by one state of its armed forces in the territory of another in contravention of an agreement reached with that state; permitting the territory of a state to be used by another state to perpetrate an act of aggression against a third state; and sending 'armed bands, groups, irregulars or mercenaries' to another state, who then perpetrate acts of armed force as grave as those already referred to or who are substantially involved in the commission of such acts.

The crime of aggression is thus a 'leadership crime': that is, it can be committed only by someone who is able to exert control over the political and military actions of a state, and hence is closely bound up with the issue of state responsibility for wrongful acts and determinations as to when (and when not) the use of force by a state is lawful. Its definition echoes that contained in the General Assembly's *Definition of Aggression*, adopted in 1974,[42] which also made clear that an act of aggression necessarily implicates state responsibility. And, as a concession to those states nervous that their actions (or, rather, those of their leaders) may be deemed to amount to an act of criminal aggression, the substantive definition of the crime incorporates a 'threshold' requirement: ie only acts that, by virtue of their 'character, gravity and scale', amount to 'a manifest violation of the Charter of the United Nations' will fall to be considered by the ICC – although this limitation on the scope of the crime still provides ample opportunity for discussion and disagreement as to exactly what actions will be deemed sufficiently serious to trigger criminal responsibility under this head.[43]

D. Scope and Operation of the ICC's Jurisdiction

Of particular importance – and often overlooked by those who accuse the ICC of meddling in matters that should properly be left to states themselves – is the fact that the Court operates according to the principle of 'complementarity' (enshrined in Article 17). That is, it is intended to complement rather than displace the role of national courts in administering justice in relation to the crimes set out in the Rome Statute, in deference to the principle of sovereignty. This means that states are primarily responsible for investigating and prosecuting those accused of the crimes in question, with the ICC acting merely as a last resort. As a result, the ICC will become involved only if a state is unwilling or unable to act in a particular case (such unwillingness may be inferred by the Court if proceedings in a particular case are unduly delayed, or are not being conducted in an independent or impartial manner, or are merely a sham, the real intention of which is to shield an individual from being held responsible for his or her criminal actions). In this respect, the Court differs substantially from the ICTY and the ICTR, both of which were granted primacy over national courts, with the latter obliged to defer to the competence of either Tribunal if requested to do so.

---

[42] UNGA Resolution 3314 (XXIX) of 1974. Article 5(2) states 'A war of aggression is a crime against international peace. Aggression gives rise to international responsibility.'

[43] A detailed discussion of the substantive elements of each of the four core crimes can be found in Schabas (n 30) 86–138; Douglas Guilfoyle, *International Criminal Law* (Oxford, OUP, 2016) chs 8–11; and Carsten Stahn, *A Critical Introduction to International Criminal Law* (Cambridge, CUP, 2019) Section 1.3.

The ICC's authority extends only to natural persons, and it therefore has no jurisdiction over juridical entities such as states or corporations. It also has no enforcement arm of any kind, and is therefore reliant on the assistance of state authorities, particularly as regards the apprehension of suspects and their subsequent imprisonment. Under the Rome Statute, states parties are obliged to co-operate fully with the Court in its investigation and prosecution of the crimes that fall within its jurisdiction, and if a state refuses to do so, the ICC can refer the matter to the ASP. If the Court is dealing with a matter that has been referred to it by the Security Council (see below), then all UN members are under a duty to co-operate, regardless of whether they are parties to the Statute or not.

The Court is unusual in that it provides victims with a voice in its proceedings. The Rome Statute contains various provisions under which victims or their legal representatives are entitled to make submissions to the Court, including at the pre-trial stage, during the trial itself, and during any appeal.

i. Jurisdiction: Genocide, Crimes against Humanity, War Crimes

Investigations by the Office of the Prosecutor into genocide-related crimes, crimes against humanity and war crimes may be triggered in one of three ways, as set out under Article 13 of the Rome Statute. First, states parties to the Statute can bring to the attention of the Prosecutor any situation apparently involving the commission of one of these crimes, provided the conduct in question has occurred on the territory of a state party or involves one or more of its nationals. Although it had initially been supposed that this provision would be used by one or more states to refer to the Prosecutor crimes involving another state, in fact there have been a number of 'self-referrals', with Uganda, the Democratic Republic of the Congo, the Central African Republic and Mali all having referred for investigation alleged criminal acts that have occurred in their respective territories. A state that is not a party to the Rome Statute can also choose to accept the Court's jurisdiction in relation to crimes involving genocide, crimes against humanity or war crimes that have occurred on its territory or involve one of its nationals. It is also possible for nationals of states that are not parties to the Statute to be referred to the ICC if they are accused of having committed one of these crimes on the territory of a state that is party to the Statute. In practice, however, this possibility is greatly reduced by the principle of complementarity described above, which places the onus for investigating and prosecuting crimes on the relevant states themselves.

Secondly, the Security Council, acting under Chapter VII of the UN Charter, can refer for investigation any situation apparently involving one or more of the specified crimes if it considers it to be a threat to international peace and security. The Council has so far exercised this power twice: in respect of

Sudan and the situation in Darfur, in 2005; and in relation to Libya, in 2011. In the case of UNSC referrals, it is irrelevant whether the state involved has ratified the Rome Statute or not. Neither Sudan nor Libya has done so. An attempt in 2014 to refer the situation in Syria to the Court, in order to investigate whether war crimes had been committed, failed when Russia and China vetoed the draft resolution. As well as being able to trigger an investigation, the Security Council can also put a stop to one. Under Article 16 of the Rome Statute, the Council can order the ICC to suspend any investigation or prosecution for a period of one year, with such suspension subject to indefinite renewal.

Thirdly, the Prosecutor can choose to launch an investigation *proprio motu* – that is, on his or her own initiative – into a genocide-related crime, crime against humanity or war crime, as long as he or she has received reliable information concerning the alleged crime and reasonably believes that an investigation is warranted. However, before such an investigation can begin, the Prosecutor must first obtain the consent of one of the Chambers of the Pre-trial division of the Court.

In respect of genocide, war crimes, and crimes against humanity, the Court can deal only with alleged criminal acts that took place on or after 1 July 2002 (i.e. the date on which the Rome Statute came into force). A state ratifying the Statute after this date is subject to the Court's jurisdiction only from the date on which the Statute enters into force for that state.

ii. Jurisdiction: Crimes of Aggression

As mentioned above, the ICC's jurisdiction over the crime of aggression was delayed (under Article 5(2)) until agreement could be reached on both a definition of the crime and the conditions under which the Court would be able to exercise its jurisdiction. Obtaining such agreement proved difficult, although a consensus was finally achieved at a special review conference in Kampala, Uganda, in 2010. It was, however, decided not to activate the Court's jurisdiction until at least 30 states parties had ratified or accepted the Kampala amendments, and only when the ASP had resolved to trigger the activation, with such a decision postponed until 2017 at the earliest. The ASP finally resolved, at a meeting in New York in December 2017, to activate the Court's jurisdiction in respect of the crime of aggression from 17 July 2018 (the twentieth anniversary of the adoption of the Rome Statute), and 37 states parties have so far ratified the amendments (as at February 2019). As well as accepting the Kampala amendments, it is possible, under Article 15*bis*(4), for a state to actively opt out of them by lodging a declaration to this effect with the Court's Registrar.

However, uncertainty persists as to the extent of the ICC's jurisdiction over the crime of aggression. This is a product of the division between those states (especially the P5) who wished to ensure that this crime could be referred to the ICC only via the Security Council (thus tightly controlling the circumstances in which an alleged act of criminal aggression could be brought before the Court) and those states that believed the ICC should be given a freer hand in investigating and prosecuting the crime.

It is accepted that, under Article 15*ter*, the Court has the power to act where a case is referred to it by the UN Security Council (regardless of whether or not the state concerned has ratified the Kampala amendments, and even if the relevant state is not actually a party to the Rome Statute). It is also clear that, in the other two situations in which the Court's jurisdiction can be triggered – state referral of a case, and the initiation of an investigation by the prosecutor him or herself – the Court is unable to act when the crime of aggression has been committed by a national or on the territory of a state that is not a party to the Rome Statute (Article 15*bis*(5)). (In this respect, the Court's power is narrower than it is in relation to the other three crimes covered by the Statute, where it can exercise jurisdiction over the national of a non-state party provided that the crime that the individual is accused of committing took place on the territory of a ratifying state.) The real problem with the extent of the Court's jurisdiction lies with state referrals or prosecutor-initiated investigations that involve a state that is party to the Rome Statute but which has neither accepted the Kampala amendments nor expressly opted out of them under Article 15*bis*(4). State and legal opinion is divided as to whether the Court is able to exercise jurisdiction over the crime of aggression in relation to such a state.

The narrow or restrictive interpretation – advocated by Canada, Colombia, France, Japan, Norway and the UK in negotiations leading up to the activation of the ICC's jurisdiction over the crime of aggression – holds that the Court is precluded from acting in such circumstances. Indeed, at the behest of France and the UK, a paragraph was included in the ASP's New York resolution stating that, where a case is referred to the Court by another state, or where the ICC has initiated its own investigation, 'the Court shall not exercise its jurisdiction regarding a crime of aggression when committed by a national or on the territory of a State Party that has not ratified or accepted these amendments.' This, it is argued, is in accordance with the need for a state to give its express consent before being bound by any new legal requirement, and is indeed simply reflective of Article 121(5) of the Rome Statute, which provides that, where a state has chosen not to ratify an amendment in relation to a crime dealt with by the Statute, the Court will then lack jurisdiction in respect of 'a crime covered by the amendment when committed by that State Party's nationals or on its territory'.

In contrast, other states, led by Liechtenstein (and including Argentina, Botswana, Samoa, Slovenia and Switzerland) adopted a broader, more expansive view of the Court's powers. They maintain that the Court will enjoy jurisdiction where a crime of aggression has been committed on the territory of a state party that has ratified the Kampala amendments even if the accused is a national of a state party that has not accepted them. The only exception will be where the state party of the national in question has specifically opted out of the Kampala amendments as provided for under Article 15*bis*(4). This view draws support from Article 12(2) of the Rome Statute, which allows the Court to exercise jurisdiction over crimes committed on the territory of a state party irrespective of the nationality of the individual responsible. The states in favour of this interpretation also emphasise that determining who is subject to the Court's jurisdiction is ultimately a matter for the Court itself, and, in deference to their wishes, the ASP's New York resolution specifically referred to Articles 40(1) and 119(1) of the Rome Statute, which specify, respectively, the independence of the ICC's judges in the performance of their functions and the power of the Court to settle disputes relating to its judicial functions.[44]

Which view ultimately prevails will have important implications for the reach of the Court's jurisdiction over the crime of aggression: does it apply to all states parties to the Rome Statute (now numbering 123) or solely to those that ratify the Kampala amendments (to date, only 37)? It will also determine the level of protection afforded to ratifying states against potential aggressor nations, depending on whether or not the latter need to have explicitly consented to the operation of the Court's jurisdiction in order for their nationals to be held guilty of this crime. Unsurprisingly, those states which, historically, have had most to fear from invasion and attack have tended to champion the broad approach, whereas those that have most to fear from a use of force being characterised as a crime of aggression are to be found in the narrow camp. This certainly explains the positions adopted by the UK and France. Indeed, many have stated that, had the crime of aggression been activated under the Rome Statute before the invasion of Iraq occurred in 2003, it is possible that the then British Prime Minister, Tony Blair, would have faced prosecution at the ICC.

For those states parties to the Rome Statute that do choose to ratify or accept the Kampala amendments in relation to the crime of aggression, such amendments will come into force for the state concerned one year after such ratification. At the present time, it is uncertain whether a state that opts to ratify the Rome Statute as a whole for the first time will be bound by these amendments or whether it will be able to exclude their application.

---

[44] For further, detailed discussion of the jurisdictional complexities in relation to the crime of aggression, see Clark 'Exercise of jurisdiction' (forthcoming); Claus Kreß, 'On the Activation of ICC Jurisdiction over the Crime of Aggression' (2018) 16 *Journal of International Criminal Justice* 1–17; and Dapo Akande, 'Treaty Law and ICC Jurisdiction over the Crime of Aggression (2018) 29 *European Journal of International Law* 939–59.

E. Current Caseload

As at February 2019, the Office of the Prosecutor (OTP) was conducting investigations into alleged war crimes and/or crimes against humanity committed in the following 10 states: Burundi (where alleged crimes committed by Burundi nationals outside of Burundi are also being investigated), Central African Republic (in respect of two separate situations: the first relating to the conflict of 2002–03, and the second concerning renewed violence beginning in 2012), Côte d'Ivoire, Democratic Republic of the Congo (DRC), Georgia, Kenya, Libya, Mali, Sudan (regarding the situation in Darfur, where the crime of genocide is also being investigated), and Uganda. In addition, the Prosecutor is carrying out a preliminary examination of information in relation to alleged crimes involving the following states in order to determine whether an investigation by the OTP is warranted: Afghanistan; Bangladesh/Myanmar (concerning the alleged deportation of the Rohingya people from Myanmar to Bangladesh); Colombia; Guinea; Iraq/UK (regarding alleged war crimes committed by British soldiers in the Iraq conflict and the subsequent occupation of that country from 2003–08); Nigeria; Palestine; the Philippines; Ukraine; and Venezuela.

There are currently two individuals on trial at The Hague. Bosco Ntaganda (alleged Deputy Chief of Staff and commander of operations of the Patriotic Force for the Liberation of the Congo) is charged with committing crimes against humanity and war crimes in 2002–03 in the north-eastern Ituri district of the DRC. (Closing statements were in fact made in August 2018 and Trial Chamber VI of the ICC is currently considering its verdict.) The other defendant, Dominic Ongwen (alleged brigade commander in the Lord's Resistance Army), is charged with committing crimes against humanity and war crimes in northern Uganda after 1 July 2002 (the date on which the ICC's jurisdiction came into force). The ICC has also formally charged Abdallah Banda (Commander in Chief of the rebel Justice and Equality Movement) with alleged war crimes carried out against African Union Mission peacekeepers in Darfur, Sudan, in 2007. However, the accused remains at large, with the trial suspended pending his arrest (the ICC has issued an arrest warrant) or voluntary appearance. A number of cases are also at the pre-trial stage, with warrants of arrest having been issued in respect of the individuals concerned.[45]

In January 2019, Trial Chamber I of the ICC, by a majority, acquitted former Côte d'Ivoire President Laurent Gbagbo and former Youth Minister

---

[45] For information on the status of cases, investigations and preliminary examinations at the ICC, visit the Court's website at www.icc-cpi.int/pages/pe.aspx#.

Charles Blé Goudé (their two cases had been joined in March 2015) of all charges in relation to crimes against humanity allegedly committed during the post-election violence in Côte d'Ivoire in 2010–11, finding that the prosecution had failed to present sufficient evidence of their guilt. As well as being a severe disappointment for victims of the violence who had appeared before the Court, the acquittal also represented a major setback for the OTP, particularly as the trial of Gbagbo represented its first prosecution of a former head of state. The acquittals of Gbagbo and Blé Goudé are being appealed.

The OTP secured its first conviction in March 2012, nearly 10 years after the establishment of the ICC, when Thomas Lubanga, former President of the Union of Congolese Patriots and founder of the Patriotic Force for the Liberation of the Congo, was sentenced to 14 years' imprisonment for the war crime of using child soldiers in an armed conflict in the DRC's Ituri region in 2002–03. Since the six years that Lubanga had already spent in detention at the ICC were deducted from his sentence, he faced a further eight years in prison, and is due to be released in 2020. In December 2015, he was transferred from The Hague to the Congolese capital Kinshasa, where he is serving the remainder of his sentence. In March 2014, the OTP obtained a further conviction in relation to the conflict in the DRC, when Germain Katanga, former commander of the Patriotic Resistance Force in Ituri, was sentenced to 12 years' imprisonment on four counts of war crimes (murder, attacking a civilian population, destruction of property, and pillaging) and acting as an accessory to one crime against humanity (murder), carried out during an attack on the village of Bogoro. Katanga was also transferred to Kinshasa in December 2015 to serve the remainder of his sentence. Reductions for time already spent in detention (nearly seven years), and for good behaviour and expressing regret to his victims, meant that Katanga was due to be released in January 2016; however, he remains in prison while the DRC authorities pursue further cases against him, including in relation to the murder of nine Bangladeshi UN peacekeepers in 2005. Finally, in September 2016, Ahmad Al Faqi Al Mahdi, an Islamic extremist, was convicted, following a guilty plea, of the war crime of intentionally directing attacks against religious and historic monuments and buildings in the city of Timbuktu, Mali, in 2012.

In a further blow to the OTP, Jean-Pierre Bemba, former President of the Movement for the Liberation of the Congo, was acquitted by a slim 3–2 majority of the Appeals Chamber in June 2018. He had initially been found guilty in 2016 of committing crimes against humanity and war crimes in the Central African Republic in 2002–03, and sentenced to 18 years in prison. The overturning of the original verdict, which had been hailed as a milestone both for securing a conviction under the doctrine of command responsibility, and for its recognition of rape as a war crime, has been widely criticised.

F. Weaknesses of the Court

In a blow to the Court's legitimacy, China, Russia and the US are not parties to the Rome Statute, despite being in a position to refer other states and their nationals to the ICC for investigation. China has never signed the Statute, while both the US and Russia, having signed it in 2000, subsequently 'unsigned' it by formally notifying the Secretary-General of their intentions not to become parties – the US in 2002 during the administration of George W Bush, and Russia in 2016, after the ICC classified the Putin Government's annexation of Crimea as an occupation. Thus, in accordance with Article 18(1) of the Vienna Convention on the Law of Treaties 1969, both are no longer 'obliged to refrain from acts which would defeat the object and purpose' of the Statute. Moreover, as India and Indonesia have also refused to sign the Statute, this means that the world's four most populous states have opted to exempt themselves from the Court's jurisdiction. Compounding its problems still further, the Philippines has recently withdrawn from the Rome Statute (having objected to the Court investigating alleged crimes against humanity committed by President Rodrigo Duterte's Government during its 'war on drugs'),[46] Burundi withdrew in 2017, and both South Africa and The Gambia have threatened to do so (see below).

The US has been especially active in ensuring that its nationals are never brought before the ICC, further weakening the Court. Asserting that its military personnel serving overseas would be vulnerable to politically motivated arrests and prosecutions (notwithstanding the safeguards built in to the Statute deliberately subordinating the powers of the ICC to those of the states themselves), the US has pressured a number of states into signing Article 98, or bilateral immunity, agreements, under which they promise never to surrender US citizens to the ICC (see chapter four). This hostility towards the Court has accelerated under the Trump administration. After learning that the Prosecutor was considering opening a formal investigation into war crimes allegedly committed by US military and intelligence personnel in Afghanistan (Afghanistan being a state party to the Rome statute, and the prosecutor being empowered to initiate an investigation where such a crime has occurred on the territory of a member state, even if the accused is a national of a non-member), US National Security Adviser John Bolton lambasted the ICC,

---

[46] Under Art 127 of the Rome Statute, a state wishing to withdraw is obliged to give a year's notice. Any duty to cooperate with the Court in relation to criminal investigations and proceedings commenced before the date on which the withdrawal takes effect will continue to bind the state, and the withdrawal shall not 'prejudice in any way the continued consideration of any matter which was already under consideration by the Court' before such date. Consequently, the ICC is free to continue its investigation into the actions of Philippine officials and also to pursue any subsequent prosecution, although, from a practical point of view – owing to the non-cooperation of the Philippine government – this will now be much more difficult.

describing it as 'illegitimate' and a danger to American sovereignty and US security interests.[47] In order to deter the Court from acting, Bolton threatened to bar ICC prosecutors and judges from entering the US, to impose sanctions on any funds they hold with US financial institutions, and even to prosecute such officials in American courts. He also sharply criticised the ICC regarding Israel (Palestine having asked the Court to open a formal investigation into alleged war crimes and crimes against humanity committed by the IDF and Israeli officials in East Jerusalem, Gaza and the West Bank), closing down the Palestine Liberation Organisation's diplomatic mission in Washington. The OTP has yet to announce whether it will begin formal investigations into either situation – ie the alleged crimes of US and Israeli nationals in Afghanistan and Palestine respectively – but the political pressure being brought to bear on the ICC is unmistakable and quite extraordinary.[48]

As noted above, under Article 16 of the Rome Statute, the Security Council is able to order the ICC to suspend any investigation or prosecution for one year, and can indefinitely renew such suspension. The awarding of such powers to the Security Council was the result of a compromise when the Statute was being negotiated, between, at the one extreme, three of the five permanent members of the Security Council – China, Russia and the US – which wanted the Council to play a prominent role both in referring situations to the ICC and also in preventing ICC investigations, and, at the other, those states, including members of the Non-Aligned Movement, which believed that the Security Council should have nothing to do with the process. Although this compromise undoubtedly helped ensure the adoption of the Rome Statute, it has led to problems in practice. And, of course, the existence of the veto power means that none of the P5 will be referred by the Council to the ICC for possible crimes committed on its territory: for example, China in relation to its actions in Tibet, or Russia in relation to possible crimes committed by its forces in Chechnya or Ukraine.

Largely debarred from holding the most powerful states to account, the ICC also faces accusations that its efforts are disproportionately targeted at some of the world's weakest nations, especially African ones. All of the ICC's initial investigations involved African states, leading some disgruntled

---

[47] See 'Full text of John Bolton's speech to the Federalist Society', *Al Jazeera*, 10 September 2018, available at www.aljazeera.com/news/2018/09/full-text-john-bolton-speech-federalist-society-180910172828633.html.

[48] In March 2019, the Trump administration further hardened its attitude towards the ICC, with US Secretary of State Mike Pompeo announcing the implementation of 'a policy of U.S. visa restrictions on those individuals directly responsible for any ICC investigation of U.S. personnel. This includes persons who take or have taken action to request or further such an investigation. These visa restrictions may also be used to deter ICC efforts to pursue allied personnel, including Israelis, without allies' consent.' He also stated that: 'We are prepared to take additional steps, including economic sanctions if the ICC does not change its course.' Michael R Pompeo, 'Remarks to the Press', US Department of State, 15 March 2019, available at www.state.gov/secretary/remarks/2019/03/290394.htm.

observers to nickname it the 'European Criminal Court for Africa'. And, notwithstanding the fact that the ICC's scope has widened since then, most of its caseload remains focused on African states and African nationals. For many, this provides yet another example of the way in which international law, in spite of its professed neutrality, fails to operate impartially, with only the poorest and weakest targeted for investigation and prosecution, while more powerful states and their nationals, or those with powerful allies, escape scrutiny.[49] Others disagree and state that it is hardly surprising that most of the Court's work should involve African nations, since these are the very countries that, owing to greater levels of impoverishment, tend to lack a fully functioning judicial system and are therefore more likely to turn to the ICC to conduct criminal trials on their behalf. As mentioned above, four African states have approached the Court themselves in respect of crimes committed on their territories, although there have been accusations of manipulation, alleging that certain leaders and governments have referred their opponents to the ICC while simultaneously shielding their own equally horrific acts from scrutiny.[50] Even those who are supportive of the ICC's work in Africa, however, worry that its over-concentration on the continent actually plays into the hands of dictators and the political elites, enabling them to portray the ICC as inherently biased or even neo-imperialist.

It is certainly true that uneasiness at the ICC's perceived preoccupation with Africa intensified as a result of the Court's actions in relation to Sudan, the subject of a UNSC referral in 2005; a case that also served to foreground the problematic nature of the relationship between the UNSC and the ICC. The Court's decision to issue an arrest warrant in respect of, among other Sudanese officials, then President Omar al-Bashir in March 2009[51] not only brought protests from the Sudanese Government at what it characterised as an unwarranted interference in its sovereign affairs (Sudan being a non-party to the Rome Statute), but also drew objections from the African Union (AU), which considered such a step disruptive to its own efforts to mediate a peaceful resolution to the conflict in Darfur. What particularly angered the AU was the failure of the UNSC to respond to the organisation's request to make use of its Article 16 powers to order a 12-month stay in the ICC's proceedings

---

[49] Archbishop Desmond Tutu drew attention to the perceived hypocrisy when he refused to attend a leadership summit in Johannesburg in 2012 in which Tony Blair was participating. In denouncing the actions of both George W Bush and Blair in ordering the invasion of Iraq in 2003, Tutu made clear his belief that both leaders should face prosecution at The Hague, noting in this respect that Western leaders were not held to account in the same way as their African and Asian counterparts.

[50] On this point, see Rajan Menon, *The Conceit of Humanitarian Intervention* (Oxford, OUP, 2018) 162–64.

[51] Citing the commission of certain war crimes and crimes against humanity in relation to Darfur. This was followed, in July 2010, by the issue of a second arrest warrant, to which the charge of genocide had been added.

against the Sudanese President. As a consequence, the AU instructed its member states not to co-operate with the ICC in securing the arrest of the President. Indeed, al-Bashir has now travelled unhindered to a large number of states, including many African and Middle Eastern countries that are parties to the Rome Statute but which have all so far refused to execute the arrest warrant.[52] Some of these states he has visited more than once. Thus, 10 years after the issuing of the first arrest warrant against him, and despite the referral of non-arresting states to the ICC's ASP and to the UNSC (which referred the situation in Darfur to the Court in the first place),[53] al-Bashir and other senior Sudanese government officials and military leaders remain at large, much to the frustration of the Prosecutor, who has repeatedly called on the Security Council to act in the matter.[54] Meanwhile, exacerbating matters still further is the fact that the war and humanitarian crisis in Darfur remains ongoing.[55]

Nor is al-Bashir the only African head of state to have been subject to an ICC arrest warrant. Uhuru Kenyatta, who was elected President of Kenya in March 2013, was indicted by the Court in 2011, charged with committing crimes against humanity in connection with the post-election violence that occurred in Kenya after the country's 2007 election. Again, the indictment proved controversial among many African states, despite the fact that the crimes in question were not the subject of a UNSC referral but had instead been referred by an investigatory body in Kenya itself, and in spite of the fact that the arrest warrant was issued before Kenyatta became president. As with the al-Bashir case, the attempt to bring Kenyatta to trial has proved less than successful. The charges against him were actually withdrawn in 2014, with the Prosecutor citing lack of cooperation from the Kenyan Government in

[52] 'States "failing to seize Sudan's dictator despite genocide charge"', Tom White, *The Observer*, 21 October 2018.

[53] Jordan, which al-Bashir visited in March 2017, has been held by a Pre-Trial Chamber of the ICC not to have complied with its obligations as a member of the Rome Statute to arrest the Sudanese leader. Jordan has appealed the decision (in a hearing that involved submissions from several organisations and individuals, including the African Union), and the Appeals Chamber of the Court is currently considering its verdict.

[54] In her most recent report to the UNSC on Darfur, the Prosecutor, having recounted that Djibouti and Uganda (both ICC members) had again played host to al-Bashir, with the Security Council having declined to take action against either state for its failure to arrest the Sudanese President during previous visits, commented: 'In the absence of any meaningful consequences for such instances of non-compliance, we are unlikely to see a change in such regrettable patterns. This status quo is hardly conducive to advancing the cause of justice in Darfur. My Office, yet again, calls on this Council to take meaningful action to give effect to non-compliance referrals by the Court.' Office of the Prosecutor, 'Twenty-Eighth Report of the Prosecutor of the International Criminal Court to the United Nations Security Council on the Situation in Darfur, Pursuant to UNSCR 1593 (2005)', 14 December 2018, paras 20 and 21.

[55] See ibid, at paras 10–12, noting a decline in violence against civilians during the reporting period, but the further commission of serious crimes, including attacks against AU and UN peacekeepers, as well as reports of 'the destruction of villages and the killing, injury and displacement of civilians' and 'sexual and gender-based violence against women and girls in Darfur'.

the collection of evidence as her reason for doing so.[56] And, as noted above, although the OTP has finally managed to prosecute a former head of state, Laurent Gbagbo, the erstwhile Ivorian President has now been acquitted (although that acquittal is currently the subject of an appeal).

The al-Bashir case prompted the AU to call for Article 16 to be amended to allow the General Assembly to order the ICC to suspend an investigation or proceedings, if, following a period of at least six months from having received a request to order such a referral, the UNSC fails to act. Although such an amendment is unlikely to be adopted (especially as it would need to be ratified by at least seven-eighths of the states parties to the Rome Statute), the fact that it was proposed signalled the level of frustration among AU members at the UNSC's inaction. The al-Bashir affair in particular has tarnished the reputation of the ICC, with it having attracted criticism from both those who believe that African states and their leaders have been unfairly targeted by the Court, which is subject to the influence of the UNSC to an unhealthy degree, and, on the other hand, from those who believe that the matter has exposed the impotence of the Court, with its own state members and the UNSC (even in respect of its own referrals to the ICC) unwilling or unable to help bring to justice the most powerful of those accused of atrocity crimes. It has also laid bare the disquiet harboured by many states and their leaders that the Court's attention extends to serving heads of state, thereby disregarding the full state immunity which such office-holders normally enjoy.

An African nation has also been the first state to leave the ICC, with Burundi's withdrawal from the Rome Statute having taken effect in October 2017. The decision of President Pierre Nkurunziza to leave the Court – made in 2016 and accompanied by claims that the ICC is used as an instrument by powerful states to punish those who do not bow to their demands – was taken shortly after the UN Human Rights Council announced the setting-up of a commission of inquiry into alleged human rights abuses that had occurred in Burundi from April 2015 onwards. (Burundi is now in fact the subject of an OTP investigation that was begun before it had formally left the ICC.) More seriously for the prestige of the Court, South Africa gave formal notification of its intention to withdraw from the ICC in 2016, under the Government of President Jacob Zuma, stating that the Court's interpretation of states parties' obligations under the Rome Statute conflicted with its commitment to the peaceful resolution of disputes. Specifically, the Government appeared stung by criticism of its refusal to comply with a High Court order to arrest the

[56] The Prosecutor also referred to a barrage of false media reports about the case, a social media campaign aimed at exposing the identity of protected witnesses, and wide-ranging witness intimidation. See 'ICC drops murder and rape charges against Kenyan president', Owen Bowcott, *Guardian*, 5 December 2014. She has pledged to reopen the case if sufficient evidence later comes to light. A case against the Deputy President of Kenya, William Ruto, and the radio host Joshua arap Sang – also in relation to alleged crimes against humanity committed during the post-electoral violence of 2007–08 – collapsed in 2016 for similar reasons to the Kenyatta case.

then Sudanese President al-Bashir during his attendance at an AU summit in Johannesburg in 2015, including a sharp rebuke from South Africa's Supreme Court of Appeal in a judgment confirming that the Government had acted unlawfully in allowing al-Bashir to leave the country.[57] The withdrawal notice was rescinded in 2017, following a High Court ruling declaring it unconstitutional, on the ground that the Government had failed to obtain parliamentary approval before issuing it. The Gambia (the home state of the current prosecutor) also opted to leave the Court in 2016, with the administration of President Yahya Jammeh pointing to double standards in its treatment of African and Western leaders (citing its failure to indict former British Prime Minister Tony Blair over the Iraq War[58]), but the notification was rescinded in 2017, under the new administration of President Adama Barrow.

A further criticism frequently levelled at the ICC is that it is too slow and too expensive. Its costs are now estimated to have exceeded $1 billion in total,[59] but its performance to date belies the size of its operating budgets. As observed above, it took nearly 10 years for the Court to obtain its first conviction; and, over 15 years later, only four convictions for the commission of grave international crimes have been achieved,[60] one of which (that of Jean-Pierre Bemba) has been subsequently overturned.

The institutional and operational defects of the ICC, and how these might possibly be rectified, have recently been the subject of an illuminating examination by Douglas Guilfoyle.[61] Among the many problems besetting the Court that he pinpoints – in addition to the costly and dilatory nature of its proceedings – are the following: a flawed pre-trial chambers process that slows down the work of the Court but nevertheless allows shaky cases to proceed

---

[57] In July 2017, a pre-trial chamber of the ICC found that South Africa had breached its obligations in failing to arrest President al-Bashir. Interestingly, however, it declined to refer this violation to the UNSC, stating that the Security Council's failure to act in respect of similar past referrals rendered such action futile.

[58] The ICC confirmed in 2006 that it was unable to take any action against Tony Blair in relation to the Iraq War (the UK being a state party to the Rome Statute) because the invasion of the country amounted to an alleged crime of aggression, and the Court's jurisdiction in respect of this category of crime had not been activated at the time of the invasion in 2003.

[59] Jessica Hatcher-Moore, 'Is the world's highest court fit for purpose?', *Guardian*, 5 April 2017.

[60] Four individuals have also been convicted by the ICC of administration of justice offences under art 70 of the Court's statute, which deals with actions that seriously jeopardise criminal proceedings, such as interference with witnesses. All these convictions relate to its investigation into the Central African Republic, and the sentences handed down ranged from six months to three years. See Douglas Guilfoyle, 'Part I – This is not fine: The International Criminal Court in Trouble', *EJIL: Talk! Blog of the European Journal of International Law*, 21 March 2019, available at www.ejiltalk.org/part-i-this-is-not-fine-the-international-criminal-court-in-trouble.

[61] ibid and Douglas Guilfoyle, 'Part II – This is not fine: The International Criminal Court in Trouble', *EJIL: Talk! Blog of the European Journal of International Law*, 22 March 2019, available at www.ejiltalk.org/part-ii-this-is-not-fine-the-international-criminal-court-in-trouble and 'Part III – This is not fine: The International Criminal Court in Trouble', *EJIL: Talk! Blog of the European Journal of International Law*, 25 March 2019, available at www.ejiltalk.org/part-iii-this-is-not-fine-the-international-criminal-court-in-trouble/#more-17007.

(and subsequently fail); a lack of trust and collegiality between the OTP and the judiciary, as well as within the judiciary itself (possibly attributable to the differing criminal legal traditions in which the various judges are nurtured, as well as their different professional backgrounds); the troubled tenure of the ICC's first Prosecutor, Luis Moreno-Ocampo;[62] and the expensive employment litigation in which the Court has become entangled, encompassing numerous successful claims of unfair dismissal by former employees of the Registry and the somewhat unseemly spectacle of several judges alleging that they are (or were) underpaid in comparison with their counterparts on the ICJ.[63] Interestingly, Guilfoyle also suggests that the Court's problems may partly stem from a shift in the zeitgeist: 'We have moved from the heady cosmopolitanism of the 1990s and its post-Cold War institution-building to a period of tribunal and law-making fatigue, along with resurgent nationalism and its emphasis on impermeable sovereignty.'[64]

Some final observations on the ICC can also be made. Clearly, only the very worst offenders can ever be prosecuted, although, ironically, this will bring them enormous privileges – excellent facilities, competent legal representation and no possibility of the death penalty. In addition, although the ICC has an important educative function in publicising the horrors that have been perpetrated and endured, this may lead to two unfortunate outcomes. The first is media 'war crime horror fatigue', with boredom being the inappropriate response to egregious crimes. The second is that the prosecutions themselves may imperil moves towards reconciliation within war-torn territories. Indeed, this was arguably the case in respect of the UNSC referral of Colonel Gaddafi and other Libyan leaders to the ICC in 2011, with such action encouraging the Libyan Government to continue fighting rather than reach an accord with opposition groups.

---

[62] Summed up by Guilfoyle as follows: 'The final verdict of history on Moreno-Ocampo is likely to be poor. He was a prosecutor who, by his own admission, did not consider securing convictions his first priority; rather, his goal was using "the shadow of the court" to prevent crimes. However, on his watch cases were mounted on the basis of very limited investigations and conducted without, it seems, either a clear eye to litigation strategy or a staff which was prepared to give him fearless advice [owing to Moreno-Ocampo's apparently overbearing attitude towards subordinates]. It is thus perhaps unsurprising that in his nine years as Prosecutor he initiated more than a dozen cases and saw only one through to a successful conclusion.' Guilfoyle, 'Part II – This is not fine: The International Criminal Court in Trouble'. Moreno-Ocampo's conduct in relation to consultancy work (worth $3 million over three years) undertaken with a Libyan businessman, Hassan Tatanaki, after he left his post as prosecutor is currently being investigated by the ICC, as is that of certain Court employees. This follows media reports that information was leaked from the ICC to Moreno-Ocampo regarding a possible investigation by the Court into his client's connection to a militia alleged to have carried out killings and other human rights violations in Libya.

[63] Guilfoyle refers to 'the open secret that six past or present ICC judges – including the current president – are litigating the alleged paucity of their €200,000 ... tax-free salaries, plus benefits and pensions when compared to those of ICJ judges'. Guilfoyle, 'Part I – This is not fine: The International Criminal Court in Trouble'.

[64] ibid.

In part, the recognition of these problems has led to the creation of so-called 'mixed tribunals', where those charged with international crimes are brought before a court in their own country, but a court that includes both domestic judges and judges from outside the state applying domestic and international criminal law. Such mixed tribunals have operated in Cambodia, Sierra Leone, East Timor, Kosovo, Bosnia-Herzegovina and Lebanon.

VIII. Conclusion

Embodied in embryonic form in the UN Charter, the concept of human rights has developed at an exponential rate in the past 60 or so years, and is now an enduring feature of the international legal landscape. The protection of various rights is now enshrined in a myriad of global and regional conventions, although the enforcement of such rights remains patchy and their implementation uneven, as states differ, according to ideological preference, as to which rights they choose to emphasise and which to downplay or ignore. In particular, and in spite of their undoubted interdependence, a divide persists between civil and political rights on the one hand, and social and economic rights on the other. Nonetheless, the increasing prominence accorded to human rights since the Second World War has meant that individuals now function, in some respects, as subjects of the international legal regime, able to benefit directly from rights conferred by international law, and liable to criminal prosecution for the gravest violations of that law. This has had an important impact not only on the place of the individual in international law, but also on the concept of state sovereignty, with governments of all stripes now forced to pay some attention to international human rights norms in their treatment of citizens.

7

The Peaceful Settlement of Disputes in International Law

I. Introduction

The Charter of the UN places considerable emphasis on the duty of member states to resolve their disputes by peaceful means: an obvious complement to the obligation it imposes on states to refrain from the use of force in settling their differences. Article 1(1) states that it is a purpose of the UN to 'bring about by peaceful means, and in conformity with the principles of justice and international law, adjustment or settlement of international disputes or situations which might lead to a breach of the peace', while Article 2(3) places an obligation upon members to 'settle their international disputes by peaceful means in such a manner that international peace and security, and justice, are not endangered'. Every member of the UN is of course a party to this Charter and is bound by it. Moreover, as Judge Christopher Weeramantry noted as a member of the ICJ, all major international disputes are finally concluded by negotiations and adjudication, and this in itself suggests that it is advantageous to have the negotiations and adjudication before, rather than after, the use of force.

The pacific settlement of disputes forms the subject matter of Chapter VI of the Charter. Under Article 33(1), state members are enjoined to settle any dispute that threatens to disrupt international peace and security by one of the following means: 'negotiation, enquiry, mediation, conciliation, arbitration, judicial settlement, resort to regional agencies or arrangements, or other peaceful means of their own choice', and the Security Council may call upon states to resolve their dispute by one of these methods if it deems it necessary to do so. What should immediately be apparent is that the means proposed for resolving disputes, while they are all obviously lawful, are not all, strictly speaking, legal methods as we defined them in chapter two. Negotiation, enquiry, mediation and conciliation, although they are defined in international law, seem to lack the quality of legal means, which, it was suggested, requires some 'translation' from the social and political world to a legal frame in which legal issues are isolated and answered. For this reason, we will primarily be concerned with judicial resolution, especially through the ICJ, and to a lesser extent with arbitration. The chapter will begin with a discussion of legal method and international dispute resolution, and will then proceed to an analysis of the International Court. It will consider the history of the Court, its composition and statute, and some cases to exemplify the points made.

Negotiation is obviously the means by which most international disputes are resolved. This is usually, but not necessarily, diplomatic and face-to-face, and any agreement will have the status intended by the parties, and will therefore be legally binding only if this is what the parties intend. Mediation and good offices depend upon the involvement of a third party or parties. Good offices from a third party precede negotiation, and mediation involves a third party mediating, or acting as an intermediary, between disputing parties. A commission of inquiry is usually a preliminary means by which facts may be impartially found in order to provide the basis for a resolution of the dispute.

II. Legal Method and International Dispute Resolution

It was observed in chapter one that international law does not provide for any compulsory adjudication in the event of disagreement or dispute. This is notwithstanding the fact that compulsory and binding jurisdiction was perceived as desirable by many international law writers for most of the twentieth century, who believed that an international court with the ability to hand down authoritative judgments in respect of issues which threatened world peace, and with the moral or physical standing to ensure compliance, would contribute directly to the UN's objective of maintaining international peace and security. Often, it is argued, the resolution of disputes by legal means is the only alternative to settling the matter by force, which frequently entails war.

Historically, there have been many efforts to persuade states that their interests lie in accepting the compulsory jurisdiction of a supranational court and giving effect to judgments even when inconvenient or worse. However, those who advocated such an approach proved to be over-optimistic for two main reasons. The first involves the distinction between politics and law, and the second (which is related) concerns the belief in the objectivity of law and its ability to provide justice. This will be illustrated through discussion of the significance of two decisions of the International Court of Justice (ICJ). The first concerns the US and its 'relations' with the Government of Nicaragua; the second, the advisory opinion given by the Court in 1996 after considering whether the threat or use of nuclear weapons is, in any circumstances, permitted under international law. Both cases illustrate the advantages, and also the pitfalls, of putting international problems into legal form.

III. The International Court of Justice

The ICJ was intended to play a vital role in ensuring the peaceful resolution of inter-state disputes. Also known as the 'World Court', the ICJ is the principal judicial organ of the UN. It was established in 1945 under Article 92 of the UN Charter, and began operating the following year, in April 1946. It sits in The Hague in the Netherlands, making it the only one of the UN's principal organs not to be based in New York.

In common with most of the other principal bodies of the UN, the ICJ is modelled to a great extent on an earlier organisation set up as part of the peace settlement of 1919. The forerunner of the ICJ was the Permanent Court of International Justice (PCIJ), established under the Covenant of the League of Nations, and active from 1922 to 1946, after which its functions were transferred to the newly created ICJ. The statute of the ICJ closely resembles that of the PCIJ; the last President of the PCIJ, Judge José Gustavo Guerrero of El Salvador, became the first President of the ICJ; the new Court assumed as its permanent seat the Peace Palace in the Hague, the former home of the PCIJ; and there is a continuity of jurisprudence between the two Courts, with ICJ decisions and opinions frequently referencing those of the earlier judicial body. However, there are also some significant differences between the two, indicative of changing attitudes to adjudication in international law.

As Judge Mohammed Bedjaoui observed when President of the ICJ, the PCIJ was more of a precursor than a predecessor. This, he explained, was because of one striking difference between the Courts. Whereas the PCIJ, which was not an organ of the League of Nations, was 'aimed essentially to do no more than establish peace in order to preserve the status quo', the ICJ was created as an integral part of the UN, with the framers of the UN Charter directing their efforts towards the establishment

> of an entirely new international society – a society consistently moving towards progress; a society more just, more egalitarian, more wont to show solidarity,

more universal; a society all of whose members were to engage in an active and collective endeavour to usher in a full and lasting peace.[1]

Indeed, the statute of the ICJ forms part of the UN Charter, so that a state that joins the UN automatically becomes party to the Court's statute (although, as will be explained below, this does not mean that it automatically becomes subject to the Court's jurisdiction).

A. The Composition of the ICJ

The Court consists of 15 judges elected by means of a simultaneous vote in the General Assembly and the Security Council, with candidates needing to attract an absolute majority of votes in both bodies in order to secure a place on the Court. Candidates for election to the Court are proposed by national groups in the Permanent Court of Arbitration (PCA) (see section IV), and UN members that are not represented on the PCA may create specially constituted groups for this purpose. Judges serve nine-year terms, and are eligible for re-election for one further term. In order to ensure a certain amount of continuity, the expiry of these terms is staggered, with five judges, or one-third of the ICJ, being elected (or re-elected) every three years.

Those elected to the Court must be 'of high moral character', and must either be qualified 'for appointment to the highest judicial offices' in their home countries or be 'jurisconsults [legal experts] of recognized competence in international law' (Article 2). No two judges may be nationals of the same state, and judges are expected to act independently and impartially: ie not as representatives of their own states or of any other state or party. They must not, during their terms of office, 'exercise any political or administrative function, or engage in any other occupation of a professional nature' (Article 16(1)), or 'act as agent, counsel, or advocate in any case' (Article 17(1)), or take part in deciding any case in which they have previously acted for one of the parties or have otherwise been involved (Article 17(2)).[2] In carrying out their duties, judges 'enjoy diplomatic

---

[1] Judge HE Mohammed Bedjaoui, Preface to AS Muller, CD Raič and JM Thuránszky, *The International Court of Justice: Its Future Role After Fifty* Years (Leiden, Brill Publishing, 1996) xxi–xxii.

[2] Outside work undertaken by serving ICJ judges in relation to arbitration disputes is to be greatly restricted following criticism of the practice, particularly as regards its potential for compromising the neutrality of the judges concerned. In the annual address of the ICJ President to the UN General Assembly in October 2018, the current President, Abdulqawi Ahmed Yusuf, confirmed that ICJ judges had decided that they would no longer 'normally accept to participate in international arbitration. In particular, they will not participate in investor–State arbitration or commercial arbitration.' In exceptional cases, ICJ judges will be allowed to act as arbitrators in inter-state disputes, but only in respect of one arbitration at a time, and only where the prior permission of the Court is obtained and the state appointing the judge as arbitrator is not also a party to a case pending before the Court. 'Speech by HE Mr Abdulqawi A Yusuf, President of

privileges and immunities' (Article 19) and are paid a tax-free salary fixed by the General Assembly.

In spite of the lofty ideals expressed in the ICJ Statute, focusing on the professional and personal qualities that potential judges must possess, political considerations intrude to a significant degree on both the nomination and election processes. Although the selection of prospective judges through the PCA groups might seem to suggest that the nomination process is free from governmental influence, in practice many of these national groups either consist of government representatives or of individuals with close links to their governments. As Mackenzie et al point out, this has resulted in a wide variance between states regarding the extent to which political considerations or connections determine who is nominated to the Court: 'Some candidates may be selected through a transparent and consultative process that focuses on merit, while their competitors may have emerged because they were the best friend of the minister, or they were the minister him or herself'.[3]

Political factors play an even more pronounced role in the election process. A state will need to 'sell' its candidate to other states in order to win votes in the General Assembly and Security Council, and this can involve years of lobbying to raise the profile of the individual concerned, perhaps involving frequent trips to UN headquarters and to foreign capitals in order to secure the necessary support from other states. Poorer states will naturally lack the funds to conduct such expensive campaigns, or, at the very least, will be severely hampered in their ability to do so. Moreover, judicial positions (whether in respect of the ICJ or the International Criminal Court) are generally subject to the same vote-trading deals as other posts within the UN, with one state supporting another state's candidate, or a state agreeing to withdraw its candidate, in return for support elsewhere: thus there appears to be little inclination on the part of states and their representatives to distinguish between judicial and purely political appointments (such as a seat on the Security Council) and to adopt a more impartial, merit-based approach in respect of the former.[4] In addition, although the elections in the General Assembly and Security Council are supposed to take place independently,

the International Court of Justice, on the Occasion of the Seventy-Third Session of the United Nations General Assembly, 25 October 2018, available at www.icj-cij.org/files/press-releases/0/000-20181025-PRE-02-00-EN.pdf, at 11–12. For the background and commentary on this, see Marie Davoise, 'Can't Fight the Moonlight? Actually You Can. ICJ Judges to Stop Acting as Arbitrators in Investor-State Disputes', *EJIL: Talk! Blog of the European Journal of International Law*, 5 November 2018. Available at www.ejiltalk.org/cant-fight-the-moonlight-actually-you-can-icj-judges-to-stop-acting-as-arbitrators-in-investor-state-disputes.

[3] Ruth Mackenzie, Kate Malleson, Penny Martin and Philippe Sands, *Selecting International Judges: Principle, Process, and Politics* (Oxford, OUP, 2010) 98. (The authors are here commenting on the use of the PCA procedure to nominate judges to both the ICJ and the ICC.)

[4] ibid 122–28.

in practice consultation between the two bodies occurs, and several rounds of voting frequently take place before a victor emerges.

The need for judicial candidates to effectively campaign for a seat on the Court is understandably viewed by many (including some of the potential candidates themselves) as wholly incompatible with the disinterested, non-partisan position a judge is supposed to adopt on appointment. Compounding matters with regard to the ICJ is the fact that a sitting judge may be elected for a further term, which raises the unedifying prospect of an individual seeking support from various states for re-election even as he or she is helping to decide disputes or shape opinions in which those states may be involved or have an interest. Even if the individual concerned is scrupulous in refusing to allow his or her judgement to be influenced in any way by such personal considerations, the very suspicion that he or she might be swayed by personal considerations is hardly calculated to inspire confidence in the Court. Not surprisingly, therefore, many take the view that ICJ judges should be appointed for one term only. Certainly, there are indications that judges deemed to have voted the 'wrong' way or to have issued opinions unpalatable to more influential states risk their services being dispensed with more quickly than might otherwise have been expected (see the discussion of the *Nuclear Weapons* Advisory Opinion below).

The ICJ as a whole is intended to be reflective 'of the main forms of civilization and of the principal legal systems of the world' (Article 9). In practice, this requirement has been satisfied by following the same geographical distribution employed for the 15-member Security Council (in turn, based on the five regional groupings in the General Assembly), with three judges drawn from Africa, three from Asia, two from Latin America and the Caribbean, two from Eastern Europe, and five from Western Europe and Other States (which includes Australia, Canada and New Zealand). By convention, the Court had traditionally included a judge from each of the nations with a permanent seat on the Security Council, although the veto power is not used in determining who is elected to the Court, and no special powers attach to these judges' positions. That the P5 states should routinely have a judge elected to the Court had, unsurprisingly, drawn resentment from other states, not least because it then reduced the number of seats available for distribution elsewhere, a problem exacerbated by the tendency for judges from Germany and Japan to also be appointed to the Court, so that, as Mackenzie et al note: 'non-P5 [Western and Other Group] and Asian states must in effect compete for one seat each'.[5] For many observers, Europe is over-represented on the Court (which is arguably a more homogeneous entity since the end of the Cold War reduced the political differences between Eastern and Western Europe), and the P5 convention ensured that the composition of the Court

---

[5] ibid 28.

(like that of the Security Council) reflected the world as it was in 1945, failing to take account of present-day power realities. However, in 2017 the convention ended, when the sitting UK judge (Sir Christopher Greenwood) had his nomination for re-election withdrawn by the UK Government after he received far fewer votes in the General Assembly than the Indian nominee (Dalveer Bhandari). For the first time in 70 years, the UK was left without a seat on the ICJ in what was undoubtedly a serious blow to British prestige. The result has been ascribed in particular to the increased willingness of non-Western states to challenge the West's hegemony at the ICJ, the growing power of India within the General Assembly, and the waning influence of the UK internationally, aggravated by a perceived isolationist stance since the country voted to leave the European Union in 2016.[6]

Unlike the governing statute of the ICC, the ICJ Statute does not contain any provision for gender balance on the Court. At present, there are three female judges on the bench: two from P5 states – Xue Hanqin from China (who is also Vice-President of the Court) and Joan Donoghue from the US, both elected in 2010 to replace judges who had resigned before the expiry of their terms, and both subsequently re-elected, from February 2012 and February 2015 respectively – and one from Uganda, Julia Sebutinde, who has been a member of the Court since February 2012. Although only accounting for one-fifth of the bench, this number of female judges is unprecedented in the history of both the ICJ and the PCIJ – previously, the only woman to be appointed on a permanent basis to the World Court was Rosalyn Higgins from the UK, who served from 1995 to 2009 (acting as President of the Court from 2006 to 2009).

Notwithstanding the apparent diversity of the Court, it arguably retains a distinctively Western legal bias. Even those judges who do not come from the West tend to have completed at least part of their legal education in the US, the UK or France; nor is it without significance that the Court's only official languages are French and English. Certainly, too, if one looks at Counsel appearing before the Court there is a predominance of US, British and French nationals and academics, and when others appear they will usually have received at least part of their legal training in those states. Moreover, as Geoffrey Palmer points out, the Court 'resides in the heart of Europe and never goes anywhere else'.[7] (The Court does have the option of

---

[6] See Report of the Foreign Affairs Select Committee of the House of Commons, '2017 elections to the International Court of Justice', available on the UK Parliamentary website at https://publications.parliament.uk/pa/cm201719/cmselect/cmfaff/860/86004.htm#_idTextAnchor005, especially paras 12 and 13. See also Prasun Sonwalkar, 'Why Britain lost to India in bid to elect judge to the ICJ', *Hindustan Times*, 22 November 2017; and Owen Bowcott, 'No British judge on world court for first time in its 71-year history', *Guardian*, 20 November 2017.

[7] Geoffrey Palmer, 'International Law and the Reform of the International Court of Justice' in Antony Anghie and Gary Sturgess (eds), *Legal Visions of the 21st Century: Essays in Honour of Judge Christopher Weeramantry* (The Hague, Kluwer Law International, 1998) 595.

'sitting and exercising its functions elsewhere' if it believes it would be desirable to do so (Article 22), but this power has yet to be used.) Furthermore, it is obvious that candidates will be selected only if they have shown a significant commitment to the structure, form and methodology of international law as it is. Neither rebels nor iconoclasts will conceivably be elected, no matter from which state they come nor with what support. This homogeneity of judicial identification is reinforced by the status, salary and privileges which are a part of their appointments. Such individuals possess the status of eminent people of ambassadorial rank, which is constantly reinforced by procedures emphasising their exalted positions, encouraging any initial diversity to evaporate.

The Court normally sits in full (nine judges being sufficient to constitute a quorum). A state party to contentious proceedings is entitled to nominate a judge ad hoc to sit with the Court if there is no member of the Court currently sitting who is a national of that party. Judges selected in this way do not necessarily have to be a national of the appointing state; the choice is a matter for the state concerned. This rule also applies if none of the parties to a case has a judge who is a national of its state currently on the bench: ie each of them is free to appoint a judge ad hoc. Thus, the ICJ operates not by disqualifying any judges who are nationals of the parties before it, but by ensuring that each party has, if it so wishes, a judge of its nationality or choice participating in the case. The rationale for this rule – bearing in mind that judges are supposed to act independently and in no way be swayed by the wishes of their home states – is that judges who are of the same nationality as a state party can help ensure its case is properly understood by the rest of the Court. However, notwithstanding the fact that ICJ judges do not always vote in favour of the position advanced by their home states (although judges ad hoc almost invariably support the views of the party that appointed them), the impression of partisanship is hard to eradicate, and is hardly diminished by the politicisation of the nomination and election process.

States can also request that their disputes be heard by a chamber of the Court, made up of three or more judges, as provided for under Article 26 of the ICJ Statute. This could be beneficial for states, since, in practice, they are able to exercise a great deal of influence over which judges are appointed to such chambers and, in principle, it should also speed up the settlement of disputes. The disadvantage is that, where the parties themselves are able to decide the composition of the chambers, overlapping membership between chambers frequently occurs, so that the resolution of cases does not proceed as quickly as might be expected.[8]

---

[8] See Hugh Thirlway, 'The International Court of Justice' in Malcolm D Evans (ed), *International Law*, 5th edn (Oxford, OUP, 2018) 577.

B. The Jurisdiction of the ICJ

As with the PCIJ before it, the Court's role is twofold. It decides legal disputes between states (and only states) that have accepted its jurisdiction, whether generally or in relation to a particular matter, and also provides advisory opinions in response to legal questions submitted to it by the UN's main organs and certain of the UN's specialised agencies. As explained in chapter one, in carrying out its duties, the Court must apply the various sources of international law provided for in Article 38(1) of the ICJ Statute, namely: international conventions; customary international law; general principles of law; and (as subsidiary means for determining the rules of law) judicial decisions and the writings of jurists.

i. The Court's Contentious Jurisdiction

Under Article 34 of the ICJ Statute: 'Only states may be parties in cases before the Court'. Thus, no other subjects of international law – whether organs or agencies of the UN, other intergovernmental organisations, NGOs, or any other legal or natural person – can appear as a party in contentious proceedings before the Court.

Being party to the ICJ Statute does not automatically mean that a state becomes subject to the Court's jurisdiction. Instead, and in keeping with the principle of sovereignty and the importance accorded to consent in international law, the ICJ can decide a dispute between states parties only if the parties concerned have voluntarily submitted to its jurisdiction. Such consent is normally indicated in one of the ways provided for under Article 36 of the ICJ Statute. First, under Article 36(1), the Court will have jurisdiction in respect of 'all cases which the parties refer to it'. Such referrals typically take the form of a special agreement concluded by the parties for this purpose, and this is a common method by which disputes concerning land and maritime borders are submitted to the Court. One such judgment, delivered in 2013, involved Burkina Faso and Niger, and was initiated by a joint agreement between the two parties asking the Court to determine the correct course of a large section of the central boundary separating their two states.[9] It is also possible for a state to make a unilateral application to the ICJ in connection with an inter-state dispute (ie without the consent of the other party). If the other state then consents to the case being heard, the Court will be deemed to possess jurisdiction in respect of the matter.

Secondly, also under Article 36(1), the Court will have jurisdiction in respect of 'all matters specially provided for ... in treaties and conventions in force'. Many treaties contain such 'jurisdictional clauses', providing that,

---

[9] *Frontier Dispute (Burkina Faso/Niger), Judgment*, ICJ Reports, 2013, 44.

if a dispute arises between any of the parties, then this is to be referred to the ICJ for determination. This type of clause is found in treaties which have as their object the peaceful settlement of inter-state disputes, as well as in other treaties, where they allow for the referral to the Court of any dispute between the parties as to the interpretation or application of the instrument or certain of its provisions. In such cases, a state may unilaterally apply to the Court, on the basis that the consent of the other party is embodied in the jurisdictional clause itself, with that other party having in effect agreed in advance that any dispute covered by the clause is to be decided by the Court.

Thirdly, under Article 36(2) of the Statute – the so-called 'optional clause' – a state may choose to confer on the Court compulsory jurisdiction in respect of any future dispute that may arise between itself and any other state that has also agreed to submit itself to the Court's compulsory jurisdiction in this way. In order to grant the Court compulsory jurisdiction a state must enter into a Declaration of Acceptance, deposited with the UN Secretary-General, conferring on the ICJ competence in relation to all legal disputes arising between itself and any other state that has also entered into such a Declaration, and which concern:

a.   the interpretation of a treaty;
b.   any question of international law;
c.   the existence of any fact which, if established, would constitute a breach of an international obligation;
d.   the nature or extent of the reparation to be made for the breach of an international obligation.

When making such a Declaration, states are also free to enter into reservations, similar to reservations in respect of treaties, excluding certain categories of dispute from consideration by the Court, including disputes that may have arisen before a certain date. These reservations have reciprocal effect, so that one state can rely on the reservation included in another state's Declaration should a dispute arise between them. Thus, in *Certain Norwegian Loans*,[10] a case concerning the claims of French holders of various Norwegian bonds, brought by France on their behalf, Norway benefited from a reservation in France's Declaration excluding the Court from entertaining any dispute which France deemed fell within its own domestic jurisdiction. Since Norway asserted that it considered the matter at hand to come within its own national jurisdiction, the Court concluded it lacked competence to deal with the matter. (It should, however, be noted that such 'self-judging' reservations, which effectively permit the state itself to determine whether a dispute is covered by its reservation or not, are controversial, since they conflict with the general principle (enshrined in Article 36(6) of the ICJ Statute) that it is for

[10] *Case of Certain Norwegian Loans (France v Norway), Judgment*, ICJ Reports 1957, 9.

the Court to determine whether it has jurisdiction in a matter.) States are also free to withdraw their Declarations (thereby removing themselves from the Court's compulsory jurisdiction) at any point, although the ICJ has suggested that any state wishing to do so may be obliged to give reasonable notice of such withdrawal. Only a relatively small number of states, 73 in total (as at February 2019), are currently part of the optional system under Article 36. Of states that are permanent members of the Security Council (and, therefore, as a matter of convention, have had judges who are nationals of their respective states sitting on the Court), only the UK is currently a member and therefore subject to the compulsory jurisdiction of the ICJ. Ironically, as noted above, the UK is now also the first P5 state to have lost its representation on the Court.

The optional system (particularly as weakened by the liberal use of reservations) is a pale imitation of what had originally been envisaged for the World Court. When the statute of the PCIJ (the ICJ's predecessor) was in the process of being drafted in 1920, the assumption had initially been made that any party to the statute would automatically be subject to the Court's compulsory jurisdiction. However, the majority of nations baulked at such a step, and the optional clause, originally embodied in Article 36 of the PCIJ's statute, represented the compromise arrived at instead. The issue of compulsory jurisdiction was revisited at the San Francisco Conference in 1945, with some delegates, most notably those from Australia and New Zealand, arguing that the ICJ should enjoy compulsory jurisdiction over all UN members, but again most state representatives were reluctant to cede such power to the Court, and the optional system was left in place.

Although in theory straightforward, the question of whether the Court possesses jurisdiction to determine a particular dispute is often less clear in practice. States frequently contest the Court's jurisdiction by raising 'preliminary objections', the effect of which is to suspend proceedings in respect of the dispute itself (the merits of the case) until the jurisdictional point or points have been dealt with.

The Court can also indicate, if it believes it necessary to do so, 'any provisional measures which ought to be taken to preserve the respective rights of either party' (Article 41). Such 'provisional measures' are somewhat akin to the issuing of an interlocutory injunction in domestic law and are intended to apply only in urgent situations in which a party may suffer irreparable damage to its rights if no action is taken until the Court has delivered its final judgment in the case. It is also possible for a state that is not a party to a case to obtain permission from the Court to intervene in the proceedings if it can demonstrate that it has an interest of a legal nature that will be affected by the Court's decision (Article 62).

All questions submitted to the Court are decided by a majority of the judges present, with the President of the Court (elected by the judges from among their number for a three-year term) able to exercise a casting vote should this prove necessary (Article 55). The Court's judgment is binding only 'between the parties and in respect of that particular case' (Article 59), again in deference to the concept of sovereignty, with no state being bound to comply with the Court's decision unless it has freely consented to do so. The Court's judgment is final, with no further appeal possible. The most that a state subject to the Court's decision can request is that the Court provide it with an interpretation of that decision if anything subsequently appears unclear (Article 60), or to ask the Court to revise its decision if facts come to light which materially affect that judgment and which were not known to the Court or to the party seeking the revision at the time the judgment was given (Article 61).

As was noted in chapter one, the common law doctrine of *stare decisis* is not part of international law, and therefore decisions of the ICJ do not create precedents as they would in domestic common law jurisdictions; however, in practice, their influence extends far beyond the instant case.

States parties to a case before the ICJ are, by virtue of Article 94(1) of the UN Charter, under a duty to comply with its decision, and the vast majority of states do so. As is usual in the international realm, there is no enforcement mechanism in the event of non-compliance, although, if a state does fail to perform any obligations imposed on it in connection with the Court's judgment, then the other state party to the case can complain to the Security Council, 'which may, if it deems necessary, make recommendations or decide upon measures to be taken to give effect to the judgment' (Article 94(2)). Of course, if the non-complying state is a permanent member of the Council, or enjoys the strong support of such a member, then, owing to the existence of the veto power, making such a complaint would be futile.

ii. The Court's Advisory Jurisdiction

In addition to its contentious role, the ICJ is also empowered, under Article 96 of the UN Charter and Chapter IV of its Statute, to provide advisory opinions on legal questions submitted to it by the UN's five principal organs and any UN specialised agency that has been authorised by the General Assembly to seek such an opinion. The General Assembly and Security Council may request an opinion 'on any legal question' (Article 96(1)), while the other main organs and the specialised agencies are confined to asking legal questions that fall 'within the scope of their activities' (Article 96(2)). States are not entitled to request advisory opinions from the ICJ, although they are allowed to take part in advisory proceedings before the Court, as are international organisations, although, in the latter case, it is normally only the UN body that has sought the opinion that is given permission by the Court to participate.

Advisory opinions are not binding, even on the entity that has requested the opinion, but they do constitute a definitive statement of the position in international law.

C. The Limited Use Historically Made of the ICJ

The fact that there are concerns over the structure and composition of the Court only partly explains the reluctance of states to grant jurisdiction. More fundamental is the very real apprehension about the usefulness of litigation and adjudication as a method of dispute resolution. By its very nature a legal case may be won by either party, and it is obvious, if usually unobserved, that no party, if given a choice, would choose to litigate unless that party believed it had a very real chance of success. Even then it might well choose negotiation and mediation rather than risk the possibility of an adverse judgment.

It was observed in chapter two that the legal method of resolving disputes brings other problems as well. In the selection of the 'legally relevant', many social facts of significance to the parties or their constituents may simply be ignored, which can be politically dangerous for governments. And the adversarial method of the ICJ often has the effect of aggravating disputes rather than mitigating them. There is also the well-founded fear that the application of international law will generally preserve the status quo rather than promoting change that might arguably be desirable. One alleged example of this concerned the legality of the NATO intervention in Kosovo. When the Government of Yugoslavia attempted to have the legality of the intervention considered by the ICJ, the UK Government refused to allow the case to be heard, as it was entitled to do. One reason advanced for the refusal was that the law relating to humanitarian intervention was still developing, and to allow the ICJ to determine the existing position might set back this development.[11]

In addition, it is seldom forgotten that international law governed the colonial world just as 'objectively' as it now governs a world of independent states. Considering the cost and the time involved in litigation, if the outcome is unpredictable, usually only those states unlikely to prevail in other fora will be prepared to chance all before the ICJ.

Two significant qualifications to this critique must, however, be addressed and allowed. The first is that while the disadvantages of the legal method of dispute resolution are clear, so too are the advantages. In structuring a dispute in terms of questions of international law, while much of the political reality and context may be lost, the advantage is that a question is formulated that is answerable. At least the dispute *as formulated by law* may be resolved. A sometimes-quoted example suggests that there are disputes in which both parties welcome any solution because of the intransigence of the situation. In the words of Nagendra Singh, a judge at the ICJ from 1973 until his death in 1988:

> The successful resolution of the border dispute between Burkina Faso and Mali in the 1986 Frontier Dispute Case illustrates the utility of judicial decision as a

---

[11] Mark Littman, *Kosovo: Law and Diplomacy* (London, Centre for Policy Studies, 1999).

means of settlement in territorial disputes. The case was submitted to a Chamber of the ICJ pursuant to a special agreement concluded by the parties in 1983. In December 1985 while written submissions were being prepared, hostilities broke out in the disputed area. A ceasefire was agreed, and the Chamber by an order of 10 January 1986 directed the continued observance of the ceasefire, the withdrawal of troops within twenty days, and the avoidance of actions tending to aggravate the dispute or prejudice its eventual resolution. The case proceeded, and in its judgment of 22 December 1986 the Chamber determined the overall course of the frontier line. The Presidents of Burkina Faso and Mali publicly welcomed the judgment and indicated their intention to comply with it.[12]

Consequently, the legal method may be useful where resolution plus authority is in the interests of all parties and it may also be appropriate in disputes between friendly states prepared to accept outside jurisdiction, as in several cases concerning the law of the sea.

The second qualification to the critique is that the record of the ICJ (such as it is, given that until recently very few cases have been referred to it) does not suggest that it has ever been less than independent. Its activities with regard to South West Africa (now Namibia) in 1966 did prompt international concern, particularly from the non-Western world, when the Court refused to rule on the question of whether South Africa was in violation of its mandate from the League of Nations in maintaining a system of apartheid within the territory (on the ground that Ethiopia and Liberia, which had brought the case, had failed to establish any legal interest or right in the matter entitling them to judgment).[13] Certainly, many African and Asian states regarded this decision as unacceptable, and it cast doubt upon both the credibility of the Court and on its ability to transition smoothly into a post-colonial era. Some of the lost ground was recovered when, in 1971, in an advisory opinion provided at the request of the Security Council dealing with some aspects of the status of Namibia in international law, the Court upheld the obligation of states to give effect to a Security Council Resolution declaring the continued presence of the South African authorities in Namibia to be unlawful.[14] Sound though this may have been, the impact of the opinion was greatly diminished by South Africa's continuing occupation of the territory until 1990, which did little to increase the standing of the Court in the eyes of those consistently offended both by apartheid and by the Western friends of the South African Government.

Overall, however, the Court is difficult to assess and appraise because it is obviously constrained by the cases referred to it. But the fact that there have

---

[12] Nagendra Singh, *Role and Record of the International Court of Justice: 1946–88 – In Celebration of the 40th Anniversary* (Dordrecht, Kluwer, 1989).

[13] *South West Africa cases (Ethiopia v South Africa and Liberia v South Africa), Judgment*, ICJ Reports 1966, 6.

[14] *Legal Consequences for States of the Continued Presence of South Africa in Namibia (South West Africa) notwithstanding Security Council Resolution 276 (1970), Advisory Opinion*, ICJ Reports 1971, 16.

been so few suggests scepticism at least over the efficacy (and desirability) of legal solutions to political disputes.

D. Law and Politics and the ICJ

As a judicial forum, the ICJ is charged with deciding 'legal disputes' between states and providing advisory opinions to various UN organs and agencies on 'legal questions'. In common, therefore, with judicial bodies at the municipal level, the Court operates (in theory, at least) above and beyond politics. Its sole concern is with international law, not international relations; politics being a matter for its sister organs the General Assembly and the Security Council. In reality, of course, the ICJ, probably more than any other judicial forum, has the most difficulty in isolating itself from political matters. And, given the ICJ's remit – adjudicating on inter-state disputes and providing opinions to institutions made up of state members – some intertwining of law and politics is obviously unavoidable. The Court itself has recognised this, and has emphasised on a number of occasions that, provided it is satisfied that a dispute or request for an advisory opinion does involve genuine questions of international law, it will not refuse to deal with the matter simply because it also has political aspects or even because the referral itself was politically motivated.

Nonetheless, the ICJ's judgments and advisory opinions – or, conversely, its decision at times to decline to hear a case or provide an opinion – have aroused the ire of various states, even prompting some that had previously consented to the Court exercising compulsory jurisdiction under Article 36 to withdraw that consent. This was the reaction of France after the Court agreed to hear cases brought by Australia and New Zealand in 1973 challenging the legality of France's actions in conducting above-the-ground nuclear tests in the South Pacific.[15]

As frequently happens when a state objects to the ICJ deciding a dispute between itself and another state or states, France contended that the Court lacked jurisdiction to entertain the matter. First, France pointed out that its most recent Declaration accepting the Court's compulsory jurisdiction under the optional clause (filed on 20 May 1966) excluded from the Court's consideration 'disputes concerning activities connected with national defence', and went on to state that it regarded its current nuclear-testing activities in the South Pacific to fall within this exemption. Secondly, France maintained, the issue in question was not juridical in nature, but rather political, and therefore ought to be resolved not by the Court but through diplomatic channels.

---

[15] *Nuclear Tests (Australia v France), Judgment*, ICJ Reports 1974, 253; *Nuclear Tests (New Zealand v France), Judgment*, ICJ Reports 1974, 457.

France therefore refused to appear before the Court or to issue pleadings in the case. The Court ultimately rejected both of France's arguments, issuing an order for interim measures of protection on 22 June 1973 that required France to desist from undertaking any further nuclear tests that could cause radioactive fallout in Australia and New Zealand. As a consequence of this ruling, France withdrew from the compulsory jurisdiction of the ICJ. In its final judgment, however, delivered in December 1974, the Court decided that it need not render a decision in the case, since the dispute had, it pronounced, been resolved by a 'supervening event': that is, an undertaking by the French Government not to carry out any further nuclear tests in the South Pacific.

The overlap between law and politics in respect of contentious proceedings before the ICJ is perhaps best exemplified by the case brought by Nicaragua against the US in 1984, which involved an initial judgment on jurisdictional issues, followed by one on the merits of the case.[16] You should be aware that any discussion of the *Nicaragua* case tends to have a polarising effect on commentators, particularly when the focus moves beyond an examination of the 'pure' points of law decided by the ICJ. This in itself is indicative of the political issues intrinsic to the case. What follows is strongly sympathetic to the Nicaraguan point of view, but many would disagree with this depiction of the case and identify with the US's position: see, for example, Shabtai Rosenne's examination of *Nicaragua* (which he uses to illustrate how a case is tried before the ICJ) in his book *The World Court: What It is and how It works*.[17]

Relations between Nicaragua and the US had long been strained, but matters entered a new phase shortly after the Sandinistas overthrew General Somoza in 1979. Installed by a military coup in 1967, the Somoza regime had been notorious both for its human rights abuses and for its corruption. Once in power, the Sandinistas implemented policies of land reform, public healthcare and education, which, although popular with the Nicaraguan people, were anathema to the Reagan administration in the US, which not only feared for the security of American investments in Nicaragua but was also worried that the country would serve as the 'threat of a good example', thereby leading to the toppling of other dictatorships in Central and South America loyal to the US. In order to counter this possibility, the US began assisting the Contra opposition in Nicaragua, consisting in the main of remnants from Somoza's oppressive army, which had been responsible for executing and torturing large numbers of peasants thought to have been

---

[16] *Military and Paramilitary Activities in and against Nicaragua (Nicaragua v United States of America), Jurisdiction and Admissibility, Judgment*, ICJ Reports 1984, 392; *Military and Paramilitary Activities in and against Nicaragua (Nicaragua v United States of America), Merits, Judgment*, ICJ Reports 1986, 14.

[17] Shabtai Rosenne, *The World Court: What It is and how It works*, 6th edn, revised by Terry D Gill (Leiden, Martinus Nijhoff, 2003) 91–125.

supporting the Sandinistas. Not only did the US provide training, arms and funding to the Contras but had also, the ICJ was to conclude (in the merits phase of the judgment), mined Nicaraguan harbours, attacked the country's oil installations, ports and shipping, and had even been responsible for the distribution of a manual on guerrilla warfare techniques that had encouraged Contra forces to commit acts contrary to general principles of humanitarian law.

The US participated in the first phase of the Court's deliberations, aimed at determining whether it possessed jurisdiction to hear the case, but, after the Court held that this requirement was satisfied, declined to take any further part in the proceedings. The US objected to the ICJ exercising jurisdiction in the case on a number of grounds. For our purposes, the most interesting was the US's contention that the ICJ was not the appropriate forum in which to consider its dispute with Nicaragua because the matter was essentially political, and therefore beyond the Court's purview. Moreover, the US argued, in so far as the countries' dispute was alleged to pose a threat to international peace and security, the appropriate UN organ for dealing with the matter was the Security Council, since, under Article 24 of the UN Charter, it is the Council that bears primary responsibility for maintaining peace and security. This argument did have its merits. There was clearly a threat to international peace and security, and, in other circumstances, the Security Council would have been the obvious main forum. In this situation, however, the argument was disingenuous because, as long as the matter was within the Security Council, the US would be able, if necessary, to exercise its veto to prevent any action which might constrain its political goals. The ICJ, however, decided that the fact that the Security Council was seized of the matter did not preclude the Court from also considering it.

When the US Government decided to withdraw from further proceedings in the ICJ, it made a public statement explaining its position. This pronouncement declared that the continuing proceedings constituted a 'misuse of the Court for political purpose ... the Court lacks jurisdiction and competence over such a case'.[18]

Quite apart from this difficulty was the fact that allowed the ICJ to conclude that it was able to consider the problem notwithstanding the Security Council's involvement. Once the Court found that the US had, under Article 36(2) of the Court's Statute (as, it was held, had Nicaragua), accepted the compulsory jurisdiction of the Court, it was scarcely open to it to suggest that the appropriate forum for dispute resolution lay elsewhere. Given that the allegations were of grave breaches of international law, the ICJ could not plausibly have declined jurisdiction within the terms of its own Statute. The US's consequent announcement that it would no longer recognise the

---

[18] Statement by US Department of State, 18 January 1985.

compulsory jurisdiction of the Court was patently in breach of treaty obligations voluntarily entered into. It was also a devastating and cynical act by the world's most powerful nation, and betrayed the US's long-held position in favour of compulsory jurisdiction.

No-one highlights more clearly just what the US's response to the action begun by Nicaragua meant than Daniel Patrick Moynihan, who had been both Professor of Government at Harvard and a US ambassador to the UN. Moynihan refers to President Eisenhower's statement in 1959 that 'the time has come for mankind to make the role of law in international affairs as normal as it is now in domestic affairs', as well as his support for global acceptance of the ICJ's compulsory jurisdiction, in which he noted that it would be much 'better to lose a point now and then in an international tribunal and gain a world in which everyone lives at peace under the rule of law'.[19] He also quotes then Vice-President Richard Nixon, who observed that the US 'should be prepared to show the world by [its] example that the rule of law, even in the most trying circumstances, is the one system which all free men of good will must support'.[20] One final quotation from Moynihan is relevant because of its poignant accuracy (and continuing pertinence). He cites Professor Louis Henkin of Columbia University as summarising the inferable position of the US Government towards international law at this time as follows:

> The United States appears to have adopted the view that under international law a state may use force in and against another country for the following reasons:
>
> to overthrow the government of that country in order to protect lives there;
>
> to counter intervention there by another state and carry the attack to the territory of the intervening state;
>
> to overthrow the government of that country on the ground that it is helping to undermine another friendly government;
>
> in reprisal for that country's suspected responsibility for terrorist activities in the hope of deterring such acts in the future;
>
> to overthrow a communist (or pro-communist) government or to prevent a communist (or pro-communist) government from assuming power, even if it was properly elected or emerged as a result of internal forces.[21]

To its credit, the ICJ ruled against the US in 1986, even though the US had refused to appear to defend its actions. Undoubtedly the judgment is highly significant for international law and international lawyers. Typically a text of cases and materials in international law will have some seven excerpts from the Merits judgment considering the sources of international law,

---

[19] Daniel Patrick Moynihan, *On the Law of Nations* (Cambridge, MA, Harvard University Press, 1990) 145.

[20] ibid.

[21] ibid 147.

the relationship between custom and treaty, *jus cogens*, sovereignty over airspace, state responsibility and private persons, the use of force, and self-defence.

However, the benefits of the judgment to the state of Nicaragua were rather less than those to international lawyers and writers. While at least some of the latter observe in passing that the US rejected the decision of the Court and refused to accept its ruling, few actively considered the aftermath. Yet this is surely crucially important both for Nicaraguan citizens and for other states contemplating adjudication of international issues through the World Court. Supposedly, one great merit of the ICJ and the rule of law is that in legal proceedings states are equal before the law. In this case of exceptionally high visibility, the US showed itself able to cock a snook at the Court with impunity, and even avoid Security Council condemnation for the clearest breach of a treaty obligation. Article 94 of the Charter of the United Nations is unequivocal:

(1) Each Member of the United Nations undertakes to comply with the decision of the International Court of Justice in any case to which it is a party.
(2) If any party to a case fails to perform the obligations incumbent upon it under a judgment rendered by the Court, the other party may have recourse to the Security Council, which may, if it deems necessary, make recommendations or decide upon measures to be taken to give effect to the judgment.

However, the aftermath of the *Nicaragua* case seems to be seen by most international law writers as a matter for political rather than legal commentators.

Although Noam Chomsky's writing (beyond the field of linguistics) is sometimes more emotive than 'dispassionate' academic audiences are used to, his comments upon the decision of the ICJ seem justified:

> The World Court condemnation of the United States evoked further tantrums. Washington's threats finally compelled Nicaragua to withdraw the claims for reparation awarded by the Court, after a US-Nicaragua agreement 'aimed at enhancing economic, commercial and technical development to the maximum extent possible', Nicaragua's agent informed the Court. The withdrawal of just claims having been achieved by force, Washington moved to abrogate the agreement, suspending the trickle of aid with demands of increasing depravity and gall. In September 1993, the Senate voted 94–4 to ban any aid if Nicaragua fails to return or give adequate compensation (as determined by Washington) for properties of US citizens seized when Somoza fell – assets of US participants in the crushing of the beasts of burden by the tyrant who had long been a US favourite.[22]

Even before these developments, Nicaragua had clearly won a Pyrrhic victory (or worse). After the US's rejection of the Court's decision in 1986,

[22] Noam Chomsky, *World Orders, Old and New* (London, Pluto Press, 1994) 136.

Nicaragua had referred the matter to the Security Council pursuant to Article 94(2) of the Charter. Here, the US vetoed a resolution calling on it to comply with the Court's judgment. In the General Assembly, a resolution calling for compliance with the ICJ ruling was passed by 94–3, with only Israel and El Salvador supporting the US. One year later, the Assembly passed a further resolution urging 'full and immediate compliance' with the ICJ's decision, with only the US and Israel voting against.

What conclusions, then, may be drawn from this case in relation to the way in which international law operates? The first is that, while the legal method allows for the depoliticisation of a dispute, the price paid may be that the legal remedy obtained fails to resolve the underlying problem. Secondly, it has become clear that for many lawyers the judgment of the Court is an end in itself, with the decision significantly more important than the illusory nature of the relief granted and the aggression directed towards Nicaragua. Thirdly, it may be seen that the ability of the law to resolve disputes in favour of the powerless is always dependent upon the acquiescence of the powerful. This does have implications for the rule of law in the international arena.

Interestingly, Moynihan's indignation in respect of the *Nicaragua* case is not directed at the foreign policy of the US, but rather at its inability to achieve, or attempt to achieve, goals in a manner that is consistent (or at least arguably consistent) with international law. It is not the attempt to remove the Sandinistas from power with which he disagrees, but the patent illegality of the methods used. Like Richard Nixon, he clearly believes that international law is an important weapon in the armoury of a powerful nation, particularly where the use of force is impractical or undesirable. That the US had usefully used the ICJ in seeking the return of the US diplomatic and consular staff being held hostage in Iran in violation of several international treaties seems to add weight to his views.[23] The US had, within two weeks of applying to the ICJ, received a provisional order establishing that the rights of the US had been violated and that the Government of Iran should restore the embassy to the US and release the hostages. Although not immediately complied with, there is no doubt that the final decision had placed the US itself in a position, pursuant to Article 94 of the Charter, to refer the matter to the Security Council. Moynihan's view that, had the Security Council not then taken action, the US itself would have been entitled to, is certainly arguably correct. In this situation, of course, there was no fear of a veto being exercised.

Nicaragua v United States is an unusual case, being one of the few in which the Court's ruling was rejected by the losing party, and without that losing party suffering any adverse consequences, if only in the form of retaliatory action taken by the other party. It does, however, provide a stark illustration of the hollowing-out effect that a severe imbalance of power has on the

---

[23] *United States Diplomatic and Consular Staff in Tehran, Judgment*, ICJ Reports 1980, 3.

notion of sovereign equality in the real world. Here, formal equality before the law means little when one state is free to disregard the Court's judgment and the other state, or even the international community at large, lacks any real means to enforce it. It also again exemplifies the point that law can be used only to solve legal problems. If the underlying difficulties are essentially political or economic in nature, then dressing them up as legal questions amenable to legal solutions will not resolve the issue, and may even exacerbate it, particularly in contentious proceedings, given their inherently adversarial nature. To this extent, and even if one does not accept that the ICJ should have declined jurisdiction, there being obvious and important questions of international law raised by the dispute, the US administration's characterisation of the matter as essentially political, and therefore to be resolved on the political rather than the legal plane, has some truth. Certainly, this was a case in which politics rather than law prevailed in the end.

This interaction between law and politics is also evident in respect of some of the advisory opinions that the Court has delivered. In 1994, the General Assembly asked the following question of the ICJ: 'Is the threat or use of nuclear weapons in any circumstances permitted under international law?'[24] This followed an earlier attempt by the World Health Organization (WHO) to obtain an advisory opinion from the Court in respect of the same issue, except that the WHO's question was framed as follows: 'In view of the health and environmental effects, would the use of nuclear weapons by a State in war or other armed conflict be a breach of its obligations under international law including the WHO constitution?'

The WHO's question had been asked particularly at the behest of Pacific members, since these states, owing to their small size and limited height above sea level, are especially vulnerable to environmental change. One reason that the question was initially posed by the WHO rather than by the General Assembly is that some of the Pacific states were members of the WHO but not the UN, owing to financial constraints. The ICJ, however, decided that the WHO was not entitled to seek the Court's opinion on the matter, since, it was held, the matter did not properly full within the agency's remit, as required by Article 96(2) of the UN Charter.

Some of the ICJ judges, such as Judge Oda from Japan, believed that the question posed by the General Assembly was really an attempt to misuse the Court to make a political point, and it is undoubtedly the case that, even if the Court were to have advised that the use of nuclear weapons was illegal, it was highly unlikely that any state possessing nuclear capability would have relinquished its weaponry on the basis of that fact. On the other hand, such an opinion would not have been inconsequential, since its effect would have been to add legal weight to the arguments of those who wanted

---

[24] *Legality of the Threat or Use of Nuclear Weapons, Advisory Opinion,* ICJ Reports 1996, 226, para 1.

the immorality and inhumanity of such weapons of mass destruction recognised and acted upon.

This again provides an example of the legal method of translation. All those involved in the case knew that what was being argued was whether the possession and potential use of nuclear weapons could ever be justified, but not justified in law, or law only, but in reality. Here was a political question par excellence; political in the sense of being imbued with policy. Debates on this policy have, of course, been prolonged and bitter, both between states that possess nuclear arms and those that do not, and within those states. And, given that every member of the Court was aware of this reality, it is not surprising that some were uncomfortable with the problem being presented as a legal one. Nor, consequently, is it a surprise that the decision of the Court was neither unanimous nor consistent. Professor Roger Clark, who acted as counsel for Samoa in the case, summarises the advisory opinion delivered by the ICJ in the case as follows:

> While the opinion strongly reflects the argument made on behalf of the Pacific coalition, what those States would have liked was a statement that the use or threat of use of nuclear weapons is illegal per se (illegal in itself), any time any place.
>
> Three of the fourteen judges – Judges Weeramantry (Sri Lanka), Koroma (Sierra Leone) and Shahabuddeen (Guyana) – said exactly that. Seven more – Judges Bedjaoui (Algeria, the President of the Court), Ranjeva (Madagascar), Herczegh (Hungary), Ski (China), Fleischhauer (Germany), Vereshchetin (Russia) and Ferrari Bravo (Italy) – said that it would 'generally' be contrary to the laws of war to use or threaten to use nuclear weapons. These judges were not sure, however, whether such a use 'would be lawful or unlawful in an extreme circumstance of self-defence, in which the very survival of a State would be at stake.' Judges Schwebel (United States), Oda (Japan), Guillaume (France) and Higgins (United Kingdom) – disagreed with both of these positions. While they conceded that a threat or use of nuclear weapons could be made only when it was compatible with the requirements of international law applicable to armed conflict, they believed that each individual case has to be considered against the relevant standards and that no general rule is possible.[25]

It is difficult not to infer that the Court, with the exception of the judges from Sri Lanka, Sierra Leone and Guyana, was not entirely at ease with the matter it had been called upon to address, and the final result was met with more than a little scepticism by many academics and commentators. The title of Professor Vaughan Lowe's note on the case in one legal journal sums up much of the response: 'Shock Verdict: Nuclear war may or may not be Unlawful'.[26] The way in which the judges divided on the issue was also less than satisfactory, apparently revealing as it did a difference in attitude between, at the

---

[25] Roger S Clark and Madeleine Sann (eds), *The Case Against the Bomb* (Camden, NJ, Rutgers University, 1996) 2.
[26] (1996) 55 *Cambridge Law Journal* 415–17.

one extreme, those states without any nuclear capability and no prospect of obtaining it, or even of sheltering under another state's nuclear umbrella, and, at the other, those states that did possess nuclear weapons or otherwise benefitted from the 'protection' afforded by another nation's nuclear arsenal. It may not be entirely coincidental that two of the judges most adamantly in favour of declaring that international law does not permit the threat or use of nuclear weapons (Judges Weeramantry and Shahabuddeen) were not re-elected to the Court.

IV. International Arbitration

Although much less influential in terms of its impact on the development of international law, international arbitration remains the favoured means for settling inter-state disputes. International arbitration has been defined by the International Law Commission as 'a procedure for the settlement of disputes between States by a binding award on the basis of law and as a result of an undertaking voluntarily accepted'. As will be noted, this definition of arbitration in international law is significantly narrower than the common meaning of the term. Arbitration differs from judicial settlement in terms of the role played by the parties to the dispute and the degree of influence they have over the process. Whereas parties have no control over the composition of a judicial body, in arbitral proceedings, the parties select the members of the tribunal that will decide their dispute. Arbitration also allows the parties to choose the law that will be applied, whereas the applicable law in the ICJ is always the principles of international law.

The modern history of arbitration began with procedures established in 1794 under the Jay Treaty between the US and the UK for the settlement of bilateral disputes. This provided for the creation of mixed commissions to which each state nominated an equal number of members, together with an umpire. In 1871, arbitration was used to determine whether breaches of neutrality had been committed by Britain during the American Civil War, and, in what represented an innovative step, not only were British and American nominees appointed to the tribunal but also three independent nominees (from Brazil, Switzerland and Italy). The 1899 Convention on the Pacific Settlement of International Disputes resulted in the establishment of an institution known as the Permanent Court of Arbitration (actually, as international lawyers like to observe, neither permanent, nor a court), the organisation and composition of which was modified in 1907. The Permanent Court of Arbitration is still in existence, and promotes the resolution of disputes involving combinations of states, state entities, intergovernmental organisations and private parties through the provision of arbitration, conciliation and fact-finding services. As with the ICJ, it can decide cases only with the consent of the states concerned, but has a number of features that make it a more preferable forum for resolving disputes than the Court.

Each of the contracting parties is entitled to nominate up to four persons to be members of the PCA panel (there are more than 300 nominated from some 80 states). Any of these may be selected by the parties for any particular dispute. Once the parties to a dispute have agreed to arbitration they must agree a *compromis*. In essence, this is an instrument that contains the agreement to arbitrate and specifies the form the arbitration is to take: thus, it will name the selected arbitrators, define the questions the tribunal is to address, define the law and procedure that is to be applied, and the period within which the award is to be made. Model rules exist as a basis for the drafting of the *compromis*.

Arbitration awards are usually binding and final, except in the event of some substantial procedural error or manifest error of fact. Should an appeal be possible and successful, the result will be to render the award of the tribunal null and void.

Although the use of arbitration is not extensive (there seem to be a much larger number of members of the PCA available to arbitrate than the number of disputes submitted for arbitration), it is clear that it does have a place. Arbitration is possible in some disputes between a state and an individual. The Convention on the Settlement of Investment Disputes between States and Nationals of Other States 1965 makes conciliation and arbitration possible (with consent) between contracting parties and companies of the nationality of another contracting party. In addition, perhaps the best-known arbitral settlement of private claims of nationals has been the Iran–United States Claims Tribunal (discussed in chapter four).

A perusal of current and recent claims at the Permanent Court suggests that, in terms of disputes between states, those that are most likely to be arbitrated involve states that generally enjoy amicable relations. There is also a close relationship between the PCA and the ICJ that is more than physical (both having homes in the Hague), with a number of judges on the ICJ also among the more than 300 members of the PCA who are available to act as arbitrators. However, following the statement of Judge Abdulqawi Yusuf during the annual presidential address to the General Assembly in October 2018 confirming that ICJ judges will no longer normally take part in international arbitrations, especially mixed ones (ie investor–state and commercial arbitrations), their role in this respect is likely to be much reduced.[27]

---

[27] See n 2 above.

V. Conclusion

Under the UN Charter, states are obliged to settle their disputes peacefully rather than resorting to the use of force. By far the majority of such disputes are settled through diplomatic channels rather than by adjudication, and hence are resolved in the political rather than legal sphere. Where a dispute is submitted for judicial settlement, this will normally be by way of arbitration, conducted with the agreement of both the parties, and with the states concerned retaining a considerable amount of control over the process, both in terms of the composition of the arbitral tribunal and the law to be applied.

This reluctance on the part of states to resolve their disputes by way of a binding legal determination explains why recourse to the ICJ remains a relatively rare occurrence, and submission to the compulsory jurisdiction of the Court even rarer. Predictably, the ICJ has been at its most successful (in terms of the parties abiding by its judgment) when a dispute has been referred to it with the agreement of both the states involved and where both have accepted that the decision of the Court will be conclusive of the matter. Where one of the parties contests the jurisdiction of the Court and, in extreme instances, refuses to participate in all or part of the proceedings, then, inevitably, the Court's decision will not resolve the underlying problem between the two states and may well aggravate it. This again highlights the fundamentally consensual nature of international law, which ultimately relies on the voluntary agreement of the states it purports to govern – especially that of the most powerful states, which are the ones most able to ignore its tenets with impunity. It is also the case that, where the tensions between states are attributable to political or economic factors, couching the problem in legal terms is unlikely to result in a satisfactory outcome, especially if one of the states is adamant that the dispute is not susceptible to a legal solution.

8

Use of Force in International Law

I. Introduction

If states cannot resolve their disputes by one of the peaceful means discussed in the last chapter, they may well resort to force in order to achieve the outcome they desire. In international law, no topic is more important than control of this use of force by states. Whereas, in the domestic sphere, governments enjoy a monopoly over the legitimate use of force, at the international level, the concept of sovereign equality and the absence of any supranational governing body means that that there is no equivalent entity able to exercise such exclusive control. Furthermore, in so far as international law acts as a medium for regulating the use of force by states, it is unable to call upon any form of enforcement mechanism to secure compliance with its rules; instead, it relies on the consent and cooperation of states in order to curb and constrain violence that has an international dimension.

Until comparatively recently, a chapter such as this would have been confined to disputes between states, but international law is now confronted more than ever by the problem of armed non-state actors bent on destabilising states or regions with which they have historical or contemporary disagreements, whether for ethnic, religious, or historic reasons. Such non-state actors, of which the Taliban, Al-Qaeda and ISIL (Islamic State of Iraq and the Levant), also known as ISIS or Daesh, are prominent examples, have been labelled or formally designated as 'terrorist' organisations by many governments. This has led to some uncertainty in current international law.

This chapter will begin with a brief history of the (restricted) role of international law in circumscribing the use of force before the creation of the UN. This history illustrates the problems in defining what is meant by 'force' and its use, and also the difficulty of creating rules for a myriad of cases in which the question of the use of force requires consideration. While there are two separate matters for regulation – first, the circumstances in which the use of force is permitted, usually described as *jus ad bellum* (the justification for going to war); and, secondly, the sort of force that may be employed, usually covered by the term *jus in bello* (the law of war that includes rules concerning the conduct of warfare and the protection of war victims) – there are also many distinct situations that trigger the application of different rules.

Thus, in considering the constraints that are to be placed on the use of force, we must first identify the circumstances in which it is proposed that such force is to be used. Does the matter concern intervention in a civil war? Does it concern the provision of help, military or otherwise, in such a situation? Does it involve an act of aggression or an act of self-defence? Is it concerned with the legitimacy of forcible intervention to save nationals or to prevent crimes against humanity or even genocide? Is it concerned with when a state may lawfully come to the assistance of one side in an existing war? Is it claimed to be a legitimate response to an act of terrorism, or a permissible course of action that is intended to pre-empt such conduct? Does it amount to an act of reprisal for acts committed by another state?

On each and all of these matters, international law has been developing rules. Not surprisingly, however, some of these rules are clearer than others, whereas some remain contentious. When NATO intervened in Kosovo in 1999 for 'humanitarian reasons', the legality of the operation was widely debated. Similarly, the actions of the US and the UK, in carrying out airstrikes against Iraq in 1998 and 2001 (to enforce the 'no-fly zones' provided for in Security Council Resolution 688 of 1991), were criticised by many. Even more obviously controversial in international law terms was the invasion and occupation of Afghanistan and, later, Iraq by the US and its few allies following the terrorist attacks of September 2001 on US territory. These controversies have been reflected in the UN-sanctioned intervention in Libya, and in the subsequent interventions in Syria, Iraq and Yemen.

II. The Use of Force in International Law before the Creation of the UN

According to the foreword of a book entitled *Right v. Might*, published by the US-based think-tank Council on Foreign Relations:

> Man's [*sic*] readiness to settle differences by force of arms has been a feature of society since prehistory. Man's attempt to place rational bounds on the use of force, emerging from his revulsion against the scourge of war, is almost as old. This struggle to impose 'rationality on reality' was a central feature of the Enlightenment and the 'Age of Reason' in the eighteenth century.[1]

---

[1] Foreword by John Temple Swing in Louis Henkin et al (eds), *Right v. Might: International Law and the Use of Force* (New York, Council on Foreign Relations Press, 1989).

While this is undoubtedly true, the fact is that a right to wage war remained unrestricted until after the First World War (1914–18). One might have thought that the Peace of Westphalia, introducing as it did the concept of sovereign equality, would have had some effect on this position. How, after all, could sovereigns be equal if the powerful states were entitled to wage war on the powerless? Such inconsistency was at the very heart of the Westphalian system, however, and the idea that international law could in any way interfere with the prerogative of sovereign states to resort to war would have been unimaginable.

War was an enduring feature of the seventeenth, eighteenth and nineteenth centuries, both in and outside of Europe. Conquest was the means by which territory was acquired and colonies won. But the ferocity of battle came to be greatly enhanced by the development of ever more fearful weaponry and the beginnings of 'weapons of mass destruction'. The ability to kill and maim enemies and civilians alike progressed in a remarkable way. Revulsion at this 'progress' led to the founding of the International Red Cross in 1863. Nevertheless, while many armies remained essentially mercenary (and, where not, the overwhelming percentage of casualties involved impoverished recruits), there was little impetus to develop rules as to when war could and could not be waged.

A further development was important. As Oppenheim observes, whereas, in the Middle Ages, 'war was a contention between the whole populations of the belligerent States ... [and] in time of war every subject of one belligerent, whether an armed and fighting individual or not, whether man or woman, adult or infant, could be killed or enslaved by the other belligerent at will', by the twentieth century war had become, almost invariably, 'a contention of States *through their armed forces*'[2]. This led to greater acceptance that private subjects of belligerent states, ie those not involved in the 'contention', were entitled to be afforded some protection.

International law responded by developing customary legal rules that dealt not with when war might (or might not) be waged, but with *how* it might be waged, and, to a lesser extent, against whom it might be waged. These were ultimately codified in treaties beginning only in the second half of the nineteenth century. The first of these was the 1856 Paris Declaration on maritime war, followed by the 1864 Geneva Convention on the wounded and the sick, and the St Petersburg Declaration of 1868, concerned with explosive projectiles. In 1874, at the instigation of Russia, an international conference was held in Brussels that adopted a declaration on the laws and customs of war. Although a lack of ratifications meant that it never entered into force, the Declaration nevertheless functioned as an important precursor

---

[2] Lassa Oppenheim in Hersch Lauterpacht (ed), *International Law: A Treatise*, Vol 2, 7th edn (London, Longmans, 1969) 204.

to the crucial Hague First International Peace Conference of 1899, and the Second International Peace Conference of 1907. These Conferences, again held at the invitation of the Russian Government, adopted numerous international instruments codifying (and sometimes adding to) international law. The 1907 Conference alone adopted 13 conventions and a declaration. Since these conventions primarily codified customary law relating to warfare, most of their provisions were binding on all states. Prominence was also given here to the so-called 'Martens Clause' that appeared in the preamble to the Hague Convention II of 1899. While the origin of the clause is disputed, its purpose was to make clear that, even in those cases that were not yet covered by appropriate rules and regulations, populations and belligerents nonetheless enjoyed the protection of international laws 'as they result from usages established among civilised peoples, from the laws of humanity, and the dictates of the public conscience'. The Martens clause was later to be reformulated in the 1949 Geneva Conventions, where it is stated that

> in cases not covered by [the Geneva Conventions and Protocols] or by other international agreements, civilians and combatants remain under the protection and authority of the principles of international law derived from established custom, from the principles of humanity and from dictates of public conscience.

Hence, before the First World War, considerable effort was expended in controlling the way in which war was conducted, but it was only after that conflict had ended, in 1918, that any real thought was given to the problem of how to deter states from waging war with one another in the first place. The initial attempt revolved around the creation of the League of Nations in 1919, followed by the negotiation and adoption of the General Treaty for the Renunciation of War in 1928, also known as the Kellogg–Briand Pact, or Pact of Paris. The Covenant of the League of Nations did not purport to abolish war but it did attempt, first, to provide a permanent forum where states could negotiate and discuss differences rather than resorting to war; and, secondly, it imposed limitations on the use of force. Member states agreed that, where they had serious disputes with one or more other states, they would submit the dispute to arbitration or judicial settlement or inquiry by the Council of the League. There was to be no resort to war until three months after the completion of such a process. Thus, the League's aim was to provide time for reflection before recourse to war – a cooling-off period for the disagreeing states. Members also undertook not to go to war with another member who complied with either an arbitral award, a judicial decision or a unanimous report from the Council. Finally, they agreed 'to respect and preserve as against external aggression the territorial integrity and existing political independence of all Members of the League' (Article 10).

One further innovation of the Covenant is to be found in Article 16, which is not unrelated to the later development of Chapter VII of the UN Charter.

Article 16 provides for collective security for League Members, with the first paragraph stating:

> Should any Member of the League resort to war in disregard of its covenants under Articles 12, 13 or 15, it shall ipso facto be deemed to have committed an act of war against all other Members of the League, which hereby undertake immediately to subject it to the severance of all trade or financial relations, the prohibition of all intercourse between their nationals and the nationals of the covenant-breaking State, and the prevention of all financial, commercial or personal intercourse between the nationals of the covenant-breaking State and the nationals of any other State, whether a Member of the League or not.

Of course, the League's attempts to limit recourse to war were scarcely successful. Unfortunately, members of the League proved unwilling to sanction a state acting in defiance of the Covenant. Other paragraphs of Article 16 had empowered the League to take such action and also to use military sanctions. The provisions were never effective, and even economic sanctions were irregularly applied, with the Assembly of the League voting in 1921 to make such economic sanctions optional for each member rather than compulsory.

Whereas the Covenant of the League of Nations had sought to limit recourse to war, the Kellogg–Briand Pact sought to abolish it altogether. Originally drawn up at the behest of the French Foreign Minister, Aristide Briand, and envisaged as a bilateral treaty with the US, this optimistic document eventually became a multilateral treaty, ratified by 15 states. By 1939, 63 states were parties, including Germany, Japan and Italy. This in itself hints at its effectiveness. It was inspired by a liberal internationalist view that war could be prevented and abolished with a combination of enlightened diplomacy and collective solidarity. War was renounced as an instrument of national policy.[3] It was accepted by the US Senate by 85 votes to one (although admittedly with the qualification that it neither affected the US's right of self-defence, nor yet committed the US to action to enforce the treaty). The Treaty has but two brief substantive articles. Article 1 states:

> The High Contracting Parties solemnly declare in the names of their respective peoples that they condemn recourse to war for the solution of international controversies, and renounce it, as an instrument of national policy in their relations with one another;

while Article 2 provides:

> The High Contracting Parties agree that the settlement or solution of all disputes or conflicts of whatever nature or of whatever origin they may be, which may arise among them, shall never be sought except by pacific means.

---

[3] For an excellent history and discussion of the Kellogg–Briand Pact, see Oona A Hathaway and Scott J Shapiro, *The Internationalists And Their Plan to Outlaw War* (London, Penguin Books, 2018).

Although the Kellogg–Briand Pact has been superseded by the UN Charter, it remains in force. The reason for its failure is in essence attributable to the fact that it remained just a pact, with no enforcement provisions, and hence was violated frequently. Its importance, however, was twofold. First, this was the first treaty that suggested that recourse to war could amount to a breach of international law. Secondly, it formed an important legal basis for the prosecutions at Nuremberg of those held responsible for instigating the Second World War. The Nuremberg judgment had this to say about the pact:

> The question is, what was the legal effect of this pact? The nations who signed the pact or adhered to it unconditionally condemned recourse to war for the future as an instrument of policy, and expressly renounced it. After the signing of the pact, any nation resorting to war as an instrument of national policy breaks the pact. In the opinion of the Tribunal, the solemn renunciation of war as an instrument of national policy necessarily involves the proposition that such a war is illegal in international law; and those who plan and wage such a war, with its inevitable and terrible consequences, are committing a crime in so doing. War for the solution of international controversies undertaken as an instrument of national policy certainly includes a war of aggression, and such a war is therefore outlawed by the pact. As Mr. Henry L. Stimson, then Secretary of State of the United States, said in 1932:

> 'War between nations was renounced by the signatories of the Kellogg–Briand Treaty. This means that it has become throughout practically the entire world ... an illegal thing. Hereafter, when nations engage in armed conflict, either one or both of them must be termed violators of this general treaty law. ... We denounce them as law-breakers.'

III. The Charter of the UN

The outbreak of the Second World War led to a renewed determination to use international law as an instrument to prevent further conflict, and, where such conflict did arise, to ensure it was terminated as swiftly as possible. The opening of the preamble to the UN Charter affirms the parties' determination 'to save succeeding generations from the scourge of war', and the overriding purpose of the UN, articulated in Article 1(1), is:

> To maintain international peace and security, and to that end: to take effective collective measures for the prevention and removal of threats to the peace, and for the suppression of acts of aggression or other breaches of the peace, and to bring about by peaceful means, and in conformity with the principles of justice and international law, adjustment or settlement of international disputes or situations which might lead to a breach of the peace.

In addition, Article 2(3) commits UN member states to settle their international disputes by peaceful means in order to ensure that international peace and security, and justice, are not endangered. Article 2(4) obliges members to refrain in their international relations from the threat or use of force 'against the territorial integrity or political independence of any State, or in any other manner inconsistent with the Purposes of the United Nations'. All of these provisions need to be read together with General Assembly Resolutions and Declarations that have sought to interpret them.

A first point to note is that the ICJ has held, in *Nicaragua v USA (Merits)*, that Article 2(4) embodies a customary rule of international law, and is there-fore applicable to all states.[4] Its effect is to prohibit all measures of force other than those permitted by the Charter. These exceptions are self-defence (Article 51), collective self-defence (also under Article 51) and measures taken pursuant to Chapter VII of the Charter as authorised by the Security Council.

The 1970 General Assembly Resolution 2625 (XXV) – Declaration on Prin-ciples of International Law concerning Friendly Relations and Co-operation among States in accordance with the Charter of the UN – is important as regards the meaning of Article 2(4). Despite being a General Assembly reso-lution, and therefore not legally binding, the Declaration is nevertheless regarded as expressing the consensus of member states on the way in which Article 2(4) is to be interpreted. It identifies the following duties:

> Every State has the duty to refrain in its international relations from the threat or use of force against the territorial integrity or political independence of any State, or in any other manner inconsistent with the purposes of the United Nations. Such a threat or use of force constitutes a violation of international law and the Charter of the United Nations and shall never be employed as a means of settling international issues.

> A war of aggression constitutes a crime against the peace, for which there is responsibility under international law.

> In accordance with the purposes and principles of the United Nations, States have the duty to refrain from propaganda for wars of aggression.

> Every State has the duty to refrain from the threat or use of force to violate the existing international boundaries of another State or as a means of solving inter-national disputes, including territorial disputes and problems concerning frontiers of States.

> Every State likewise has the duty to refrain from the threat or use of force to violate international lines of demarcation, such as armistice lines, established by or pursuant to an international agreement to which it is a party or which it is other-wise bound to respect. Nothing in the foregoing shall be construed as prejudicing the positions of the parties concerned with regard to the status and effects of such lines under their special regimes or as affecting their temporary character.

---

[4] *Military and Paramilitary Activities in and against Nicaragua (Nicaragua v United States of America), Merits, Judgment*, ICJ Reports 1986, 14, para 188.

States have a duty to refrain from acts of reprisal involving the use of force.

Every State has the duty to refrain from any forcible action which deprives peoples referred to in the elaboration of the principle of equal rights and self-determination of their right to self-determination and freedom and independence.

Every State has the duty to refrain from organizing or encouraging the organization of irregular forces or armed bands, including mercenaries, for incursion into the territory of another State.

Every State has the duty to refrain from organizing, instigating, assisting or participating in acts of civil strife or terrorist acts in another State or acquiescing in organized activities within its territory directed towards the commission of such acts, when the acts referred to in the present paragraph involve a threat or use of force.

Obviously, Article 2(4) goes beyond proscribing war, referring as it does to the 'threat or use of force'. 'Force', however, is undefined, and opinions differ as to how the term should be interpreted. Does it refer, narrowly, to the use of physical force only, or does it have a wider meaning, encompassing those situations in which political or economic pressure is brought to bear against a state? Not surprisingly, those states capable of exerting economic or political force (or coercion, to use one possible interpretation of 'force') have resisted such an interpretation, while those lacking such capability (primarily smaller and developing states) have been reluctant to see the term confined to 'armed force'. General Assembly Resolution 2625 does, in its interpretation of Article 2(7) (the duty not to interfere in matters within the domestic jurisdiction of any state), proscribe 'economic, political or any other type of measures to coerce another State in order to obtain from it the subordination of the exercise of its sovereign rights [or] to secure from it advantages of any kind'. However, in *Nicaragua v US*, the ICJ held that economic sanctions imposed by the US on Nicaragua did not constitute a breach of the *customary law principle* of non-intervention. The generally held view (and one consistent with the interests of the powerful) is that Article 2(4) cannot encompass situations beyond those involving armed force.

Another General Assembly resolution relevant to the interpretation of Article 2(4) is the 1974 Resolution on the Definition of Aggression.[5] As set out in the annex to the Resolution: 'Aggression is the use of armed force by a State against the sovereignty, territorial integrity or political independence of another State, or in any manner inconsistent with the Charter of the United Nations'. Moreover, the use of armed force in violation of Article 2(4) 'shall constitute prima facie evidence of an act of aggression' (albeit that the Security Council is free to determine, in accordance with the Charter, that an act of aggression has not actually taken place, taking into account other factors, such as the fact that 'the acts concerned or their consequence are not of

---

[5] UNGA Resolution 3314 (XXIX) of 14 December 1974.

sufficient gravity'). Conduct identified as amounting to an act of aggression includes an invasion or armed attack; any annexation of territory; bombardment of the territory of a state by the armed forces of another state; an attack on the land, sea or air force, marine and air fleets of another state; and the sending of armed bands, groups, irregulars or mercenaries by or on behalf of a state which then carry out acts of armed force against another state so grave as to be comparable to other acts of aggression listed in the Charter. Significantly, the Declaration also states that: 'No consideration of whatever nature, whether political, economic, military or otherwise, may serve as a justification for aggression'. The examples given of acts of aggression were explicitly stated not to be exhaustive, and the task of determining the existence of any act of aggression remains with the Security Council under Article 39 of Chapter VII of the UN Charter.[6]

This, then, is the framework put in place by the UN to eliminate the use of force in international relations. The fact that provision was made for exceptions demonstrates that the Charter, unlike its predecessors (in particular, the Kellogg–Briand Pact), was not simply a utopian construct. Those who drafted the document recognised that situations would arise that contravened the terms of the Charter, and that consequently it was necessary to cater for legitimate responses for when such breaches did occur. However, one subsequent development which was not foreseen was the rise of 'terrorism' by non-state actors and the implications this would have for international law.

IV. Chapter VII of the UN Charter

What should by now be clear is that, when the UN was formed, the intention was that this should be the body responsible for maintaining international peace and security. Both the prohibition on the threat and use of force (Article 2(4)) and the prohibition on intervening in matters essentially within the domestic jurisdiction of a state (Article 2(7)) were designed to achieve this aim. However, those who drafted the Charter recognised that these provisions would, in themselves, be insufficient to prevent or halt international strife and thus awarded the Security Council (UNSC) the role of making these provisions effective. The UNSC is defined and created by Chapter V of the Charter. This not only specifies the membership of the UNSC, both permanent and elected, granting the power of veto to permanent members (see chapter five), but also, and crucially, confers on the UNSC 'primary responsibility for the maintenance of international peace and security' (Article 24). Article 25

---

[6] See ch 6 for a discussion of the definition of 'aggression' for the purposes of the International Criminal Court.

obliges all members to accept and carry out UNSC decisions. Its powers with regard to threats to the peace, breaches of the peace and acts of aggression are to be found in Chapter VII of the Charter.

Chapter VII gives the UNSC the power to determine the existence of any threat to the peace, breach of the peace, or act of aggression. Upon making such a determination, the UNSC is then empowered to issue recommendations or to decide what measures shall be taken to maintain or restore international peace and security. It is important to note that this power 'to determine' is unfettered: once the UNSC has made its decision, there is no possibility of it being subject to review, whether by a judicial body or by any other means. While some writers have argued that the position should be otherwise, being of the view that the power of the UNSC should be constrained in order to ensure that there is some objective evidence justifying its determinations (often pointing to the ICJ as the appropriate reviewing body), this does not seem a possible interpretation of the power given to the Council. The measures available to the UNSC under Chapter VII to achieve its goals range from the imposition of economic sanctions to authorising the use of military force against states that fail to comply with its decisions.

The onset of the Cold War, coupled with the veto power conferred on the permanent members of the Security Council, ensured that the Chapter VII powers remained largely in abeyance until 1990. The two occasions on which they were used were wholly exceptional. The first occurred in 1950, after hostilities had broken out between North and South Korea, when the UNSC 'recommended' in Resolution 83 that the member states of the UN give such assistance to South Korea 'as may be necessary to repel the armed attack [by North Korea] and to restore international peace and security in the area'. It was therefore a recommendation rather than an authorisation. Moreover, it was passed in the absence of the one permanent UNSC member that would otherwise have blocked the Resolution through the exercise of its veto: North Korea's ally, the Soviet Union. (The Soviets were at that time boycotting UNSC meetings in protest at the refusal of the other UNSC powers to agree to award China's seat on the Council to the government of the People's Republic of China in place of the Nationalist government of Chiang Kai-shek.) The second exceptional case concerned the attempt by Ian Smith's Government in Southern Rhodesia (now Zimbabwe) to declare independence from British rule with a white-minority government in 1965. The UNSC condemned this action,[7] described the resulting situation as a 'usurpation of power by a racist settler minority',[8] and deemed the imminent supply of oil to Southern Rhodesia a 'threat to the peace', calling upon the UK 'to prevent, by the use of force if necessary, the arrival at Beira [in neighbouring

---

[7] UNSC Resolution 216 of 12 November 1965.
[8] UNSC Resolution 217 of 20 November 1965.

Mozambique] of vessels reasonably believed to be carrying oil destined for Southern Rhodesia'.[9] The UNSC later imposed mandatory economic sanctions on the country.[10]

The end of the Cold War in the early 1990s led many to hope that a new era had dawned in which the UNSC might at last perform the role allotted to it in 1945. However, such optimism quickly faded. The main reason for this relates to the failure of UN member states to implement an important part of Chapter VII, detailed in Articles 43 to 47 of the Charter. Under Article 43, 'in order to contribute to the maintenance of international peace and security', member states were to 'undertake to make available to the Security Council ... armed forces, assistance, and facilities'. In order to ensure that the UN could 'take urgent military measures', members were also to 'hold immediately available national air-force contingents for combined international enforcement action' (Article 45). The UNSC was to be responsible for the deployment of armed force provided by the member states, acting with the assistance of a Military Staff Committee (Article 46). As described in Article 47, this Military Staff Committee was to comprise 'the Chiefs of Staff of the permanent members of the Security Council or their representatives', and was to 'be responsible under the Security Council for the strategic direction of any armed forces placed at the disposal of the Security Council'. If a member state not represented on the UNSC was asked to contribute forces to a UNSC military operation, then the UNSC was to allow that member, if it so wished, to take part in determining how its forces were to be used (Article 44). Hence, if the provisions set out in Articles 43 to 47 had been put into effect, the UNSC would essentially have been given its own military force to command. These articles have yet to become operational, however, with member states remaining reluctant to cede control of their armed forces to the UNSC, notwithstanding having the right to participate in decisions regarding their deployment. As a consequence, while the UNSC has authorised military action, such action has always been carried out entirely under the control of the participating states, not the UNSC's own military command force, as originally envisaged. Not surprisingly, it has proved difficult to obtain the agreement of all permanent members to a proposed course of action when the mission is to be controlled not by the UN but by designated coalitions of states. Even if this were not the case, however, there is little to suggest that the international community is sufficiently united for the UN to have been more effective in its peacekeeping role.

Notwithstanding this failure to equip the UNSC with its own military force, Chapter VII has been used more widely since the end of the Cold War. In 1990, the UNSC authorised member states to use 'all necessary means'

[9] UNSC Resolution 221 of 9 April 1966.
[10] UNSC Resolution 232 of 16 December 1966.

to restore international peace and security in the Gulf by forcing Iraq to withdraw from Kuwait, reinstating Kuwait's sovereignty.[11] Other Resolutions have authorised particular states or sometimes organisations of states (such as the Organization of American States) to use all necessary means to achieve particular ends.

The two principal provisions under which the UNSC takes enforcement decisions are Article 41 (enforcement not involving the use of armed force) and Article 42 (providing for enforcement with the use of armed force). Under Article 41:

> The Security Council may decide what measures not involving the use of armed force are to be employed to give effect to its decisions, and it may call upon the Members of the United Nations to apply such measures. These may include complete or partial interruption of economic relations and of rail, sea, air, postal, telegraphic, radio, and other means of communication, and the severance of diplomatic relations.

As with outright military action, the Cold War ensured that this provision was under-employed, although it was used against Southern Rhodesia in 1965 and South Africa in 1977. In the case of Southern Rhodesia, its effect was limited by the refusal of South Africa and also of Portugal (then a colonial power with control over Mozambique and Angola) to support UN sanctions. With regard to South Africa, Resolution 418 of 1977 called for an arms embargo, but there was little enthusiasm among powerful states for effective monitoring to ensure that the Resolution was implemented properly. Wider sanctions have always been controversial, partly because many state governments are cynical about their effect, partly because many are unwilling to give up trading with the targeted state, and partly because many believe that sanctions simply inflict further misery on the poorest citizens of the country concerned. The exposure of the corruption that accompanied the sanctions imposed on Iraq after its expulsion from Kuwait in 1991 strengthened the arguments of those opposed to such measures. With the recognition that sanctions were an extraordinarily blunt instrument, frequently hurting the most vulnerable, so-called 'smart sanctions' have been developed, which can target specific imports or exports, or particular individuals, who may be denied the right to travel to countries which have imposed the sanctions. For example, the late Kim Il-sung of North Korea had his personal luxury imports embargoed, certain Russian nationals believed by the US to be responsible for the death of a corruption whistleblower have been refused entry visas to the US, and Iran's oil exports and financial and banking sectors have been the subject of UN sanctions.

---

[11] UNSC Resolution 678 of 29 November 1990.

If measures taken under Article 41 fail to have the desired effect, or are dispensed with altogether in the belief that they would simply be ineffective, the UNSC can always have recourse to Article 42, which allows it to:

[T]ake such action by air, sea, or land forces as may be necessary to maintain or restore international peace and security. Such action may include demonstrations, blockade, and other operations by air, sea, or land forces of Members of the United Nations.

Technically, this provision has never been used. As mentioned above, the resolution concerning Korea in 1950 was no more than a 'recommendation' that action be taken to assist South Korea in repelling the attack mounted on it by North Korea. As for the authorisation of the use of force against Iraq in 1990, following Saddam Hussein's invasion of Kuwait, Article 42 was not referred to in Resolution 678, prompting some cynics to suggest that action had been taken under Article 41½. Since the UNSC's own military command structure envisaged under Articles 43 to 47 was never put into place, the Council is reduced to authorising others – whether a state, a group of states, or a regional organisation such as NATO – to use armed force to restore international peace and order. The effect has been to pass control of the exercise of the use of force from the UN, as originally intended, to other states or bodies. This was not contemplated in the Charter, although the authority to act in this way is arguably implicit in Chapter VII.

V. Self-defence in International Law

The other main exception to the UN Charter's proscription of the use of force is concerned with self-defence, and is to be found in Article 51. This states:

Nothing in the present Charter shall impair the inherent right of individual or collective self-defence if an armed attack occurs against a Member of the United Nations, until the Security Council has taken measures necessary to maintain international peace and security. Measures taken by Members in the exercise of this right of self-defence shall be immediately reported to the Security Council and shall not in any way affect the authority and responsibility of the Security Council under the present Charter to take at any time such action as it deems necessary in order to maintain or restore international peace and security.

Article 51 raises a number of points. First, from a historical perspective, when recourse to war was not inconsistent with international law, there was no need for a specific right of self-defence: it was no more and no less lawful than the act that provoked it. Having said this, it is equally clear that the principles governing this 'inherent right' were in fact laid down in an era when war remained lawful. The identification of the rights and limitations of self-defence first appeared in a rather oblique way from an incident concerning the destruction of a US steamboat, the *Caroline*, in 1837. The *Caroline* was being used by US private militia to provide aid to rebels fighting the British in Upper Canada. While the *Caroline* was docked in New York State, the British set the vessel on fire and cast it adrift, causing it to plummet over Niagara Falls. Two members of the crew were killed and two were taken prisoner. In response to a formal protest issued by the US Government, ·the British insisted that the destruction of the *Caroline* was an act of 'necessary self-defence'. The dispute was finally resolved in 1842, when a British diplomat, Lord Ashburton, accepted the contention of the then US Secretary of State, Daniel Webster, that actions of self-defence should be restricted to those situations in which there is 'a necessity of self-defence, instant, overwhelming, leaving no choice of means, and no moment of deliberation'.[12] In addition, the force used would have to be proportionate to the threat encountered, and not 'unreasonable or excessive; since the act, justified by the necessity of self-defence, must be limited by that necessity, and kept clearly within it'.[13]

This was, of course, a peculiar case, since property belonging to citizens of a third entity (the US) was destroyed in the territory of that third entity in order to prevent it from being used to assist a rebellion in a second entity (Upper Canada) against the forces of a first (Great Britain). Despite this, these principles of necessity and proportionality had, at least until the 21st century, come to be accepted as appropriate criteria against which to judge the lawfulness of a claimed act of self-defence. Nevertheless, Article 51 is situated within the framework of the UN Charter, the intention of which was essentially to grant the UNSC a monopoly over the use of force in international relations. Thus, although a right of self-defence is recognised as 'inherent', it is a right that was expected to exist only until such time as the UNSC was able to take the measures necessary to maintain or restore international peace and security. Such is the theory, but in practice the failure to create the structures that would have enabled the UNSC to play this role, together with political disagreements as to when the use of force is warranted, has led to the right of self-defence being invoked to a much greater extent than was contemplated when the Charter was drafted.

In addition, there has been a great deal of discussion as to whether, given Article 51's reference to an 'armed attack', states are now permitted to use force in self-defence in relation to anything other than an attack that is already underway – ie whether it is now lawful for states to use force to forestall even an imminent attack, as allowed under the *Caroline* formula (normally

---

[12] Letter from Daniel Webster to Lord Ashburton, 27 July 1842 (enclosing extract from letter of 24 April 1841); available at: http://avalon.law.yale.edu/19th_century/br-1842d.asp#web1.
[13] ibid.

referred to as a right of 'anticipatory self-defence').[14] One point is certainly clear, however. The Bush administration's assertion, in its *National Security Strategy of 2002*, of a proclaimed right of 'pre-emptive' self-defence allowable under customary international law was disputed by practically all states and the vast majority of international lawyers, including the large number who believe that states are still permitted to respond to an imminent threat. This is because the use of force to counter more remote or 'emergent' threats – as set out in the Strategy – does not meet the strict *Caroline* criterion of imminence. Nor have many been convinced by the argument that the concept of 'imminence' must be reinterpreted or reconceptualised in light of a new type of threat – ie that posed by WMDs, terrorists and 'rogue states'. Indeed, many have objected to the Bush administration's use of the term 'pre-emptive' in this context, insisting that the term properly refers to a response to an imminent attack as traditionally defined in customary international law, and that what the administration was seeking to justify is more accurately characterised as 'preventive' self-defence. Such 'pre-emptive' or 'preventive' use of force is discussed further below.

Another unfortunate aspect of Article 51 concerns its failure either to define 'armed attack' or to specify whether such an attack must be made on the actual territory of the state being threatened. What is the situation, for example, when the nationals of a state are attacked, but that attack takes place beyond the state's borders? This situation arose in 1976 when an Air France aircraft with 251 passengers on board was hijacked by pro-Palestinian militants and taken to Entebbe in Uganda. The hijackers released the majority of the passengers but continued to hold some 60 individuals, most of whom were Israeli citizens. The Ugandan Government (under Idi Amin) did little to bring the hijacking to an end, and, shortly before a deadline set by the hijackers expired, an Israeli commando raid took place, with members of the Israel Defence Force arriving unannounced at Entebbe, where they stormed the hijacked craft, released the passengers and killed the hijackers (and some Ugandan soldiers in the process) before returning with the passengers to Israel, after a stopover in Nairobi. Did international law permit such a rescue? Israel claimed that Article 51 allowed it to use force in such circumstances in order to protect its citizens abroad if the state in which they found themselves was either unable or unwilling to protect them. International opinion was divided (less upon international law lines than upon individual states' attitudes to Israel), but, since this incident took place, it has become implicitly accepted that if a state has sufficient power to rescue its citizens, then, provided the intervention represents a proportionate response, it will not be regarded as inconsistent with Article 51. However, it should again be

---

[14] For a detailed discussion of the current scope of the right of self-defence, see Christine Gray, *International Law and the Use of Force*, 4th edn (Oxford, OUP, 2018) 124–75.

clear that the ability to exercise such a right lies only with those states with the means to effect such a rescue. It should also be apparent that claims of entitlement to act in self-defence in such circumstances are obviously open to abuse – as, for example, when the US invaded Grenada in 1983, supposedly to rescue its nationals, or when it intervened in Panama in 1989. In neither case was the primary objective of the US's invasion the safeguarding of American citizens.

In conclusion, it is probably correct to say that intervention to rescue nationals will not be contrary to Article 2(4), but only if the threat to the citizens of the intervening state is real and imminent, the state where they are being held is unwilling or unable to protect them, the sole purpose of the intervention is to rescue the individuals concerned, and the response is proportionate, in the sense that more lives may be expected to be saved than lost.

On occasions, the self-defence justification has been used when the response to the original offensive act has nevertheless been delayed. At first sight, this would appear to be contrary to Article 51, since it would seem that, if there is time for reflection, then there must also be time to refer the matter to the UNSC. The advantage of not making such a referral (that is, treating the matter as falling within Article 51) is that there will then be no need to wait for the UNSC to take action (by means of a resolution), and, if the right of self-defence is being exercised, only a UNSC resolution will suffice in order to halt the act of self-defence. Two examples are instructive here. The Argentinian invasion of the Falkland Islands/Islas Malvinas in 1982 did not provoke an immediate response from the British Government, owing to the time required to assemble and dispatch a substantial naval force, and also because of the additional time it then took that force to travel from the UK to the South Atlantic. The argument could have been made that, rather than carry out this delayed 'act of self-defence', the British should have simply put the matter in the hands of the UNSC. However, for transparently political reasons, this course of action was rejected. Such an outcome was probably inevitable: had the matter been referred to the Council, a resolution empowering action would have been most unlikely – a veto would have prevented it. The second example concerns the attempted assassination of President George HW Bush in 1993, when a car bomb was discovered in Kuwait. Some two months later, the US launched a substantial cruise missile attack against Iraqi Military Intelligence Headquarters in Baghdad, causing much death and destruction. Although this attack appeared more an act of reprisal than one of self-defence, the US argued that its response was permitted under Article 51. The delay in carrying out the act of self-defence arose, it was claimed, because of the need to obtain proof of Iraqi involvement in the assassination attempt. The US's stance received considerable support from within the UNSC, but the international community was deeply divided at such a unilateral use of force in the absence of the Council's authorisation.

Acts of reprisal are generally thought to have been outlawed by the UN Charter, but they do still occur. Since they are unlawful, such acts tend to be cloaked in the language of self-defence, although this is not always the case. In 1968, in response to an attack the year before by Palestinian guerillas on an El Al aircraft in Athens, in which an Israeli citizen died, Israeli commandos destroyed 13 civil aircraft in Beirut valued at more than $40 million. By way of justification, the Israeli Chief of Staff simply said that the objective was to make clear 'to the other side that the price they must pay for terrorist activities can be very high'. Notwithstanding the UNSC's unanimous condemnation of Israel's 'premeditated military action in violation of its obligation under the Charter' (in Resolution 262[15]) no further action was taken, in spite of calls for Israel to pay compensation for the attack.

More recently, on 6 April 2017, the US, in response to an alleged chemical attack by the al-Assad Government against its own citizens, responded by bombing the Syrian airbase from which it claimed the attack had emanated. Such a chemical weapons attack by Syria would undoubtedly have been a clear contravention of Article 1 of the Chemical Weapons Convention 1993 – a Convention to which Syria was by then a party.[16] A statement released by the Pentagon stated that the strike was intended to 'deter the [Syrian] regime from using chemical weapons'.[17] No claim was made by the US that it was acting in self-defence. This was therefore a forcible counter-measure, otherwise known as a reprisal. Unsurprisingly, and notwithstanding the vocal disapproval of some states (especially Syria and Russia, both of which denied that chemical weapons had been used), there was little in the way of international condemnation and the matter was not discussed by the UNSC. In 2018, following an alleged chemical attack in the Syrian town of Douma, in which dozens of civilians were killed, the US, the UK and France responded with air strikes against Syrian targets, primarily sites around Damascus thought to be linked to Syria's chemical weapons production. Although the US did not seek to bring its actions within international law, the UK Government of Theresa May sought to rely on humanitarian intervention as lawful justification, stating that

> as an exceptional measure on grounds of overwhelming humanitarian necessity, military intervention to strike carefully considered, specifically identified targets in order effectively to alleviate humanitarian distress by degrading the Syrian regime's

---

[15] UNSC Resolution 262 of 31 December 1968.

[16] Syria acceded to the Convention in 2013. This followed accusations that it had used chemical weapons in an earlier attack, in August 2013, on Ghouta, near Damascus. In order to avert US air strikes against the country on that occasion, Syria had agreed, as part of a deal brokered by Russia, to the destruction of its chemical weapons arsenal, overseen by the Organization for the Prohibition of Chemical Weapons.

[17] US Department of Defence, 'U.S. Strike Designed to Deter Assad Regime's Use of Chemical Weapons', 7 April 2017, available at https://dod.defense.gov/News/Article/Article/1145665/us-strike-designed-to-deter-assad-regimes-use-of-chemical-weapons.

chemical weapons capability and deterring further chemical weapons attacks was necessary and proportionate and therefore legally justifiable. Such an intervention was directed exclusively to averting a humanitarian catastrophe caused by the Syrian regime's use of chemical weapons, and the action was the minimum judged necessary for that purpose.[18]

However, as explained in section VI below, even when carried out for avowedly humanitarian purposes, such attacks cannot be said to form a justifiable exception to the prohibition on the use of force enshrined in Article 2(4).

In conclusion, therefore, it is essential to recognise the limits that international law has imposed on the right of states to resort to the use of force in self-defence, and also to be aware of the various ways in which states have ignored or evaded the application of those rules. In theory, self-defence is limited to a necessary and immediate (and proportionate) response until such time as the UNSC is able to consider the matter. In reality, if a state has sufficient power or the support of a powerful actor, it is possible either to put forward a justification of self-defence even when this is obviously inappropriate, or even concede that the act is one of reprisal, in the knowledge that condemnation by the UNSC is highly unlikely (especially where the attack has been perpetrated by one or more P5 members).

A. Collective Self-defence

As its wording makes clear, Article 51 envisages not only acts of self-defence on the part of an individual state in response to an attack on its territory or citizens, but also acts of collective self-defence, in which one or more states use force in order to defend another state or states from attack. Collective self-defence typically occurs in the context of a formal alliance created for the purpose of mutual protection. During the Cold War, the Warsaw Pact (formed by the Soviet Union and several Eastern European states) and the North Atlantic Treaty Organization or NATO (comprising the US, Canada and various Western European states) were the most prominent examples of this kind of collective alliance, but they were by no means unique. Under Article 5 of the North Atlantic Treaty, the contracting parties:

> [A]gree that an armed attack against one or more of them in Europe or North America shall be considered an attack against them all and consequently they agree that, if such an armed attack occurs, each of them, in exercise of the right of individual or collective self-defence recognised by Article 51 of the Charter of the United Nations, will assist the Party or Parties so attacked by taking forthwith, individually and in concert with the other Parties, such action as it deems

---

[18] Prime Minister's Office, 'Syria action – UK government legal position', Policy paper, 14 April 2018, available at www.gov.uk/government/publications/syria-action-uk-government-legal-position/syria-action-uk-government-legal-position.

necessary, including the use of armed force, to restore and maintain the security of the North Atlantic area.

Since Article 51 applies, the same requirements as to what constitutes an armed attack in cases of individual self-defence are relevant, and NATO members remain under an obligation to report any defensive measures taken to the UNSC. (The use of force by members of NATO against Yugoslav forces in Kosovo in 1999 is considered in section VI.A below.)

As to the right of states to make regional arrangements, Article 52 of the UN Charter provides as follows:

1. Nothing in the present Charter precludes the existence of regional arrangements or agencies for dealing with such matters relating to the maintenance of international peace and security as are appropriate for regional action, provided that such arrangements or agencies and their activities are consistent with the Purposes and Principles of the United Nations.

2. The Members of the United Nations entering into such arrangements or constituting such agencies shall make every effort to achieve pacific settlement of local disputes through such regional arrangements or by such regional agencies before referring them to the Security Council.

Again, in accordance with Article 51, the actions of such regional arrangements must either be consistent with an act of collective self-defence or must conform to the purposes and principles of the UN. Most importantly, the power of the UNSC remains superior to any regional arrangement.

In the past few years, the US and a number of other states have invoked collective self-defence (among other grounds) to justify the taking of military action against ISIS/ISIL targets in Iraq and Syria. In the latter case, this has proved particularly controversial, quite apart from the question of when states are permitted to use force against non-state actors (discussed further below). Although capable of justification when carried out with the consent of the state subject to the intervention (as with the Iraqi Government's request to the US to assist it in its fight against ISIS in 2014), such claims ring hollow when the state concerned has issued no such invitation, and more so when it positively objects to the actions or presence of an intervening state on its territory. Claims to be engaging in the collective self-defence of an adjacent country, as the US and many other Western states asserted they were doing in respect of Iraq when bombing ISIS targets in neighbouring Syria, is controversial absent the permission of the state in which the military action is actually being undertaken. Syria in fact objected that such a rationalisation amounted to a distortion of the meaning of Article 51,[19] and it is difficult to see how the actions concerned did not amount to both an unlawful use of force and a violation of Syria's sovereignty. Turkey's claim to be participating in the collective self-defence of Iraq as justification for its military action in

---

[19] Gray, *International Law* (2018) 190–92.

Syria was even more dubious in the absence of evidence that Iraq had even requested such assistance[20] (indeed Iraq has frequently objected to Turkey's military incursions across its northern border).[21] (In fact, many of these states also put forward a right of individual self-defence in their letters to the Security Council, claiming that the radical terrorist groups operating in Syria posed a threat to their own nations and nationals.[22] Again, it is difficult to see how such assertions fall within the ambit of Article 51.)

B. Pre-emptive/Preventive Self-defence

Since Article 51 refers to a situation where 'an armed attack occurs', this would logically seem to confine the right of self-defence to responding to an attack that has already taken place, or is at least under way. This has traditionally been the view of most writers since the creation of the Charter. As a consequence, states have seldom attempted to justify any use of force on their part as an act of pre-emptive self-defence. When Israel adopted this line of argument after its bombing of the Osirak nuclear reactor in Iraq in 1981, the UNSC was unimpressed, condemning the attack in Resolution 487 as a 'clear violation of the Charter of the United Nations and the norms of international conduct'. The Resolution attracted unanimous support, with even Israel's staunch ally, the US, voting in favour. It may seem unreasonable, however, that states should have no right to take action to counter a threatened attack. The *Caroline* principle has been cited in this respect, although it is relevant only where the necessity for self-defence is 'instant, overwhelming, leaving no choice of means and no moment of deliberation', and where the response is proportionate to the imminent threat. And, as was noted above, anything that does not conform to this is really more accurately described as 'preventive' self-defence.

Any attempt to define a right of pre-emptive/preventive self-defence is, however, fraught with difficulty. As it has such potential for abuse – and often by states in unstable relationships (India and Pakistan, Israel and Iran, North and South Korea) and in possession of powerful, even nuclear, weaponry – its use must be tightly circumscribed. Most states accept this, and, of course, few states have the military power to undertake a preventive strike. Following the terrorist attacks on American soil in 2001, however, the US proclaimed for itself rights of 'pre-emptive self-defence'. The position was spelt out by the administration of President George W Bush in *The National Security*

---

[20] ibid 194–95.

[21] The same can be said of the military interventions carried out in support of various rebel groups, simply because these have (obviously) been carried out without the permission of the government of Syria.

[22] Gray (n 14) 192–95.

Strategy of the United States of America, published under the presidential seal in September 2002 (*NSS* 2002). Although many have taken issue with the document's assertions, denying that they provide an accurate representation of when the use of force in self-defence is permitted under international law, they are undoubtedly reflective of the US Government's views at that time. Some of the claims made are startling. On page 15 of the document, it is stated:

> For centuries, international law recognized that nations need not suffer an attack before they can lawfully take action to defend themselves against forces that present an imminent danger of attack. Legal scholars and international jurists often conditioned the legitimacy of preemption on the existence of an imminent threat – most often a visible mobilization of armies, navies, and air forces preparing to attack.

> We must adapt the concept of imminent threat to the capabilities and objectives of today's adversaries. Rogue states and terrorists do not seek to attack us using conventional means. They know such attacks would fail. Instead, they rely on acts of terrorism and, potentially, the use of weapons of mass destruction – weapons that can be easily concealed and delivered covertly and without warning.

> The targets of these attacks are our military forces and our civilian population, in direct violation of one of the principal norms of the law of warfare. As was demonstrated by the losses on September 11, 2001, mass civilian casualties is the specific objective of terrorists and these losses would be exponentially more severe if terrorists acquired and used weapons of mass destruction.

> The United States has long maintained the option of preemptive actions to counter a sufficient threat to our national security. The greater the threat, the greater is the risk of inaction – and the more compelling the case for taking anticipatory action to defend ourselves, even if uncertainty remains as to the time and place of the enemy's attack. To forestall or prevent such hostile acts by our adversaries, the United States will, if necessary, act preemptively.

> The United States will not use force in all cases to preempt emerging threats, nor should nations use preemption as a pretext for aggression. Yet in an age where the enemies of civilization openly and actively seek the world's most destructive technologies, the United States cannot remain idle while dangers gather.

Significantly, this position was used by the US as one reason for its unauthorised invasion of Iraq in 2003. More telling, however, was the fact that the US's major allies chose to justify their part in the Iraqi invasion only on the basis that this was authorised (so they argued) by prior UNSC resolutions. Yet again, this is a situation where the power of the US enabled it to advance a position in international law not shared by other states and certainly rejected by the UN.

The *Caroline* principle was, of course, formulated at a time when attacks using technologically advanced weaponry, and emanating from sources other than states themselves, could not have been imagined. This has led some governments and many lawyers and writers (Western ones, at least) to ponder in what circumstances pre-emptive or preventive self-defence might be permissible, and regardless of whether the threat is posed by a state or non-state actor. In the words of Michael Doyle, the dilemma is:

> Should a responsible government try to deter a potential foe, or should it strike first – that is, preventively – to spare itself from a blow that the other seems to intend, has delivered before, and could again deliver? Is it safer to wait and threaten punishment than to throw the first punch? Or is it wiser to strike now, before the risks increase, even though that means taking the chance that danger might not materialize?[23]

However, if it is left to the discretion of individual states to determine when action needs to be taken against a putative threat, discarding even the need for imminence, then this arguably leaves too much to the subjective views of an incumbent administration, and its potential for abuse is evident. Moreover, as mentioned above, very few states have the capacity to carry out military action (pre-emptive) or otherwise, which in turn greatly reduces the likelihood of the international community as a whole accepting an expansive interpretation of the right of self-defence. This is even more so when many smaller and weaker states contemplate the possibility that they themselves might one day be the object of a pre-emptive/preventive strike.

As Christine Gray explains, since the publication of President Barack Obama's National Security Strategy in 2010, the US appears to have retreated from advocating a right of pre-emptive action, instead favouring a wider interpretation of the imminence principle: a position that has been echoed in the UK.[24] Indeed, in January 2017, the then Attorney-General in Prime Minister Theresa May's Government, Jeremy Wright, gave a speech setting out the UK Government's understanding of how it might lawfully determine whether an attack is 'imminent', thereby permitting an armed response, whether against another state or a non-state actor.[25] It clearly purported to redefine the *Caroline* concept of imminence.

According to the Attorney-General, although, where possible, threats from non-state actors should be dealt with via the criminal justice system, in other situations, an armed (and, if necessary, lethal) state response may be justified. In determining whether the necessary imminence threshold has been met, the Attorney-General suggested posing the following question: 'is action

---

[23] Michael Doyle, *Striking First: Preemption and Prevention in International conflict* (Princeton, Princeton University Press, 2008), 95. Harold Hongju Koh's response, included within Doyle's book, is also well worth reading, with his conclusion 'that we should move to a per se ban on unilateral anticipatory war making, with any post hoc justification of such anticipatory actions being asserted as a defense and not in the form of prior permission': 101.

[24] Gray (n 14) 252–53.

[25] 'Attorney General's speech at the International Institute for Strategic Studies', 11 January 2017, available on the UK Government website at https://assets.publishing.service.gov.uk/government/uploads/system/uploads/attachment_data/file/583171/170111_Imminence_Speech_.pdf.

necessary now?'[26] In order to formulate a justifiable response to this question, he proposed that the following factors be taken into account (drawing on an article by Sir Daniel Bethlehem, former Legal Adviser to the Foreign and Commonwealth Office[27]):

(a)   the nature and immediacy of the threat;
(b)   the probability of an attack;
(c)   whether the anticipated attack is part of a concerted pattern of continuing armed activity;
(d)   the likely scale of the attack and the injury, loss or damage likely to result therefrom in the absence of mitigating action; and
(e)   the likelihood that there will be other opportunities to undertake effective action in self-defense that may be expected to cause less serious collateral injury, loss or damage.[28]

However, as discussed when we consider the law applicable to the use of unmanned aerial vehicles (drones) in international law (in section VII below), other members of the UK Parliament believe this reconsideration of 'imminence' to be problematic and potentially dangerous.

C. Self-defence and Terrorism in International Law

The attacks perpetrated by members of Al-Qaeda against US targets on 11 September 2001, killing almost 3,000 people, did not, of course, constitute the first major instance of international terrorism. However, these attacks were seminal in the effect they had upon international law. Before 9/11, the typical response to an act of national or international terrorism was to interpret the conduct in question as being the responsibility of individuals, and therefore criminal in nature. This stemmed from the recognition that, while different states might support different acts of terrorism, it would be rare indeed that an act of terror could be attributed to such a state. As will be seen, however, that position was not absolute, nor were responses to terrorism uniform.

International law has had considerable difficulty in defining what is meant by terrorism. Some have considered such a definition unnecessary, believing that any act of so-called terrorism was better defined according to the individual circumstances of the case. Adopting this logic, an act of terrorism might amount to murder, arson, causing explosions, or related offences, each giving rise to charges of a recognised crime. There were also some state representatives who were unwilling to define terrorism in a way that condemned the

---

[26] ibid 7.
[27] Daniel Bethlehem, 'Self-Defense Against an Imminent or Actual Armed Attack by Nonstate Actors' (2012) 106 *American Journal of International Law* 770–77.
[28] 'Attorney General's speech' (n 25) 15.

'freedom fighter' – those concerned with pursuing a legitimate goal of self-determination – as well as the religious fanatic or politically disaffected. In the words of Antonio Cassese: 'Third World countries staunchly clung to their view that this notion [terrorism] could not cover acts of violence perpetrated by the so-called freedom fighters, that is individuals and groups struggling for the realization of self-determination'.[29]

More recently, members of the Organisation of the Islamic Conference continued to insist that the armed struggle 'for liberation and self-determination' be excluded from a definition of terrorism because of their empathy with the Palestinian cause. Nevertheless, it was recognised that acts of terrorism amounted to more than simple, if terrible, crimes under other names. In the mid-1990s, in a declaration attached to a General Assembly resolution dealing with measures to eliminate international terrorism (and which was adopted unanimously without a vote), the following statement was made, encapsulating a definition of terrorism:

> Criminal acts intended or calculated to provoke a state of terror in the general public, a group of persons or particular persons for political purposes are in any circumstance unjustifiable, whatever the considerations of a political, philosophical, ideological, racial, ethnic, religious or any other nature that may be invoked to justify them.[30]

Both earlier and later attempts to define terrorism have been made. In an unadopted League of Nations Convention of 1937, terrorism was described as: 'All criminal acts directed against a State and intended or calculated to create a state of terror in the minds of particular persons or a group of persons or the general public.' In 1996, in another resolution aimed at preventing international terrorism, the General Assembly reiterated that it:

1. Strongly condemns all acts, methods and practices of terrorism as criminal and unjustifiable, wherever and by whomsoever committed;
2. Reiterates that criminal acts intended or calculated to provoke a state of terror in the general public, a group of persons or particular persons for political purposes are in any circumstance unjustifiable, whatever the considerations of a political, philosophical, ideological, racial, ethnic, religious or other nature that may be invoked to justify them.[31]

Finally, it is worth quoting a comparatively short legal definition proposed by Alex Schmid:

> Terrorism is an anxiety-inspiring method of repeated violent action, employed by (semi-) clandestine individual, group or state actors, for idiosyncratic, criminal or political reasons, whereby – in contrast to assassination – the direct targets of

---

[29] Antonio Cassese, *International Law*, 2nd edn (Oxford, OUP, 2005) 449.
[30] 'Declaration on Measures to Eliminate International Terrorism', operative paragraph 3, annexed to UNGA Resolution 49/60 of 9 December 1994.
[31] UNGA Resolution 51/210 of 17 December 1996.

violence are not the main targets. The immediate human victims of violence are generally chosen randomly (targets of opportunity) or selectively (representative or symbolic targets) from a target population, and serve as message generators. Threat- and violence-based communication processes between terrorist (organization), (imperilled) victims, and main targets are used to manipulate the main target (audience(s)), turning it into a target of terror, a target of demands, or a target of attention, depending on whether intimidation, coercion, or propaganda is primarily sought.[32]

The need to define terrorism arises from the legal consequences of a terrorist act. If an act fulfils the necessary criteria to be deemed terrorist, then it will be classified as an international crime. Of most importance here, however, is the question of when acts of terrorism may give rise to the use of force in international law and whether that use of force is to be regarded as lawful. It will no doubt quickly be realised that an assertion of a right of self-defence to a terrorist attack does not dispose of the question of legality. Such a claim has often been made, particularly by the US, Israel and the apartheid regime that governed South Africa prior to that country's first democratic elections in 1994. Israel used this justification when invading Lebanon in 1982, arguing that the invasion was an act of self-defence in response to terrorist attacks, and resorted to it again in 1985, when it attacked the Palestine Liberation Organization's headquarters in Tunis, killing 60 people, after three Israeli citizens on a yacht in Larnaca harbour in Cyprus were murdered, supposedly by a Palestinian task force. The US claimed to be responding to an act of terrorism in 1986, after a terrorist bomb exploded in a West Berlin nightclub frequented by US service personnel, killing two Americans and injuring many others. Ten days later, the US bombed Tripoli, stating that it was in possession of information showing that this was the source of the terrorist attack. Fifteen people were killed. The then US Secretary of State, George Shultz, asserted that this action fell within the ambit of Article 51, but there was little international support for his argument. Both Israel and the US have insisted that this right of self-defence extends even to attacks on states not directly involved in the terrorist activity, as, for example, with Tunisia in 1985.

The 11 September attacks were foreshadowed by the bombing of the US embassies in Nairobi and Dar es Salaam in August 1998. Twelve Americans were killed, but more than 200 non-Americans also lost their lives, while thousands were injured. The response clearly illustrates the importance of power in determining action appropriate to the terrorist attack. While the governments of Kenya and Tanzania, whose citizens had suffered grievously in the bombings, were incapable of mounting a counter-attack by way of self-defence (as would almost certainly have been available to them if the identity of the bombers could have been ascertained), the US concluded that

---

[32] In Alex P Schmid and Albert J Jongman, *Political Terrorism: A New Guide to Actors, Authors, Concepts, Data Bases, Theories, and Literature* (Amsterdam, Transaction Books, 2005) 28.

responsibility lay with Osama bin Laden and Al-Qaeda. Some two weeks later, the US launched 79 cruise missiles at what they claimed were terrorist training camps in Afghanistan and at a factory in Sudan. As with Israel's operation in Tunis, it was claimed that Article 51 permitted action in self-defence against the territory of a state from which terrorists had been operating, even though the terrorists in question were not identified in any way with the states that were targeted.

Michael Byers, in his book *War Law*, describes how the then US president, Bill Clinton, in an attempt to deflect international criticism, took the precaution of communicating with the US's close allies (the UK, France and Germany) to warn them in advance of the attack and to seek their support.[33] Protest was therefore generally muted. Byers suggests that, at least until the second Bush administration:

> Whenever the US government wishes to act in a manner that is inconsistent with existing international law, its lawyers regularly and actively seek to change the law. They do so by provoking and steering changing patterns of state practice and *opinio juris*, with a view to incrementally modifying customary rules and accepted interpretations of treaties such as the UN Charter.[34]

He goes on to suggest that this is the best explanation for the US's behaviour after the 11 September attacks, since other, more obviously legitimate, courses of action were available to the US Government instead of the path it chose to follow. Instead of attempting to bring its attack on Afghanistan in October 2001 within the framework of Article 51, the US could, for example, almost certainly have secured a UNSC resolution authorising its action.[35] Adopting such an approach would, however, have had a distinct downside, since it would have entailed acknowledging the supremacy of the UNSC and its authority over the US's actions. As we will discuss in the final chapter, this would not have been acceptable to the Bush administration.

How much better, then, for the US to depict its attack on Afghanistan as an act of self-defence. Furthermore, although the real intention was to target the Taliban – then in control of most of Afghanistan – this course of action was made more palatable by the Taliban's refusal to cooperate with the US in apprehending and handing over those thought responsible for the events of 9/11. Byers argues that this enlargement of the meaning of 'self-defence' is amenable to yet further expansion, and, taken to extremes, can be used to justify 'targeted assassinations', as carried out by Israel against those whom it believes are involved in acts of violence against its citizens.[36] Indeed, this form of 'extra-judicial killing' (so-called because it disregards the due process

---

[33] Michael Byers, *War Law* (London, Atlantic Books, 2005) 63.
[34] ibid 64.
[35] ibid 65.
[36] ibid 67–68.

of law, including an individual's right to receive a fair trial) was a particular favourite of the previous US administration of President Obama in its efforts to combat the Taliban and members of Al-Qaeda and its affiliates. Most famously, Osama bin Laden, the architect of the 9/11 attacks, was the subject of a targeted assassination carried out by US Navy Seals in Abbottabad, Pakistan in May 2011, a mission that was executed without the consent, or even knowledge, of the Pakistani Government. The Obama administration also made liberal use of drones (unmanned aerial vehicles) in Yemen, Afghanistan and north-western Pakistan, to bomb groups and individuals believed to be terrorists. The decision to track down and kill an American citizen, Anwar al-Awlaki, by this method in Yemen in September 2011 caused particular outrage in the US.[37] Owing to its contemporary importance, the use of drones is discussed in section VII below.

It can therefore be seen that the precise scope of Article 51 in defining permissible responses to terrorist attacks is unclear, and this is perhaps not surprising in view of the fact that the UN Charter was drafted at a time when the principal threat to international peace and security was inter-state hostility rather than conflict between states and non-state actors. Two final points should also be borne in mind. The first is that any 'right' of self-defence is of little practical consequence unless the state under attack has the military means to respond, whether directly or through powerful allies. Secondly, terrorism is almost always a manifestation of an asymmetric struggle between irregular and often ill-equipped forces on the one hand and a state with access to armed forces and weapons on the other. While this is not to condone terrorist activity, it does highlight the fact that labelling one side of a struggle 'terrorists', as for instance with Chechnyans, Palestinians or Tamil Tigers, while exempting the other from the same charge because of its identification with governmental authority, is excessively simplistic. Indeed, some of the most repressive states have been enthusiastic about the so-called war against terror, precisely because it can be used to justify additional suppression and a refusal to negotiate under any circumstances.

A clear example of the sort of definitional problems posed by the appellation 'terrorism' is provided by the Israeli attack upon Gaza in December 2008 and January 2009. Under the operational title of 'Operation Cast Lead' Israel, claiming self-defence against terrorist acts (a small number of Hamas rockets had been fired from Gaza into Israel causing few injuries and little damage), mounted a massive attack upon Gaza, destroying much of its infrastructure, many buildings and killing 1,338 Palestinians (including 333 children), while suffering 13 Israeli deaths. The subsequent Report of

---

[37] See, eg, 'Secret U.S. Memo Made Legal Case to Kill a Citizen', *New York Times*, 9 October 2011, A1. A number of other American citizens have since perished in drone strikes, and the UK has similarly (and controversially) used such strikes to kill British citizens in Syria.

the UN Fact Finding Mission on the Gaza Conflict (*the Goldstone Report*)[38] concluded, in the words of Avi Shlaim:[39]

> The Goldstone team investigated 36 incidents involving the IDF. It found 11 incidents in which Israeli soldiers launched direct attacks against civilians with lethal outcomes; seven where civilians were shot leaving their homes waving white flags; a 'direct and intentional' attack on a hospital; numerous incidents where ambulances were prevented from attending to the severely injured; and nine attacks on civilian infrastructure with no military significance, such as flour mills, sewage works, and water wells – all part of a campaign to deprive civilians of basic necessities. In the words of the report, much of this extensive damage was "not justified by military necessity and carried out unlawfully and wantonly".

> In conclusion, the 575-page report noted that while the Israeli government sought to portray its operations as essentially a response to rocket attacks in the exercise of the right to self-defence, 'the Mission itself considers the plan to have been directed, at least in part, at a different target: the people of Gaza as a whole.' Under the circumstances, 'the Mission concludes that what occurred in just over three weeks at the end of 2008 and the beginning of 2009 was a deliberately disproportionate attack designed to punish, humiliate and terrorise a civilian population, radically diminish its local economic capacity both to work and to provide for itself, and to force upon it an ever-increasing sense of dependency and vulnerability.'

What can be stated with some certainty, however, is that Article 51 is being used to justify the use of armed force in circumstances never contemplated by those who drew up the Charter.

VI. From Humanitarian Intervention to Responsibility to Protect

As mentioned above, international law seems generally to permit the use of force by a state to rescue its citizens if they are being held improperly on the territory of another state, although, of course, the usual qualifications relating to necessity and proportionality apply, not to mention whether the relevant state has the capacity to carry out such a rescue. The issue of humanitarian intervention is related to this point, but here the purpose of the operation is not to secure the welfare of nationals of the intervening

---

[38] Available on the UN Human Rights Council website at www.ohchr.org/EN/HRBodies/HRC/SpecialSessions/Session9/Pages/FactFindingMission.aspx.

[39] Avi Shlaim, 'Ten years after the first war on Gaza, Israel still plans endless brute force', *Guardian*, 7 January 2019.

state or states but instead to protect the citizens of the state subject to the intervention in cases where mass atrocities or other grave human rights violations are being perpetrated by that state's government or other actors within the country. The question, then, is when, if ever, it is permissible for one state to interfere in the affairs of another (without that state's permission) when the object is not the safeguarding of its own nationals but rather that of 'saving strangers', in Nicholas Wheeler's memorable phrase.[40] On the one hand, recognising a right of humanitarian intervention would seem to be admirably in accord with the importance placed on human rights in the UN Charter and, more particularly, in the 1948 Universal Declaration of Human Rights and the succeeding covenants of 1966. On the other, it can be difficult to reconcile the practice of humanitarian intervention with either Article 2(4) of the Charter, which forbids UN member states from using 'the threat or use of force against the territorial integrity or political independence of any state' or Article 2(7), which precludes the UN from interfering 'in matters which are essentially within the domestic jurisdiction of any state' unless the provisions of Chapter VII of the Charter are engaged: that is, the situation must, in the opinion of the UNSC, amount to a threat to international peace and security.

Those who would like to see intervention on humanitarian grounds established as an international norm, including the former UN Secretary-General Kofi Annan, view such a step as part of a natural, and desirable, evolution of international law and the principles enshrined in the Charter, in which a concern for individual human rights, and, in particular, protecting those rights from gross violations, must necessarily trump the right of a state to conduct itself as it pleases within the confines of its own borders.[41] States whose governments grievously abuse the rights of their citizens, or which have ceased to function as effective polities – so-called 'failed states' – leaving their populations at the mercy of various warring factions, have, it is argued, forfeited their sovereign status and with it any entitlement to respect for their territorial integrity. It was this perspective that informed the outlook of former British Prime Minister Tony Blair, as articulated in his widely publicised 'Doctrine of the International Community' speech, delivered in Chicago in 1999:

> On the eve of a new Millennium we are now in a new world. ... The most pressing foreign policy problem we face is to identify the circumstances in which we should get actively involved in other people's conflicts. Non-interference has long been considered an important principle of international order. And it is not one we would want to jettison too readily. One state should not feel it has the right to change the political system of another or foment subversion or seize pieces

[40] Nicholas J Wheeler, *Saving Strangers: Humanitarian Intervention in International Society* (Oxford, OUP, 2000).

[41] Kofi Annan, *Interventions: A Life in War and Peace* (New York, Penguin Press, 2012).

of territory to which it feels it should have some claim. But the principle of non-interference must be qualified in important respects.[42]

Complicating matters, however, is the persistent problem of the unequal distribution of power in the international realm. In reality, only some states – most notably permanent members of the UNSC, and especially the US – possess the military capability to intervene, and hence are able to decide in what circumstances and against which states intervention on humanitarian grounds is justified. Conversely, some states, simply because they are powerful, will never be subject to a humanitarian intervention, no matter how egregious their human rights abuses become. Again, this is true of the permanent members of the UNSC, with China and Russia in particular able to treat their nationals as they wish without fear of international intervention. This inevitably concerns the less powerful states, particularly those that were formerly subject to colonial domination and consequently remain suspicious of any purported 'right' to forcibly interfere in the affairs of another state for the supposed good of its indigenous population.

Balanced against this fear that an intervention may take place when it is not warranted is the opposite concern: that an intervention may not materialise when it is badly needed. States that possess the resources (military and financial) to intervene in another country in order to relieve a humanitarian crisis are often reluctant to do so when their own security or economic interests are not at stake. In democratic contexts, pressure from national media and domestic constituents may play a role in prompting a hesitant administration to act, although it can also have the opposite effect, especially after an intervention is under way. A government that is urged to intervene abroad by members of the public shocked by TV pictures of dead and starving civilians is equally likely to face demands for immediate withdrawal when that same public is confronted by images of the nation's soldiers returning in body bags. This helps to explain the growing popularity of intervening via airstrikes and drones rather than by deploying soldiers on the ground, thereby minimising the number of troop casualties. Saving strangers, therefore, is ordinarily only an option when a state is not putting its own nationals unduly at risk. The ongoing conflict in Syria bears witness to this lack of enthusiasm among the general public in intervening nations, or in those with the capacity and will to intervene (essentially the US and Western Europe), with support for military action ebbing away even as the numbers dying rose.[43] This is probably

---

[42] Tony Blair, 'Doctrine of the International Community', 24 April 1999, available on the website of the National Archives at https://webarchive.nationalarchives.gov.uk/+/http://www.number10.gov.uk/Page1297. See also John Mearsheimer, *The Great Delusion: Liberal Dreams and International Realities* (New Haven, Yale, 2018), especially ch 6, 'Liberalism as a Source of Trouble'.

[43] See Rajan Menon, *The Conceit of Humanitarian Intervention* (Oxford, OUP, 2016) 38. Drawing on a German Marshall Fund poll conducted in the summer of 2013, Menon reports

indicative not only of frustration and fatigue among Western citizens with the lack of progress made in resolving the Syrian crisis itself, but also of a cumulative disillusion with the way in which Western military interventions have played out across the Middle East and North Africa over the past two decades. Such interventions, whether undertaken for avowedly humanitarian reasons or not, have in the opinion of most, left the states affected (Somalia, Afghanistan, Iraq, Libya), together with their neighbours, in a much more chaotic and violent condition than they were in before, making the loss of life (both military and civilian) even more difficult to justify.

In fact, humanitarian intervention has always had a very mixed history. Such interventions have not been undertaken consistently, nor have they always been handled well. The UNSC-authorised intervention in Somalia in 1993 may have begun with good intentions – to ensure that humanitarian aid reached Somalian citizens in the midst of the civil war that engulfed the country after the overthrow of President Siad Barre in 1991 – but it ended in fiasco. After the mission's objective was expanded to restore law and order in Somalia through the disarmament of the various warring militias, UN peace-keeping troops from Pakistan came under attack when searching a weapons storage site. Twenty-five of the troops died and over 50 were wounded. An operation was then launched, mainly at the instigation of the US, to hunt down the warlord deemed responsible. Further disaster then ensued when a US Rangers team involved in the assignment came under attack, losing two helicopters. Eighteen US soldiers were killed and scores more were wounded. Even more shocking, and captured in images transmitted on TV screens around the globe, was the treatment meted out to certain of the soldiers' corpses, which were dragged through the streets of Mogadishu. The resulting public outcry hastened the departure of US troops from Somalia, prompting the eventual collapse of the UN mission, with other troop-contributing nations also withdrawing their forces. The calamitous events that occurred in Somalia help explain the paralysis that afflicted the UN Secretariat and members of the UNSC the following year, when reports of wholesale slaughter began emanating from Rwanda, as extremists within the Hutu governing party began calling for the extermination of the country's Tutsi minority. Around a million Rwandan civilians were massacred before any outside intervention was entertained.

that 'American and European public support for intervention, or even for arming the opposition to Assad [Syrian President Bashar al-Assad], declined even as the death toll increased between 2012 and 2013. Opposition grew in every country surveyed and ranged from 61 percent in Sweden to 85 percent in Slovakia. The 2013 average for the entire EU was 72 percent – up from 59 percent in 2012 – while the percentage of Americans opposing intervention increased from 55 to 62 percent.' Menon goes on to explain that an apparent change of heart registered in 2014, when a *Washington Post*–ABC News poll showed the American public supportive of air strikes in Syria, was actually attributable to the fact that such strikes were to be directed against ISIS strongholds, and hence was motivated by support for self-defence against a terrorist threat rather than by concern for Syrian civilians.

A. Intervention with and without UNSC Authorisation

International law distinguishes humanitarian interventions undertaken pursuant to UNSC resolutions from those that are carried out without the UNSC's imprimatur. Only the former are in compliance with international law. Moreover, strictly speaking, the UNSC can authorise an intervention only if the humanitarian emergency in the relevant state is, or is likely to have, a destabilising effect beyond the state itself and thus constitutes a threat to international peace and security, thereby bringing the crisis within the UNSC's Chapter VII mandate. However, although many may deplore the fact, once an intervention has been authorised by the UNSC, then it must be regarded as legitimate (if not necessarily wise), even if doubts are expressed as to whether the Security Council has been correct in its characterisation of the situation as one that jeopardises international peace and stability. As we have observed, there is no court or other body with the power to review UNSC decisions, and hence the concept of ultra vires (ie that the UNSC has acted beyond its permitted powers) is of no practical relevance. Thus, the contentious situations continue to be those in which a state or a number of states wish to intervene militarily in order to protect a population or part of a population at risk but lack Security Council approval to do so.

The majority of the international community still seems to have little appetite for such unauthorised interventions. The General Assembly issued its interpretation of the principle of non-interference embodied in Article 2(7) in a Declaration on the Inadmissibility of Intervention in the Domestic Affairs of States and the Protection of Their Independence and Sovereignty in 1965,[44] restating it in a further declaration in 1981.[45] According to the Declaration:

> No State has the right to intervene, directly or indirectly, for any reason whatever, in the internal or external affairs of any other State. Consequently, armed intervention and all other forms of interference or attempted threats against the personality of the State or against its political, economic and cultural elements, are condemned.

The strength of international feeling on this subject explains why there is so little evidence of a developing law permitting humanitarian intervention, certainly prior to Kosovo in 1999. Indeed, it is important to understand that, in each case of intervention before Kosovo, the intervening state justified its actions not in terms of any right of humanitarian intervention, but largely on the ground of self-defence.[46] While this was no doubt partly owing to a

---

[44] UNGA Resolution 2131 (XX) of 21 December 1965.

[45] UNGA Resolution 36/103 of 9 December 1981.

[46] Although see Wheeler, *Saving Strangers* (2000) 60–62, who argues that India sought to justify its invasion of East Pakistan not in terms of a right of self-defence under Article 51 but rather as a legitimate response to Pakistan having committed 'refugee aggression', which had caused millions of Bengalis to flee to India, threatening India's stability.

determination to bypass the difficulties of securing UNSC authorisation, the refusal to rely upon any right of humanitarian intervention has had the effect of negating any evidence of changing *opinio juris.* As a result, each of the examples normally cited as providing evidence of a developing norm of humanitarian intervention does not in fact support any such contention. Three instances typically referred to are India's intervention in East Pakistan (now Bangladesh) in 1971 after widespread atrocities had been committed by the army of West Pakistan; Vietnam's invasion in 1978 of Kampuchea (now Cambodia), after hundreds of thousands of the country's citizens had been murdered by the Kampuchean army; and Tanzania's invasion of Uganda in 1979 to overthrow the regime of Idi Amin, responsible for the mass murder of Ugandan citizens and the expulsion of the country's South Asian population. In each case, not only did the invading state claim self-defence as the reason for its actions, it also refrained from suggesting that it had in any way been motivated by humanitarian concerns. The removal of tyrannical and murderous regimes was never offered as justification for these interventions, nor did the beneficial outcome in each case win any approval in those terms. Indeed, Vietnam was roundly criticised for its use of force against the territorial integrity and political independence of Kampuchea, even as the atrocities of the Pol Pot government were attracting widespread condemnation.

In fact, before NATO's intervention in Kosovo, there had been only one occasion when a state had been prepared to portray its actions in terms of a response to a humanitarian crisis. When the UK deployed forces, together with the US, Italy, the Netherlands and France, in northern Iraq after the Gulf War of 1991, with the object of providing safe havens for the Kurdish people under attack from Saddam Hussein's regime, the British Foreign Office gave the following rationale for its government's actions: 'We believe that international intervention without the invitation of the country concerned can be justified in cases of extreme humanitarian need.'[47] Significantly, it was not suggested that this justification was a legal one. Such a proposition would seem immediately incompatible with Article 2(4) of the UN Charter.

How, then, should NATO's intervention in Kosovo in 1999 be regarded? Could it, and did it, represent a change in international law? Brief facts are relevant. When Yugoslavia's Constitution was drafted in 1945, Kosovo was accorded the status of an autonomous region. It was inhabited by people who were divided by their religion and, to some extent, by their ethnicity. By the 1990s, some 90 per cent of the 2.2 million population of Kosovo was Muslim and ethnically Albanian. The remaining 10 per cent was made up of Orthodox Christian Serbs. Many of the religious and national sites most revered by the Serbs are to be found in Kosovo, which has exacerbated tensions between the two groups. Significantly, Kosovo was the poorest part of Yugoslavia,

---

[47] Gray (n 14) 43.

and the Serbs met with little success in persuading ethnic Serbs to live there. A major reason for the election of Slobodan Milošević as president in 1989 was his promise to promote Serbian interests in Kosovo. After his election, Milošević immediately withdrew Kosovo's autonomous status, which led to increased tension and violence between the two communities.

While opinions differ, the evidence suggests that Serbian aggression was provoking defensive action, which in turn prompted yet more Serb violence, culminating, it was alleged, in ethnic cleansing and other atrocities, including both murder and rape. In fact, it is difficult to obtain clear evidence of exactly what was done to each community by the other, but the UNSC was concerned by the violence, and in 1998 imposed a mandatory arms embargo on the whole of the Federal Republic of Yugoslavia (FRY).[48] A series of resolutions followed. Resolution 1199 of 23 September 1998, expressly referring to the authority of Chapter VII, determined that the situation in Kosovo 'constitute[d] a threat to peace and security in the region'. However, it was clear that no resolution could be obtained that would expressly authorise the use of force, since Russia would exercise its veto. Under threat from NATO for failing to comply with the demand of Resolution 1199 for the cessation of hostilities and a return to negotiations, the Serbian-dominated FRY eventually agreed to comply. Resolution 1203 of 24 October 1998 followed, again under Chapter VII, endorsing the two agreements made by the FRY to comply with UNSC resolutions and to accept a verification mission from the Organization for Security and Co-operation in Europe (OSCE), and also an agreement with NATO creating an air-verification mission. Notwithstanding this, the violence escalated, NATO resumed its threats, and, after the failure of talks aimed at resolving the Kosovan problem held in Rambouillet near Paris,[49] NATO began its campaign of aerial bombardment against FRY targets on 23 March 1999, which lasted until the withdrawal of Serbian forces following an agreement reached on 9 June 1999. The agreement was notified to the UN, and the UNSC passed Resolution 1244, which endorsed the end of hostilities and also the plan for restoring peace to the region, most notably through the establishment of an interim administration in Kosovo under the auspices of the UN.

The NATO airstrikes caused immense concern to international lawyers. The intervention was clearly not consistent with international law, and yet many felt that if the facts of the human rights abuses were as NATO claimed, intervention was both necessary and moral. Some thought that

---

[48] UNSC Resolution 1160 of 31 March 1998.

[49] The projected Rambouillet Agreement (Interim Agreement for Peace and Self-Government in Kosovo) was in many ways a strange document, demanding effectively that a NATO occupation force be accepted in Kosovo by the Serbs. Even more peculiar was a provision (Ch 4, Art 1) that stated: 'The economy of Kosovo shall function in accordance with free market principles.' The Agreement is available on the US Department of State website at https://1997-2001.state. gov/regions/eur/ksvo_rambouillet_text.html.

the intervention, although not legal, was justified by subsequent international reaction: in particular, the attempt by Russia and Belarus to have the NATO bombing declared illegal was rejected by a large majority of the UNSC, and the General Assembly failed to condemn NATO's actions. Even the UN Secretary-General at the time of the intervention, Kofi Annan, has acknowledged his ambivalence on the matter, believing that the international community should have intervened in Kosovo even as he was equally clear that, under the UN Charter, such intervention could take place only with the prior approval of the UNSC.[50] It should also be pointed out that the NATO powers themselves stated at the time that their actions were not to be viewed as setting any sort of precedent.

What this example usefully illustrates once more is the distinction between (international) law and morality. International humanitarian intervention is lawful only if consistent with the UN Charter. But the issue of legality does not finally dispose of the matter, even if many think that it should. Although international law is a major consideration in determining a course of action, other factors may well be considered more important by state officials and diplomats, particularly in cases where egregious breaches of humanitarian or human rights law are believed to be occurring. Here, we can also observe the different weight of veto. The knowledge that Russia would prevent any resolution empowering forcible intervention (with or without the support of China) was not viewed as tantamount to a threat of war if the authority of the Charter was ignored. The use by the US of the veto to prevent the condemnation of Israel under Chapter VII is altogether more powerful. Even where the US's stance is not supported by any other member of the UNSC, no other party or parties would seriously consider challenging its position.

To return to the purely legal position, it is apparent that the overwhelming majority of states do not accept that unilateral military intervention for humanitarian purposes is lawful under the UN Charter, being adamant that it does not represent one of the permitted exceptions to the prohibition on the use of force contained in Article 2(4). Nor does there appear to be much likelihood of this changing in the near future.

It appears that only the UK has been willing to expressly champion humanitarian intervention, with, as Gray points out, its position having evolved since the mid-1980s from regarding the doctrine as, at best, 'not unambiguously illegal' to suggesting, from 1992 onwards, that 'international intervention without the invitation of the country concerned can be justified in cases of extreme humanitarian need',[51] to producing a framework document in 2000 for the UN Secretary-General on intervention in response to mass violations of humanitarian law or where crimes against humanity are

---

[50] Annan, *Interventions* (2012) 91–100.
[51] Gray (n 14) 40–41, 43.

being committed.[52] The Government of David Cameron again returned to the theme in response to the chemical attack carried out on Ghouta in Syria in August 2013, describing in some detail the criteria that, if met, would justify intervention on humanitarian grounds without UNSC authorisation.[53] In particular, the Government stated:

> If action in the Security Council is blocked, the UK would still be permitted under international law to take exceptional measures in order to alleviate the scale of the overwhelming humanitarian catastrophe in Syria by deterring and disrupting the further use of chemical weapons by the Syrian regime. Such a legal basis is available, under the doctrine of humanitarian intervention, provided three conditions are met:
>
> (i)   there is convincing evidence, generally accepted by the international community as a whole, of extreme humanitarian distress on a large scale, requiring immediate and urgent relief;
>
> (ii) it must be objectively clear that there is no practicable alternative to the use of force if lives are to be saved; and
>
> (iii) the proposed use of force must be necessary and proportionate to the aim of relief of humanitarian need and must be strictly limited in time and scope to this aim (i.e. the minimum necessary to achieve that end and for no other purpose).[54]

It then went on to conclude that, in its opinion, all three criteria had been met in the case of the Ghouta attack. (In fact, no military intervention took place, after the UK Parliament, chastened after the country's involvement in the Iraq intervention in 2003, voted against taking military action.[55])

And, as was seen in section V above, in 2017 the UK again invoked humanitarian intervention as justification for carrying out air strikes in Syria after the Assad regime's alleged use of chemical weapons against its own citizens. More cynically, it could be said that, lacking a conventionally lawful ground for its bombing mission (eg, authorisation contained in a UNSC resolution or an invitation from the country itself) the UK appealed to humanitarian intervention as a useful *ex post facto* justification for its actions. Whether this was the case or not, it will confirm the view of many states that recourse to the doctrine should be severely curtailed rather than encouraged.

Indeed, suspicion over the (mis)use of humanitarian intervention may explain why, since the turn of the millennium, another doctrine has emerged

---

[52] ibid 55.

[53] ibid 57.

[54] Prime Minister's Office, 'Chemical weapon use by Syrian regime: UK government legal position', Policy Paper of 29 August 2013, para 4, available on UK Government website at www.gov.uk/government/publications/chemical-weapon-use-by-syrian-regime-uk-government-legal-position/chemical-weapon-use-by-syrian-regime-uk-government-legal-position-html-version.

[55] As mentioned above (n 16), the US (under President Obama) also ultimately decided not to take military action, with Syria, in a deal negotiated by Russia, agreeing to dispose of its chemical weapons arsenal.

alongside it, and may even be displacing it: responsibility to protect. However, as explained below, this new concept is beset with some of the same problems as humanitarian intervention.

B. Responsibility to Protect

Devised by the International Commission on Intervention and State Sovereignty (ICISS) – a body set up in 2000 under the auspices of the Canadian Government to consider how to respond to gross human rights violations – responsibility to protect (commonly abbreviated to R2P) has sought to reorient the debate on how to deal with humanitarian catastrophes. As set out in the ICISS's 2001 report,[56] R2P places the onus for protecting individuals from severe human rights violations primarily on the state in which those individuals reside, seeking to avoid outside military intervention wherever possible. In particular, it champions a preventive rather than reactive strategy, in that states are encouraged to take pre-emptive steps to eliminate the conditions likely to give rise to humanitarian crises rather than focusing upon the consequences of those crises.

Where a state is unable or unwilling to deal with a humanitarian catastrophe, then the international community has a responsibility to help through a variety of responses, which may include coercive measures, such as the imposition of sanctions or prosecuting individuals alleged to have committed grave human rights abuses. Military intervention, however, is envisaged only as a last resort and in clearly defined circumstances. Emphasis is also placed on following up any military intervention with measures aimed at rebuilding and restoring order to the society subject to the intervention and, significantly, 'addressing the causes of the harm that the intervention was designed to halt or avert',[57] thereby engaging with a criticism frequently levelled at humanitarian interventions: that, whatever their outcome, they do little if anything to tackle the underlying causes of human rights violations, with the result that such violations simply recur.

The ICISS's recommendations have had an appreciable impact on UN and state thinking on how to deal with (or at least talk about) grave human

---

[56] International Commission on Intervention and State Sovereignty, *The Responsibility to Protect: Report of the Commission on Intervention and State Sovereignty* (Ottawa, International Development Research Centre (IDRC), 2001), available on the IDRC website at www.idrc.ca/en/book/responsibility-protect-report-international-commission-intervention-and-state-sovereignty. See also Gareth Evans, *The Responsibility to Protect: Ending Mass Atrocity Crimes Once and For All* (Washington DC, Brookings Institution Press, 2008). Evans, a former foreign minister of Australia, chaired the Commission, along with Mohamed Sahnoun, a special adviser to the UN Secretary-General.

[57] ICISS, *The Responsibility to Protect* (ibid) 11.

rights transgressions. The UN's High-level Panel on Threats, Challenges and Change, in its own report published in 2004, endorsed

> the emerging norm that there is a collective international responsibility to protect, exercisable by the Security Council authorising military intervention as a last resort, in the event of genocide and other large-scale killing, ethnic cleansing or serious violations of humanitarian law which sovereign governments have proved powerless or unwilling to prevent.[58]

The Panel's report also set out five minimum criteria that it believes the UNSC should take into account when deciding whether or not a military intervention is justified:

a)   *Seriousness of threat.* Is the threatened harm to State or human security of a kind, and sufficiently clear and serious, to justify prima facie the use of military force? In the case of internal threats, does it involve genocide and other large-scale killing, ethnic cleansing or serious violations of international humanitarian law, actual or imminently apprehended?

b)   *Proper purpose.* Is it clear that the primary purpose of the proposed military action is to halt or avert the threat in question, whatever other motives or purposes may be involved?

c)   *Last resort.* Has every non-military option for meeting the threat in question been explored, with reasonable grounds for believing that other measures will not succeed?

d)   *Proportional means.* Are the scale, duration and intensity of the proposed military action the minimum necessary to meet the threat in question?

e)   *Balance of consequences.* Is there a reasonable chance of the military action being successful in meeting the threat in question, with the consequences of action not likely to be worse than the consequences of inaction?[59]

The General Assembly, at its 2005 World Summit, celebrating the sixtieth anniversary of the UN, approved the concept of R2P, albeit limiting its application to cases in which the following atrocities are taking place, or are believed to be at risk of occurring: genocide; war crimes; ethnic cleansing; and crimes against humanity.[60] It confirmed that responsibility for preventing such crimes lies primarily with a population's own state, but also acknowledged that the international community as a whole has a collective responsibility to support individual states in order to ensure that such atrocities do not occur. Such support, it explained, should take the form of 'appropriate diplomatic, humanitarian, and other peaceful means', and that, should such approaches

---

[58] Report of the Secretary-General's High-level Panel on Threats, Challenges and Change, 'A More Secure World: Our Shared Responsibility', UN Doc A/59/565, 2 December 2004, para 203.

[59] ibid para 207.

[60] 2005 World Summit Outcome, UN Doc A/60/L.1, para 138.

prove to be insufficient, states 'are prepared to take collective action ... through the Security Council ... on a case-by-case basis'.[61] Thus, resort to any unilateral use of force is expressly ruled out. In fact, as many writers have observed (and some deplored), the R2P that emerged from the World Summit process was a much paler imitation of the version championed by the ICISS, with states unwilling to commit to a responsibility to take military action in situations where such atrocities are taking place.[62]

The conclusions of the World Summit on the responsibility to protect were in turn reaffirmed by the UNSC in a 2006 resolution on the subject of protecting civilians in armed conflict,[63] and were drawn on by the then Secretary-General, Ban Ki-Moon, in a report presented to the General Assembly in 2009. Entitled 'Implementing the Responsibility to Protect',[64] the report sets out a three-pillar strategy aimed at preventing crimes against humanity, which:

1. recognises that responsibility for protecting populations from genocide, war crimes, ethnic cleansing and crimes against humanity lies principally with the states in which those populations are located;
2. emphasises the important part to be played by the international community in helping states fulfil that responsibility; and
3. acknowledges the need for UN members 'to respond collectively in a timely and decisive manner when a state is manifestly failing to provide such protection'.[65]

Since then, the Secretary-General has issued annual reports concentrating on and seeking to clarify different aspects of R2P. The most recent report (the tenth in the series), issued in June 2018,[66] focused on the need to further improve systems for early warning and assessment in order to avert atrocities, and also emphasised the importance of closing the gap between early warning and early action, advocating i) the strengthening of existing preventive capacities, especially through regional and sub-regional arrangements; ii) holding states accountable to their populations for failures to protect them from atrocity crimes; and iii) much better use of the contribution that civilian

---

[61] ibid para 139.
[62] 'By the time the concept emerged from the United Nations, there was little responsibility left in the responsibility to protect.' Saira Mohamed, 'Syria, the United Nations, and the Responsibility to Protect' (2012) 106 *Proceedings of the Annual Meeting (American Society of International Law)* 223–26, 224. See also Menon, *Humanitarian Intervention* (2016) 92–93.
[63] UNSC Resolution 1674 of 28 April 2006.
[64] Report of the Secretary-General, 'Implementing the responsibility to protect', UN Doc A/63/677, 12 January 2009.
[65] ibid para 9.
[66] Report of the Secretary-General, 'Responsibility to protect: from early warning to early action', UN Doc A/72/884–S/2018/525, 1 June 2018. All the Secretary-General's reports on R2P can be accessed on the website of the UN Office on Genocide Prevention and the Responsibility to Protect: www.un.org/en/genocideprevention.

organisations and actors can make to atrocity prevention. The Secretary-General's reports have subsequently been debated by the General Assembly.

It should also be noted that, as far back as 2000, the African Union recognised the right to intervene in a member state where gross human rights violations are occurring. Hence, even as the organisation's Constitutive Act (its constitution or founding principles) places great emphasis on respect for each member's sovereignty and the principle of non-interference (as might well be expected on a continent where colonialist exploitation ended only a comparatively short time ago), so it also enshrines a right for the Union to intervene in a member state where 'war crimes, genocide, and crimes against humanity' are taking place.[67] In practice, however, it has shown itself reluctant to use these powers.

In spite of the undoubted impact that R2P has had on the debate concerning how best to prevent people from suffering gross human rights violations, it is still far from establishing itself as a principle of international law. Although there has been a general willingness to support the concept as encapsulated in the 2005 World Summit Outcome document, the absence to date of widespread and consistent state practice, a dearth of evidence indicating that states consider it to amount to a binding obligation, and the difficulties that persist at present in relation to reconciling R2P (at least in regard to its third, 'interventionist' pillar) with respect for state sovereignty all indicate that it is far from crystallising into a legal norm.[68] Many states (especially weaker nations and former colonies) harbour misgivings that the doctrine, as with humanitarian intervention, will be abused by more powerful states in order to provide a semblance of legitimacy to military actions that are, in reality, undertaken for other, more self-interested motives. Counterbalancing this is the fear – particularly prevalent among those nations that possess the means to intervene – of being drawn into situations that will prove costly in terms of 'blood and treasure' but will yield few if any benefits for the intervening state and its nationals. Hence, as Rajan Menon notes:

> Objections to R2P did not ... come solely from non-Western and authoritarian states. The United States, through its pugnacious UN ambassador, John Bolton [now National Security Adviser to President Trump], also opposed any formulation that might be interpreted as obligating states to stop mass killings.[69]

---

[67] Constitutive Act of the African Union, Art 4(h). Under a protocol containing various amendments to the Constitutive Act, adopted in 2003, this Article is widened to allow the Union to also intervene to deal with 'a serious threat to legitimate order', so as 'to restore peace and stability to the Member State of the Union upon the recommendation of the Peace and Security Council'. The protocol has yet to come into force, however, having so far failed to attract the necessary number of ratifications: two-thirds of the Union's member states. (As at February 2019, 28 of the 55 member states had ratified the protocol.)

[68] See Spencer Zifcak, 'The Responsibility to Protect' in Malcolm D Evans (ed), *International Law*, 5th edn (Oxford, OUP, 2018) 512–15.

[69] Menon (n 43) 92.

In common with humanitarian intervention, R2P has been invoked selectively and not always appropriately. As Alex Bellamy points out, the concept has been referred to by a number of actors (various states, the UN and other entities, such as NGOs) in the context of certain humanitarian crises, including Darfur and Kenya, but ignored in others where the loss of life, displacement of persons and general suffering have been equally applicable, such as Somalia,[70] and, subsequently, Yemen. It has also made an appearance in circumstances where its applicability is much more doubtful, having been appealed to by Russian Foreign Minister Sergei Lavrov to justify Russia's intervention in the South Ossetian region of Georgia in 2008, shortly before Russia recognised the independence of South Ossetia and Abkhazia, and by French Foreign Minister Bernard Kouchner, again in 2008, in an attempt to persuade the UNSC to intervene in Myanmar after the country's military rulers had been slow to accept foreign aid following the devastation wreaked on the country by Cyclone Nargis.[71] In both cases, the relevance of R2P was strongly disputed by significant elements of the international community. This echoes the attempt a few years earlier by a number of American and British politicians to characterise the 2003 invasion of Iraq as partly a humanitarian venture (citing the brutality of Saddam Hussein's regime towards Iraq's citizens and neighbours, and the lack of democracy in the country), which generally met with very short shrift.[72]

It would certainly seem that the cause of R2P, and of humanitarian intervention in general, has suffered a setback as a result of the 2011 intervention in Libya's civil war, undertaken pursuant to UNSC authorisation.[73] In sanctioning the NATO-led coalition 'to take all necessary measures … to protect civilians and civilian populated areas under threat of attack',[74] the Security Council did seem to be referencing R2P, even if it did not expressly refer to the concept. In the opinion of many states, not least P5 members China and Russia (supported by fellow sitting UNSC members Brazil, India and

---

[70] Alex J Bellamy, 'The Responsibility to Protect – Five Years On' (2010) 24 *Ethics & International Affairs* 143–69.

[71] Bellamy (ibid) 150–53.

[72] Evans, *The Responsibility to Protect* (2008) 69–71; Annan, *Interventions* (n 41) x–xi. See also Jeremy Moses, Babak Bahador and Tessa Wright, 'The Iraq War and the Responsibility to Protect: Uses, Abuses and Consequences for the Future of Humanitarian Intervention' (2011) 5 *Journal of Intervention and Statebuilding* 347–67, who point out that humanitarian-type arguments were deployed by politicians in the UK and US in the run-up to the Iraq war, not merely, as is often asserted, after the invasion had taken place, when no WMD were unearthed.

[73] UNSC Resolution 1973 of 17 March 2011.

[74] UNSC Resolution 1973, operative paragraph 4. The fourth preambular paragraph had reiterated Libya's prime responsibility for the protection of its citizens. This onus on Libya to protect its citizens had been recited in the Security Council's earlier resolution (UNSC Resolution 1970 of 26 February 2011 (preambular paragraph 9)), which had imposed an arms embargo on the country; introduced a travel ban and asset freeze in respect of Gaddafi, certain of his family members and a number of senior politicians and military leaders; and referred the situation in Libya to the ICC.

South Africa), the NATO-led campaign went far beyond the protection of civilians mandated by the Security Council, and instead facilitated 'regime change': ie the overthrow of the government of Muammar Gaddafi, which in turn led to the eventual capture and killing by rebel forces of Gaddafi himself. Such 'mission creep' in the case of Libya has undoubtedly made other R2P-inspired interventions far more difficult to achieve.[75] China and Russia have repeatedly blocked the passing of any UNSC resolution they believe might pave the way for a similar intervention in Syria, now approaching the eighth year of its devastating civil war. Both vetoed, at an early stage in the conflict, a draft resolution that alluded to R2P, with Russia referring pointedly to the Libyan example: 'The international community was alarmed by statements that Libya is a model for the future actions of NATO in implementing the responsibility to protect.'[76]

Syria also demonstrates the problem of implementing R2P when the geopolitical interests of UNSC members are clearly engaged. Despite manifestly failing to protect its civilians from the commission of atrocity crimes (and having apparently perpetrated some of those crimes itself), the government of President Bashar al-Assad is unlikely to be held accountable owing to its close relationship with Russia. In addition, Russia's own military intervention in the conflict (together with Iran and Hezbollah) in support of the Syrian Government, mirrored by the intervention of the US-led coalition, primarily to target ISIL, but also in support of certain of the rebel groups seeking to overthrow the al-Assad regime, makes it much harder to agree on a course of action in the Security Council aimed at protecting civilians and respecting the rules of warfare. Thus, in spite of the UNSC having passed multiple resolutions calling for an end to the conflict, the granting of access for humanitarian purposes, and a prohibition on the use of chemical weapons, the war continues, over 400,000 Syrians have now been killed, and millions more have either fled the country or are internally displaced.

Nor has R2P proved effective in preventing the violence committed by military forces in Myanmar against the Rohingya Muslim minority, which various states and UN officials say amounts to genocide,[77] and which has prompted around 700,000 Rohingya to flee from their homes in Rakhine state into

---

[75] According to Menon (n 43) 95–96, Brazil's 2011 proposal 'Responsibility While Protecting', although ostensibly concerned with limiting the harm suffered by non-combatants in R2P-type military interventions, really sought to ensure that the UNSC exerted greater control over such situations, so as to prevent misuse of the doctrine, as Brazil believed had occurred in Libya. See also Deepak Bhojwani, 'Responsibility to Protect: Issues of Legality and Legitimacy' (2012) 47 *Economic and Political Weekly* 28–30.

[76] Cited in Gray (n 14) 64. China and Russia have also vetoed attempts to refer the situation in Syria to the International Criminal Court for investigation.

[77] The Independent International Fact-Finding Mission on Myanmar, established by the UN Human Rights Council to investigate the situation in the states of Rakhine, Kachin and Shan, concluded that serious violations of human rights and international humanitarian law had been committed, principally by the Tatmadaw, Myanmar's security forces, and especially the military. It recommended that Myanmar's Commander-in-Chief and other senior military leaders be

neighbouring Bangladesh. Neither the Myanman Government itself, which bears primary responsibility for protecting its citizens from atrocity crimes (in accordance with the first pillar of R2P) nor UN member states, responsible (under the third pillar of R2P) for taking collective action 'when a state is manifestly failing to provide such protection', have so far taken measures to resolve the situation, including facilitating the return of the Rohingyan refugees to Myanmar. China, with the backing of Russia, has resisted attempts within the UNSC to take action against Myanmar, such as imposing an arms embargo, implementing targeted sanctions, or referring military leaders to the ICC or an ad hoc tribunal for investigation regarding the alleged commission of atrocity crimes.[78] China's position is reflective of its long-standing adherence to the principle of non-interference in the affairs of other states, but is doubtless also influenced by its economic ties to neighbouring Myanmar and by its unwillingness to set any precedent that could be applied to the treatment of its own Muslim minority population, the Uighur.

Meanwhile, although quick to call for action to be taken against Myanmar for its treatment of the Rohingya, or for military intervention in Syria to protect civilians against chemical attacks allegedly committed on behalf of the al-Assad administration, the UK and US have been much less vocal with regard to Saudi Arabia's aerial bombardment of Houthi-held areas in its neighbour Yemen, conducted with little regard for the lives of non-combatants.[79] Oil-rich and geopolitically important Saudi Arabia is, of course, a long-standing ally of both states, and also represents a lucrative market for arms sales. That the

investigated for genocide, crimes against humanity and war crimes. UN Human Rights Council, A/HRC/39/CRP.2, 17 September 2018. According to the former UN High Commissioner for Human Rights, Zeid Ra'ad Al Hussein, the treatment of the Rohingya 'seems a textbook example of ethnic cleansing'. OHCHR, 'Darker and more dangerous: High Commissioner updates the Human Rights Council on human rights issues in 40 countries', 11 September 2017, available at www.ohchr.org/EN/NewsEvents/Pages/DisplayNews.aspx?NewsID=22041&LangID=E.

[78] See 'U.N. Security Council mulls Myanmar action; Russia, China boycott talks', *Reuters*, 17 December 2018 and 'China fails to stop U.N. Security Council Myanmar briefing', *Reuters*, 24 October 2018.

[79] Air strikes by the Saudi Arabian-led coalition in Yemen began in March 2015, escalating the civil war between the forces of Yemeni President Abd Rabbu Mansour Hadi (whom the Saudi coalition supports) and the Houthis, an armed rebel group that belong to the Zaydi sect of Shi'a Islam, and which is supported by Iran. Accurate figures are difficult to obtain, but an independent research group, the Armed Conflict Location and Event Data Project, has estimated that 60,000 civilians and combatants died between January 2016 and December 2018. See 'Yemen death toll now exceeds 60,000 according to latest ACLED data, *Reliefweb*, 11 December 2018, available at https://reliefweb.int/report/yemen/yemen-war-death-toll-now-exceeds-60000-according-latest-acled-data. A UN report examining the conflict in Yemen between September 2014 and June 2018 concluded there were reasonable grounds for believing that human rights violations had been committed by the governments of Yemen, Saudi Arabia and the United Arab Emirates, and also by Houthi rebel forces. Human Rights Council, 'Situation of Human Rights in Yemen, including violations and abuses since September 2014, UN Doc A/HRC/39/43, 17 August 2018. With regard to the coalition air strikes, it found that these had caused 'most of the documented civilian casualties' (at 5), and that there were reasonable grounds for believing that some of these attacks amounted to war crimes.

current UK Government would seek to advocate humanitarian intervention in order to safeguard Yemeni civilians is therefore inconceivable. In fact, the government of Theresa May has been sharply criticised for continuing to sell weapons to Saudi Arabia that may well have been used in violation of human rights law and international humanitarian law in Yemen.

Libya, now controlled by rival factions, also serves as an unfortunate example of a further problem with R2P and other military interventions as practised to date: a failure of post-conflict planning that can leave the affected state in a more dangerous and violent situation than before the intervention took place, magnifying rather than reducing the 'threat to peace and stability' in the relevant region, and further jeopardising the security of its citizens and those of neighbouring countries.[80]

Thus, while the then UN Secretary-General Ban Ki-Moon was able to say in 2011: '[I]t is a sign of progress that our debates are now about how, not whether, to implement the responsibility to protect. No Government questions the principle',[81] such an assertion is now much harder to justify. As with its older sibling, humanitarian intervention, R2P is now regarded with some suspicion by a large part of the international community. Ultimately, as Jeremy Moses notes, it is impossible to ignore the question of sovereign power in relation to both types of intervention:

> [T]he much-vaunted change in language, from 'right to intervene' to 'responsibility to protect', does not change the contours of the problem, nor does it alter the meaning and significance of *de facto* sovereignty. While state sovereignty remains 'real', interventions will remain imperialist; that is, they will be motivated and carried out primarily in the interests of powerful states who are themselves not subject to the universal 'ethic' of responsibility ...
>
> To the extent that modern international law maintains a coercive force, it is provided by agreement of these powers who are themselves not subject to the law. We might say, then, that the use of RtoP principles to justify the actions of the great powers represents continuation of power politics by other norms.[82]

VII. Rules Constraining the Type of Force Permissible

As we observed at the beginning of this chapter, historically, international law has been more concerned with the rules of warfare – that is, *how* wars should

---

[80] On the post-conflict chaos in Libya, see Menon (n 43) 141–47.

[81] 'Effective Prevention Requires Early, Active, Sustained Engagement, Stresses Secretary-General at Ministerial Round Table on "Responsibility to Protect"', UN Doc SG/SM/13838, 23 September 2011.

[82] Jeremy Moses, 'Sovereignty as irresponsibility? A Realist critique of the Responsibility to Protect' (2013) 39 *Review of International Studies* 113–35, 133 and 134.

be fought – rather than with the question as to *when*, if ever, it is permissible for a state to wage war in the first place. In a further development, as inter-state conflicts, or wars between states, became less common, so intra-state conflicts – fighting among factions within states – increased, with the effect that rules relating to the use of force began to concentrate on armed conflict more generally rather than simply being concerned with war as tradition-ally defined. As already noted, the rules of international humanitarian law are to be found primarily in the four Geneva Conventions of 1949, and the Hague Conventions of 1899 and 1907. These two sources focus on different aspects of the rules of armed conflict. The Hague Conventions are primarily concerned with the methods and means of warfare, and with limiting (though not to a very great extent) the sort of weapons deemed 'acceptable' for use in wars. The Geneva Conventions are mainly preoccupied with the protec-tion of persons who are not participating in the armed conflict, or who have ceased to do so, whether because of injury or surrender. It is sometimes said that 'Hague law' encompasses the laws of war or the law of armed conflict, whereas 'Geneva law' is concerned with humanitarian law. Nevertheless, this is not entirely correct, as we shall see when we consider the use of armed unmanned aerial vehicles (drones).

Underlying all of the rules concerning the ways and methods by which war may be waged are, first, the principle of humanity and, second, that of the protection of non-combatants and civilians. As the term suggests, the princi-ple of humanity is intended to ensure that individuals are treated humanely in all circumstances. Although the phrase 'humane warfare' appears oxymo-ronic, in essence it means that any violence not justified by 'military necessity' is prohibited by the law of armed conflict. In particular, if violence or destruc-tion is unnecessary, disproportionate, indiscriminate or intended to spread terror, it will not meet the criteria of lawful armed conflict. Similarly, certain kinds of weapon are unlawful and their use is banned. Both chemical and biological weapons are incompatible with international law, although the use of nuclear weapons remains unprohibited – at least, in some imaginary scenarios, according to the ICJ.[83] Conventional weaponry may be unlaw-ful if those weapons have a disproportionately inhumane effect (such as 'dum-dum' bullets, which are designed to expand upon impact, or, arguably, anti-personnel land mines).

The four Geneva Conventions of 12 August 1949 were drafted after the Second World War, but they drew upon earlier developments in international law. The first Geneva Convention is the Convention for the Amelioration of the Condition of the Wounded and Sick in Armed Forces in the Field, being the natural successor to the Geneva Convention with a similar name of 1864. The second – the Geneva Convention for the Amelioration of the Condition of Wounded, Sick and Shipwrecked Members of Armed Forces

---

[83] *Legality of the Threat or Use of Nuclear Weapons, Advisory Opinion*, ICJ Reports 1996, 226.

at Sea – built on the first to provide similar protection for those affected by maritime warfare. The third concerned prisoners of war,[84] and was based on the Prisoners of War Convention of 1929, while the fourth dealt with the protection of civilians,[85] having been developed from the draft Tokyo Convention of 1934. An overwhelming majority of states (196 in total as at February 2019) are party to these Conventions; as a result, they undoubtedly represent customary international law, and hence are binding on all states, even those that are not actually party to them.

Supplementing the Geneva Conventions are the two Additional Protocols of 1977. These provide enhanced protection for, in the first Protocol, victims of international armed conflict,[86] and, in the second, victims of non-international armed conflict.[87] The first Protocol now has 174 states parties, and the second 168 (as at February 2019). Arguably, therefore, both are now reflective of customary international law. A third Additional Protocol was adopted in 2005, and came into force in 2007. As at February 2019, this has 76 states parties. This added a further emblem – the Red Crystal – to those of the Red Cross and the Red Crescent to denote that its bearer enjoys special protective status in any conflict (because, for example, he or she is providing medical services[88]).

It is probably accurate to state that, until the aftermath of the US-led invasion of Iraq in 2003, no international lawyer considered the Geneva Conventions to be other than binding on all parties to any conflict. It was surprising, therefore, to witness some lawyers representing the administration of George W Bush asserting that, as neither the Taliban (in Afghanistan), nor members of Al-Qaeda, were parties to the Conventions, they were not entitled to benefit from their protection. This seems demonstrably wrong. The Conventions were intended to protect all in situations of warfare, not simply nationals of states whose governments had ratified the instruments. The principle of humanity is of universal application, and the Bush administration's description of the Geneva Conventions as 'quaint' was forcefully rejected in both academia and the political world.

Since the Geneva Conventions and their Protocols, the most important developments in this field have concerned the use of ad hoc tribunals created by the UNSC: namely, the International Criminal Tribunal for the Former Yugoslavia (1993) and the International Criminal Tribunal for Rwanda (1994),

---

[84] Geneva Convention relative to the Treatment of Prisoners of War.

[85] Geneva Convention relative to the Protection of Civilian Persons in Time of War.

[86] Protocol Additional to the Geneva Conventions of 12 August 1949, and relating to the Protection of Victims of International Armed Conflicts, 8 June 1977.

[87] Protocol Additional to the Geneva Conventions of 12 August 1949, and relating to the Protection of Victims of Non-international Armed Conflicts, 8 June 1977.

[88] Protocol additional to the Geneva Conventions of 12 August 1949, and relating to the Adoption of an Additional Distinctive Emblem, 8 December 2005.

intended to try those accused of committing international crimes in those two states, as well as the International Criminal Court (ICC), established in 2002 as a permanent forum to deal with individuals accused of genocide, crimes against humanity, war crimes, and the crime of aggression (see chapter six). Suffice it to say that the US is not a party to the treaty which established the ICC (the Rome Statute), and has done its best to impede the development of the Court. Both the tribunals and the Court are concerned to criminalise conduct that is in breach of humanitarian law.

A. Unmanned Aerial Vehicles ('Drones')

There continues to be a great deal of controversy surrounding a comparatively new weapon of war: armed unmanned aerial vehicles, or drones. The controversy helps illustrate how controls over types of weapons develop, and also exemplifies the interplay between international law and international politics in such situations.[89]

As we observed earlier, the history of attempting to control the types of weapons available to parties in violent conflict stretches back more than 160 years, with efforts to outlaw weapons regarded as unacceptably cruel or random in their effects preceding any attempt to prohibit recourse to war or the use of force. The legal status of newly invented weaponry continues to be the subject of intense debate, with chemical, biological and nuclear weapons the object of particular scrutiny. That notwithstanding, the almost unimaginable sums of money dedicated to armament research, manufacture and development worldwide each year continues to lead to the production of ever more 'efficient' means of defence and warfare. New inventions and modifications are the one constant feature of such expenditure. International law has continued to play a role in such development. In particular, Additional Protocol 1 of 1977 to the Geneva Conventions of 1949 provides continuing constraints on the sorts of weapons that are permissible. Article 35(1) and (2) of that Protocol state as basic rules that:

1. In any armed conflict, the right of the Parties to the conflict to choose methods or means of warfare is not unlimited.
2. It is prohibited to employ weapons, projectiles and material and methods of warfare of a nature to cause superfluous injury, or unnecessary suffering.

Article 36 is concerned with new weapons, and provides that, in the study, development, acquisition or adoption of a new weapon, a state party to the Protocol is under an obligation to determine whether its employment would in any circumstances be prohibited by the Protocol 'or by any other rule of

[89] See especially Chris Woods, *Sudden Justice: America's Secret Drone Wars* (London, Hurst, 2015).

international law applicable [to the state party]'. One such invention has been unmanned aerial vehicles, now commonly known as drones.

The evolution of drone technology has a longer history than might be supposed. Shortly after aircraft useful for warfare had been developed during the First World War, attempts were made to construct unmanned aircraft that could be sent over enemy lines to acquire photographic evidence of enemy deployment. It was, however, during the Second World War that German scientists invented the forerunners of modern drones. These were the so-called 'V weapons' ('V' being short for 'Vergeltungswaffen', meaning 'retaliatory weapons'). The first of these (the V1) was an unmanned aerial weapon directed by a pre-set magnetic compass and gyroscopic auto-pilot. The second, the V2, was a rocket-propelled missile carrying a ton of high explosive and with a terminal velocity in excess of 3,000 mph. While the V2 was the precursor of 'inter-continental ballistic missiles', the V1 preceded the drone, travelling much more slowly and without rocket propulsion. Before the V1, drones were used for surveillance, but now they may be used either for surveillance or for targeted attacks, sometimes euphemistically described as 'surgical strikes'. The essence of the current drones is that they are no longer, as a rule, simply a flying bomb with an autopilot. Instead, they are vehicles (which may carry missiles) that are controlled by a desk-bound 'pilot', who may be thousands of miles from the drone he or she controls, often able to 'see' through the remarkably sensitive high-definition camera lens installed on the drone, which transmits instantly what is observed. Because of the speed at which they travel, drones may themselves be vulnerable to attack, but of course their great advantage is that it is only equipment and not the pilot that may be destroyed. As such, they have become a weapon of choice – many thousands have been manufactured, and are now deployed by more than 50 states.

Before considering the relationship between drones and international law, it is necessary to make some obvious but important distinctions. The first is that drones may be used either for surveillance or in order to launch a targeted attack, and one might expect rules to develop differently depending upon the end use. Secondly, questions as to when the use of drones internationally is permissible will clearly be affected by the relationship between the states concerned. If states are at war with each other, then the use of drones might be regarded very differently from their use by states supposedly at peace. Thirdly, while there is a clear distinction between surveillance and the use of force, the intention or effect in the use of force might differ. Most controversially, drones have been used not only to destroy physical targets, but also to target and kill certain individuals. It is this latter purpose – the killing of selected individuals beyond the jurisdiction of the state operating the drone – on which we wish briefly to concentrate.

Targeted extra-judicial killings have been an increasing phenomenon since the Second World War. According to a UN Human Rights Council Report prepared by the Special Rapporteur on extra-judicial, summary or arbitrary executions, Philip Alston:

> A targeted killing is the intentional, premeditated and deliberate use of lethal force, by States or their agents acting under colour of law, or by an organized armed group in armed conflict, against a specific individual who is not in the physical custody of the perpetrator. In recent years, a few States have adopted policies, either openly or implicitly, of using targeted killings, including in the territories of other States.[90]

Although 'targeted killing' is not a term distinctly defined under international law, the term gained currency in 2000 after Israel made public a policy of targeting alleged terrorists in the Palestinian territories.[91] The particular act of lethal force can vary widely, but it is with those committed through the use of drones in a state beyond the jurisdiction of the drone-operating state with which we are concerned.

Before 9/11, there would undoubtedly have been a consensus among international lawyers that such killings, except where a state of war existed between the drone-sending state and the state whose territory was attacked, were contrary to international law. The infringement of territorial integrity would have been decisive, unless the agreement of the 'receiving' state had first been obtained – and even then the legality of assassination rather than capture and trial would be highly problematic. However, after 9/11, the US acted in a way which denied that this was still the position. Significantly, the US did not simply assert that it would now ignore the accepted position, but rather moved to have new rules accepted as being consistent with international law. How did it do this? First, it must be observed that the US was at greater pains to define the circumstances in which it would be entitled in international law to use lethal force in a foreign country outside the area of active hostilities if that force was to be used against a US citizen. The Obama administration set out its position in a US Department of Justice White Paper produced in 2011 and finally released in February 2013. This basically applied domestic legal concepts concerned with public authority justification for the use of lethal force within the US where such force is essential to preserve the innocent. It did not address the problem of the infringement of foreign territorial integrity; it merely said that sovereignty concerns could be avoided if the consent of the host state could be obtained, and that, if it could not, then a determination would be required that the host nation 'is unable or unwilling to suppress the threat posed by the individual targeted'.

---

[90] UN Human Rights Council, 'Report of the Special Rapporteur on extrajudicial, summary or arbitrary executions, Philip Alston', A/HRC/14/24/Add.6, 28 May 2010, 3 para 1.

[91] For a discussion of Israeli attempts to formulate a legal justification for such assassinations before 9/11, see Ronen Bergman, *Rise and Kill First: The Secret History of Israel's Targeted Assassinations* (New York, Random House, 2018) 508–15.

As to the use of drones to eliminate perceived foreign enemies elsewhere, further reference to international law has been made. The use of drones for such purposes originally became significant in Afghanistan, where the US argued that it was engaged in a war of self-defence following 9/11 (against the Taliban government that the US held responsible for the actions of Al-Qaeda). This justification of self-defence ended when Hamid Karzai was selected as Interim President of Afghanistan in 2002 by a *loya jurga*, and since then drones have been used within Afghanistan with the permission of the Afghan Government, now headed by Ashraf Ghani. Beyond Afghanistan, drones have been used extensively by the US in Pakistan, as well as in Somalia and Yemen. In Pakistan, drones were first used in 2004, against targeted individuals believed to be senior Al-Qaeda leaders. According to the Bureau of Investigative Journalism, by July 2018 there had been 430 US drone strikes carried out in Pakistan, with estimates of the number of people killed ranging from 2,500 to 4,000, of which an estimated 424 to 969 were civilians, including 172 to 207 children.[92] While the actual figures are contested (and unprovable), there is no dispute that the casualty list is substantial.

The use of drones expanded greatly under President Obama, being deployed not only by the US military but also under the clandestine auspices of the CIA. Attempts to impose a greater degree of transparency and accountability on the use of drones towards the end of President Obama's tenure, including limiting the role of the CIA, have apparently been abandoned by the Trump administration, which has opted to relax the guidelines for the employment of drones beyond active combat zones, sidelined traditional channels of authorisation, and reinstated the secrecy surrounding such operations.[93]

There are two different, if related, disputes that have arisen from this exercise of drone power. The first concerns itself with the efficacy of drone attacks, and might be described as the military considerations. Evidence suggests that a significant number of senior Al-Qaeda figures were indeed 'eliminated' by attacks from unmanned aerial vehicles. Given, however, the undisputed 'collateral damage' (resulting in the deaths and injuries of untargeted civilians) caused by this course of action, the cost to the US might well have outweighed the benefits. The effect of the attacks in terms of radicalising Pakistanis who were indignant at such activities by a foreign power, and also in making it difficult for Pakistani governments to be seen to be giving support to the US – widely perceived to be acting in an arrogant and high-handed manner – should not be underestimated. A further military/political consideration relates to the ability of other states either now or in the future

---

[92] For an analysis of the yearly numbers of US drone strikes, see the website of The Bureau of Investigative Journalism at www.thebureauinvestigates.com/projects/drone-war.

[93] See, for example, Daniel J Rosenthal and Loren Dejonge Schulman, 'Trump's Secret War on Terror', *The Atlantic*, 10 August 2018, and Brett Max Kaufman, 'Trump is unshackling America's drones thanks to Obama's weakness', *Guardian*, 17 September 2018.

to emulate the US in its use of drones. The proliferation of drone technology means that many other states are now in a position to attack targets in other nations with which they are not actually in a state of armed conflict. Both Pakistan and India have such capability, as does Turkey – should it wish to attack Kurdish bases in Iraq – and Russia – should it wish to select targets in Georgia.

The second dispute is concerned with legality. Could the US defend its actions by arguing that the weapon used and the outcome achieved were consistent with international law? On the assumption (considered below) that drones are not inconsistent with Articles 35 and 36, there are two ways in which this argument might be made. First, the US has consistently maintained that it is at war with 'terrorism'. Certainly, until 9/11, international law had made a clear distinction between the activities of states with which other states might be at war; and the activities of non-state actors, whether individuals or groups, who were traditionally understood to have criminal responsibility but be incapable of being 'at war'. After 9/11, the US denied the inevitability of this distinction, and was perhaps supported by international opinion. Indeed, the preamble to the Security Council resolution passed the day after 9/11 expressly refers to 'the inherent right of individual or collective self-defence in accordance with the Charter',[94] and the Russian Federation representative stated that the US 'had come up against an unprecedented act of aggression from international terrorism'.[95] Some would claim that the constant assertion that the meaning of self-defence now encompasses the taking of defensive action against organised non-state actors has actually led to a change in international law, legitimating what would previously have been regarded as unlawful. If this is the case, then it could also be argued that the use of drones to respond to non-state actors could have become lawful subject only to the other requirements for a self-defence justification (particularly proportionality).

The second legal argument is, however, even more problematic. The US is still faced with the issue of sovereignty and territorial integrity. Here, international law is quite clear in stating that each state enjoys control over its airspace. Indeed, in 1960, when the Soviet Union shot down a high-altitude espionage 'U2' craft piloted by Gary Powers, the US did not protest either the shooting-down or the subsequent trial of the pilot. (Of course, these rights have been held to extend only within the sub-orbital atmosphere, which is why Sputnik and subsequent orbiting satellites do not infringe territorial rights.) It was long accepted that such airspace territorial rights disappeared only in the case of armed conflict, and this was thought to occur only when a state of war

---

[94] UNSC Resolution 1368 of 12 September 2001, third preambular paragraph.
[95] UNSC Press Release, SC/7143, 'Security Council condemns "in strongest terms" terrorist attacks on United States', 12 September 2001.

existed between states. This position has almost certainly been modified since the adoption of a report by the International Law Association in 2010, which

> was motivated by the United States' position following the attacks of 11 September 2001 that it was involved in a 'global war on terror'. In other words, the U.S. has claimed the right to exercise belligerent privileges applicable only during armed conflict [these include the abrogation of territorial integrity between states involved in armed conflict] anywhere in the world where members of terrorist groups are found. The U.S. position was contrary to a trend by states attempting to avoid acknowledging involvement in wars or armed conflicts.[96]

It concluded that, as a matter of international customary law, a situation of armed conflict required that two essential criteria be met: first, the existence of organised armed groups; and, secondly, the presence of fighting of some intensity.

The US's assertion that those who sheltered or assisted or even tolerated its enemies in the 'war on terror' would themselves incur liability certainly seems to go well beyond the ICJ's 2005 ruling in *Congo v Uganda*.[97] In that case, the ICJ held that cross-border incursions by armed groups based in the Congo did not justify Uganda's reciprocal use of force on the territory of Congo, which remained unlawful. The decision was based on the finding that Congo was not legally responsible for the armed groups, as it did not control them.

A final legal consideration should be noted, which concerns Articles 35 and 36 of Geneva Protocol I. As there are today more than 170 states parties to the Protocol, some argue that Article 36 now represents customary international law. The US's position on this point is unclear, although it does seem to accept, despite not being party to the Protocol, the obligation to conduct a review of a new weapon to ensure that its use will not contravene international law. It has been suggested, however (perhaps disingenuously) that, as the Predator drone (when used for surveillance) had already passed such a review, as had, separately, the Hellfire missile with which the Predator was to be equipped, there was no need to carry out a review of the two combined.

Hence, there are two separate legal questions. One relates to the legality of armed drones as such. The other relates to the legality of their use according to whether they are or are not governed by the Geneva Protocol. The purpose of the foregoing discussion is not to provide answers to these questions, but rather to illustrate the input of international law into the consideration by a state as to when it will elect to use drone technology. While the legal and the military considerations are severable, they are also clearly interrelated.

---

[96] International Law Association, Use of Force Committee, 'Final Report on the Meaning of Armed Conflict in International Law' (2010) 1. The report is available on the website of the Rule of Law in Armed Conflicts (RULAC) project of the Geneva Academy of International Humanitarian Law and Human Rights at www.rulac.org/assets/downloads/ILA_report_armed_conflict_2010.pdf.

[97] *Armed Activities on the Territory of the Congo (Democratic Republic of the Congo v Uganda)*, *Judgment*, ICJ Reports 2005, 168.

In July 2018, after a two-year inquiry, the UK All-Party Parliamentary Group on Drones published its report into the UK's use of armed drones.[98] Although this does not resolve all legal issues, it does usefully and cogently consider them. The stated intention of the inquiry was to 'help create a strong international protocol on the use of drone technologies and particularly in relation to their lethal use'. Although the full contents of the Report are beyond the scope of this book, it is of interest that one area of discussion centred on the UK Government's expansive interpretation of "imminence", as expounded in the Attorney-General's speech in January 2017 (considered in section V above).

The All-Party Parliamentary Group noted that, until the Attorney-General's speech, the UK's position had been that the right of anticipatory self-defence was governed by the *Caroline* understanding of 'imminence' – namely, 'force may be used if there is a: "necessity of self-defense instant, overwhelming, leaving no choice of means, and no moment for deliberation"'.[99] The relevant question that such a definition demands, the Report stated, is: 'Is the attack about to happen?'.[100] (This is, of course, very different from the question said by the Attorney-General to be appropriate: 'Is action necessary now?'.) The Report explained that the problem with the Attorney-General's expanded definition is that it unjustifiably moves away from the purely temporal question embodied in the *Caroline* principle, adding the non-temporal factors found originally in Daniel Bethlehem's article.[101] In this respect, the Report observed: 'the Principles set out by Sir Daniel have by no means been accepted as an authoritative statement on the law in this area. Rather, they have been the subject of significant criticism', and stated that some writers had suggested that their purpose was to set 'a new standard of imminence to enable preemptive military strikes against threats'.[102] It concluded that 'the UK is moving closer to the dangerously expansive interpretation espoused by the US',[103] and warned that this could potentially lead to the UK acting unlawfully, as well as possibly encouraging other states to ignore current constraints on the use of force. It also noted that such behavior on the part of the US, UK and some other states might represent

> a concerted push towards establishing a legal framework which permitted more frequent use of military force unilaterally without Security Council approval. Without a temporal requirement ... there was no clear threshold for the use of

---

[98] All-Party Parliamentary Group on Drones Inquiry Report, 'The UK's Use of Armed Drones: Working with Partners', July 2018, available at http://appgdrones.org.uk/wp-content/uploads/2014/08/INH_PG_Drones_AllInOne_v25.pdf.

[99] ibid 36.

[100] ibid.

[101] Bethlehem, 'Self-Defense' (2012).

[102] All-Party Parliamentary Group on Drones, 'The UK's Use of Armed Drones' (2018) 36–37.

[103] ibid 36.

force which would prevent an entirely preemptive strike, based on a mere possibility, probability or likelihood of future attack.[104]

And it suggested that the new test might in turn enable 'the use of force by a small number of powerful states where previously it would not have been justified, with no input or consent from the less powerful states who may be the subject of attack'.[105]

The report is also helpful in its summary of the contemporary law relating to the use of drones, suggesting, firstly, that if drones are being used as part of an armed conflict:

- International humanitarian law and international human rights law both apply.
- IHL will provide the primary legal framework for assessing whether the person targeted is a legitimate target and for assessing the legality of incidental civilian casualties.
- In an armed conflict, a person constitutes a legitimate target under IHL if they are a member of an organised armed group that is a party to the conflict.
- Under IHL, it is not illegal to use force that would cause civilian casualties or civilian damage as long as those casualties or damage are not disproportionate.
- IHL can modify the application of IHRL and will usually provide a more permissive framework for the use of force than would be the case outside of armed conflict.

And, secondly, that if drones are not being used as part of an armed conflict:

- International humanitarian law does not apply, but international human rights law does.
- The circumstances in which an individual can be targeted are much narrower than would be the case in armed conflict.
- The standards to be applied are much the same as would apply to a policeman targeting a civilian on the streets of the UK in a law enforcement operation.
- Outside of armed conflict a person can only be targeted if

    1. their conduct constitutes a threat to life or other lethal threat;
    2. the threat posed is imminent;
    3. the use of force is a last resort; and
    4. the benefit to be derived from the use of force would outweigh the dangers posed by the force to be used by the state authorities.[106]

---

[104] ibid 37.
[105] ibid.
[106] ibid 39.

VIII. Conclusion

Many readers may well be surprised to learn that, almost 75 years after the adoption of the UN Charter, legal rules concerning such a fundamental area of international law as the use of force should remain in a state of flux and uncertainty. Reflection should counter the surprise. International law and the use of force represent opposite means of resolving disputes. As has been observed earlier, the simple fact is that nations 'with the bigger stick' will have to be persuaded of the advantages of peaceful dispute resolution in confrontations with weaker competitors. But, as Daniel Moynihan argues convincingly, and perhaps counterintuitively, because that bigger stick can never be sufficient to achieve all the goals of a powerful state, a commitment to law rather than force might bring its own reward.[107] Avoiding the need to use force is itself a gain, and a demonstrated commitment to the rule of law might well bring real, if intangible, rewards. At the very least, perhaps, we are in a position to deny Cicero's verdict that *inter arma enim silent leges*: in times of war, the law falls silent.

---

[107] Daniel Patrick Moynihan, *On the Law of Nations* (Cambridge, MA, Harvard University Press, 1990).

9

The Misery and Grandeur of International Law[1]

I. Introduction

> We are witnessing the beginnings of the greatest presidential onslaught on international law and international institutions in American history.[2]

From the illustration at the beginning, by the New Zealand cartoonist David Low, a central concern of this book has been to explore the relationship between international law and the exercise of power. Or, to put it another way, what is the relationship between 'might' and 'right'? What we have argued is that the concept of the 'rule of law' in international law is an assertion of the supremacy of 'right' over 'might'. As we saw in chapter two, crucial to that concept is the acceptance of the sovereign equality of states, upon which the United Nations (UN) is based (Article 2(1) of the UN Charter). Of course, as in domestic law, this formal equality is simply that. It makes no comment upon the actual relative power or impotence, wealth or poverty, of different states. Thus, its effect is to hide, at least in international law terms, the question of 'who wields the bigger stick?' in favour of 'whose arguments are validated by international law?'. An understanding of this point should immediately suggest that its effect does not apparently favour those states which do in fact have more power. They will be constrained in obtaining goals through the exercise of that power. (This is not to suggest that advantage lies entirely with

[1] The title of Professor Georg Schwarzenberger's inaugural lecture at University College London in 1964.

[2] Jack Goldsmith, Henry L Shattuck Professor at Harvard Law School, 'The Trump Onslaught on International Law and Institutions, *Lawfare*, March 2017, available at www.lawfareblog.com/trump-onslaught-international-law-and-institutions.

weaker states, because, arguably, all states, no matter the disparity between them, gain from an orderly system, and one based upon *pacta sunt servanda.*)

Until comparatively recently, the previous paragraph would have simply observed the factual situation, although it would have been necessary to make some comment about those occasions when power trumps law (so to speak). When, in the last edition of this book, we spent some time discussing the extreme neo-conservative views of John Bolton on international law, we had not anticipated either his promotion to National Security Adviser to the current President, nor the acceptance of many of his views by the US administration. In essence, the positions adopted really do threaten both the concept of the rule of law in international law, and the centrality of the UN. With the unilateral withdrawal from such multilateral treaties and agreements as the Paris Agreement on Climate Change and the nuclear agreement with Iran, not to mention the enforced modification of the North American Free Trade Agreement (NAFTA), together with the expressed suspicion of multilateral treaties which may have their own legal dispute resolution mechanisms, even the validity of *pacta sunt servanda* is called into question. In 2019, misery seems to have the upper hand over grandeur.

Some brief elaboration of these examples is now appropriate if that rather dramatic assertion is to be sustained. The Paris Agreement on Climate Change of December 2015, intended to control global warming, was made under the UN Framework Convention on Climate Change of 1992. The Agreement was signed by 165 states and now has 197 states parties (as at February 2019). President Trump, a climate change sceptic, who viewed the Agreement as unfair to the US in the controls it had undertaken to apply, announced the withdrawal of the US from the agreement in July 2017. Under the Agreement (Article 28), the earliest effective date of withdrawal is November 2020, but some policy changes in contravention of the Agreement have already taken effect. As explained in chapter four, the ability of the US administration to withdraw from such a treaty in accordance with its domestic law, even if not in conformity with international law, is dependent upon whether the US legislature has duly ratified that treaty after it has been concluded by the executive. That notwithstanding, for the international community the implications of a unilateral and unauthorised withdrawal from a multilateral agreement strikes at the heart of *pacta sunt servanda.*

The implications and ramifications of the unilateral withdrawal of the US from the Iran nuclear deal are at least as significant. In 2015, Iran entered into a long-term agreement with the P5+1 (the US, China, Russia, the UK, France and Germany), known as the Joint Comprehensive Plan of Action (JCPOA), which places various restrictions on Iran's nuclear programme in return for the lifting of economic sanctions. The JCPOA was widely applauded, though certainly not by the Israeli administration of Benjamin Netanyahu. In May 2018, President Trump denounced the Agreement as 'terrible' (as he had throughout his presidential campaign) and announced both the US's withdrawal and its intention to reimpose draconian sanctions on Iran and its regime. This withdrawal was contrary to the wishes of all other parties to the JCPOA, and, despite the Trump administration asserting otherwise, no evidence of a breach of the agreement by Iran was ever substantiated. If this action were not dramatic enough, the US also announced that, in order to ensure the efficacy of the sanctions it was imposing, other states would also have to comply with them, and would face financial and other penalties if they did not do so. (The legality of such extra-territorial measures is discussed in the section on jurisdiction in chapter two.) Other states have responded indignantly, with threats of reciprocal action in the event of the imposition of US punitive measures. European Commissioner Věra Jourová, speaking in the European Parliament in November 2018, stated:

> We Europeans cannot accept that a foreign power – not even our closest friend and ally – takes decisions over our legitimate trade with another country. The ongoing work – led by France, Germany and the United Kingdom – aims at preserving the full and effective implementation of the JCPOA in all its aspects and in line with UN Security Council Resolution 2231. But protecting legitimate trade is also a basic element of our own sovereignty, and it is only natural that we are working in this direction.[3]

This reference to Security Council Resolution 2231[4] is important. That Resolution endorsed the Iran nuclear deal and urged full implementation. National Security Adviser John Bolton has now stated that the US would also cease to abide by that Resolution. Remembering that Article 25 of the UN Charter states categorically that 'The Members of the United Nations agree to accept and carry out the decisions of the Security Council in accordance with the present Charter', the threat to the central role of the UN Charter and organisations seems irrefutable. Other developments since the US's withdrawal from the JCPOA are equally ominous. In an attempt to mitigate the severity of the sanctions, Iran asked the International Court of Justice (ICJ) for a ruling to the effect that curbs on humanitarian trade announced by the Trump administration after withdrawing from the Iran nuclear deal were illegal under international law. In support of this, the Iranians had cited the 1955 treaty of friendship between the US and Iran,[5] Article 1 of which states that 'There shall be firm and enduring peace and sincere friendship between the United States of America and Iran'. In a preliminary ruling, the ICJ stated

---

[3] Věra Jourová, European Commissioner for Justice, Consumers and Gender Equality, on behalf of the High Representative of the European Union for Foreign and Security Policy, Federica Mogherini, 'Speech on the extraterritorial effects of US sanctions on Iran for European companies, at the European Parliament', 14 November 2018, available here: https://eeas.europa.eu/headquarters/headquarters-homepage/53860/speech-extraterritorial-effects-us-sanctions-iran-european-companies-european-parliament_en.

[4] UNSC Resolution 2231 of 20 July 2015.

[5] Treaty of Amity, Economic Relations and Consular Rights between United States of America and Iran 1955.

that the US must remove 'any impediments arising from' the re-imposition of sanctions on the export to Iran of medicine and medical devices, food and agricultural commodities, and spare parts and equipment necessary to ensure the safety of civil aviation. Within hours, US Secretary of State Mike Pompeo announced that the US was pulling out of what he referred to as an 'obsolete' 63-year-old treaty.[6]

Similarly, at a press briefing in the White House, John Bolton, while stating that the administration had blocked a legal challenge lodged at the ICJ to its decision to move the US embassy from Tel Aviv to Jerusalem, called the case a political stunt by 'the so-called state of Palestine', and went on to add that the US would withdraw from the optional protocol on dispute resolution to the Vienna Convention on Diplomatic Relations. Even more dramatically, he informed reporters that: 'We will commence a review of all international agreements that may still expose the United States to purported binding jurisdiction dispute resolution in the International Court of Justice.' For good measure, he went on to add that the US would 'not sit idly by as baseless politicized claims are brought against us'.[7]

The Trump administration's attitude to the 25-year-old NAFTA, while rather different to its approach in respect of the Paris Agreement and the JCPOA, is nevertheless significant. NAFTA came into effect in January 1994, and its effect was to lift tariffs on goods traded between the US, Canada and Mexico. Consequently, trilateral trade came to exceed $1 trillion annually. In July 2018, President Trump, as part of his 'America First' trade policy, notified Congress of his intention to scrap NAFTA and to sign separate United States–Mexico and United States–Canada trade agreements – a further attempt to replace a multilateral (in this case trilateral) agreement with a bilateral one. Unlike the Iranian nuclear deal and the Paris Agreement, however, NAFTA was a treaty that had been ratified by Congress. Thus, while theoretically the US could have exercised its right to withdraw from NAFTA (provided for under Article 2205 and requiring six months' notice), it was highly arguable that such withdrawal would also require Congressional agreement, which might well not have been forthcoming. In fact, this proposition was never put to the test, as Mexico and Canada separately consented to enter into a significant new agreement, intended (by the US) to reduce the US's trade deficit with both Mexico and Canada. The new agreement, the United States–Mexico–Canada Agreement (USMCA), was signed on 30 September 2018, but has yet (as at February 2019) to be ratified by the parties. It is certainly far less of a 'free trade' agreement than that which it is intended to replace.

---

[6] See 'U.S. cancels 1950s treaty with Iran after international court rules against sanctions', *Washington Times*, 3 October 2018.

[7] John Bolton, 'Remarks on the withdrawal from the Optional Protocol on Dispute Resolution to the Vienna Convention on Diplomatic Relations', White House Press Briefing, 3 October 2018. (The instrument's formal title is the Optional Protocol to the Vienna Convention on Diplomatic Relations, concerning the Compulsory Settlement of Disputes 1961.)

But while these developments may be discombobulating for doctrinal international lawyers, hopefully readers of this book will be less surprised, recognising that current developments simply serve to unmask the facts which were discoverable. As will have been seen, examples are legion where formal 'rights' are unexercisable. Hence, although all states enjoy the right of self-defence, that right is exercisable only by those states which have sufficient resources, military or otherwise, to resist an attack. Again, although treaties will be invalid if they are produced through coercion, unequal bargaining power has always been a political reality, bringing with it many bilateral treaties which favour those able to exert greater leverage. When the concept of universal jurisdiction was considered (in chapter two), it was observed that its exercise is available to every state, but, of course, smaller states have neither the power nor the temerity to indict foreign miscreants of the worst order. And, as a final example, just as Nicaragua found itself unable to enforce the judgment of the ICJ against the US (as explained in chapter seven), so too are states with territorial claims in the South China Sea unable to have their claims to the Spratley Islands and the Paracels internationally definitively adjudicated in the face of intransigence by China.[8] Indeed, in common with the US, China has recently shown itself to be predisposed to bilateral agreements rather than allowing neutral arbitration arising from multilateral treaties, as was seen in the position adopted by China in the face of attempts to seek a solution to conflicting territorial claims.

Having made these preliminary comments on contemporary developments affecting the international legal regime, it is now appropriate to develop something of a brief (and partial) critique of international law. What is meant by 'critique' is that we will attempt to stand back from the method and detail and rules of international law and institutions, in order to identify some academic questions about public international law that might help to reveal perspectives that would otherwise remain hidden. The task may seem paradoxical, because this book has tried throughout to understand the politics with which it maintains international law is imbued, and one theme we have pursued is that international law achieves what it does by 'depoliticising' the facts to which it is to be applied. To some extent this 'critique' approach may be unsettling because it does call into question the objectivity of at least parts of the preceding analysis and certainly that of many leading international law textbooks. For any reader studying the subject of international law this perspective might feed dissatisfaction with such textbooks that often hint at the political aspects of international law but only occasionally explore them.

---

[8] See *South China Sea Arbitration, Philippines v China*, PCA Case 2013–19 of 12 July 2016, which determined that there was no legal basis for China to claim historic rights to resources within its 'nine-dash line' and that the United Nations Convention on the Law of the Sea (UNCLOS) does not provide for a group of islands such as the Spratley Islands to generate maritime zones collectively as a unit (at 473–74). The ruling was rejected by China (and by Taiwan).

Such feelings are important because they reflect the intellectual challenge of having, on the one hand, to study the rules and methods of international law as objective phenomena and, on the other, to question the neutrality of the results achieved.

Some readers will probably be disappointed with international law because it seems so malleable, indeterminate and infinitely arguable. Even where the rules do seem clear (as in chapter eight, when we looked at the rules governing the use of force in international law), if they are broken, particularly by a powerful state, not only does retribution, reparation and enforcement seem to be beyond the ability and will of the international community, but a legal argument will often be 'constructed' in order to avoid a clear legal position. A very good example of this concerns the intervention in Iraq by the US, the UK and their allies in 2003. The response of the British academic international law community was to be found in an unequivocal letter to the British newspaper the *Guardian* on 7 March 2003, signed by many of the most prominent UK international lawyers not in government service. It stated:

> We are teachers of international law. On the basis of the information publicly available, there is no justification under international law for the use of military force against Iraq. The UN charter outlaws the use of force with only two exceptions: individual or collective self-defence in response to an armed attack and action authorised by the security council as a collective response to a threat to the peace, breach of the peace or act of aggression. There are currently no grounds for a claim to use such force in self-defence. The doctrine of pre-emptive self-defence against an attack that might arise at some hypothetical future time has no basis in international law. Neither security council resolution 1441 nor any prior resolution authorises the proposed use of force in the present circumstances.

> Before military action can lawfully be undertaken against Iraq, the security council must have indicated its clearly expressed assent. It has not yet done so. A vetoed resolution could provide no such assent. The prime minister's assertion that in certain circumstances a veto becomes 'unreasonable' and may be disregarded has no basis in international law. The UK has used its security council veto on 32 occasions since 1945. Any attempt to disregard these votes on the ground that they were 'unreasonable' would have been deplored as an unacceptable infringement of the UK's right to exercise a veto under UN charter article 27.

> A decision to undertake military action in Iraq without proper security council authorisation will seriously undermine the international rule of law. Of course, even with that authorisation, serious questions would remain. A lawful war is not necessarily a just, prudent or humanitarian war.

The conclusion was thus inevitable. Because Article 2(4) of the UN Charter proscribes the use of force except pursuant to Article 51 (allowing self defence), or pursuant to a Security Council resolution under Chapter VII of the Charter (the Council having been persuaded of the reality of a 'threat to the peace, breach of the peace, or act of aggression' (Article 39)) an invasion of Iraq could not be lawful. QED.

So strong, clear and seemingly incontrovertible was this position that, when the UK Government sought to justify intervention, it purported to accept that legal analysis while finding room for manoeuvre within it. Advice accepted by the Government argued the legality of the intervention because of non-compliance by Iraq with earlier (1990) Chapter VII resolutions which had authorised the use of force. In the UK, the Government accepted the need for its actions to be legal, accepted the constraints upon the use of force arising from the UN Charter, and argued within that circumscription. Hence, in the UK, the governance by the UN of the use of force was accepted as representing international law, and any illegality was denied.

The important point here is that arguments in international law for almost any course of action can be constructed, and generally there is no final adjudication as to their legality. It is very rare for such a body as the ICJ to be able to conclude authoritatively on the validity of legal argument, as it is only able to do so when a matter comes before it, and it is this very fact which dictates that matters coming before it are few and far between, while the questions it addresses are narrowly framed. As a result, states may hold on to tenuous legal argument even when it seems quite unsustainable. (The UK, for instance, refused to allow the legality of its Kosovan intervention to be tested in the ICJ when the opportunity arose, arguing, remarkably, that the law relating to humanitarian intervention was in a state of development and that the ICJ might arrest that development![9]) Equally obviously, no case will come before the ICJ unless each party feels itself (rightly) to have been able to construct a legal argument which could be accepted as stating the law. The ICJ only adjudicates where there is a genuine legal dispute. Just as, in the UK, no case comes before the Supreme Court unless each party believes that it has a good chance of having its legal argument accepted (otherwise they would have conceded the case and saved the legal fees), so too in international disputes states will only accept judicial settlement where its legal representatives are persuaded that the case may be decided legally (ie in accordance with international law) in their favour.

In response to such criticism of international law, there is the often-proffered defence that, for every situation in which international law remains arguable, there is a myriad of other instances where international law either pre-empts disputes or even resolves them. However, this is not wholly convincing in view of the ability of some states to ignore the international community and its rules with almost total impunity.

Other readers may well be disappointed with international law because, as was suggested in chapter one, it seems to reflect a very European way of seeing the world – and perhaps even a European (Western) way of dominating the

---

[9] See Mark Littman, *Kosovo: Law and Diplomacy* (London, Centre for Policy Studies, 1999).

world, only now being challenged by a rising China and the other so-called Brics (Brazil, Russia, India and South Africa), together with South East Asia. Certainly many international rules and much international legal methodology were created in a time of Western hegemony and colonialism, and arguably some of the consequences of this remain.

Yet others may feel that public international law is a very 'gendered' way of making sense of world events. International law takes as a premise that nations constantly compete in order to maximise national advantage. Consequently, international legal rules are about creating, structuring and managing competition and competitiveness. The desirability, healthiness and inevitability of competition (or conflict) over cooperation are not only taken for granted but even seem 'natural', and the consequent conflicts that arise seem all too often resolved by power, force or the threat of force – all causes and means which many would suggest are more redolent of a male rather than female outlook.[10]

Finally, much of this book has been preoccupied with the relationship between power and law, and underlying the whole of this book has been the paradox of sovereign equality. That concept is at once at the heart of the rule of law way of organising the international community by emphasising the superiority of justice over power, and yet all too often irrelevant in the face of the reality of unequal power. It is not insignificant that when the UN Charter was being drafted the most bitter disagreement was between the states that were to become the permanent five and the less powerful state delegations, who were suspicious of the veto power and foresaw problems if one of the veto states menaced world peace. The smaller powers wanted greatly restricted veto powers, and it was only when the US delegate threatened to tear up the proposed Charter if there was no agreement on this issue that opposition was overcome. Many of the smaller powers also wanted an ICJ with an enhanced role providing for the compulsory referral of disputes for resolution.

The conclusion drawn from this reality of unequal physical power could be seen as an attack upon the actions of powerful states and upon the US in particular. This would be a misinterpretation. While it is not improper to be critical of the policies of any state, the fact of a nation's status is always important. Nearly every state pursues foreign policy goals that its government believes to be in the state's interest to the maximum of its ability almost all of the time. How effective this is, depends upon both power and diplomacy. It should therefore be clear that the US is not acting exceptionally in attempting to achieve its foreign policy goals. It is, however, the goals themselves that

---

[10] This statement does, of course, make enormous generalisations, which, in a book other than a merely introductory one, would require considerable elaboration and justification. Further discussion is to be found in Wade Mansell, *A Critical Introduction to Law*, 4th edn (London and New York, Routledge, 2015).

are politically questionable – though this is generally beyond the range of a course in international law.

The aim of this chapter is to consider two problematic areas that go to the heart of the reality of international law. The first concerns the place of the US in an international law regime in what was, perhaps briefly, a 'unipolar' world, and the second considers the significance of the demonstrable ability of one client state of the US (Israel) to flout international law at will and without sanction.

II. The Paradox of Sovereign Equality

In chapter two we considered the concepts of sovereignty and sovereign equality. In various places we have observed how dramatically the Westphalian system (at least the theoretical Westphalian system) has changed with the rise of the UN and the centrality of human rights. Even in 1967, however, Oppenheim's Treatise on International Law felt able to define sovereignty as follows:

> Sovereignty as supreme authority, which is independent of any other earthly authority, may be said to have different aspects. Inasmuch as it excludes dependence upon any other authority, and in particular from the authority of another State, sovereignty is *independence*. It is *external* independence with regard to the liberty of action outside its borders in the intercourse with other States which a State enjoys. It is *internal* independence with regard to the liberty of action of a State within its borders. As comprising the power of a State to exercise supreme authority over all persons and things within its territory, sovereignty is *territorial* supremacy (*dominium, territorial sovereignty*). As comprising the power of a State to exercise supreme authority over its citizens at home and abroad, sovereignty is *personal* supremacy (*imperium, political sovereignty*).[11]

In fairness, the work does go on to recognise limits to external independence arising from treaty obligations, and internal independence through the obligation of a state to respect the fundamental human rights of its own citizens. Nevertheless, the emphasis upon liberty of action seems to warrant much more qualification in the twenty-first century, at least with regard to the majority of states. It is here appropriate to note that the constraints upon sovereignty will depend not only upon treaty commitments, but upon power. This will be explored below but first necessitates a brief discussion of sovereign equality.

---

[11] Lassa Oppenheim, *International Law: A Treatise* edited by Hersch Lauterpacht (London, Longman, 1967) 286.

An important book on the concept of sovereignty which is of direct relevance to this chapter is Gerry Simpson's *Great Powers and Outlaw States: Unequal Sovereigns in the International Legal Order*, published in 2004.[12] Critically for our discussion, Simpson takes the view that sovereign equality has three distinct aspects, not all of which lead to assumptions of real equality. The first aspect is 'formal equality', defined as no more than 'equality before the law' and which 'extends neither to forms of jurisdictional equality nor to equal capacity to vindicate rights outside the judicial context'.[13] We say 'no more than', but, as was suggested in chapter two, this is a truly crucial feature, necessary for any international rule of law. The second aspect is legislative equality, to be found, for example, in the UN General Assembly, with its single vote for each state. In truth, as Simpson recognises, this is one of the few places where legislative equality is accepted and enjoyed. More typically, strength and wealth will dictate legislative power, as is all too clear both in the Security Council and in the deliberative bodies of the international financial institutions.

Existential equality is the third aspect of sovereign equality. This is really an equal right to existence, with the accompanying corollary of the principle of non-intervention (and immunity from externally brought-about regime change). Simpson shows that, historically as well as contemporaneously, this has been more problematic than some might wish to believe. The claimed anti-pluralist (that is, universal) virtue of 'liberal democracies' (as Fukuyama would argue) resonates, Simpson suggests, with times of proclaimed 'Christian', 'European' or 'civilised' superiority used as a justification for intervention. Pariah or rogue states have replaced the heathen, the primitive and the uncivilised states which were historically beyond the realm of 'unintervenability'.[14]

Simpson's point here is an important one. He is suggesting that sovereign equality in the existential sense (roughly equivalent to 'independence') has

---

[12] Gerry Simpson, *Great Powers and Outlaw States: Unequal Sovereigns in the International Legal Order* (Cambridge, CUP, 2004).

[13] ibid 47.

[14] Manifestations of this world-view are not difficult to discern. Preceding the assertion that 'humanitarian intervention' should be replaced by 'Responsibility to Protect' was the so-called 'Blair Doctrine', laid out by Tony Blair in a speech in Chicago in 1999 (see chapter eight), where he outlined a 'doctrine of the international community' based on the idea of a 'just war'. In order to decide when and where to intervene, he proposed that five major questions should be asked – illustrative of the kinds of issues that should be taken into account in the decision-making process, rather than as absolute tests: 1) Are we sure of our case?; 2) Have we exhausted all diplomatic options?; 3) Are there military operations we can sensibly and prudently undertake?; 4) Are we prepared for the long term?; 5) Do we have national interests involved? And, he argued, where the answer to all five questions is 'yes' there would be a strong case for intervention. Tony Blair, 'Doctrine of the International Community', 24 April 1999, available on the website of the National Archives at https://webarchive.nationalarchives.gov.uk/+/http://www.number10.gov.uk/Page1297. Related views are to be found in Oliver Kamm, *Anti-Totalitarianism: The Left-Wing Case for a Neoconservative Foreign Policy* (London, Social Affairs Unit, 2005).

never in fact achieved the uncontroversial status often claimed for it, not least under the UN Charter. Historically, the reality is that powerful states have always curbed the freedom of action of lesser states if it was in their interests so to do and the constraints were not counterproductive. Both US hegemony in Central and South America, sometimes formalised under the 'Monroe Doctrine'; and Soviet hegemony in Eastern Europe between 1945 and 1990 are very clear examples. In both cases direct intervention was sometimes resorted to (usually with a highly doubtful claim to legitimacy) and on occasion regimes were changed. Simpson's argument is that powerful states are now questioning the sovereign rights of states without democratic governance in the same way that colonial powers in the nineteenth century justified territorial acquisition on the assumption that all 'civilised' peoples would approve.

III. The United States of America and International Law

Having briefly dwelt on the complexity of sovereign equality, it is now necessary to contemplate the role of the US, currently still the world's only 'superpower', at least in military terms, in the international legal regime. The question to be considered is whether the US should be viewed simply as another 'sovereign equal' in international relations and international law, or whether its singular power, both military and economic, necessitates a recognition of a special status beyond sovereign equality, and even beyond the special status already accorded as a permanent member of the Security Council. Although the claim that we live in a 'unipolar' world is less plausible than it was at the turn of the new century – given the rise of China and the US's enormous indebtedness – the US's military superiority remains.[15] Nonetheless, in light of the increasing strength of China in particular, any claim for special status must take account of the fact that other states may want to make similar claims in due course.

In many of the earlier chapters we saw that the US does not always behave as other states tend to. This was most obvious when we examined international law relating to the use of force, where the US made clear that it was prepared to do what it thought necessary for its own security without feeling any need to seek or obtain international approval, even if this might be interpreted as flouting international law. There are many other examples where the

---

[15] Not everyone subscribes to the view that the US's days in a unipolar world are numbered. See Michael Beckley, *Unrivaled: Why America Will Remain the World's Sole Superpower* (Ithaca, NY, Cornell University Press, 2018).

US has failed to ratify (or even sign) international treaties that have received widespread support even from its allies, the most prominent examples being the Rome Treaty that created the International Criminal Court (ICC), the Kyoto Protocol on Climate Change, and now the Paris Agreement on Climate Change.

A body of opinion has developed in the US (particularly among the neo-conservatives) that argues that America's unique strength and role in international relations must be recognised, and that some form of 'exceptionalism' (referred to sometimes as 'exemptionalism' and sometimes as 'American particularism') is not only desirable but inevitable. Those of that opinion could draw upon some international law jurisprudence. In early editions of Oppenheim's *International Law* (for example, the edition of 1912), the argument had been made that it is of the essence of international law that there is both community of interest and a balance of power, without which there can be no international law. This position was adopted by Hans Morganthau, the prominent international relations theorist in the 1960s. In a chapter promisingly entitled 'The Problem of International Law', Morganthau quoted Oppenheim as stating:

> The first and principal moral [in the history of the development of the Law of Nations] is that a Law of Nations can exist only if there be an equilibrium, a balance of power, between the members of the Family of Nations. If the Powers cannot keep one another in check, no rules of law will have any force, since an over-powerful State will naturally try to act according to discretion and disobey the law. As there is not and never can be a central political authority above the Sovereign States that could enforce the rules of the Law of Nations, a balance of power must prevent any member of the Family of Nations from becoming omnipotent.[16]

Given that international law is, as Shabtai Rosenne put it, a system of 'co-ordination', rather than 'subordination' (see chapter one), it is dependent on, at the very least, the formal equality of states. If one state is in a position, or believes itself to be in a position, to act unilaterally without fear of the consequences, the force of law may seem to have disappeared. The US, neo-conservatives and others have argued, is now in this position. Indeed, as early as 1992, in a document entitled *Defence Planning Guidance Draft* (drawn up under the supervision of Paul Wolfowitz and subsequently revised by soon-to-be Vice-President Dick Cheney), the idea was introduced that the US was now uniquely strong enough to be able to contemplate with equanimity unilateral military action, the pre-emptive use of force and 'the maintenance of a US nuclear arsenal strong enough to deter the development of nuclear programmes elsewhere'. As has been pointed out, what that document did

---

[16] Hans J Morgenthau, *Politics Among Nations: The Struggle for Power and Peace*, 7th edn (New York: McGraw-Hill, 1993) 256.

not do was to explain how such policies might be reconcilable with the many international agreements and obligations the US had voluntarily entered into or undertaken since the Second World War.

The Project for the New American Century's letter to President Clinton in 1998,[17] arguing for unilateral action to overthrow Saddam Hussein's regime in Iraq regardless of the lack of unanimity in the Security Council, and signed by many who had played a part in the administration of Ronald Reagan and/or the first Bush administration (including Elliott Abrams,[18] John Bolton, Robert Kagan, Richard Perle, Donald Rumsfeld and Paul Wolfowitz), ensured that the *Defence Planning Guidance Draft* came into its own after the terrorist attacks of 11 September 2001. In *The National Security Strategy of the United States*, published under the seal of the President in September 2002, it was asserted that the US now claimed the right of pre-emptive (or preventive) action, leaving the limitations on the international use of force in the UN Charter in utter disarray. And, in claiming this right, it was asserted that the 'United States will use this moment of opportunity to extend the benefits of freedom across the globe. We will actively work to bring the hope of democracy, development, free markets, and free trade to every corner of the world.'

A. American Exceptionalism

Writing in 2003, Harold Hongju Koh, then Dean and Professor of International Law at Yale University, sought to analyse the content and significance of American exceptionalism.[19] Before considering the relevance of this analysis, some preliminary comments are called for. The concept of exceptionalism seems to have two broad meanings. The first, which relates to the Oppenheim proposition that any system of international law requires an

---

[17] Letter to President Clinton on Iraq', 26 January 1998, available at www.information-clearinghouse.info/article5527.htm. The Project for the New American Century (PNAC), a neo-conservative think tank of which John Bolton was a Director, was dissolved in 2006. According to its erstwhile website, the PNAC believed that: 'American leadership is good both for America and for the world; and that such leadership requires military strength, diplomatic energy and commitment to moral principle.'

[18] In common with John Bolton, Elliott Abrams has returned to the White House – as US Special Envoy for Venezuela. Abrams was pardoned by George HW Bush after pleading guilty to lying to Congress over his role in the secret funding of the Contra rebels in Nicaragua. Linked to a failed attempt to topple former Venezuelan leader Hugo Chávez, Abrams is now keen to see Chávez's successor, Nicolás Maduro, replaced by opposition leader Juan Guaidó. See Julian Borger 'US diplomat convicted over Iran–Contra appointed special envoy for Venezuela', *Guardian*, 26 January 2019; and Lesley Wroughton, 'U.S. envoy warns Maduro that actions against Guaido would be "foolish"', *Reuters*, 30 January 2019.

[19] Harold Koh, 'On American Exceptionalism' (2003) 55 *Stanford Law Review* 1479. Koh later occupied the post of Legal Adviser to the US Department of State (from 2009–13) under President Barack Obama.

equilibrium between states, seems to assert that such is the power of the US that, as a matter of fact, it cannot be a party to international law because any consequent restraints are simply unreal and would have to depend for their effectiveness upon voluntary, but disadvantageous, compliance. This proposition entails two possible conclusions. If the US is above and beyond international law, where does this leave lesser states? Either the entire system falls, and international law, failing to constrain the mightiest, similarly fails to constrain any state with the power to reject such restrictions in any particular case with impunity, or international law retains its distinctive character for all states but the US. The first interpretation really is the cataclysmic one: every principle of international law would lose its legal character and become indistinguishable from general rules of international relations. The second suggests that lesser states continue to be bound by *pacta sunt servanda* and only the US enjoys impunity and immunity. Both scenarios have significant implications for the US itself.

Although the first scenario has obvious advantages for the US, it also brings with it a number of dangers and difficulties. In moving from the international rule of law to power relationships unmediated by law, it may be expected that, if the US is to persuade other states to do its bidding, force and the threat of force will become a much more prominent feature of US foreign policy – in itself an option with significant cost. In the second scenario, where only the US is outside of the international legal regime, the perils are not much diminished. The greatest power exempting itself from the rules of international law while requiring the compliance of other states would be highly hypocritical, and a risky position to adopt. It may be possible, at a cost, to police such a system if the US really believed it to be in its interests to do so. But when second-order states seek to follow the principle espoused by the US, then, for all its power, the US could not uniformly prevail.[20]

The second and more limited meaning of exceptionalism suggests that, because of its power (and perhaps other reasons such as the US Constitution and the country's federal structure), the US either must necessarily be, or should be, in a position to accept the rules of international law with a discretion not appropriate to other states. Two examples are pertinent. The US might argue that, notwithstanding the number of states that have already signed and ratified the treaty creating the ICC, with its overtones of the acceptance of universal jurisdiction, the US's own exceptional international responsibilities and powers, together with its confidence in its own special needs and abilities, mean that it must claim exemption for itself alone. This in no sense condones atrocity crimes. It simply asserts that, for the US, this is

---

[20] For an analysis of the strains to which the US's world-power status is subject, and the challenge posed by competing powers, particularly China, see Gideon Rachman, *Easternisation: War and Peace in the Asian Century* (London, Bodley Head, 2016).

more appropriately dealt with in its own domestic jurisdiction. Even with the Kyoto Protocol on Climate Change, and the subsequent Paris Agreement, the argument might have been that, given the explicit intention of the Defence Strategy to ensure that the US remains the supreme global power, it is inappropriate for the US to risk any lessening of its industrial power, regardless of environmental cost. Of course, both these examples have many arguments in favour of compliance, and many of the problems of hypocrisy remain, but some argument is perhaps maintainable.

Koh, in his analysis, distinguishes four manifestations of American exceptionalism, which range from the least problematic to that deserving of the most opprobrium. Koh seems to assume that exceptionalism is much more limited in its effect than we have suggested. For Koh, the two most difficult aspects of exceptionalism concern, firstly, what Louis Henkin named 'America's Flying Buttress mentality'. By this, Henkin meant that the US often identified with the values expressed in international human rights documents and, indeed, often complied with their requirements, yet remained unwilling to subject itself to the critical examination processes provided for in such conventions. The effect was external support (like a flying buttress), but not the internal support of a pillar. In other words, the US was willing to comply (and in fact did) with the provisions of such instruments, but would not want to recognise any external authority as having the power to examine and judge its conduct. One sees a parallel in the US's decision to intervene in Afghanistan post 9/11 without the authority of a Security Council resolution, notwithstanding the fact that it would almost certainly have been forthcoming had it been requested. The US does not want to look to any external authority to sanction its domestic or foreign policy choices. Koh's view is that this often results in unwarranted condemnation of the US, with it sometimes relegated to pariah status for appearing to align itself with other states not ratifying, or not complying with, conventions – states with appalling human rights records.

However, the real problem of exceptionalism, according to Koh, arises when the US uses its power to promote a double standard, by which it is proposed 'that a different rule should apply to itself than applies to the rest of the world':

> Recent well-known examples include such diverse issues as the International Criminal Court, the Kyoto Protocol on Climate Change, executing juvenile offenders or persons with mental disabilities, declining to implement orders of the International Court of Justice with regard to the death penalty, or claiming a Second Amendment exclusion from a proposed global ban on the illicit transfer of small arms and light weapons. In the post 9/11 environment, further examples have proliferated: America's attitudes toward the global justice system, holding Taliban detainees on Guantanamo without Geneva Convention hearings, and asserting a right to use force in pre-emptive self-defence.[21]

---

[21] Koh, 'American Exceptionalism' (2003), 1486 (internal footnotes omitted).

Perhaps the first two examples – the ICC and the Kyoto Protocol – should be distinguished from the rest, because in those cases the US did not (publicly) accept the usefulness of either of them for the world as a whole or for the US. But for the rest the problem is not only the appearance of hypocrisy but the reality. For the US to ignore ICJ decisions in contentious cases (the only nation to have done so), and to assert that it may continue to act in a way contrary to internationally accepted standards because of its unique position, leaves open similar arguments to every pariah state in the world. While the US's response is that these other states lack democratic validation, this has no necessary truth.

B. The United States, Radical Exceptionalism and International Law

Within recent US legal thinking, there are even some who are prepared to argue that in fact international law is not really law at all. This is hardly a new perspective. The entry for 'International Law' in the 1889 *Encyclopaedia Britannica* reads as follows:

> International Law is the name now generally given to the rules of conduct accepted as binding [between themselves] by the nations – or at all events the civilized nations – of the world. International law as a whole is capable of being very differently interpreted according to the point of view from which it is regarded, and its rules vary infinitely in point of certainty and acceptance. According to the ideas of the leading school of jurists it is an impropriety to speak of these rules as being laws – they are merely moral principles, positive, it is true, in the sense that they are recognised in fact, but destitute of the sanctioning force which is the distinguishing quality of law.

As indicated at the beginning of this chapter, one influential and powerful holder of these views is John Bolton, an American lawyer often in the employ of Republican US administrations, and US Ambassador to the UN from 2005–06. At the time of writing, he holds the position of President Trump's National Security Adviser. The immense power of this role makes it worthwhile engaging seriously with Bolton's perception of international law, if only to make sense of some of his actions. For international lawyers outside of the US (and undoubtedly for a good few within it), this is not always easy, but it is important. And it must be conceded that, distasteful though many of us might find his arguments, they do have an internal coherency which cannot be dismissed.

Whereas the 1889 author had the grace to add that the problem with the proposition found in the *Encyclopaedia* is that it may 'unduly depreciate the actual force and effect of the system as a whole', Bolton would accept no such qualification. For him, the legal positivism of the Austinian kind (understanding law to be defined as commands from a sovereign backed by the threat or use of coercion, sanctions or force) is an obvious truth with significant implications for international 'law' and its influence on US policies generally and on the attitude of the US administration to human rights in particular.

Bolton's attack on international law is comprehensive. It is an attack on treaty law and customary international law, along with the other usually claimed sources of international law as found in Article 38 of the Statute of the International Court of Justice of 1945.

As we have often reiterated, almost all international lawyers and all state governments are in agreement that at the heart of international law is the crucial principle of *pacta sunt servanda*. Acceptance of this principle is one immediate means of distinguishing international law from international relations. It is because it is a legal principle that it is generally accepted uncritically. This, however, does not mean that a state will invariably comply with the principle, just as in domestic jurisdictions not all will obey all laws. But two obvious points need to be made. The fact of occasional non-compliance in the domestic realm does not negate the law. The same is true internationally. Secondly, even if there is no direct sanction, the price of breaking treaty obligations will rarely be cost-free, even if it involves nothing more than enduring a certain amount of disapprobation from other states, or a hesitancy upon their part to enter into future international legal relations. Universally accepted though this is, Bolton disputes it. When he claimed, in 1997, that, regardless of the UN Charter, the US was not bound to pay its United Nations dues, the response from Robert F Turner of the University of Virginia Law School was as follows:

> How do we know that international treaty commitments are legally binding? Because every single one of the 185 [now 193] states that are members of the United Nations, and every one of the few states that are not, acknowledge that fact. Article 26 of the Vienna Convention on the Law of Treaties recognizes the fundamental and historic principle of pacta sunt servanda: 'Every treaty in force is binding upon the parties to it and must be performed by them in good faith.'
>
> To be sure, like some of our own citizens, members of the international community of states do on occasions violate their legal obligations. But when they do, they never assert that treaty commitments are merely non-binding 'political' undertakings. Stalin, Hitler, Kim Il Sung, Gadhafi and Saddam Hussein all either denied the allegations against them, pretended that their acts of flagrant international aggression were really in 'self-defence' to a prior attack by their victims, or proffered some other legal basis for their conduct. Not one of them asserted that treaties 'were not binding,' because they realized that no country would accept such a patently spurious assertion – it simply would not pass the straight-face test.[22]

Why then does Bolton want to argue that treaties are not legally binding on the US, and what are the implications? There are two aspects to his

---

[22] 'US and UN: The Ties That Bind', Letter to the Editor, *Wall Street Journal*, 1 December 1997.

arguments here. The first is concerned with the status of treaties in the international world, and the second with the status of treaties within the domestic jurisdiction of the US. Internationally, it is the lack of sanction which persuades Bolton that the obligation to comply can be moral or political only (neither to be underestimated, but, he says, not to be confused with the legal). If one accepts his premise that it is only the threat or use of sanctions which makes an obligation legal then his argument is irrefutable. Few would accept the premise, however. Legality is not in essence necessarily linked with sanction or punishment. Rather, most lawyers would accept that the legal quality arises from the universal acceptance of the legal aspect. This is not as circular as it sounds. It is because of the acceptance of the legal quality of *pacta sunt servanda* that overwhelmingly most states, almost all of the time, accept their treaty obligations automatically and only very rarely subject them to unilateral reconsideration. Bolton attempts to avoid this argument by emphasising that his position does not mean that the US should not ordinarily comply with its treaty obligations, only that it need not do so. With this position the debate might seem to be purely semantic, arising from his understanding of the term 'legal'. It is more than that, however, simply because, by avoiding using the term 'legal', Bolton hopes both to elevate the US's right to ignore treaties, and to downgrade the need for compliance.

Bolton effectively admits this intention when, in an article in *Transnational Law & Contemporary Problems*,[23] having observed that: 'In the rest of the world, international law and its "binding" obligations are taken for granted',[24] he goes on to state of US citizens: 'When somebody says: "That's the law", our inclination is to abide by that law. Thus if "international law" is justifiably deemed "law", Americans will act accordingly.'[25] Conversely, he adds:

[I]f it is not law, it is important to understand that our flexibility and our policy options are not as limited as some would have us believe. It follows inexorably, therefore, that the rhetorical persuasiveness of the word 'law' is critically important.[26]

It is manifest then, and admitted, that the argument he makes is driven by the end he wishes to achieve: the return of international law to the political world.[27]

---

[23] 'Is There Really "Law" in International Affairs?' (2000) 10 *Transnational Law & Contemporary Problems* 1.

[24] ibid 8.

[25] ibid 9.

[26] ibid.

[27] In fairness, it must be conceded that this view is not without (rational) support. In the words of Oliver Kamm, when writing about the discussion of the lawfulness of the invasion of Iraq, he states: 'I am not competent to discuss the legality of the Iraq War, but arguments about the role of international law in relations between states ought not to be left to lawyers alone. In particular, the American unease at the notion of a rule-based system that stands outside and above politics is not groundless or reactionary.' Kamm, *Anti-Totalitarianism* (2005) 114, fn 9.

If Bolton's arguments about the international obligations arising from treaties are therefore specious, what of customary international law? For Bolton, the phrase 'customary international law' deserves, at the least, inverted commas expressing incredulity. Of course, debates over customary international law are familiar and continuing. There are problems in defining when customary international law comes into existence and in proving *opinio juris*, and there are difficulties with the position of 'the persistent objector', and with the flexibility and malleability of customary international law. Such nice jurisprudential questions have no place in Bolton's mind, however. He denies the very existence of customary law. For him, practice is practice, and custom is custom; neither one is law.

Again, this extraordinarily extreme position is driven by the conclusion at which Bolton wishes to arrive: namely, the view that the US is not, and should not be, constrained in its policy decisions or conduct by any customary international law, whether in its international relations or domestically. Internationally, Bolton's view is that the US must pursue its own path. If this path should coincide with what other states regard as customary international law, then that is all well and good, but it is the product of coincidence, not compliance.

As with treaty law, any recognition of customary international law has both international and domestic significance and implications. This is particularly true in the area of human rights. Bolton's fear is that, through means other than internal democratic approval, changes in standards created by 'the international community' might affect the US. Thus, internally, he fears, for example, that US courts could (though he approves the fact that they have generally not) look to developing international customary law in determining whether the US death penalty might constitute cruel or unusual punishment. Internationally, the effect might be to incur international legal condemnation for acts seen by the US administration as necessary for its own security or interests.

It might be thought that so extreme are these views that they tell us little about the US, even in a 'unipolar' world. In fact, however, they are effectively proffered as a justification enabling the US to choose to remain outside of the international legal regime. After all, not only has John Bolton been the holder of important US government posts, invariably concerned with international law, but his opinions were probably representative of those of the majority of members of the George W Bush administration and are now consonant with the views of President Trump (although the President may not be able to articulate them as cogently as John Bolton).[28] Furthermore, Bolton is not without friends in the academic community. To give examples, we turn first

---

[28] See also John Bolton, *Surrender Is Not An Option: Defending America at the United Nations and Abroad* (New York, Threshold Editions, 2007), not least for his pejorative reference to 'High Minded European States'.

to Professor Michael Glennon of the Fletcher School of Diplomacy. His concern with the state of international law predates the events of September 2001, and he would regard these events as simply reinforcing his earlier arguments. In a book published in 2001, he directed his attention to the intervention in Kosovo in particular and the question of the use of force in general. The title of the book, *Limits of Law, Prerogatives of Power*, with its sub-title *Interventionism After Kosovo*,[29] summarises its content remarkably accurately. Glennon's argument is that it is no longer proper, sensible or accurate to speak of the Charter of the UN as exerting legal control over the use of force in international relations. His conclusion begins thus:

> With the close of the twentieth century, the most ambitious of international experiments, the effort to subordinate the use of force to the rule of law, almost came to an end – the victim of a breakdown in the consensus among member states concerning the most basic of issues: the scope of state sovereignty. Never a true legalist order, the use-of-force regime of the UN Charter finally succumbed to massive global disagreement pitting North against South and East against West over when armed intervention in states' internal affairs was permissible.[30]

He went on to hold that such had been the extent of the violation of Charter rules that it made little sense to speak any more of a legal regime. Such views, which seem extraordinary to most international lawyers beyond the US, continue to be held by a significant number of influential American academics. At their most moderate, perhaps, they are to be found in the work of Andrew Guzman,[31] who argues that, in essence, the choice for a state to comply with international law depends upon a cost–benefit analysis, and recognises that a decision not to comply will not be cost-free, but on occasions the benefit gained will outweigh the cost incurred. No doubt, every state makes these calculations, but, of course, the more powerful the state, the more able it might be to bear the cost of non-compliance. The possible costs of non-compliance that he enumerates include reciprocal non-compliance, retaliation and damage to a state's reputation consequent upon failure to comply with international legal commitments. Thus, perhaps unwillingly reflecting Bolton, the implication is that 'the primary sources of international commitment – formal treaties, customary international law, soft law, and even international norms – must be understood as various points on a spectrum of commitment rather than wholly distinct legal structures'.

This argument was not inconsistent with that made by Jack Goldsmith and Eric Posner in *The Limits of International Law*, published in 2005,[32] in which they contended that international law was less significant than

---

[29] Michael Glennon, *Limits of Law, Prerogatives of Power* (New York, Palgrave, 2001).

[30] ibid 207.

[31] Andrew Guzman, *How International Law Works: A Rational Choice Theory* (New York, OUP, 2008).

[32] Jack L Goldsmith and Eric A Posner, *The Limits of International Law* (Oxford, OUP, 2005).

government officials, lawyers and even the media might conclude. Whereas most international lawyers had long concluded that international law 'pulled towards compliance' simply by virtue of being law, Goldsmith and Posner suggest that international law results simply from states pursuing their own interests, and that states are not persuaded to comply with international law if it is not in their interests to do so.

Posner developed these arguments in his 2009 book *The Perils of Global Legalism*.[33] Here, he suggests that there is an American–European divide in attitudes towards international law. While Americans (government, elites and the general public) 'think of international law in instrumental terms', viewing it as 'consist[ing] of agreements and norms that reflect the mutual interests of states involved, and [which] can and ought to be changed as the interests of states change', Europeans (though not necessarily their governments he suggests):

> [R]efuse to think of international law in purely instrumental terms. While acknowledging that many treaties reflect instrumental goals these global legalists believe that instrumental thinking about international law can only erode global confidence in it, and that the core of international law is 'constitutional' in the following sense. Certain norms – basic human rights norms – cannot be violated under any circumstances. The Charter of the United Nations is also higher law, to which all other international law (except human rights norms) is subordinated. As to mainly American fears that this conception leads to rule by international elites and the devaluation of democracy, Europeans offer certain accommodations – a commitment to transparency, the involvement of NGOs in policy-making, and so forth – but not the still-impossible-to-imagine global democracy.[34]

Unsurprisingly, then, Posner concludes that the US will continue to resist efforts to constrain its policy choices by the implementation of international legal norms in the belief that it needs freedom of action if it is to protect its interests and 'advance liberty and democracy around the world' (even at the expense of human rights) while Europe 'will continue to argue that international law serves American as well as global interests in the promotion of human rights and international security'.[35] This claimed difference in perception again reflects John Bolton's view of international law, which he sees as an aspect of intended global government, as he observed when addressing a conference in 2000:

> Even the apparently simple act of entitling a conference 'Trends in Global Governance: Do They Threaten American Sovereignty?' is likely to expose the vast disparities which exist between two quite different factions within the United States. One party, small but highly educated, voluble and tireless, knows instinctively (and often emotionally) what global governance is and why it is desirable.

---

[33] Eric A Posner, *The Perils of Global Legalism* (Chicago, University of Chicago Press, 2009).
[34] ibid 227.
[35] ibid 228.

Consisting of academics (largely, but not exclusively, law and international relations professors) and media professionals; members of self-styled human rights, environmental and humanitarian groups; rarified circles within the 'permanent government', and at present even in the White House; and a diverse collection of people generally uneasy with the dominance of capitalism as an economic philosophy and individualism as a political philosophy, these 'Globalists' find allies all around the world. Their agenda is unambiguously statist, but typically on a worldwide rather than a national level.

The other faction, consisting silently of virtually everyone else in the United States, has no clue whatever that 'global governance' is even an issue worth discussing, since, among other things, it has formed no part of any political campaign in recent memory. This large party cannot define global governance, does not think about it, and – when it is explained – typically rejects it unhesitatingly. Although overwhelmingly predominant numerically, these Americans (who are comfortable with individualism and capitalism) are little recognized abroad, lost from view beneath the prolific production of academic papers, endless international conferences, and international media appearances of the diverse and often contradictory views of those whose primary urge, if not their ultimate objective, enrolls them in the party of global governance. Accordingly, when the 'Americanists' speak out, foreigners often assume that they are simply the knee-jerk voice of reaction, the great unlettered and unwashed, whom the cultured and educated Globalists simply have not yet gotten under proper control. Europeans in particular will instantly recognize the disjunction between elite and mass political opinions that has characterized their societies for almost their entire democratic experience, and they will empathize, needless to say, with their elite, Globalist counterparts.[36]

There are, therefore, influential American academics and government officials readily prepared to argue that international law should first and foremost be seen as merely an aspect of international relations. This book has argued that such an argument threatens to destroy the concept of the rule of law in the international community. The result of this in our view (as 'Europeans') is the great danger of what has been called 'blowback' – undesired and unforeseen results in a world without international law. In the following section, we consider one result of such a cavalier view of international law, the disaster of the Israeli–Palestine conflict.

IV. The Case of Israel and International Law

The Israeli statesman Abba Eban is often quoted as having observed that: 'If Algeria introduced a resolution in the General Assembly declaring that the earth was flat and that Israel had flattened it, it would pass by a vote

[36] John R Bolton, 'Should We Take Global Governance Seriously?' (2000) 1 *Chicago Journal of International Law* 205.

of 164 to 13 with 26 abstentions.' While times have changed, Israel's continuing disillusionment with the UN has, if anything, grown stronger. The attitude of the Israeli Government and its supporters is almost unanimous in regarding the UN (and indeed the majority of the international community) as both judging Israel unfairly when compared with other states, and as being a major source of the relentless criticism it receives over its alleged human rights abuses. After all, so the argument goes, Israel commits grave human rights abuses, but it is by no means the worst offender (with situations such as those in Darfur, the DRC and Myanmar furnishing contemporary examples). Notwithstanding this, Israel does hold itself out as a European (and Jewish) state in the Middle East. From trivial identifications with Europe, ranging from football to the Eurovision song contest, to, more importantly (if not significantly), its insistence that it is the only democracy in the Middle East, committed to the rule of law, Israel makes clear that it is different (and superior) to the rest of the states in the region. As expressed by Lorna Finlayson in an article considering the accusations of anti-Semitism directed towards the UK leader of the Labour Party, Jeremy Corbyn:

> The argument that it is antisemitic to apply 'double standards' to Israel is one that is often used to brand criticism of the country as racist, on the grounds that Israel is singled out although many nations commit human rights abuses. There are very good reasons for singling Israel out, such as the deep complicity of Western liberal democracies in its violence. The point is especially pertinent in Britain, which is implicated in everything that is happening in Israel and Palestine today, as in the Middle East more broadly. Britain, after all, occupied Palestine for the thirty years between the Balfour Declaration of 1917 and the founding of the state of Israel, overseeing and facilitating the construction of Jewish settlements. Yet Palestine is conspicuously absent from the sporadic conversation about 'coming to terms' with our imperial legacy – Rhodes must fall, but what about Balfour?[37]

No dispassionate observer could but be impressed with the extent to which Israel has repeatedly acted in contravention of the clearest principles of international law without apparent penalty. Not only has it flouted the most important international rules, but it has refused to accept the judgment of any international body as to its conduct. It is arguable that such conduct has not been cost-free, either for Israel or its American protector, with the majority of the Middle East convinced of hypocrisy, which does little to further Middle Eastern peace hopes. Israel's reliance upon power rather than law makes universal condemnation of states that attempt to do likewise – North Korea currently being an excellent example – very much more problematic.

We have chosen to illustrate this argument by briefly considering only the most blatant violations of international law by Israel, concerned with land

---

[37] 'Corbyn Now' (2018) 40 *London Review of Books* 17.

'acquisition', and breaches of international criminal law, although we will also consider Israel's singular relationship with nuclear weapons.

A. Israeli Land Acquisition, Occupation and Annexation

This section is concerned only with territory that was brought under Israel's control after the war of 1967. This is not because of an absence of controversy over territory acquired in the 1948 war rather than allocated to Israel by UN resolution, but because the prospect of any Palestinian state recovering any land beyond the pre-1967 borders seems remote and probably unrealistic. It should, however, be mentioned that Israel is the only state in the world not to have a defined and bounded territory, which does lead to continuing debate even within Israel. Thus, the territory which falls for consideration is East Jerusalem, the Golan Heights, the West Bank and (until comparatively recently) Gaza.

As already noted, international law dealing with the acquisition of territory seems, at first sight, deceptively clear and straightforward. According to Article 2(4) of the UN Charter:

> All Members shall refrain in their international relations from the threat or use of force against the territorial integrity or political independence of any state, or in any other manner inconsistent with the Purposes of the United Nations.

This proscription of the use of force has been interpreted as meaning that, where use of force contrary to Article 2(4) does occur, any consequential territorial gain would be unlawful and, while it might amount to an occupation, could not give rise to a transfer of sovereignty. Moreover, although Article 51 does allow for the use of force in self-defence, this is for the limited purpose of repelling aggression. Consequently, even when a state acting in self-defence occupies territory, it cannot then acquire sovereignty over that territory. And Security Council Resolution 242, passed in the aftermath of the 1967 conflict, stressed the inadmissibility of the acquisition of territory by war. In addition, the 1970 Declaration of Principles of International Law, annexed to UN General Assembly Resolution 2625, provides that: 'The territory of a state shall not be the object of acquisition by another state resulting from the threat or use of force. No territorial acquisition resulting from the threat or use of force shall be recognised as legal.' The immediate inference might therefore be that Israel could never acquire territory permanently that it had conquered in 1967. This position is certainly held by governments of the overwhelming majority of states in the UN. But it is not, as we shall see, one which goes unchallenged either explicitly (as in the case of Israel) or implicitly (in the case of the US).

Of the remaining three territories occupied since 1967, two – East Jerusalem and the Golan Heights – are distinct in the claims Israel has made over them. Although East Jerusalem had been an integral part of the East Bank within Jordan, upon conquest steps were quickly taken by Israel with a view to ensuring that it became effectively not merely occupied territory but Israeli territory. On the very day of the conquest, the then Defence Minister, Moshe Dayan, visited the Jerusalem Western Wall, proclaimed that Jerusalem had been 'liberated' and stated: 'We have united Jerusalem, the divided capital of Israel. We have returned to the holiest of our Holy Places, never to part from it again.' West Jerusalem had been declared by the Israeli Knesset to be Israel's capital city in 1950, while in the same year Jordan had formally incorporated the West Bank (including East Jerusalem) into Jordan. Jordan's assertion of sovereignty was, however, qualified by its parliament, which stated that it acted 'without prejudicing the final settlement of Palestine's just case within the sphere of national aspirations, inter-Arab co-operation and international justice'.

In 1967, the 1950 Israeli declaration of the status of West Jerusalem as Israel's capital was effectively amended to extend Israel's jurisdiction over East Jerusalem, not as an area of occupation but as an integral part of Israeli Jerusalem. Very quickly some 6,000 Palestinians were evicted from the Old City in order to create an open space before the Western Wall. When the UN General Assembly called upon Israel to 'rescind all measures already taken and to desist forthwith from taking any action which would alter the status of Jerusalem',[38] Israel responded by confiscating significant quantities of Palestinian land in East Jerusalem (some 450 acres in the first three years of occupation).

Worse still for the Palestinians, whereas the municipal boundaries of East Jerusalem as administered before 1967 included 6.5 km^2, Israel added an additional 70 km^2 to the land it purported effectively to annexe. The annexation was made formal by the Israeli Government on 30 July 1980 in a declaration that stated that Jerusalem was the 'eternal undivided capital' of Israel. Condemnation of the declaration came quickly from the UN Security Council. Within a month, a resolution was passed declaring

> that all legislative and administrative measures and actions taken by Israel, the occupying Power, which have altered or purport to alter the character and status of the Holy City of Jerusalem ... are null and void and must be rescinded forthwith.[39]

Remarkably, the resolution was passed by 14 votes to zero, with the US abstaining.

In spite of this, the assertion of annexation was never withdrawn, and from 1967 Israel has determinedly promoted the policy of settling Jewish people within its defined Jerusalem municipal borders. Much land owned by

---

[38] UNGA Resolution 2253 (ES-V) of 4 July 1967.
[39] UNSC Resolution 478 of 20 August 1980, para 3.

Palestinians has been confiscated and expropriated, and, perhaps most significantly of all, Israel has always refused to allow the sovereignty of its defined
Jerusalem to be a part of any peace negotiations.

The other territory occupied after the 1967 war which Israel has purported
to annex is the Golan Heights, captured from Syria. The purported annexation took place in the Israeli Knesset in December 1981. The motivation for
this action was twofold. The first was that the area 'annexed' had important
security and strategic significance, and had, between 1948 and 1967, been
used as a base from which to shell Israel. This was contrary to the Israel–Syria
Armistice Agreement concluded after the 1948 conflict, but the Commission
which oversaw the implementation of the Agreement reported many violations
by each side. Indeed, Moshe Dayan himself once observed that the shelling
was most often a response to Israeli provocations in the demilitarised zone.
The second incentive for annexation concerned the water resources of the
region. In an area of 1,860 km^2, the Golan contains some 80 springs; the head
waters of the Jordan River, together with tributaries; and the Masada Lake.
The Golan Heights currently provides a third of the fresh water consumed
by Israel. The annexation was rationalised partly in defence terms and partly
(by Menachim Begin) by suggesting that the original borders had been arbitrarily defined, and that this action should be seen as a rectification.[40]

Here again, the response of the UN and the international community was
immediate and ineffective. Security Council Resolution 497[41] made all the
appropriate noises: it reaffirmed the inadmissibility of the acquisition of territory by force; it stated that Israel's attempt to incorporate the Syrian Golan
Heights was null and void and without international legal effect; it confirmed
the continuing relevance of the Fourth Geneva Convention; and resolved,
in the event of non-compliance, to meet again to consider taking appropriate measures. The non-compliance led to a further meeting of the Security
Council and the consideration of a draft resolution calling upon all states to
take steps to ensure compliance with Resolution 497. Significantly, but not
unexpectedly, the proposed resolution was vetoed by the US.

In the period of occupation after 1967, the Golan Heights has also been
the object of Israeli settlement. By 2016, there were over 30 settlements with
more than 22,000 settlers claiming a reconnection to a Jewish heritage in the
region. At the time of the 1967 war, many of the Syrian inhabitants fled and
have not been permitted to return. Building work is continuing and there
seems no immediate prospect of compliance with international law. The position remains, even as Syria has been engulfed in civil war.

In the Gaza Strip, meanwhile, although Israeli forces and settlers were
withdrawn in 2005, such is the control and the constraints that continue to

---

[40] Quite extraordinarily, in March 2019, President Trump announced the intention of the
United States to recognise Israeli sovereignty over the 'annexed' Golan Heights.
[41] UNSC Resolution 497 of 17 December 1981.

be exercised over the Strip that it has in effect remained in occupation, as we will see below. In the West Bank itself, Israeli settlements, now with more than 400,000 settlers, have occupied some of the prime sites and most fertile ground. The continued growth of settlements is in direct and continuing contravention of the Fourth Geneva Convention, Article 49, which provides that in situations of occupation 'The occupying power shall not deport or transfer parts of its own population into the territories it occupies.' Israel is alone in arguing that such settlements are not illegal.[42]

B. Israel and Nuclear Weapons

In a time of unprecedented proliferation of all things nuclear (including nuclear weapons), the position of Israel remains remarkable. India and Pakistan are now in possession of nuclear weapons, North Korea has not only apparently developed nuclear weapons but has threatened to use them, and Iran's suspected development of a nuclear weapons programme led to the conclusion of the JCPOA (discussed in section I above). The position of India and Pakistan now seems to be regarded by the international community as a fait accompli, and attempts to sanction them for their nuclear weapons development have been effectively abandoned. North Korea and Iran have been informed, implicitly and explicitly, that the acquisition of nuclear weapons is unacceptable, and will result in action aimed at preventing such acquisition or destroying any resulting weaponry. Through all of this, however, Israel has possessed nuclear weapons and the means to deploy them while being subjected to very little criticism from its powerful friends.

An overwhelming number of states (currently 190[43]) are party to the Nuclear Non-Proliferation Treaty of 1968 (NPT), which entered into force in 1970. The NPT acknowledged the reality that, by 1 January 1967, five states (the current veto powers of the Security Council) had conducted nuclear weapons tests, and they were defined as 'existing nuclear weapons states'. Article 1 of the NPT provided these five states with particular obligations not to transfer these weapons or to assist in their acquisition by other states. They were also obliged to pursue nuclear disarmament (Article 6). Other states were able to join or accede to the NPT, and their obligations were to not receive or seek to acquire nuclear weapons, and to accept safeguards (verification of non-acquisition and/or development) from the International

---

[42] For a contemporary consideration by an Israeli academic of the law relating to occupation, see Aeyal Gross, *The Writing on the Wall: Rethinking the International Law of Occupation* (Cambridge, CUP, 2017).

[43] For information on the status of the treaty, see the website of the United Nations Office for Disarmament Affairs at: http://disarmament.un.org/treaties/t/npt.

Atomic Energy Agency (IAEA). The reward for such states was access to nuclear energy technology for 'peaceful' purposes. Neither Pakistan nor India is a party to the treaty, but while they were briefly sanctioned for having developed nuclear weapons, these sanctions have been abandoned. North Korea, which was a party, declared its withdrawal from the NPT in 2003, and has carried out a number of nuclear weapons tests. Iran has been a party since 1970. Both North Korea and Iran have incurred the wrath of the US for what it regards as breaches of treaty obligations. North Korea has now apparently agreed under US pressure to 'denuclearise', and both the US and Israel have issued pronouncements at various times to the effect that force might be necessary to prevent Iran from completing the development of nuclear weapons.[44]

In an interview in January 2005, the Israeli defence minister, Shaul Mofaz, who in the past had stated that Israel had operational plans in place for a (preventive) strike against Iranian nuclear facilities, argued that the US should take such a step. Seymour Hersh, the American investigative journalist, had by then reported that the US already had special forces in Iran scouting out its nuclear facilities. The case of Israel is very different. By the time the NPT was concluded (to which Israel is not a party), there is strong evidence that the country had already developed, or was on the point of developing, a small number of nuclear weapons. Production was located at Israel's nuclear facility in Dimona, in the Negev Desert, south of Jerusalem. Hersh argues convincingly that Israel's nuclear developments were made possible owing to major assistance from France, beginning even before the Suez War of 1956.[45] It is clear that, during the earliest period of Israel's existence, a number of influential Israelis were convinced that nuclear weapons would be crucial in providing a guarantee in a hostile world. Ernst David Bergmann, the Chairman of the Israel Atomic Energy Commission, formed in 1952, had long advocated an Israeli nuclear bomb as being crucial in ensuring 'that we shall never again be led as lambs to the slaughter'. David Ben-Gurion, the most powerful Israeli statesman at the time, similarly laid emphasis upon the security 'the bomb' would bring.

The role of the US in Israel's development of nuclear weapons is neither clear nor consistent. Certainly, all the initial development was carried out with France, and Israel was at pains to hide its plans and actions from the US. When the US became suspicious of activities at Dimona, Israel carefully misled any who asked questions, and even went to the lengths of substantial subterfuge when Dimona was visited. Occasionally, even the President of the

---

[44] See Ronen Bergman, *Rise and Kill First: The Secret History of Israel's Targeted Assassinations* (New York, Random House, 2018) 608–09. According to Bergman, Israel's targeted assassinations extended to Iranian nuclear scientists.

[45] Seymour Hersh, *The Samson Option: Israel, America and the Bomb* (London, Faber and Faber, 1991).

US was lied to, as when Shimon Peres told John F Kennedy in April 1963, in answer to a direct question:

> I can tell you forthrightly that we will not introduce atomic weapons into the region. We certainly won't be the first to do so. We have no interest in that. On the contrary, our interest is in de-escalating the armament tension, even in total disarmament.

Kennedy did his best to ensure that this was the case, but ineffectually. Finally, when, in 1963, it became clear that both France and Israel were in the at least preliminary process of bomb manufacture, the US seems to have been persuaded to take what was seen as a 'pragmatic' approach. This primarily meant not seeking explicit answers to explicit questions.

While subsequent US presidents differed in the detail of what they did, none was prepared to publicly state what increasingly became public knowledge. Indeed, when Israel cooperated with apartheid South Africa to test a nuclear device in the Indian Ocean,[46] the Carter administration (probably the presidency most concerned to encourage non-proliferation) took steps to ensure that the event received minimal publicity. Even when the Israeli nuclear technician Mordechai Vanunu provided the British newspaper the *Sunday Times* with descriptions and photographs of Israeli nuclear warheads – information which suggested to informed observers that Israel was in possession of between 100 and 200 nuclear devices – disinterested publication, particularly in the US, was limited. Israel has never been placed under pressure to accede to the NPT by the US or its allies, nor yet to agree to inspections from the IAEA. Furthermore, 'for many years [the US] Congress has made it clear to the Nuclear Regulatory Commission and other responsible parties that they did not want to have anything revealed in an open hearing related to Israel's nuclear capability'.

In brief then, Israel's position with regard to nuclear weapons is unique. It has been determined both to possess a large arsenal of nuclear weapons and to refuse either to admit to the existence of such weapons or to tolerate inspection. And yet, ironically, it is this state of affairs that has arguably persuaded states such as Iraq and Iran of the need to obtain nuclear weapons themselves. There is evidence, too, that Israel even contemplated the use of nuclear devices in 1973. While not everyone would share Israel Shahak's thesis that the possession of nuclear weapons is intended to make Israel not merely defensively secure but also secure as *the* regional power in the Middle East,[47] it is clear that such 'defensive' ability has implications beyond defence.

---

[46] See Sasha Polakov-Suransky, *The Unspoken Alliance: Israel's Secret Relationship with Apartheid South Africa* (New York, Pantheon Books, 2010).

[47] Israel Shahak, *Open Secrets: Israeli Foreign and Nuclear Policies: Expansionism and Israeli Foreign Policy* (London, Pluto Press, 1997).

It is scarcely surprising that the then IAEA Director-General, Mohamed El Baradei, when addressing a meeting in Israel in 2004, should have observed that

> he is constantly questioned about Israel's refusal to sign on to the Non-Proliferation Treaty that would put its nuclear facilities under IAEA supervision. He said this perceived double standard is leading to an erosion of the legitimacy of the NPT in the Arab world.

Two final points arising from Israel's nuclear policies need to be mentioned for their international law implications. Israel's insistence that it should remain the only state in the region with nuclear capability led of course to two manifestations of its policy of pre-emptive (or preventive) use of force. Saddam Hussein's Iraqi Government had, with French help and with French design, built a light-water nuclear-materials-testing reactor known as Osirak (or, to the Iraqis, as Tammuz 1). The Israelis doubted Iraqi claims that the reactor was for peaceful purposes, although it was under IAEA supervision and had been regularly inspected. It was destroyed by an Israeli airstrike in June 1981. In 2007, the Israeli air force similarly destroyed an unfinished nuclear reactor in the Deir ez Zor region of Syria. Secondly, of course, the kidnapping, drugging and returning to Israel of the informant Mordechai Vanunu was hardly consistent with Italian sovereignty (Vanunu was seized in Rome).

C. Operation Cast Lead and the *Mavi Marmara* Incident

The reaction of the international community to the so-called *Mavi Marmara* 'incident' is not only inherently interesting but also of considerable significance to international law. This is not least because of the apparent 'disconnect' between legal analyses of the event on the one hand, and the primarily social analyses and reaction on the other. This contrast is nowhere better illustrated than by the reports produced by two UN bodies each concerned with these events. The first of these is the report of the Human Rights Council,[48] and the second is the Report of the Secretary-General's Panel of Inquiry on the 31 May 2010 Flotilla Incident.[49] While the difference between these two reports is highly significant, their body of agreement is sufficient for us to reach conclusions about the illegality of much, if not all, of the Israeli intervention.

---

[48] UN Human Rights Council, 'Report of the international fact-finding mission to investigate violations of international law, including international humanitarian and human rights law, resulting from the Israeli attacks on the flotilla of ships carrying humanitarian assistance', UN Doc A/HRC/15/21, 27 September 2010.

[49] 'Report of the Secretary-General's Panel of Inquiry on the 31 May 2010 Flotilla Incident', September 2011, available at: www.un.org/News/dh/infocus/middle_east/Gaza_Flotilla_Panel_Report.pdf.

Although the background to this incident is well known, it is necessary to provide a short summary. At the time of writing, the Hamas Government is in its twelfth year of power in the Gaza Strip, a small enclave (around 365 km^2) populated by some 1.8 million people, having won Palestinian legislative elections in January 2006, and then forcibly taken power in June 2007. The result of this assumption of power by a government that refused to recognise the legality of the state of Israel was that intense pressure was brought to bear by the Israeli Government on Gaza with the intention of forcing Hamas from power. This pressure resulted in a drastically tightened economic blockade, which allowed for the entry of humanitarian goods only, and this further devastated an already impoverished territory. In September 2007, the Israeli security cabinet declared the Gaza Strip an 'enemy entity' controlled by a 'terrorist organisation'. This was used to justify further sanctions, and in the autumn of 2008 Israel imposed a ban on fuel imports. Something of a watershed in relations between Israel and Gaza was reached in December 2008, when, in what was claimed to be a response to the firing of Qassam rockets from Gaza into Israel, Israel launched Operation Cast Lead. (It should be noted that while the launching of these rockets is uncontested, the best estimates are that between June 2004 and November 2012 they resulted in 26 deaths in Israel. More than 500 Palestinians were killed in Gaza by Israel between November 2006 and March 2008.) Operation Cast Lead resulted in the devastation of the Gaza Strip. Some 1,300 Palestinians were killed, of whom 430 were children, and a further 4,500 were injured. Thirteen Israelis were killed – 10 soldiers and three civilians. In addition, infrastructure, including electricity and water supplies, was targeted; more than half the hospitals were struck; schools were destroyed; and government buildings, especially police stations, were attacked. Gaza was in every sense devastated. Even the UN compound in Gaza that contained the United Nations Relief and Works Agency for Palestine Refugees in the Near East (UNRWA) warehouse was destroyed – a warehouse that, according to the UNRWA director, contained 'hundreds of tons of emergency food and medicines set for distribution to shelters, hospitals and feeding centres'.

The UN's response to Operation Cast Lead involved the Human Rights Council appointing a 'fact-finding mission' with the mandate to 'investigate all violations of international human rights law and international humanitarian law that might have been committed at any time in the context of the military operations that were conducted in Gaza during the period from 27 December 2008 and 18 January 2009'. The head of the Mission was Richard Goldstone, a South African former judge of the South African Constitutional Court. (Only because, after the report was published, Goldstone attracted such opprobrium that he partially, if unclearly, resiled from the conclusion which his report reached, it is relevant to add that he is himself Jewish, and said in an interview published in December 2009: 'I'm certainly a friend of Israel – I don't mind being called a Zionist.') He accepted the position only after the mandate was rewritten (by himself) to include investigation not only of Israeli violations, but violations on all sides. Notwithstanding Goldstone's links with Israel, Israeli cooperation with the Mission was withheld, with allegations that the Mission was biased.

When the Human Rights Council Report was completed in September 2009, it proved to be a substantial and appalling indictment both of the Cast Lead invasion and of the continuing Israeli occupation. In essence, in addition to the conclusion that the operation constituted a disproportionate attack designed to punish, humiliate and terrorize a civilian population, it listed many war crimes that Israel had committed. It concluded that, among other matters, its actions denied Palestinians access to the basic necessities of life, including food, medicine, housing and water; severely restricted their freedom of movement; and prevented recourse to effective legal remedies; and could justify a competent court finding that crimes against humanity had been committed. (It came to a similar conclusion about the rocket attacks fired by Hamas, but the effect was so quantitatively different that understandably this received much less consideration.)

This is the background to the essential facts of this section. After Operation Cast Lead, Israel yet again tightened the blockade by which it controlled all goods and persons entering or leaving Gaza. Israel attempted to prevent the importation of almost all construction materials and other raw materials. The tunnels between Gaza and Egypt (illegal in Israel's view) had alleviated the situation to some extent, but as it is Gazans live with extremely high levels of unemployment; electricity and water shortages; and the constant threat of further military intervention. Israel also controls Gaza's coastal waters, preventing importation by this route.

Against this background, the Gaza Freedom Flotilla was planned in an attempt both to bring humanitarian relief to Gaza and also to publicise the plight of the Gazan population. Six ships finally made up the flotilla, the largest of which was the Turkish-owned *Mavi Marmara*, carrying around 580 passengers. (Two further ships suffered mechanical problems; one turning back and the other sailing on at a later date.) The flotilla carried volunteer humanitarian workers and 10,000 tons of humanitarian aid, and all cargo was inspected at the point of departure to ensure that no weapons were being carried, and indeed none was ever found. The volunteers on the flotilla were a mixture of people from 40 nations and included parliamentarians, politicians, artists, journalists and activists.

From the first news of the intended flotilla, the Israeli authorities made it plain that they would not tolerate any violation of the blockade they had imposed on Gaza. This was to become a matter of some importance in one of the two UN reports on the events that followed. In brief, while the flotilla, led by the *Mavi Marmara*, was still some 70 miles off the Israeli coast in international waters, having ignored Israeli orders to change course, Israeli commandos forcibly boarded the ship and, when an attempt was made to resist the boarding, they opened fire, killing nine Turkish activists and injuring scores of others. The 700 people on board the flotilla were taken forcibly to Israel and were then deported, many of them having been severely maltreated. The possessions of those detained were retained by the Israelis, who made an effort to ensure that all camera and other recordings of what had happened were destroyed or confiscated. Such was the international outcry, that the two UN Reports were commissioned.

The Human Rights Council Report was prepared by a fact-finding mission that had been charged by the Human Rights Council in June 2010

> to investigate violations of international law, including international humanitar-ian law and human rights law, resulting from the interception by Israeli forces of the humanitarian aid flotilla bound for Gaza on 31 May 2010 during which nine people were killed and many others injured.[50]

The second report was announced by the Secretary-General of the UN on 2 August 2010, but this was to be a Panel of Inquiry given the mandate to receive and review the reports of the national investigations (Israeli and Turkish) with a view to recommending ways of avoiding 'similar incidents in the future'.

The Human Rights Council fact-finding mission was informed by Isra-el's Permanent Representative at Geneva on 18 August 2010 'in writing ... that the position of his Government was one of non-recognition of, and non-cooperation with, the Mission'.[51] The Mission interviewed more than 100 witnesses, and came to a series of damning conclusions. It determined that, before the forcible intervention against the *Mavi Marmara* took place, there was overwhelming evidence that a humanitarian crisis existed in Gaza, and for that reason alone the blockade was unlawful. Consequently, the interception was unlawful and unjustifiable. Although it acknowledged that the firing of rockets into Israel from Gaza constituted 'serious violations of international law and international humanitarian law', it held that Israel's response consti-tuted collective punishment of the civilian population of Gaza, and could not therefore be regarded as lawful. Furthermore, it concluded that the use of force against the flotilla passengers was utterly disproportionate and brutal and that there was evidence to support prosecutions under Article 147 of the Fourth Geneva Convention for the following crimes: wilful killing; torture or inhuman treatment; and wilfully causing great suffering or serious injury to body or health. For good measure it also found that Israel had violated a number of obligations under international human rights law, particularly

---

[50] UN Human Rights Council, 'Report of the international fact-finding mission to investigate violations of international law' (2010) 1.
[51] ibid para 16.

those to be found in the International Covenant on Civil and Political Rights (in Articles 6, 7, 9, 10 and 19) and the Convention against Torture.

The response of the Human Rights Council upon receiving the Report was to endorse its conclusions, and it called upon the parties to implement them – that is, to take action to bring prosecutions against those who had committed the offences the Report identified. Israel, however, ignored the resolutions of the Council, which it had already decided was inherently biased in its attitudes and actions. It took this position even though a resolution of March 2012 repeating the call for implementation was passed by 38 votes to one (the US voting against) with eight abstentions.[52] Among the states supporting the call for implementation were many not usually regarded as unfriendly towards Israel, including France, Japan, Norway, Spain and Switzerland. Apart from the US, all the permanent Security Council states supported the resolution.

It would therefore seem to be the case that the independent international fact-finding mission reached legal conclusions derived from witness interrogation. The structuring of the events to enable the application of international law is what was important, but Israel escaped sanction because of its ability to rely on the power of the US (although Israel's own power should not be underestimated), thereby revealing the impotence of international law in such circumstances.

Meanwhile, what of the Secretary-General's Panel of Inquiry? Strangely, perhaps, its report scarcely alludes to the work of the Human Rights Council. The Panel heard no witnesses, instead relying for its information upon the internal inquiries into the relevant events conducted by Israel and Turkey respectively. In addition to the internal reports, the Panel had access to 'Points of Contact' in both Turkey and Israel, and these were to provide clarification where necessary. Thus, rather than consider the facts on the basis of evidence provided, what was considered were conclusions from two inevitably partial inquiries. The result is peculiar. Inferences are drawn which seem to attempt to bridge the very different conclusions of the two inquiries, even where such a compromise is unsupportable. An example of this concerns the role of one of the primary organisers of the flotilla, the Turkish NGO İnsan Hak ve Hürriyetleri Vakfi. Relying upon no discoverable evidence, the Panel implies that the organisation was somehow dishonest:

> 86. However, the Panel seriously questions the true nature and objectives of the flotilla organizers, a coalition of non-governmental organizations. The leading group involved in the planning of the flotilla was the Turkish NGO 'İnsan Hak ve Hürriyetleri Vakfi' (IHH), a humanitarian organization. It owned two of the ships; the *Mavi Marmara* and the *Gazze I*. There is some suggestion that it has provided support to Hamas, although the Panel does not have sufficient information to

---

[52] UNGA Doc A/HRC/19/L.36 of 19 March 2012.

assess that allegation. IHH has special consultative status with ECOSOC, a status which in the Panel's view raises a certain expectation with respect to the way in which it should conduct its activities.

87. On the basis of public statements by the flotilla organizers and their own internal documentation, the Panel is satisfied that as much as their expressed purpose of providing humanitarian aid, one of the primary objectives of the flotilla organizers was to generate publicity about the situation in Gaza by attempting to breach Israel's naval blockade. The purposes of the flotilla were clearly expressed in a document prepared by IHH and signed by all flotilla participants as follows:

Purpose: Purposes of this journey are to create an awareness amongst world public and international organizations on the inhumane and unjust embargo on Palestine and to contribute to end this embargo which clearly violates human rights and delivering humanitarian relief to the Palestinians.[53]

Compounding this apparent misunderstanding of the purpose of the flotilla, the report also suggests that the number of passengers on board was excessive if the exercise was one which was purely humanitarian. With due respect, the objective was obviously not just to deliver aid, but, as was stated, to draw attention to the asserted unjustifiable suffering caused by Israel's blockade, described in the Human Rights Council Report as 'clearly unlawful'.

None of this, however, is as significant as the decision of the Panel that the central issue to be considered was the legality of the Israeli blockade in international law. Indeed, the chair and vice-chair of the Panel appended a 26-page analysis of the principles of public international law that they regarded as relevant to the events under review. Central to this is a consideration of the law of blockade. Remarkably and controversially, the Panel concluded that the Israeli blockade was not inconsistent with international law, bearing in mind that:

It is important to note that a 'blockade, in order to be of itself illegal, must have the *sole purpose* of starving the population.' In practice, there can be difficulties in ascertaining whether this was the intention of the State imposing the blockade.[54]

If this was indeed the law it would seem curiously out of step with modern sentiment, which might suggest that starving a population, even 'merely' as collateral damage, could not be consistent with international law, whether human rights law or humanitarian law. (It would also seem to ignore concepts of proportionality.) Fortunately, subsequent analysis in an article in the *British Yearbook of International Law* demonstrated that such a conclusion was ill-founded, both because the conflict between Israel and Gaza (still effectively under Israeli occupation) had to be seen as a 'non-international

---

[53] 'Report of the Secretary-General's Panel of Inquiry on the 31 May 2010 Flotilla Incident' (2011) paras 86 and 87 (internal footnotes omitted).

[54] ibid para 16. Emphasis in original; internal footnotes omitted.

armed conflict' at most, and thus a blockade could be legitimate only under circumstances that were not present, and because the blockade did not represent a proportionate response.[55]

This is obviously a rather specialised area of international law, but the significance of the Panel's conclusion is what is important. It effectively ignored the facts that gave rise to the flotilla – the immense difficulty for 1.7 million inhabitants of living in a devastated and blockaded territory. Few observers could argue that the treatment of the Gazans was anything other than 'collective punishment'. If indeed the Panel had been correct in its analysis, these social facts would have been beyond the scope of its report – as they actually were.

At the same time, the conclusions to be drawn from these reports are significant in illustrating the centrality of international law in imposing an understanding of a contemporary international dispute, and in illustrating the inability of law to finally do more than structure arguments to be made. Even if international law is reasonably lucid on a particular point, this will not necessarily provide an answer of finality in the social and political world.

Much the same result was achieved when, in July 2004, the ICJ, having been asked by the UN General Assembly to provide an advisory opinion on Israel's construction of a wall in the Occupied Palestinian Territory, confirmed that the wall and 'its associated régime' was contrary to international law, and stated the legal consequences arising from that illegality.[56] The Court acknowledged that the question it had been asked meant that the opinion it provided would necessarily have political implications, but stated that this could not in itself mean that the Court should not respond to the request. The Court was remarkably united in its opinion, with only Judge Buergenthal (from the US) dissenting from the central holdings.

Importantly, the Court concluded that the building of the wall violated customary international law; that Israel was under an obligation to restore the position *ante*, with an obligation to provide reparation for the damage caused; that all states were under an obligation not to recognise the illegal situation arising from the wall's construction; and, finally, that the General Assembly and the Security Council should consider what further action was required to bring to an end the illegal situation resulting from the construction of the wall. In coming to its conclusions, the Court drew upon the relationship between international human rights law and international humanitarian law, and the application of human rights treaties, as well as the right of self-defence in international law. It is difficult to conceive of a clearer advisory

---

[55] Douglas Guilfoyle, 'The *Mavi Marmara* Incident and Blockade in Armed Conflict' (2011) 81 *British Yearbook of International Law* 171.

[56] *Legal Consequences of the Construction of a Wall in the Occupied Palestinian Territory, Advisory Opinion*, ICJ Reports 2004, 136.

opinion. The General Assembly responded with a resolution in August 2004, part of which states:

> *Considering* that respect for the Court and its functions is essential to the rule of law and reason in international affairs, [the General Assembly:]
>
> 1. *Acknowledges* the advisory opinion of the International Court of Justice of 9 July 2004 on the *Legal Consequences of the Construction of a Wall in the Occupied Palestinian Territory*, including in and around East Jerusalem;
> 2. *Demands* that Israel, the occupying Power, comply with its legal obligations as mentioned in the advisory opinion;
> 3. *Calls upon* all States Members of the United Nations to comply with their legal obligations as mentioned in the advisory opinion.[57]

Notwithstanding this, and although the Resolution was passed by 150 votes to six, with 10 abstentions, Israel continued to build the wall and has not fulfilled its obligations as defined by the Court.

D. Israel and 'Targeted Assassinations'

Since the Second World War, there has been a substantial increase in so-called 'targeted assassinations', in which a state authorises and carries out extra-territorial and extra-judicial killings of those it perceives to be its enemy. Russia is accused of having colluded in the murder of a number of its citizens residing in the UK; there is strong evidence that North Korea arranged the murder of Kim Jong-nam, the half-brother of its leader, Kim Jong-un, at Kuala Lumpur International Airport in Malaysia in 2017, and it is accepted that Israel arranged for the deaths of at least six Iranian nuclear scientists. Russia stood accused of attempting to murder one of its ex-spies, Sergei Skripal, in March 2018 in Salisbury in the UK, by means of a nerve agent.[58] Even more widely publicised was the gruesome 'targeted assassination' by Saudi Arabian agents of Jamal Khashoggi, a Saudi dissident residing in the US, who was killed in Saudi Arabia's consulate in Istanbul, with the murder exposed by the Turkish authorities. Arguably in a different league, both the UK and the US have used drones to kill their own citizens extraterritorially when they have claimed to have clear evidence that those killed were either collaborating with terrorists or that it had been established that they posed

---

[57] UNGA Resolution of 20 July 2004, UN Doc A/RES/ES–10/15, 2 August 2004 (internal footnote omitted).

[58] Mr Skripal, along with his daughter, Yulia, and a police officer, fell dangerously ill after being exposed to the Novichok nerve agent, but later recovered. Unfortunately, a British citizen, Dawn Sturgess, died a few months later, after coming into contact with a Novichok-filled container believed to have been discarded by those responsible for the Skripal attack. The British Government accused Russia of perpetrating the attack; and, unsurprisingly, the Russian Government denied any involvement in the affair.

a clear and imminent danger either to their fellow citizens or to the state to which they owed allegiance.

Coincidentally, in 2018, a quite remarkable book appeared which detailed the history of Israel's 'targeted assassinations'.[59] It is remarkable because it is authored by someone who gained the cooperation of 'many current and former members of the Israeli government, including Prime Ministers Shimon Peres, Ehud Barak, Ariel Sharon, and Benjamin Netanyahu, as well as high-level figures in the country's military and intelligence services',[60] but is equally remarkable for the story it tells. Written as it is, by an Israeli reporter, it is unsurprising that the overall tone of the book is supportive of these many extra-judicial killings, citing Israel's insecurity (or security) as justification. But when placed in the context of the struggle for Palestinian human rights and statehood this is a book which gives rise to considerable qualms. Israel has assassinated more people than any other state since the Second World War, with no less than 800 assassination operations in the last decade. The vast majority of those killed have been Palestinians, usually leaders with whom Israel might have been expected to negotiate rather than eliminate. Whether the effect of these murders has been to increase or decrease Israel's security is a moot point, but is obviously not one that will be resolved in a book concerning international law.

But this does not mean that international law is silent as to the legality of targeted assassinations. Both the UK and the US have attempted to provide a legal justification for their extra-territorial assassinations (see the discussion in chapter eight on the use of drones), but Israel has simply denied its involvement in such activities and refuses to discuss such matters, even in the face of incontrovertible evidence.

V. Conclusion

The purpose of this chapter has been to try to understand the implications of a world in which those with sufficient power regard themselves as above international law and feel free to disregard it when compliance is deemed inconvenient. Evidence indicates that the result of such conduct in the case of the US has certainly come at a price. International interventions have proved costly both in lives lost and the amount of expenditure required, and the gains have yet to be demonstrated. Although it cannot be proved that compliance with international law would have brought a happier result, it certainly

---

[59] Bergman, *Rise and Kill First* (2018).
[60] ibid.

seems likely. As to Israel, even though it claims to be held to different standards of conduct than other states, so egregious are its consistent breaches of international law that it can scarcely complain. Indeed, it is ironic that a state that came into existence through decisions of the UN now treats that body with ill-disguised contempt. If the grandeur of international law is its emphasis upon the maintenance of peace and the protection of human dignity, the misery is that compliance is claimed by some states to be optional.

Select Bibliography

Abouharb, M. Rodwan and David Cingranelli, *Human Rights and Structural Adjustment* (Cambridge: CUP, 2007).

Adams, Patricia, *Odious Debts: Loose Lending, Corruption, and the Third World's Environmental Legacy* (Earthscan, London and Toronto, 1991).

Akande, Dapo, 'Treaty Law and ICC Jurisdiction over the Crime of Aggression, (2018) 29(3) *European Journal of International Law* 939.

Alston, Philip and Crawford, James (eds), *The Future of UN Human Rights Treaty Monitoring* (Cambridge, CUP, 2000).

Amnesty International, *Universal Jurisdiction: A Preliminary Survey of Legislation Around the World – 2012 Update* (London, Amnesty International Publications, 2012).

Anghie, Antony, *Imperialism, Sovereignty and the Making of International Law* (Cambridge, CUP, 2005).

Annan, Kofi, *Interventions: A Life in War and Peace* (New York, Penguin Press, 2012).

Aust Anthony, *Modern Treaty Law and Practice* (Cambridge, CUP, 2000).

Beazer, Quintin H and Woo, Byungwon, 'IMF Conditionality, Government Partisanship, and the Progress of Economic Reforms', (2016) 60(2) *American Journal of Political Science* 304.

Beckley, Michael, *Unrivaled: Why America Will Remain the World's Sole Superpower* (Cornell University Press, 2018).

Bellamy, Alex J, 'The Responsibility to Protect – Five Years On' (2010) 24 *Ethics & International Affairs* 143.

Benvenisti, Eyal, 'Domestic Politics and International Resources: What Role for International Law?' in Michael Byers (ed), *The Role of Law in International Politics* (Oxford, OUP, 2001).

Bergman, Ronen, *Rise and Kill First: The Secret History of Israel's Targeted Assassinations* (New York, Random House, 2018).

Bethlehem, Daniel, 'Self-Defense Against an Imminent or Actual Armed Attack by Nonstate Actors' (2012) 106 *American Journal of International Law* 770.

Bhojwani, Deepak, 'Responsibility to Protect: Issues of Legality and Legitimacy' (2012) 47 *Economic and Political Weekly* 28.

Bolton, John, 'Is There Really "Law" in International Affairs?' (2000) 10 *Transnational Law & Contemporary Problems* 1.

——, 'Should We Take Global Governance Seriously?' (2000) 1 *Chicago Journal of International Law* 205.

——, *Surrender Is Not An Option: Defending America at the United Nations and Abroad* (New York, Threshold Editions, 2007).

Bosco, David, *Five to Rule Them All: The UN Security Council and the Making of the Modern World* (New York, OUP, 2009).

Bowring, Bill, *The Degradation of the International Legal Order?* (Oxford, Routledge–Cavendish, 2008).

Boyle, Alan and Chinkin, Christine, *The Making of International Law* (Oxford, OUP, 2007).

Bradlow, Daniel D, 'The World Bank, the IMF, and Human Rights' (1996) 6 *Transnational Law and Contemporary Problems* 67.

Brierly, James L, *The Outlook for International Law* (Oxford, Clarendon Press, 1944).

Byers, Michael, *Custom, Power and the Power of Rules: International Relations and Customary International Law* (Cambridge, CUP, 1999).

——, (ed), *The Role of Law in International Politics: Essays in International Relations and International Law* (Oxford, OUP, 2000).

——, *War Law: Understanding International Law and Armed Conflict* (London, Atlantic Books, 2005).

—— and Nolte, Georg (eds), *United States Hegemony and the Foundations of International Law* (Cambridge, CUP, 2003).

Cassese, Antonio, *International Law in a Divided World* (Oxford, Clarendon Press, 1986).

——, *International Law*, 2nd edn (Oxford, OUP, 2005).

——, *Cassese's International Criminal Law*, 3rd edn, revised by Antonio Cassese, Paola Gaeta, Laurel Baig, Mary Fan, Christopher Gosnell and Alex Whiting (Oxford, OUP, 2013).

Chang, Ha-Joon, *Kicking Away the Ladder: Development Strategy in Historical Perspective* (London, Anthem Press, 2003).

——, *Bad Samaritans: Rich Nations, Poor Policies and the Threat to the Developing World* (London, Random House Business Books, 2007).

Charlesworth, Hilary and Chinkin, Christine, *The Boundaries of International Law: A Feminist Analysis* (Manchester, Manchester University Press, 2000).

Chen, Lung-Chu, *An Introduction to Contemporary International Law*, 2nd edn (New Haven, Yale University Press, 2000).

Chomsky, Noam, *Year 501: The Conquest Continues* (London, Verso, 1993).

——, *World Orders, Old and New* (London, Pluto Press, 1994).

——, *A New Generation Draws the Line: Humanitarian Intervention and the 'Responsibility to Protect' Today* (Boulder, CO, Paradigm Publishers, 2012).

Christie, Kenneth and Roy, Denny, *The Politics of Human Rights in East Asia* (London, Pluto Press, 2001).

Ciorciari, John D, 'China's Structural Power Deficit and Influence Gap in the Monetary Policy Arena' (2014) 54 *Asian Survey*, 869.

Clagett, Brice, 'Just Compensation in International Law: The Issues Before the Iran-United States Claims Tribunal' in Richard B Lillich (ed), *The Valuation of Nationalized Property in International Law* (Charlottesville, VA, University of Virginia Press, 1987).

Clark, Roger S, 'Exercise of jurisdiction over the crime of aggression', *Max Planck Encylopedia of International Procedural Law* (forthcoming).

—— and Sann, Madeleine (eds), *The Case Against the Bomb* (Camden, NJ, Rutgers University, 1996).

Clarke, Richard, *Against All Enemies: Inside America's War on Terror* (New York, Free Press, 2004).

Collier, John, and Lowe, Vaughan, *The Settlement of Disputes in International Law: Institutions and Procedures* (Oxford, OUP, 1999).

Comeaux, Paul and Kinsella, Stephen, *Protecting Foreign Investment Under International Law: Legal Aspects of Political Risk* (New York, Oceana Publications, 1997).

Crawford, James, *The International Law Commission's Articles on State Responsibility: Introduction, Text and Commentaries* (Cambridge, CUP, 2002).

—— and Koskenniemi, Martti (eds), *The Cambridge Companion to International Law* (Cambridge, CUP, 2012).

Davies, Norman, 'How States Die' (2011–12) 32 *New England Review* 68.

Dixon, Martin, *Textbook on International Law*, 7th edn (Oxford, OUP, 2013).

——, McCorquodale, Robert and Williams, Sarah, Cases & Materials on International Law (Oxford, OUP, 2016).

Doyle, Michael W, *Striking First: Preemption and Prevention in International Conflict* (Princeton, NJ, Princeton University Press, 2008).

Dunoff, Jeffrey L and Trachtman, Joel P (eds), *Ruling the World? Constitutionalism, International Law and Global Governance* (Cambridge, CUP, 2009).

Eatwell, Roger and Goodwin, Matthew, *National Populism: The Revolt Against Liberal Democracy* (London, Pelican, 2018).

Eichengreen, Barry and Woods, Ngaire, 'The IMF's Unmet Challenges' (2016) 30 *Journal of Economic Perspectives*, 29.

Evans, Gareth, *The Responsibility to Protect: Ending Mass Atrocity Crimes Once and For All* (Washington DC, Brookings Institution Press, 2008).

Falk, Richard, *Human Rights Horizons: The Pursuit of Justice in a Globalizing World* (New York, Routledge, 2000).

Fassbender, Bardo, 'The United Nations Charter as Constitution of the International Community' (1998) 36 *Columbia Journal of Transnational Law* 529.

Finlayson, Lorna, 'Corbyn Now', *London Review of Books*, 27 September 2018, 62.

Flamini, Roland, 'Scotland's Independence bid: History, Prospects, Challenges' (2013) 176 *World Affairs* 57.

——, 'European Disunion: Cameron, the EU, and the Scots' (2014) 177 *World Affairs* 8.

Fox, Gregory H and Roth, Brad R, *Democratic Governance and International Law* (Cambridge, CUP, 2000).

Franck, Thomas M, *Fairness in International Law and Institutions* (Oxford, OUP, 1995).

Fukuyama, Francis, *The End of History and the Last Man* (New York, Free Press, 1992).

Galeano, Eduardo, *Open Veins of Latin America* (New York, Monthly Review Press, 1997).

Glennon, Michael J, *Limits of Law, Prerogatives of Power: Interventionism After Kosovo* (New York, Palgrave, 2001).

Goldsmith, Jack L and Posner, Eric A, *The Limits of International Law* (Oxford, OUP, 2005).

Goodwin-Gill, Guy S and Talmon, Stefan (eds), *The Reality of International Law: Essays in Honour of Ian Brownlie* (Oxford, OUP, 1999).

Gray, Christine, *International Law and the Use of Force*, 4th edn (Oxford, OUP, 2018).

Gray, John, *False Dawn: The Delusions of Global Capitalism* (Granta, London, 2009).

Gross, Aeyal, *The Writing on the Wall: Rethinking the International Law of Occupation* (Cambridge, CUP, 2017).

Grotenhuis, René, *Nation-Building as Necessary Effort in Fragile States* (Amsterdam, Amsterdam University Press, 2016).

Guibernau, Montserrat, 'Prospects for a European Identity' (2011) 24 *International Journal of Politics, Culture and Society* 31.

——, 'Prospects for an Independent Catalonia' (2014) 27 *International Journal of Politics, Culture and Society* 5.

Guilfoyle, Douglas, 'The Mavi Marmara incident and blockade in armed conflict' (2011) 81 *British Yearbook of International Law*, published online 12 May 2011.

——, *International Criminal Law* (Oxford, OUP, 2016).

Guzman, Andrew, *How International Law Works: A Rational Choice Theory* (New York, OUP, 2008).

Halper, Stefan and Clarke, Jonathan, *America Alone: The Neo-Conservatives and the Global Order* (Cambridge, CUP, 2004).

—— and ——, *The Silence of the Rational Center: Why American Foreign Policy is Failing* (New York, Basic Books, 2007).

Hamm, Bernd (ed), *Devastating Society: The Neo-Conservative Assault on Democracy and Justice* (London, Pluto Press, 2005).

Hanhimäki, Jussi M, *The United Nations: A Very Short Introduction* (Oxford, OUP, 2008).

Harris, David, *Cases and Materials on International Law*, 7th edn (London, Sweet & Maxwell, 2010).

Hathaway, Oona A and Shapiro, Scott J, *The Internationalists And Their Plan to Outlaw War* (London, Penguin Books, 2018).

Henderson, Conway W, *Understanding International Law* (Chichester, Wiley-Blackwell, 2010).

Henig, Ruth, *The League of Nations* (London, Haus, 2010).

Henkin, Louis, *International Law: Politics and Values* (The Hague, Kluwer Law, 1995).

——, Hoffmann, Stanley, Kirkpatrick, Jeane J, Gerson, Allan, Rogers, William D and Scheffer, David J, *Right v. Might: International Law and the Use of Force* (New York, Council on Foreign Relations Press, 1989).

Heraclides, Alexis, *The Self-determination of Minorities in International Politics* (London, Frank Cass, 1991).

Hersh, Seymour M, *The Samson Option: Israel, America and the Bomb* (London, Faber and Faber, 1991).

——, *Chain of Command: The Road from 9/11 to Abu Ghraib* (London, Allen Lane, 2004).

Hickman, John, *News From the End of the Earth: A Portrait of Chile* (London, Hurst & Co, 1998).

Higgins, Rosalyn, *Problems and Process: International Law and How We Use It* (Oxford, OUP, 1994).

Hiscocks, Richard, *The Security Council: A Study in Adolescence* (London, Longman, 1973).

Hoge, James F and Rose, Gideon (eds), *How Did This Happen? Terrorism and the New War* (New York, PublicAffairs, 2001).

Hollis, Rosemary, *Britain and the Middle East in the 9/11 Era* (London, Wiley–Blackwell, 2010).

Ignatieff, Michael (ed), *American Exceptionalism and Human Rights* (Princeton, NJ, Princeton University Press, 2005).

Issacharoff, Samuel, 'Democracy's Deficits' (2018) 85 *University of Chicago Law Review* 485.

Johnson, Chalmers, *Blowback: The Costs and Consequences of American Empire* (London, Time Warner Books, 2000).

——, *The Sorrows of Empire: Militarism, Secrecy, and the End of the Republic* (London, Verso, 2004).

Judah, Tim, *Kosovo: War and Revenge* (New Haven, Yale University Press, 2000).

Kamm, Oliver, *Anti-Totalitarianism: The Left-Wing Case for a Neoconservative Foreign Policy* (London, Social Affairs Unit, 2005).

Khan, Rahmatullah, *The Iran–United States Claims Tribunal: Controversies, Cases and Contribution* (Dordrecht, Martinus Nijhoff, 1990).

King, Jeff, *The Doctrine of Odious Debt in International Law: A Restatement*, Cambridge Studies in International and Comparative Law (Cambridge, CUP, 2016).

Kinzer, Stephen, *All the Shah's Men: An American Coup and the Roots of Middle East Terror* (Hoboken, NJ, John Wiley & Sons, 2003).

Klein, Naomi, *The Shock Doctrine* (London, Penguin, 2007).

Koh, Harold Hongju, 'On American Exceptionalism' (2003) 55 *Stanford Law Review* 1479.

Koskenniemi, Martti, *The Gentle Civilizer of Nations: The Rise and Fall of International Law 1870–1960* (Cambridge, CUP, 2001).

Kreß, Claus, 'On the Activation of ICC Jurisdiction over the Crime of Aggression' (2018) 16 *Journal of International Criminal Justice* 1.

Lauterpacht, Hersch, *The Function of Law in the International Community* (Oxford, OUP, 1933).

Littman, Mark, *Kosovo: Law and Diplomacy* (London, Centre for Policy Studies, 1999).

Lowe, Vaughan, 'Shock Verdict: Nuclear War May or May Not be Unlawful' (1996) 55 *Cambridge Law Journal* 415.

——, *International Law* (Oxford, OUP, 2007).

——, Roberts, Adam, Welsh, Jennifer and Zaum, Dominik (eds), *The United Nations Security Council and War: The Evolution of Thought and Practice since 1945* (Oxford, OUP, 2008).

MacDonald, Ronald St John, 'The Charter of the United Nations and the Development of Fundamental Principles of International Law' in Bin Cheng and ED Brown (eds), *Contemporary Problems of International Law: Essays in Honour of Georg Schwarzenberger on his Eightieth Birthday* (London, Stevens & Sons, 1988).

Mackenzie, Ruth, Malleson, Kate, Martin, Penny and Sands, Philippe, *Selecting International Judges: Principle, Process, and Politics* (Oxford, OUP, 2010).

MacQueen, Norrie, *The United Nations: A Beginner's Guide* (Oxford, Oneworld, 2010).

McWhinney, Edward, *The World Court and the Contemporary International Law-Making Process* (Alphen aan den Rijn, Sijthoff & Noordhoff, 1979).

——, *Judicial Settlement of International Disputes: Jurisdiction, Justiciability and Judicial Law-Making on the Contemporary International Court* (Dordrecht, Martinus Nijhoff, 1991).

——, 'International Law' in Mary Hawkesworth and Maurice Hogan (eds), *Encyclopaedia of Government and Politics* (London, Routledge, 1992).

Magaisa, Alex T, 'The Land Question and Transitional Justice in Zimbabwe: Law, Force and History's Multiple Victims', *Oxford Transitional Justice Working Paper Series*, 30 June 2010.

Malone, David (ed), *The UN Security Council: From the Cold War to the 21st Century* (Boulder, CO, Lynne Rienner Publishers, 2004).

Mamdani, Mahmood, *Saviors and Survivors: Darfur, Politics and the War on Terror* (London, Verso, 2009).

Mansell, Wade, 'Two Cheers for the International Criminal Court' in John Carey, William V Dunlap and R John Pritchard (eds), *International Humanitarian Law: Prospects* (Ardsley, NY, Transnational, 2006).

——, *A Critical Introduction to Law*, 4th edn (London, Cavendish, 2015).

—— and Scott, Joanne, 'Why Bother about a Right to Development?' (1994) 21 *Journal of Law and Society* 171.

Mapp, Wayne, *The Iran–United States Claims Tribunal: The First Ten Years, 1981–1991* (Manchester, Manchester University Press, 1993).

Marks, Susan (ed), *International Law on the Left: Re-examining Marxist Legacies* (Cambridge, CUP, 2008).

Mattei, Ugo and Nader, Laura, *Plunder: When the Rule of Law is Illegal* (Oxford, Blackwell Publishing, 2008).

Mearsheimer, John, *The Great Delusion: Liberal Dreams and International Realities* (New Haven, Yale, 2018).

Menon, Rajan, *The Conceit of Humanitarian Intervention* (Oxford, OUP, 2018).

Meron, Theodor, *War Crimes Law Comes of Age: Essays* (Oxford, OUP, 1998).

Merrills, JG, *International Dispute Settlement*, 3rd edn (Cambridge, CUP, 1998).

Miller, Lynn H, *Global Order: Values and Power in International Politics*, 2nd edn (Boulder, CO, Westview Press, 1990).

Mohamed, Saira, 'Syria, the United Nations, and the Responsibility to Protect' (2012) 106 *Proceedings of the Annual Meeting (American Society of International Law)* 223.

Morgenthau, Hans J, *Politics Among Nations: The Struggle for Power and Peace*, 7th edn (New York, McGraw-Hill, 1993).

Moses, Jeremy, 'Sovereignty as irresponsibility? A Realist critique of the Responsibility to Protect' (2013) 39 *Review of International Studies* 113.

—— and Bahador, Babak and Wright, Tessa, 'The Iraq War and the Responsibility to Protect: Uses, Abuses and Consequences for the Future of Humanitarian Intervention' (2011) 5 *Journal of Intervention and Statebuilding* 347.

Mosler, Hermann, 'Political and Justiciable Legal Disputes: Revival of an Old Controversy?' in Bin Cheng and ED Brown (eds), *Contemporary Problems of International Law: Essays in Honour of Georg Schwarzenberger on his Eightieth Birthday* (London, Stevens & Sons, 1988).

Mouri, Allahyar, *The International Law of Expropriation as Reflected in the Work of the Iran–US Claims Tribunal* (Dordrecht, Martinus Nijhoff, 1994).

Moyn, Samuel, *Not Enough: Human Rights in an Unequal World* (Cambridge, Harvard University Press, 2018).

Moynihan, Daniel Patrick, *On the Law of Nations* (Cambridge, MA, Harvard University Press, 1990).

Muller, AS, Raič, CD and Thuránszky, JM (eds), *The International Court of Justice: Its Future Role After Fifty Years* (Leiden, Brill Publishing, 1996).

Müller, Jan-Werner, *What is Populism?* (London, Penguin Books, 2017).

Murphy, John F, *The United States and the Rule of Law in International Affairs* (Cambridge, CUP, 2004).

Newhouse, John, *Imperial America: The Bush Assault on World Order* (New York, Alfred A Knopf, 2003).

Northedge, FS, *The League of Nations: its Life and Times, 1920–1946* (Leicester, Leicester University Press, 1986).

O'Connell, DP, *The Law of State Succession* (Cambridge, CUP, 1956).

Openshaw, Karen S and Terry, Patrick CR, 'Zimbabwe's odious inheritance: Debt and unequal land distribution' (2015) 11 *McGill International Journal of Sustainable Development Law and Policy*, 39.

Oppenheim, Lassa, *International Law: A Treatise*, 8th edn, edited by Hersch Lauterpacht (London, Longman, 1967).

——, *International Law: A Treatise*, Vol 2, 7th edn, edited by Hersch Lauterpacht (London, Longman, 1969).

Orford, Anne, 'Globalization and the Right to Development' in Philip Alston (ed) *Peoples' Rights* (Oxford, OUP, 2005).

——, *International Authority and the Responsibility to Protect* (Cambridge, CUP, 2011).

Pakenham, Thomas, *The Scramble for Africa* (London, Weidenfeld & Nicolson, 1991).

Palmer, Geoffrey, 'International Law and the Reform of the International Court of Justice' in Antony Anghie and Gary Sturgess (eds), *Legal Visions of the 21st Century: Essays in Honour of Judge Christopher Weeramantry* (The Hague, Kluwer Law International, 1998).

Parker, Karen, 'Understanding Self-Determination: The Basics', available at www.guidetoaction.org/parker/selfdet.html.

Parsi, Trita, *Treacherous Alliance: The Secret Dealings of Israel, Iran, and the US* (New Haven, Yale University Press, 2007).

Polakow-Suransky, Sasha, *The Unspoken Alliance: Israel's Secret Relationship with Apartheid South Africa* (New York, Pantheon Books, 2010).

Posner, Eric A, *The Perils of Global Legalism* (Chicago, University of Chicago Press, 2009).

Prunier, Gérard, *The Rwanda Crisis: History of a Genocide* (London, Hurst, 1995).

Rachman, Gideon, *Easternisation: War and Peace in the Asian Century* (London, Bodley Head, 2016).

Rajagopal, Balakrishnan, *International Law from Below: Development, Social Movements, and Third World Resistance* (Cambridge, CUP, 2003).

Reinhart, Carmen M. and Trebesch, Christoph, 'The International Monetary Fund: 70 Years of Reinvention' (2016) 30 *Journal of Economic Perspectives*, 3.

Reus-Smit, Christian (ed), *The Politics of International Law* (Cambridge, CUP, 2004).

Rickard, Stephanie J and Caraway, Teri L, 'International Negotiations in the Shadow of National Elections' (2014) 68 *International Organization*, 701.

Rosenne, Shabtai, *Practice and Methods of International Law* (New York, Oceana, 1984).

——, *The World Court: What It is and how It works*, 6th edn, revised by Terry D Gill (Leiden, Martinus Nijhoff, 2003).

Ross, Alf, *Constitution of the United Nations: Analysis of Structure and Function* (New York, Rinehart & Co, 1950).

Roth, Brad R, *Governmental Illegitimacy in International Law* (Oxford, OUP, 1999).

Sampson, Thomas, 'The Economics of International Disintegration' (2017) 31 *Journal of Economic Perspectives* 163.

Sands, Philippe, *Lawless World: America and the Making and Breaking of Global Rules* (London, Penguin Books, 2006).

Scahill, Jeremy, *Dirty Wars: The World Is a Battlefield* (New York, Nation Books, 2013).

Schabas, William A, *An Introduction to the International Criminal Court*, 5th edn (Cambridge, CUP, 2017).

Schlesinger, Stephen, *Act of Creation: The Founding of the United Nations* (Boulder, CO, Westview Press, 2003).

Schmid, Alex P and Jongman, Albert J, *Political Terrorism: A New Guide to Actors, Authors, Concepts, Data Bases, Theories, and Literature* (Amsterdam, Transaction Books, 2005).

Schrijver, Nico, *Sovereignty Over Natural Resources: Balancing Rights and Duties* (Cambridge, CUP, 1997).

Sellars, Kirsten, *The Rise and Rise of Human Rights* (Stroud, Sutton Publishing, 2002).

Shahak, Israel, *Open Secrets: Israeli Foreign and Nuclear Policies: Expansionism and Israeli Foreign Policy* (London, Pluto Press, 1997).

Shaw, Malcolm, *International Law*, 8th edn (Cambridge, CUP, 2017).

Simpson, AWB, *Human Rights and the End of Empire* (Oxford, OUP, 2001).

Simpson, Gerry, *Great Powers and Outlaw States: Unequal Sovereigns in the International Legal Order* (Cambridge, CUP, 2004).

Singh, Nagendra, *Role and Record of the International Court of Justice: 1946–88 – In Celebration of the 40th Anniversary* (Dordrecht, Kluwer, 1989).

Sloan, Blaine, 'The United Nations Charter as a Constitution' (1989) 1 *Pace Yearbook of International Law*, 61.

Slobodian, Quinn, *Globalists: The End of Empire and the Birth of Neoliberalism* (Cambridge, MA, Harvard University Press, 2018).

Soederberg, Susanne, *The Politics of the New Financial Architecture: Reimposing Neoliberal Domination in the Global South* (London, Zed Books, 2004).

Stahn, Carsten, *A Critical Introduction to International Criminal Law* (Cambridge, CUP, 2019).

Starke JG and Shearer IA (eds), *Starke's International Law* (London, Butterworths, 1994).

Steiner, Henry J, Alston, Philip and Goodman, Ryan, *International Human Rights in Context: Law, Politics, Morals* (Oxford, OUP, 2008).

Stiglitz, Joseph E, *Globalization and its Discontents* (London, Penguin Books, 2002).

Story, Alan, 'Property in International Law: Need Cuba Compensate US Titleholders for Nationalising Their Property?' (1998) 6 *Journal of Political Philosophy* 306.

Terry, Patrick CR, 'The Return of Gunboat Diplomacy: How the West has Undermined the Ban on the Use of Force' (2019) 10 *Harvard National Security Journal* 75.

Thirlway, Hugh, 'The International Court of Justice' in Malcolm D Evans (ed), *International Law*, 5th edn (Oxford, OUP, 2018).

Tripp, Charles, *A History of Iraq*, 3rd edn (Cambridge, CUP, 2007).

United Nations, *Basic Facts about the United Nations* (New York, United Nations Department of Public Information, 2011).

Valli, Vittorio, *The American Economy from Roosevelt to Trump* (London, Palgrave Macmillan, 2018).

Vidmar, Jure, 'Conceptualizing Declarations of Independence in International Law' (2012) 32 *Oxford Journal of Legal Studies* 153.

Villiger, Mark E, *Commentary on the 1969 Vienna Convention on the Law of Treaties* (Leiden, Martinus Nijhoff, 2008).

von Glahn, Gerhard and Taulbee, James Larry, *Law Among Nations: An Introduction to Public International Law*, 8th edn (New York, Pearson Longman, 2007).

Waldron, Jeremy (ed), *Nonsense upon Stilts: Bentham, Burke and Marx on the Rights of Man* (London and New York, Methuen, 1987).

Wallace, Rebecca and Martin-Ortega, Olga, *International Law*, 6th edn (London, Sweet & Maxwell, 2009).

Ward, Lee, 'Thomas Hobbes and John Locke on a Liberal Right of Secession' (2017) 70 *Political Research Quarterly* 876.

Weale, Albert, 'Brexit and the improvised constitution' in Benjamin Martill and Uta Staiger (eds) *Brexit and Beyond: Rethinking the Futures of Europe* (London, UCL Press, 2018).

Weart, Spencer, *Never at War: Why Democracies Will Not Fight One Another* (New Haven, Yale University Press, 1999).

Weller, Marc, 'Undoing the global constitution: UN Security Council action on the International Criminal Court' (2002) 78 *International Affairs*, 693.

——, *Contested Statehood: Kosovo's Struggle for Independence* (Oxford, OUP, 2009).

——, *Iraq and the Use of Force in International Law* (Oxford, OUP, 2010).

Wheeler, Nicholas J, *Saving Strangers: Humanitarian Intervention in International Society* (Oxford, OUP, 2000).

Williams, Paul D and Bellamy Alex J, 'Principles, Politics and Prudence: Libya, the Responsibility to Protect, and the Use of Military Force' (2012) 18 *Global Governance* 273.

Woods, Chris, *Sudden Justice: America's Secret Drone Wars* (London, Hurst, 2015).

Woods, Ngaire, *The Globalizers: The IMF, the World Bank, and Their Borrowers* (Ithaca, Cornell University Press, 2006).

Zifcak, Spencer, 'The Responsibility to Protect' in Malcolm D Evans (ed), *International Law*, 5th edn (Oxford, OUP, 2018).

Index